Engineering Computation

with **MATLAB**®

Third Edition

DAVID M. SMITH

Georgia Institute of Technology

PEARSON

Boston   Columbus   Indianapolis   New York   San Francisco   Upper Saddle River
Amsterdam   Cape Town   Dubai   London   Madrid   Milan   Munich   Paris   Montreal   Toronto
Delhi   Mexico City   São Paulo   Sydney   Hong Kong   Seoul   Singapore   Taipei   Tokyo

Editorial Director: Marcia Horton
Editor in Chief: Michael Hirsch
Editorial Assistant: Emma Snider
Director of Marketing: Patrice Jones
Marketing Manager: Yez Alayan
Marketing Assistant: Kathryn Ferranti
Vice President of Production: Vince O'Brien
Managing Editor: Jeff Holcomb
Production Project Manager: Kayla Smith-Tarbox
Production Editor: Pat Brown
Senior Operations Supervisor: Alan Fischer
Manufacturing Buyer: Pat Brown

Art Director: Anthony Gemmellaro
Creative Director: Jayne Conte
Designer: Kathy Foot
Manager, Visual Research: Karen Sanatar
Manager, Rights and Permissions: Michael Joyce
Media Director: Daniel Sandin
Full-Service Project Management: Kailash Jadli/ Aptara®, Inc.
Composition: Aptara®, Inc.
Printer/Binder: Courier/Westford
Cover Printer: Lehigh-Phoenix Color
Text Font: Palatino Lt Std

Photo Credits: Cover image: The cover image is of a three-dimensional model of HMS Victory developed entirely in Matlab by the Author. Page 4: Fig. 1.1: David Smith; Fig 1.2: Courtesy of the UK Government. Page 25: Fig 2.1: Screenshots copyright © 2011 by MathWorks. Reprinted with permission. Page 28: Fig 2.2, Fig 2.3: Screenshots copyright © 2011 by MathWorks. Reprinted with permission. Page 29: Fig 2.4, Fig 2.5: Screenshots copyright © 2011 by MathWorks. Reprinted with permission. Page 30: Fig 2.6: Screenshots copyright © 2011 by MathWorks. Reprinted with permission. Page 31: Fig 2.7: Screenshots copyright © 2011 by MathWorks. Reprinted with permission. Page 32: Fig 2.8: Screenshots copyright © 2011 by MathWorks. Reprinted with permission. Page 37: Fig. 2.9: AP Photo/Scaled Composites. Page 200: Fig 9.3: © PhotoDisc. Page 302: Fig 13.10: David Smith. Page 397: Fig 17.4: jorgen mcleman/Shutterstock.

Many of the designations by manufacturers and sellers to distinguish their products are claimed as trademarks. Where those designations appear in this book, and the publisher was aware of a trademark claim, the designations have been printed in initial caps or all caps.

Library of Congress Cataloging-in-Publication Data

Smith, David M.
  Engineering and computation with MATLAB/David M. Smith.—3rd ed.
    p. cm.
  ISBN 978-0-13-256870-8
  1. Engineering mathematics—Data processing. 2. MATLAB. I. Title.
  TA345.S585 2013
  620.00285'53—dc23

                              2012000377

10 9 8 7 6 5 4 3 2 1

PEARSON

ISBN 10:   0-13-256870-5
ISBN 13: 978-0-13-256870-8

This book is dedicated to the
glory of Almighty God

~David M. Smith

Contents

Contents

Appendices

About the Author

David Smith has been teaching introductory computer science classes for engineers at the Georgia Institute of Technology since 1997 when he retired from industry. Previously, he worked 31 years for Lockheed-Martin at its Marietta, Georgia, facility as a systems and software specialist with a focus on intelligent systems. He was active in designing and developing software for the C-130J, C-27J, F-22, and C-5 aircraft and was the technical leader of the Pilot's Associate program, a $64 million research project sponsored by the Defense Advanced Research Projects Agency.

Mr. Smith has a bachelor's degree in aeronautical engineering from Southampton University and a master's degree in control systems from Imperial College, London.

Preface

> *"That of all the several ways of beginning a book which are now in practice throughout the known world, I am confident my own way of doing it is the best—I'm sure it is the most religious—for I begin with writing the first sentence, and trusting to Almighty God for the second."*

Laurence Sterne (1713–1768), British author, clergyman

This book introduces the power, satisfaction, and joy of computing to beginning engineering students who have little or no previous computing experience. It began as a snapshot of the content of a Georgia Tech course that introduces engineers to computing. However, it has been extensively enhanced to meet the needs of a wider audience of students and educators who want to understand programming for other reasons. In this book, to understand computing, we use the basic syntax and capabilities of MATLAB, a user-friendly language that is emerging as one of the most popular computing languages in engineering.

New to the Third Edition

Many engineering disciplines use the concept of graphs to represent specific ideas. We have added a chapter that deals with the fundamentals of graph manipulation from an engineering standpoint—specifically, how to find a minimum spanning tree, and both exact and approximate methods for finding the best path from one point to another. We also try to note those new features of MATLAB that are relevant to students in an introductory programming class. For examples, features were added recently allowing a user to manipulate plotted data by adjusting and saving values. Although interesting, one can achieve the same result with more traceability and repeatability by editing to the source data and repeating the plots.

One interesting observation emerged when refreshing the analysis of sorting algorithms in Chapter 16. In older versions of MATLAB (prior to R2008), our crude recursive implementations of Merge Sort and Quick Sort did not achieve the expected performance. The reason we deduced was that when data are passed into and out of a function, they must be copied between the workspaces of the calling and called functions. With R2011, however, the same code works splendidly, suggesting that the earlier inefficient parameter passing mechanisms have been significantly improved.

Pedagogical Style

Computing is not a spectator sport. Students learn computing by using a computing system to solve problems. This text not only presents computing concepts and their MATLAB implementation, but also offers students extensive hands-on exercises. The text illustrates the ideas with examples from the world of engineering, provides style points, and presents sample problems that students might encounter. Each chapter includes topics that go a step beyond the basic content of an introductory class. This gives professors the choice to progress slowly, and more thoroughly, through the material in two semesters. It also offers advanced students enrichment materials for their personal study.

The overall philosophy of this text approaches programming tools in the following manner:

1. Explain a computing concept in general
2. Discuss its implementation in MATLAB
3. Provide exercises to master the concept

To help facilitate students' understanding of the concept and its implementation, the text uses two features: general templates and MATLAB listings. The general templates provide a foundation for students to understand concepts in general and can be applied to any language. The MATLAB listings show students how to implement concepts in MATLAB and are followed by detailed explanations of the code.

Features of the Text

- **Exercises:** Allow students a "Do It Yourself" approach to master concepts by trying what they just learned. Exercises follow each new topic.
- **Style Points:** Advise students about writing quality code that is easy to understand, debug, and reuse.
- **Hints:** Enrich students' understanding of a topic. Hints are interspersed through the book at points where students may benefit from a little extra "aside."
- **Engineering Examples:** Provide robust models and apply to real-world issues that will motivate students. Examples from different engineering disciplines are presented at the end of each chapter.
- **Special Characters, Reserved Words, and Functions:** Provides a quick reference for the key MATLAB principles discussed in each chapter.
- **Self Test:** Helps students to check their understanding of the material in each chapter.
- **Programming Projects:** Offer a variety of large-scale projects that students can work on to solidify their skills.

Chapter Overview

Chapter 1: *Introduction to Computers and Programming* discusses the history of computer architectures as they apply to computing systems today. The chapter provides an overview of computer hardware and software and how programs execute.

Chapter 2: *Getting Started* discusses some basic concepts of computing and then introduces the basic operation of the MATLAB user interface. The chapter also describes how to capture simple MATLAB programs in the form of scripts.

Chapter 3: *Vectors and Arrays* introduces the fundamental machinery that sets MATLAB apart from other languages—its ability to perform mathematical and logical operations on homogeneous collections of numbers.

Chapter 4: *Execution Control* describes the common techniques used to control the execution of code blocks—conditional operation and iteration.

Chapter 5: *Functions* describes how to implement procedural abstraction by defining reusable code blocks.

Chapter 6: *Character Strings* discusses how MATLAB operates on variables containing text.

Chapter 7: *Cell Arrays and Structures* discusses two kinds of heterogeneous data collections accessed by index and by name.

Chapter 8: *File Input and Output* describes three levels of ability provided in MATLAB for transferring data to and from data files—saving workspaces, specific tools that read and write specific data files, and general-purpose tools for processing any kind of file.

Chapter 9: *Recursion* discusses and illustrates a widely used alternative approach to repetitive code execution.

Chapter 10: *Principles of Problem Solving* introduces ideas that help students design solutions to new problems and avoid the "blank sheet of paper" syndrome—how to start a program.

Chapter 11: *Plotting* takes the student from basic plotting in two dimensions to the advanced tools that draw representations of three-dimensional objects with smooth shading and even multiple light effects.

Chapter 12: *Matrices* describes specific MATLAB capabilities that implement matrix algebra.

Chapter 13: *Images* discusses how to use vector and array algebra to manipulate color pictures.

Chapter 14: *Processing Sound* shows how to analyze, synthesize, and operate on sound files.

Chapter 15: *Numerical Methods* introduces numerical techniques that commonly occur in engineering: interpolation, curve fitting, integration, and differentiation.

Chapter 16: *Sorting* presents five algorithms for ordering data, each of which has applicability under certain circumstances—Insertion Sort, Bubble Sort, Quick Sort, Merge Sort, and Radix Sort—and then compares their performance on large quantities of data.

Chapter 17: *Processing Graphs* discusses how to represent graphs in general and then how to solve two important engineering problems—finding a minimal spanning tree and finding an optimal path between two nodes of the graph.

Appendices provide a summary of the MATLAB special characters, reserved words, and functions used throughout the text, the ASCII character set, the internal number representation inside the computer, and answers to the True or False and Fill in the Blank questions.

Paths through the Book

Not all courses that cover programming and MATLAB follow the same syllabus. *Engineering Computation with MATLAB* is designed to facilitate teaching the material with different styles and at different speeds. For example, Chapters 3, 4, and 5 cover MATLAB array manipulation, iteration, and writing your own functions. There are three schools of thought about the appropriate way to introduce these concepts. One would introduce array constructs first and follow up with the more "traditional" concept of iteration; another would teach iteration first and deal with the MATLAB-specific array operations later; and the third would treat functions first. I chose to order the book according to the arrays-first approach, to suit a particular teaching style. However, should you prefer iteration or functions first, Chapters 3, 4, and 5 can be used in any order you wish. In practice, over the years, our course has shifted to a functions-first approach so that we can use function interfaces to isolate students' code for automated code grading. Chapters 6–9 should be taught in sequence—there are dependencies between chapters that would make it awkward change the order. Chapter 10 is an important chapter that is difficult to place on a class schedule. Where it stands in the book appears to be a logical position. However, at that point in the semester, beginning students are still not ready to think about larger problems. I have usually covered this material (if at all) at the end of each semester by way of review. Chapter 11 provides basic plotting capability and is necessary for the remaining chapters. After that, Chapters 12–17 are virtually independent and can be taught in any order, but should follow Chapters 2–9 and 11.

Supplements

Various supplemental materials for this text are available at the book's Companion Web site: www.pearsonhighered.com/smith. The following are accessible to all readers:

- Solutions to selected Programming Projects
- Selected full-color figures
- Source code for all MATLAB listings
- Bonus chapters including: Object-Oriented Programming, Linked Lists, N-ary Trees and Graphs, and the Cost of Computing

In addition, the following supplements are available to qualified instructors at Addison-Wesley's Instructor Resource Center. Please visit www.pearsonhighered.com/irc, or send an e-mail to computing@aw.com.

- Solutions to all of the Programming Projects
- PowerPoint lecture slides

Acknowledgments

The underlying philosophy of this book and the material that forms its skeleton originated in the work of Professor Russell Shackelford around 1996. Dr. Melody Moore, currently an Associate Professor in the Interactive Computing department of the College of Computing at Georgia Tech, was instrumental in creating many of the teaching materials (then as overhead transparencies) from which this class was first taught. I am deeply indebted to Professor James Craig from the Aerospace Engineering department at Georgia Tech, who joined me in co-teaching the first engineering version of CS1, taught me much about MATLAB, and pioneered this class from the original 35 students to its current size of over 1,000 engineering students per semester. This engineering class became a vessel for introducing the students to the MATLAB language.

I would like to thank the following reviewers for their insight and wisdom during the process of manuscript development:

Kenneth Rouse, *Auburn University*

Suparna Datta, *Northeastern University*

Gerardine G. Botte, *Ohio University*

Mica Grujicic, *Clemson University*

Kuldip S. Rattan, *Wright State University*

Y.J. Lin, *The University of Akron*

Mark Nagurka, *Marquette University*

Michael Peshkin, *Northwestern University*

Howard Silver, *Fairleigh Dickinson University*

Steve Swinnea, *The University of Texas at Austin*

The material has benefited from the efforts of every Georgia Tech teaching assistant (TA), graduate student, instructor, and professor who has taught CS1, a list too long to enumerate. In particular, those wonderfully creative TAs who developed the ideas for examples used in this text have enriched it immeasurably. I wish to credit Professor Aaron Bobick with an important contribution made in the course of one short conversation. That conversation was responsible for pulling the class back from the brink of being merely a MATLAB programming class to one with roots in CS concepts. Professor Bobick taught CS1 with me in the fall of 2004. Early in the semester he made a very simple request: he said it would be easier for him to teach the class if we explicitly expressed the computing concepts inherent in each lesson, rather than leaving him—and the students—to tease the concepts out of the teaching materials.

I cannot adequately express my appreciation for the team at Addison-Wesley that helped bring this book to fruition. Many of them have done, and I am sure continue to do, their work "behind the scenes": Michael Hirsch, Emma Snider, Yez Alayan, Kayla Smith-Tarbox, Pat Brown, and Jeff Holcomb. I also really appreciate the work of Kailash Jadli and his team at Aptara®, Inc. for the care with which they designed the third edition.

Most important, I would like to acknowledge the personal contributions of those people without whom this book would not exist. My wife and best friend, Julie, has been an unwavering source of strength and encouragement during the process of writing this text. Bill Leahy was a student in the first CS1 class I taught in the spring of 1998. In spite of this beginning, he continued to a master's in computer science from Tech and is now an instructor in the College of Computing. Beyond his uncountable technical contributions to the material in this book, I want to acknowledge his friendship, encouragement, and wise judgment, all of which have been an inspiration to me during the process of developing this text.

CHAPTER 1

Introduction to Computers and Programming

Chapter Objectives

This chapter presents an overview of the historical background of computing and the computer hardware and software concepts that build the foundation for the rest of this book:

- Hardware architectures

- Software categories

- Programming languages

- Anticipated outcomes

1.1 Background

Advances in technology are achieved in two steps as follows:

- A visionary conceives an idea that has never been tried before
- Engineers find or invent tools that will bring that vision to reality

The search for new software tools is therefore an inescapable part of an engineer's life. The process of creating these tools frequently spawns subproblems, which themselves require creative solutions. The pace of change in our world is increasing, and nowhere is this phenomenon more dramatically obvious than computer science. In the span of just a few generations, computers have invaded every conceivable aspect of our lives, and there is no indication that this trend is slowing.

This book will help you become familiar with one specific programming tool: MATLAB. It is intended to bring you to a basic proficiency level so that you can confidently proceed on your own to learn the features of other programming languages that are useful to your interests.

A word of caution: Learning a programming language is very much like learning to speak a foreign language. In order to find something to eat in Munich, you must be able to express yourself in terms a German can understand. This involves knowing not only some vocabulary words, but also the grammatical rules that make those words comprehensible—in German, for example, this means putting the verbs at the ends of phrases.

If languages were a strictly theoretical exercise, you could make up your own vocabulary and grammar, and it would undoubtedly be an improvement over existing languages—especially English, with its incredibly complex spelling and pronunciation rules. However, language is not a theoretical exercise; it is a practical tool for communication, so we can't make up our own rules, but are constrained to the vocabulary and grammar expected by the people with whom we want to converse.

Similarly, this book is not an abstract text about the nature of computer languages. It is a practical guide to creating solutions to problems. Accomplishing this involves expressing your solutions in such a form that the computer can "understand" your solutions; therefore, it requires that you use the vocabulary (i.e., the appropriate key words) and grammar (the syntax) of the language.

To become proficient in this, as in any other language, it is not enough to merely know the grammar and vocabulary. You have to practice your language skills by communicating. For foreign languages, this means traveling to the country, immersing yourself in the culture, and talking with people. For computer languages, this means actually writing programs, seeing what they do, and determining how to use their capabilities to solve your engineering problems.

1.2 History of Computer Architectures

Computing concepts developed as tools to solve previously intractable problems. This section will trace the growth of computing architectures, review the basic organization of computer hardware components, and emphasize the implementation of the data storage and processing capabilities by highlighting three milestones on the road to today's computers: Babbage's difference engine, Colossus, and the von Neumann architecture.

1.2.1 Babbage's Difference Engine

Charles Babbage (1791–1871) is generally recognized as the earliest pioneer of the modern computer. Babbage's **difference engine**—a relatively simple device that can subtract adjacent values in a column of numbers—is a good example of a computing device designed to improve the speed and repeatability of mathematical operations. Babbage was concerned about the process engineers used to develop the tables of logarithms and trigonometric functions. In his day, the only way to develop these tables was for mathematicians to calculate the values in the tables by hand. While the algorithms were simple—combining tables of the differences between adjacent values—the opportunity for human error was unacceptably high. In 1854 Babbage designed a difference engine that could automate the process of generating tables of mathematical functions. Since the objective was to create numerical tables, the output device was to be a set of copper plates ready for a printing press. The memory devices for storing numerical values were wheels arranged in vertical columns. The arithmetic operations were accomplished by ratchet devices cranked by hand.

Sadly, the manufacturing tools and materials available then prevented him from actually building his machine. However, in 1991 the Science Museum in London built a machine to his specifications, as shown in Figure 1.1. With only minor changes to the design, they were able to make the machine work. Although limited in its flexibility, the machine was able to compute difference equations up to the seventh order with up to 13 significant digits.

1.2.2 Colossus

Colossus was a computing machine developed to solve large, complex problems quickly. Early in the Second World War, Britain was losing the Battle of the Atlantic—German U-boats were sinking an enormous number of cargo ships that were resupplying the Allied war effort. The Government

Figure 1.1 *Babbage's difference engine*

Code and Cypher School was established at Bletchley Hall in Britain with the goal of breaking the German codes used to communicate with their U-boats in the North Atlantic. They were using Enigma machines, relatively simple devices that encrypted messages by shifting characters in the alphabet. However, to crack the code they needed to exhaustively evaluate text shifted by arbitrary amounts. Although the algorithm was known, the manual solution took too long, and it was often too late to make use of the information. A computer later named Colossus (see Figure 1.2) was designed by Max Newman and was custom built for this purpose. While not a general-purpose processor, Colossus was fast enough to crack all but the most sophisticated Enigma codes. Sadly, due to security concerns, the machine was destroyed when the war ended. However, the dawn of ubiquitous computing was breaking, and general-purpose computers were soon to be available.

1.2.3 The von Neumann Architecture

These and other contemporary achievements demonstrated the ability of special-purpose machines to solve specific problems. However, the creativity of John von Neumann ushered in the current era of general-purpose computing in which computers are flexible enough to solve an

Figure 1.2 *Colossus*

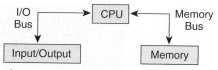

Figure 1.3 *von Neumann architecture*

astonishing array of different problems. Dr. von Neumann proposed a computer architecture that separated the Central Processing Unit (CPU) from the computer memory and the Input/Output (I/O) devices (see Figure 1.3).

Together with binary encoding for storing numerical values, this was the genesis of general-purpose computing as we know it today. Although the implementation of each component has improved beyond recognition, the fundamental processing architecture remains unchanged today.

1.3 Computing Systems Today

Today's computing systems—the combination of hardware and software that collectively solve problems—retain many of the key characteristics of these inventions: they process more data than is humanly possible, quickly enough for the results to be useful, and they basically follow the von Neumann architecture. Computer **hardware** refers to the physical equipment: the keyboard, mouse, monitor, hard disk, and printer. The **software** refers to the programs that describe the steps we want the computer to perform.

1.3.1 Computer Hardware

All computers have a similar internal organization, as shown in Figure 1.4, that is closely related to the von Neumann architecture. The CPU is usually separated into two parts: the Control Unit, which manages the flow of data between the other modules, and the Arithmetic and Logic Unit (ALU), which performs all the arithmetic and logical operations required by the software.

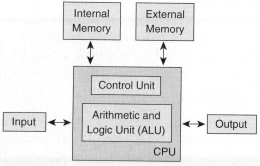

Figure 1.4 *Internal organization of a computer*

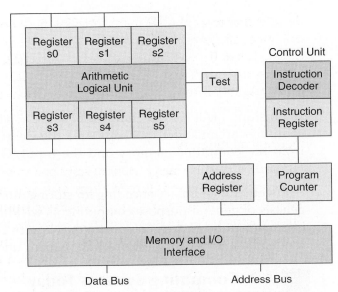

Figure 1.5 *Internal computer details*

The individual logic devices that comprise the electronic components of the computer operate in a binary mode, which is represented electrically by the presence or absence of voltage at a connection. These states, called **bits**, have the value of 1 (present) or 0 (absent). Most computer operations assemble these bits into larger collections—a **byte** being 8 bits, and **words** consisting of 16, 32, 64, or more bits. We refer to the data items coming into the computer as the **input**, and the results coming from the computations as the **output**.

Input and output (I/O) is accomplished by moving data between the memory and external equipment designed to communicate with users or other computers. In the early days, all devices had to be individually installed in the computer with dedicated wiring—a process called **hardwiring**. In contrast, today this is usually accomplished merely by plugging devices into one of many **data buses** (see Figure 1.5). A data bus is an electronic "pathway" for transporting data between devices. Since most devices expect to be able to send data on the bus as well as receive data from it, data bus design always involves a protocol that ensures that only one device is writing to the bus at any given time.

1.3.2 Computer Memory

Memory comes in many forms. Not long ago it could be nicely divided into two categories—solid state and mechanical. Solid-state memory modules were directly connected to the processor and used digital addresses to save and restore data. Mechanical memory relied upon devices that moved rewriteable storage media past sensors that converted the impressions on the storage media to digital form. Tape drives, floppy disks, hard drives, and optical disks (CDs and DVDs) share this architecture, and they are usually externally connected to the input/ output system. Recently, however, these distinctions have been blurred by the arrival of devices like **flash cards** that are solid-state memory devices but attach to the computer's I/O ports and behave as if they were mechanical memory.

Today, CPUs use many forms of solid-state memory. The first instructions executed when power is turned on are usually stored in **Read-Only Memory (ROM)**, sometimes referred to as the **Basic Input/Output System (BIOS)**. These instructions are just enough to wake up the keyboard and screen in basic mode and look around for a memory device containing the real programs. These real programs are transferred from the memory device, frequently referred to as "mass memory," to **Random-Access Memory (RAM)**—large amounts of high-speed, solid-state memory used to hold all of the programs and data users need immediately.

Most processors achieve significant performance improvement by using smaller amounts of even higher speed memory as **cache**. Cache memory processors are smart devices that "guess" what instructions and data the computer needs next, and preload those guesses into cache memory where the CPU can reach them quickly. These guesses are based on the likelihood that the program will continue linearly through the program as opposed to branching to go somewhere else for the next instruction. A significant amount of today's computer architecture design effort focuses on the effective use of cache memory to improve performance.

As programs become larger and process more data, and the systems allow more than one program to run simultaneously, RAM occasionally fills up. Most operating systems today use **virtual memory**—a data file usually on the hard drive that contains an image of everything you would like to have in RAM divided into **pages**. When the CPU requires access to a page that is not actually in RAM, it has to take the time to find a special area in RAM referred to as a "page buffer" that it can safely use, write its contents back to virtual memory, and read in the page needed. No matter how smart this process might be about looking ahead and predicting required pages, there is always a huge performance loss when a computer begins using virtual memory.

Figure 1.6 illustrates some aspects of how computer memory is managed. The operating system (UNIX, Windows, Mac OS X, or whatever) consumes some memory and determines from the I/O devices available what internal software **(drivers)** must be present to enable the application programs to communicate with the outside world. As mentioned earlier, many programs

Heap		
Stack A	Stack B	Stack C
Program A	Program B	Program C
Operating System		
Driver	Driver	Driver	Driver	Driver

Figure 1.6 *Typical memory layout*

are loaded automatically when the operating system starts, and others are loaded upon user request. In addition to the memory needed to store the instructions, each program is allocated some **stack** space for storing local static data. The remaining memory, the **heap**, is accessible to all programs upon request to the operating system. The heap is typically used to store most of the data being manipulated by the programs. When a program finishes with a block from the heap, it is usually released by that program for other programs to use as necessary.

1.3.3 Computer Software

Computer software contains the instructions that the CPU uses to run programs. There are several important categories of software, including operating systems, software applications, and language compilers. Not all processors need all these facilities. Figure 1.7 illustrates the interactions among these categories of software and the computer hardware, and the following sections describe each in more detail.

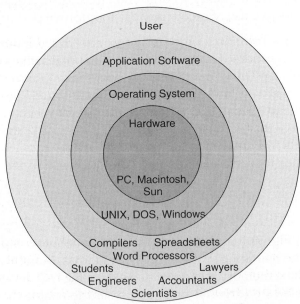

Figure 1.7 *Interactions between computer hardware and software*

Operating Systems The **operating system (OS)** serves as the manager of the computer system as a whole. It controls access to the processor by users and networked devices, and it organizes the hardware and software according to the users' specifications. The operating system is the first major software component fetched by the BIOS from mass storage, and it automatically loads and starts the myriad programs that make computers "user friendly." It also provides the tools for making the computer's peripheral devices—such as printers, scanners, and DVD drives—available to other software. Common modern operating systems are Microsoft Windows, Linux, UNIX, and Apple Mac OS.

Operating systems also contain a group of programs called **utilities** that allow you to perform functions, such as printing files, copying files from one disk to another, and listing the files that you have saved on a disk. Although these utilities are common to most operating systems, the commands themselves vary from operating system to operating system.

While computer systems give the appearance of stability, like automobiles, they require periodic maintenance to maintain peak performance.

- You should protect your computer by installing and configuring utilities that protect it from viruses, intrusive advertising, and external influences that make illegal use of the processor or its data. Refer to the documentation for your specific operating system.
- Over time, most disk drives become fragmented—the available space gets chopped up into smaller and smaller pieces—and the performance of your system begins to suffer. Defragmentation of a large disk drive may be an overnight effort, but should be done periodically.
- While very reliable, computers are not indestructible. You should establish a regular policy of backing up your personal files onto removable media. Most operating systems provide such utilities, and a number of services are now available at a modest cost that automatically back up your files to encrypted storage whenever your computer is connected to the Internet. You do not need to back up commercial software that can be reloaded from the manufacturer's installation disks.

Software Tools Software tools are commercial programs that have been written to solve specific problems. They are highly sophisticated, complex applications that use the facilities provided by the operating system to enable you to create, save, recall, manipulate, and present ideas in the form of data files on your computer. The specific nature of those files depends on the nature of the problem. If you need a well-formatted document or report, **word processors** are programs that enable you to enter and format text and graphics. They allow you to develop documents in outline form; move words, sentences, and paragraphs; and check your spelling and grammar. **Desktop publishing** combines a very powerful word processor with a high-quality printer to produce professional-grade documents.

If you need sophisticated results from tabular data, **spreadsheets** let you work easily with data that can be displayed in a grid of rows and columns. Most spreadsheet packages include plotting capabilities to create charts and graphs, so they can be especially useful in analyzing and displaying information.

If you need to store, quickly retrieve, and format large amounts of data, **database management** programs are useful tools. They are used by large organizations, such as banks, hospitals, universities, hotels, and airlines, to store and organize crucial information; they are also used to analyze large amounts of scientific data. Meteorology and oceanography are examples of scientific fields that commonly require large databases for the storage and analysis of data.

Computer-aided design (CAD) packages let you define computer models of real-world objects, assemble groups of such models, and then manipulate them graphically. CAD packages are frequently used in engineering applications, and the designs of most automobiles and aircraft are now "paperless"—the essential information is in a CAD database rather than on paper.

Programming Languages All programming languages are merely tools a programmer uses to express the logic for a computer to implement. Like any spoken language, a computer language is defined by its grammar **(syntax)** and its vocabulary. There are three necessary attributes of a computer language: the scope of the logic expressed in each line of code (the **power** of the language), the clarity of each line of code from the human viewpoint, and its **portability** between different types of processor. Computer languages are frequently described in terms of **generations** that reflect the development of language power, clarity, and portability.

First-generation, or **machine languages**, are the most primitive languages, usually tied closely to the nature of the computer hardware. Since the basic logic of the CPU is binary, the syntax of machine language is expressed as sequences of 0s and 1s. This maximizes the control over the processor, but results in programs that are completely incomprehensible to anyone, including the original programmer, and are absolutely not portable.

A **second-generation** language, frequently called **assembly language**, is a means of expressing machine language in symbolic form where each line of code usually produces a single machine instruction. While programming in assembly language is easier than machine language, it is still a tedious process that requires each detailed instruction to be specified; and like the first-generation languages, it is completely tied to the nature of the CPU.

Third-generation languages such as C, FORTRAN, and BASIC have commands and instructions that are more similar to spoken languages. One line of code of these languages creates many machine level instructions. Consequently, they are much clearer expressions of the logic of a program, and the power of each instruction is significantly increased. The resulting programs are to some degree portable between processor types. Third-generation languages and beyond are referred to as **high-level languages**.

The **fourth-generation** languages that include Ada and Java take this trend to the next level. They are completely portable between supported processor types, and each line of code creates a significant amount of machine instructions. MATLAB and its close competitors, Mathematica, Mathcad, and Maple, are very powerful fourth-generation languages that combine mathematical functions and commands with extensive capabilities for presenting results in a graphical form. This combination of computation and visualization power makes them particularly useful tools for engineers.

The current language development trend is to allow the programmer to express the overall program logic in a graphical form and have the programming tools automatically convert the diagrams to working programs. Programmers involved with these implementations still need language skills to complete the implementation of the algorithms. The goal of the fifth generation of languages is to allow a programmer to use natural language. Programmers in this generation would program in the syntax of natural speech. Implementation of a fifth-generation language will require the achievement of one of the grand challenges of computer science: computerized speech understanding.

1.3.4 Running a Computer Program

For most computer languages, getting the program to run involves compilation, linking, loading, and then executing the program. These processes are outlined in Figure 1.8.

> *Compilation:* Programs written in most high-level languages, such as C or Java, need to be compiled (i.e., translated into machine language) before the instructions can be executed by the computer. A special program called a **compiler** performs this translation. Thus,

Figure 1.8 *Program compilation, linking, loading, and execution*

in order to write and execute C programs on a computer, the computer's software must include a C compiler. If any errors[1] are detected by the compiler during compilation, the compiler generates corresponding error messages. Programmers must correct the program statements and then perform the compilation step again. The errors identified during this stage are called **compile-time errors**. For example, if you want to divide the value stored in a variable called sum by 3, the correct expression in C is sum/3. If you incorrectly write the expression using the backslash, as in sum\3, you will get a compiler error. For non-trivial programs, the process of correcting statements (or **debugging**) and recompiling often must be repeated several times before the program compiles without compiler errors. When there are no compiler errors, the compiler generates a program in machine language that performs the steps specified by the original C program. The original C program is referred to as the **source code**, and the machine-language version is called the **object code**. Thus, the source code and the object code specify the same logic, but the source code is specified in a high-level language and the object code is specified in machine language.

Linking: Once the program has compiled correctly, additional steps are necessary to prepare the object code for **execution**. A **linker** will search libraries of built-in capabilities required by this program and collect them in a single executable file stored on the hard drive. Errors generated in this phase are typically caused by the programmer referring to program modules that are not, in fact, defined in the current context.

Loading: A **loader** is then used to copy the executable program into memory where its instructions can be executed by the computer.

Execution: New errors, synonymously called **execution errors**, **runtime errors**, **logic errors**, or **program bugs**, may be identified in this stage. Execution errors often cause the termination of a program. For example, the program statements may attempt to perform a division by zero, which usually generates an execution error. Some execution errors, however, do not stop the program from executing, but they cause incorrect results to be computed. These types of errors can be caused by programmer errors in determining the correct steps in the solutions and by errors in the data processed by the program. When execution errors occur because of errors in the program statements, you must correct the errors in the source program and then begin again with the compilation step. Even when a program appears to execute

---

[1]often called **bugs**, a reference to an unidentified insect that caused a short in one of the early digital computers

properly, you must check the results carefully to be sure that they are correct. The computer will perform the steps precisely as you specify them. If you specify the wrong steps, the computer will execute these wrong (but syntactically legal) steps and present you with an answer that is incorrect.

1.4 Running an Interpreted Program

An interpreted language is one that does not appear to require compilation. Rather, the environment in which it is used gives the user the impression that the instructions are taken one at a time and executed directly. The advantage of interpreted code is that the programmer can run programs a line at a time or from a stored text file, see the results immediately, and apply a number of tools to find out why the results were not as expected. Programmers can rapidly develop and execute programs (scripts) that contain commands and executable instructions that allow them to gather data, perform calculations, observe the results, and then execute other scripts. This interactive environment does not require the formal compilation, linking/loading, and execution process described earlier for high-level computer languages.

The disadvantages of interpreted code are numerous. The code is very slow to run relative to compiled code because every line must be syntactically analyzed at run-time. In order to reduce the impact of this as much as possible, the interpreter will often make use of a compilation step that is hidden from users. Also, because there is no explicit compilation step, the programmer does not have the compiler's protection from syntax errors. Typographical errors that cause unknown assets to be referenced from a program cannot be caught by the linker. In fact, all programming errors—syntactic, typographical, and logical—are postponed until the moment the interpreter tries to deal with the offending line of code. They all become run-time errors.

1.5 Anticipated Outcomes

To conclude this chapter, we list in increasing order of importance three outcomes for a diligent student: a brief introduction to MATLAB, some understanding of programming concepts, and improvement in their problem-solving skills.

1.5.1 Introduction to MATLAB

MATLAB is a highly successful engineering programming language that includes not only the capabilities needed in this text to introduce programming to novices, but also a vast collection of tools in toolboxes that enable professional engineers to be highly productive. It is very likely that you will encounter MATLAB in your career as an engineer. The concepts you learn in this book will ensure that you know what to do when faced with a MATLAB program.

1.5.2 Learning Programming Concepts

Even if you never see MATLAB again, you will certainly either need to use other programming languages or be able to converse effectively with other engineers who do. Converting to, or writing accurate specifications for, other languages is greatly simplified if you have a general idea of the capabilities of that language. When faced with a different programming language, if the student has an understanding of the basic underlying programming concepts, the transition from MATLAB to the new language becomes just one question—"How do I express the concepts I need in the new language?" We therefore have chosen to explain each programming concept in a language-independent way before discussing the MATLAB implementation of that concept.

1.5.3 Problem-Solving Skills

More important even than the computing concepts inherent in all computer languages is the ability to use those concepts as tools to solve a problem. Before we even start to program, we have to develop an idea of how to solve the problem before us. If we think about a computer program as a logical component that consumes data in one form and produces data in another, we can think about problem solving as the process of designing a collection of solutions to sub-problems. A brief illustration and example will suffice.

In general terms, solutions to nontrivial problems are found by the two-pronged approach illustrated in Figure 1.9. We can consider the original information and ask ourselves what could be done with that information using existing tools, and we can also consider the objective and the different ways in which that objective might be achieved. The process of creative problem solving then becomes a search for a match between states that can be achieved from the given data and states from which the answer can be achieved.

For example, say you have a big collection of baseball cards and you want to find the names of the 10 "qualified" players with the highest lifetime

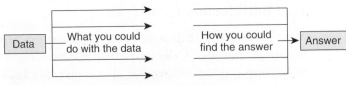

Figure 1.9 *Generalized problem solving*

batting averages. To qualify, the players must have been in the league at least five years, had at least 100 plate appearances per year, and made fewer than 10 errors per year. The cards contain all the relevant information for each player. You just have to organize the cards to solve the problem. Clearly there are a number of steps between the stack of cards and the solution. In no particular order, these are:

a. Write down the names of the players from some cards

b. Sort the stack of cards by the lifetime batting average

c. Select all players from the stack with five years or more in the league

d. Select all players from the stack with fewer than 10 errors per year

e. Select all players from the stack with over 100 plate appearances per year

f. Keep the first 10 players from the stack

When you think about it from right to left as shown in Figure 1.9, step a is probably the last step and step f is probably the step before that. The hard work starts when you think about it from left to right. Intuitively, when you think about sorting the stack of cards, this seems like a lengthy process. Since the sorting should probably be done on a small number of cards, you should do all the selecting before the sorting. Continuing that line of reasoning, you would reduce the total effort if the first selection pass was the criterion that eliminated most cards. You might even consider combining all three selection steps into one.

One logical way to find the players' names that you need would be to perform the steps in this order: c, d, and e in any order, followed by b, f, and then a.

Chapter Summary

This chapter presented an overview of the historical background of computing and the computer hardware and software concepts that build the foundation for the rest of this book:

- The spectrum of software products, ranging from operating systems to the many flavors of specific programming tools
- The rich variety of programming languages currently in use, and the place of interpreted programs in that spectrum as a legitimate fourth-generation language
- The basics of problem solving as a search for a path from the data provided to the answers required

Self Test

Use the following questions to check your understanding of the material in this chapter:

True or False

1. Computers were originally conceived as tools for solving specific problems.
2. Bill Gates designed the first working computer.
3. Programs cannot interact with the world outside the computer without an operating system.
4. Programs cannot interact with the world outside the computer without drivers.
5. Programs cannot interact with the world outside the computer without hardware interfaces.
6. Application programs have access to shared memory.
7. An algorithm bridges the gap between the available data and the result to be achieved.

Fill in the Blanks

1. A computer language is not a(n) _____ exercise; it is a _____ tool for communication and problem solving.
2. Together with the use of binary encoding for storing numerical values, _____ was the genesis of general-purpose computing as we know it today.
3. Most operating systems today use_____, which is actually a data file containing an image of everything you would like to have in RAM.
4. Operating systems contain a group of programs called _____ that allow you to perform functions, such as printing, copying files, and listing the file names.
5. Many _____ are loaded automatically when the operating system starts, and others are loaded upon user request.
6. Even when a program appears to execute properly, you must check the results carefully to find _____ errors.
7. Problem solving is the process of designing a collection of _____ .
8. The process of problem solving is a search for a match between _____ one can achieve from the given data and _____ from which the answer can be achieved.

Getting Started

Chapter Objectives

This chapter introduces you to some of the fundamentals of computing that apply to all programming languages, and specifically to the programming environment used for program development. The fundamentals of programming include:

■ How to use abstraction to think in a general way about a collection of data and procedural steps

■ How to describe the solution of a problem as an algorithm

■ The three paradigms of computing and the position of MATLAB in that spectrum

■ Three aspects of the apparently simple task of assigning a value to a variable

As you study the MATLAB user interface, you will understand:

■ How to use the Command window to explore single commands interactively and how to recall earlier commands to be repeated or changed

■ Where to examine the variables and files created in MATLAB

■ How to view data created in MATLAB

■ How MATLAB presents graphical data in separate windows

■ How to create scripts to solve simple arithmetic problems

Introduction

The name MATLAB is a contraction of **Mat**rix **Lab**oratory. It was developed for engineers to create, manipulate, and visualize matrices—rectangular arrays of numerical values. At its most basic level, MATLAB can perform the same functions as your scientific calculator, but it has expanded far beyond its original capabilities and now provides an interactive system and programming language for many applications, including financial analysis as well as general scientific and technical computation.

The following are the fundamental components of MATLAB:

- A computing system that accepts one instruction at a time in text form and implements the logic of that instruction. Instructions must conform to a specific syntax and vocabulary, which will be the topic of Chapters 3–9.
- A large library of modules that provide high-level capabilities for processing data. These modules will be the major topic of Chapters 10–17.
- A graphical user interface (GUI) that lets users assemble and implement programs that solve specific problems. The rest of this chapter will describe the basic behavior of these windows.

MATLAB offers a number of advantages to users over conventional, compiled languages like C++, Java, or FORTRAN:

- Because MATLAB programs are interpreted rather than compiled, the process of producing a working solution can be much quicker than with compiled languages.
- MATLAB excels at numerical calculations, especially matrix calculations.
- MATLAB has built-in graphics capabilities that produce professional-looking images for reports.

However, the very attributes that make MATLAB convenient for a user to develop quick solutions to certain problems make it unsuitable for other kinds of projects. For example:

- MATLAB does not work well for large computing projects where a number of developers share coding responsibilities.
- Professional GUIs and windowing applications (like the MATLAB system itself) are best written in a compiled language.

2.1 Programming Language Background

Before learning about concepts in computing, you need to understand the background of programming languages. This section discusses the following aspects of programming languages: abstraction, algorithms, programming paradigms, and three fundamental concepts of programming—assigning values to variables, data typing, and the difference between classes and objects.

2.1.1 Abstraction

For the purpose of this text, we will define **abstraction** as "expressing a quality apart from a particular implementation." We use the concept of abstraction in everyday conversation without thinking about it:

> "To convert from degrees Celsius to Kelvin, you add 273 to *the temperature*."

> "He *drove home* from the office."

The first is an example of **data abstraction**. "The temperature" could mean a single reading from the thermometer hanging outside the window or a table of temperature readings for the month of August. The specifics are unimportant; the phrase captures all you need to know.

The second example is actually much more complex—an example of multiple levels of **procedural abstraction**. To a businessperson taking the same route home every night, "drive home" is all that is required to understand the idea. To a competent driver unfamiliar with the route, the next level of abstraction might be necessary—turn right out of the parking lot, left onto Main Street, and so on. For instructions to guide a future robotic commuter vehicle, an incredibly fine-grained level of abstraction will be required. Everything taken for granted in the higher level abstractions will need to be meticulously spelled out for the robotic vehicle—start the engine, accelerate the vehicle, look out for traffic, keep in the lane, find the turn, steer the vehicle, control the speed, observe and obey all signs, and so on.

2.1.2 Algorithms

Chapter 1 defined problem solving as the ability to isolate sub-problems that seem simple and appropriate to solve, and then assemble the solutions to these sub-problems. The solutions to each of these sub-problems would be expressed as an **algorithm**, which is a sequence of instructions for solving a sub-problem. The process of solving each sub-problem and assembling the solutions to form the solution to the whole problem would also be expressed as an algorithm at a higher level of abstraction.

The level of abstraction needed to describe an algorithm varies greatly with the mechanism available. For example, describing the algorithm (recipe) for baking cookies might take the following forms:

- To your grandmother, who has been baking cookies for the last 50 years, it might be "Please bake some cookies."
- To others it might be "Buy a cookie mix and follow the directions."
- To a young person learning to cook from scratch, the algorithm might include an intricate series of instructions for measuring, sifting, and combining ingredients; setting the oven temperature and preheating the oven; forming the cookies and putting them on the cookie sheet; and so on.

In programming terms, algorithms are frequently expressed first conceptually at a high level of abstraction, as demonstrated in Section 1.5. The solutions to each sub-problem would then be expressed at lower and lower levels of abstraction until the description is sufficient to write programs that solve each sub-problem, thereby contributing the pieces that, when assembled, solve the whole problem.

2.1.3 Programming Paradigms

From the Greek word *paradeigma*—"to show alongside"—the *American Heritage Dictionary* defines a paradigm as "a set of assumptions, concepts, values, and practices that constitutes a way of viewing reality for the community that shares them, especially in an intellectual discipline." So a programming paradigm becomes a codified set of practices allowing the community of computing professionals to frame their ideas. This section considers three radically different paradigms: functional programming, procedural programming, and object-oriented programming.

Functional programming is typically associated with languages like Lisp and Forth, in which every programming operation is actually implemented as a function call with no side effects (changes of state of the program surroundings) permitted or implemented in the language. Without side effects, a programming solution can be mathematically proven to be correct—an enormous advantage. Except for the discussion of recursion, this paradigm will not be mentioned again.

Procedural programming is typical of languages like FORTRAN, C, and MATLAB, where the basic programs or sub-programs are sequences of operations on data items that are generally accessible to all programs. Although side effects from sub-programs—such as changing the values of variables outside that sub-program—are considered poor practice, they are not prohibited by the language.

Object-oriented programming (OOP), typical of languages like C++, Ada, and Java, is a relatively new addition to the world of programming paradigms. It is characterized by the concept of encapsulating, or packaging, data items together with the methods or functions that manipulate those data items. In this paradigm, side effects are explicitly managed by controlling access to the data and methods in a particular grouping. The major theme in true OOP is that "everything is an object." You will see MATLAB exhibiting many traits of OOP as you work through this book, but you will not need to use this programming paradigm.

2.2 Basic Data Manipulation

In order to use MATLAB to demonstrate basic data manipulation, we begin with an exercise in starting and stopping the MATLAB system.

2.2.1 Starting and Stopping MATLAB

Exercise 2.1 shows you how to start and stop the MATLAB user interface. We will soon see the details of all the program's windows. For the moment,

Exercise 2.1 Starting and stopping MATLAB

If you have not installed MATLAB on your computer yet, follow the directions that came with your license for performing and testing the installation.

To start MATLAB, double-click on its icon. In the Interactions window you should see the MATLAB prompt (>>), which tells you that the MATLAB system is waiting for you to enter a command.

To exit MATLAB, type exit at the MATLAB prompt, choose the menu option File > Exit, or click the close icon (x) in the upper-right corner of the screen.

however, we will interact with MATLAB by typing instructions in the large Command window that occupies the left side of your screen.

2.2.2 Assigning Values to Variables

The concept of assigning values to variables is the first challenge facing novice programmers. The difficulty arises because many programming languages (including MATLAB) present this simple concept in a syntax that is very similar to conventional algebra, but with significantly different meaning. Consider, for example, the following algebraic expression:

```
z = x + y
```

In normal algebra, this is a two-way relationship that is an identity for the duration of the problem. If you knew the values of z and x, you could derive the value of y with no further analysis. To a programmer, however, this statement has a different meaning. It means that you want to sum the values given to the variables x and y, and store the result in a variable called z. If either x or y is unknown at the time of executing this statement, an error ensues. In particular, this relationship is true *only for this statement*. The relationship can be revoked in the next instruction, which might be:

```
z = 4*x - y
```

In algebra, this pair of statements collectively constrains the values of x, y, and z. In programming, the only significance is that the programmer decided to calculate the current value of z differently. A few computer languages are sensitive to this dilemma and use a different symbol for assigning values to a variable. For example, in Pascal or Ada, an instruction to assign the value z = x + y would be written as follows:

```
z := x + y
```

The ":=" operator clearly indicates that this is an assignment statement, not an algebraic identity.

Variable names: In general, variable names may contain any combination of uppercase and lowercase alphabetic letters, numbers, and the special

Exercise 2.2 Assigning variables

When you start MATLAB, you should see the prompt '>> ' in the Interactions window. This is your invitation to type something. Text that you should type will be shown like this throughout this book:

```
>> radius = 49
```

Note that all entries in the Interactions window terminate with the Enter key. The system response will be shown like this:

```
radius =
    49
>>
```

This response indicates that the value **49** has been stored in a variable named `radius`. To retrieve the value of `radius`, you just type its name and press Enter.

```
>> radius
ans =
    49
```

This response shows that the value **49** has been retrieved. Since you didn't specify where to put this result, it was stored in a default variable named `ans`.

characters _ (underscore) and $ (dollar). The underscore character is frequently used to represent a space in a variable name because spaces are not allowed. However, variable names may not begin with a numeric character, and even though the names may be hundreds of characters long, the first 64 characters must be unique. Exercise 2.2 demonstrates the assignment of values to variables.

2.2.3 Data Typing

It is important to understand how MATLAB treats the data stored in a variable. Different languages take varying approaches to this problem, and languages in general fall into two broad categories: untyped and typed. In general, interpreted languages like Lisp, Forth, Python, and MATLAB determine the type of data contained by a variable based on the type of data being stored there. Such languages are referred to as **untyped languages**. Each assignment

Style Points 2.1

1. Some early versions of the FORTRAN and Basic languages severely restricted the number of characters you could use for variable names. It is no longer necessary to program as if you were still in the "bad old days." Choose names for variables that describe their content. For example, a variable used to store the velocity of an object should be named `velocity_in_feet_per_second` rather than `v`.

2. Since the space character is not permitted in variable names, there are two conventions for joining multiple words together to make a single variable name. One uses the underscore character to separate the words (`file_size`), and the other capitalizes the first letter of additional words (`fileSize`). You should choose one convention and be consistent with it. You cannot use a hyphen to concatenate words—MATLAB treats the name `file-size` as the arithmetic operation subtracting the value of the variable `size` from the value of the variable `file`.

statement is presumed to be correct. If the variable already exists, both its type and value are reassigned; if it did not exist before, a new variable is created. Exercise 2.3 illustrates the effect of performing simple mathematical operations in MATLAB. By putting 49 into the variable `radius`, you established its type as numeric and enabled it to be used in normal arithmetic operations. Character strings are specified by including arbitrary characters between single quote marks. These have the type `char`, and must be handled differently, as discussed fully in Chapter 6. When you stored a character string in the variable `radius`, adding 1 to it did not cause an error in MATLAB as it would in some other languages, because addition is actually defined for character strings. It just did something radically different—it actually converted the individual characters to numbers and then added 1!

While this ability to assign data types dynamically is good for interpreted languages, it has two undesirable consequences that are really hard to unravel as the program runs:

- Typographical errors that misspell variable names in assignment statements cause new variables to be declared unintentionally and without the user noticing the error
- Logical errors that assign incompatible data to the same variable can cause obscure runtime errors

Typed languages require that programmers declare both the name and type of a variable before a value can be assigned to it. With this information, a compiler can then do a better job of ensuring that the programmer is not using a variable in an unintended way. Typed languages fall into two categories: weak typing and strong typing. If programmers decide to use only the normal data types, such as `double` and `char` as we saw above, this

---

Exercise 2.3 Performing basic mathematical operations

Make the following entries in the Interactions window. You should see the responses as shown here:

```
>> radius = 49
radius =
    49
>> radius + 1
ans =
    50
>> radius = 'radius of a circle'    ← string
radius =
    radius of a circle
>> radius + 1
ans =
  115  98  101  106  118  116  33  112  103 ...
```

is known as **weak typing** and is the usual approach to typing. In some extreme circumstances, programmers may choose to be more restrictive and define specific data types with a limited set of permitted interactions. This is called **strong typing**. For example, programmers might define the following data types, all of which are actually of type `double`: `meters`, `seconds`, and `meters_per_second`. The compiler would then be provided with a set of rules specifying the legal relationships between these types. For example, assignments can only be made to a variable of type `meters_per_second` from another variable of the same type, or by dividing a variable of type `meters` by a variable of type `seconds`.[1]

2.2.4 Classes and Objects

This section discusses two different attributes of a variable: its type and its value. In Section 2.2.2 you saw that a variable is a container for data, whose **value** is determined by what is assigned to the variable. In Section 2.2.3 you saw that by making that assignment to a variable, MATLAB also infers the **type** of data stored in that variable. You will see that while MATLAB is an untyped language, the programs you write will behave differently if applied to data of different types. For example, the type `double` specifies the form and expected behavior of a number. Adding 1 to a variable of class `double` containing 4 will, as expected, produce the result 5. Similarly, the type `char` is intended to hold a single character. Adding 1 to a `char` variable containing the value `'d'` will produce the numerical equivalent of the character `'e'`. MATLAB refers to the type of data in a variable as its **class**, and the value contained in the variable at any time as an **object**, an instance of that class. So in the operation:

```
this_number = 42.0
   object          class: double
```

the variable `this_number` would be defined (if it didn't already exist); its class would be set to `double`, the inherent type of a floating point number; and its value to `42.0`. So the word `double` corresponds to a type definition or `class`, while the variable `this_number` is a variable of that type, which is an instance of that class or, in programming terms, an `object`.

2.3 MATLAB User Interface

MATLAB uses several display windows (see Figure 2.1). The default view includes a large Command window on the left, and stacked on the right are the Files, Workspace, and Command History windows. The tabs near the

---

[1]Before rushing to judge on the pickiness of this approach, note that this would have avoided the loss in 1999 of the Mars Climate Orbiter, which crashed into Mars because one group of programmers used English units while another used metric.

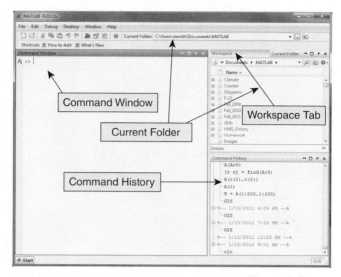

Figure 2.1 *The MATLAB default window configuration*

Hint 2.1

If you are using MATLAB, you can customize how your initial window will display. If you make a mistake and close an essential window, you can always restore the default configuration by choosing Desktop > Desktop Layout > Default.

Hint 2.2

When you make a mistake, you cannot easily correct it as you would in a word processor. The Interactions window really is functioning like a calculator, performing one instruction at a time exactly as you specify them. When you enter the command, it is immediately executed, regardless of whether that is what you intended. MATLAB offers several ways to correct erroneous commands. One way is to use the arrow keys on your keyboard. The up and down arrows let you move through the list of commands you have executed. Once you find the appropriate command, you can edit it and then press Enter to execute your new version.

---

middle of the windows on the right indicate which views are layered in that particular window. Selecting a tab will bring that view to the top. Other windows, such as an Editor window or a Figure window, will automatically open when needed.

2.3.1 Command Window

You can use MATLAB in two modes: Command mode, which is useful if you need instant responses to specific MATLAB commands, and Edit mode, in which practical solutions are developed. When working in Command mode, we use the Command window, which offers an environment similar to a scientific calculator. This window lets you save any values you calculate, but you cannot permanently save the commands used to generate those values. You will see in the next section how to use the Editor window to create and execute a text file of commands as the first step to unleashing the full programming capability of the language. The Command window is useful for performing quick experiments to discover the effects of different commands in MATLAB before embedding them in a larger program. You can perform calculations in the Command window much like doing calculations on a scientific calculator. Most of the

Exercise 2.4 Using the Interactions window

To compute the value of 5^2, type this command:

```
>> 5^2
```

The following output will be displayed:

```
ans =
      25
```

To find the cosine of π, type:

```
>> cos(pi)
```

which results in the following output:

```
ans =
-1
```

syntax is even the same. Exercise 2.4 shows how you might use the Command window to test two simple calculations.

Notice that in both of the examples in Exercise 2.4, MATLAB echoes the result as if it were saved in a variable called `ans`. This is the default variable used to save the result of any calculation you perform in the Command window that is not specifically assigned to another variable. Notice also the use of one of MATLAB's many built-in functions, `cos(...)`, that compute the cosine of an angle in radians, and of the built-in constant `pi`.

2.3.2 Command History

The Command History window records the commands you issued in the Command window in chronological sequence. When you exit MATLAB or when you issue the `clc` (Clear Commands) instruction, the commands listed in the Command window are cleared. However, the Command History window retains a list of all the commands you issued. You can clear the Command History using the Edit menu if you need to by selecting Edit and then Clear Command History. If you entered the sample commands in Exercise 2.4, notice that they are repeated in the Command History window. This window lets you review previous MATLAB sessions, and you can transfer the commands to the Command window by copying and pasting. Exercise 2.5 demonstrates the use of the Command History window. You will find the Command History window useful as you perform more and more complicated calculations in the Command window.

Hint 2.3

As a security precaution, if you use MATLAB on a public computer, you can set its defaults to clear the Command History window when you exit MATLAB or when you log off the computer.

Exercise 2.5 Using the Command History window

In the Interactions window, type:

```
>> clc
```

This should clear the Interactions window but leave the data in the Command History window intact. You can transfer any command from the Command History window to the Interactions window by double-clicking it (which also executes the command) or by clicking and dragging the line of code into the Interactions window. Try double-clicking:

```
cos(pi)
```

This should result in the following display in the Interactions window:

```
ans =
    -1
```

Now click and drag 5^2 from the Command History window into the Interactions window. The command won't execute until you press the Enter key, and then you'll get the following result:

```
ans =
    25
```

2.3.3 Workspace Window

The Workspace window keeps track of the variables you have defined as you execute commands in the Command window. As you have seen in the exercises so far, because you have not created other variables yet, the Workspace window should just show one variable, ans. The columns in the window display the name of the variable, its current value, and an entry in the class column (see Figure 2.2). In this case, the variable ans has a value of 25 and is a double array. Actually, even a single number you would usually consider a scalar is a 1 × 1 array to MATLAB. Exercise 2.6 shows how to obtain more information about a particular variable. Figure 2.2 shows the normal Variable window display for the variable ans. Figure 2.3 shows that the variable ans is a 1 × 1 array, uses 8 bytes of memory, and is an object of class double.

row × column

In Exercise 2.7, variable A has been added to the Workspace window, which lists variables in alphabetical order. Variables beginning with capital

 Exercise 2.6 Showing more details in the Workspace window

Set the Variables window to show more about the variable ans by right-clicking on the bar with the column labels. On the drop-down menu, check the boxes next to Size and Bytes, so that these will display in addition to Name, Value, and Class. Your Variables window should now look like Figure 2.3.

Figure 2.2 *The Workspace window*

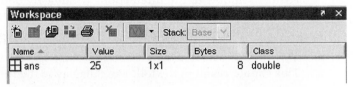

Figure 2.3 *Additional information in the Workspace window*

letters are listed first, followed by variables starting with lowercase letters, as shown in Figure 2.4.

Exercise 2.8 added the variable B to the Workspace window, and in Figure 2.5 you can see that its size is a 1 × 4 array.

You define two-dimensional arrays in a similar fashion. Semicolons are used to separate rows, as illustrated in Exercise 2.9. As you can see in

Exercise 2.7 Defining other variables

You can define additional variables in the Interactions window, and they will be listed in the Variables window. For example, type:

```
>> A = 5
```

This returns:

```
A =
    5
```

Exercise 2.8 Creating a vector

Entering matrices is not discussed in detail in this section. However, you can enter a simple one-dimensional matrix by typing:

```
>> B = [1, 2, 3, 4]
```

This returns:

```
B =
  1  2  3  4
```

The commas are optional. You would see the same result from:

```
>> B = [1 2 3 4]
```

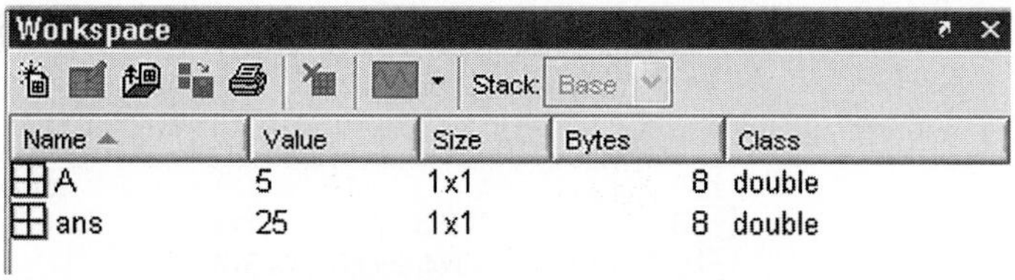

Figure 2.4 *Additional variables*

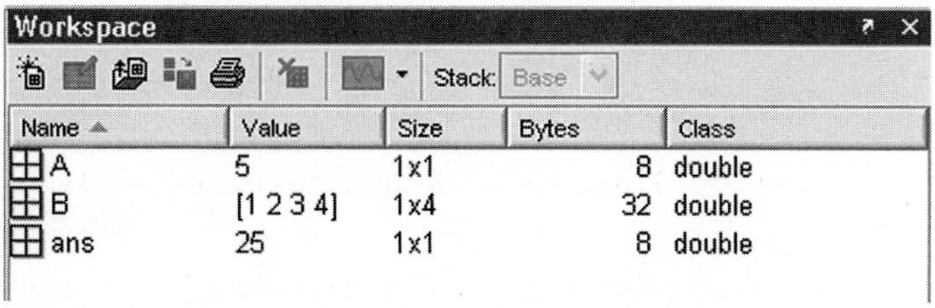

Figure 2.5 *Vector added in the Workspace window*

Figure 2.6, variable c appears in the Workspace window as a 3 × 4 array. Vectors and arrays are discussed fully in Chapter 3.

Note:

MATLAB presents numerical results in the following default format: if the value is an integer, there are no decimal places presented; but if there is a fractional part, four decimal places appear. You can change this by using the format command. See MATLAB help for details.

You can recall the values for any variable by just typing in the variable name, as shown in Exercise 2.10.

If you prefer to have a less cluttered desktop, you can close any of the windows (except the Command window) by clicking the x in the upper-right corner of each window.

Exercise 2.9 Creating a 3 × 4 matrix

```
>> C = [ 1 2 3 4; 10 20 30 40; 5 10 15 20]
```

returns:

```
C =

     1     2     3     4
    10    20    30    40
     5    10    15    20
```

Now, enter

```
>> C = [1 2 3 4; 10 20 30 40];
```

You will see the value of C change in the Variables window, but not echoed in the Interactions window. The semicolon on the end of the line suppresses presentation of the result.

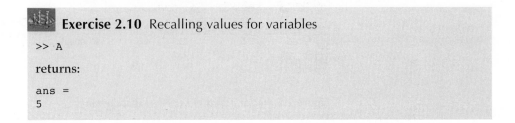

Figure 2.6 *Array added in the Workspace window*

Exercise 2.10 Recalling values for variables

```
>> A
```

returns:

```
ans =
5
```

You can also personalize which windows you prefer to keep open by selecting View from the menu bar and checking the appropriate windows. If you suppress the Workspace window, you can still find out what variables have been defined by using the commands who or whos. The command who lists the variable names, and whos lists the variable names together with their size and class. Exercise 2.11 illustrates this capability.

2.3.4 Current Directory Window

When MATLAB accesses files from and saves information to your hard drive, it uses the current directory. The default for the current directory depends on your version of the software and how it was installed. The current directory is listed at the top of the main window (see Figure 2.7). This can be changed by selecting another directory from the drop-down list to the right of the current directory name, or by browsing through your

Exercise 2.11 Using the whos command

```
>> whos
```

You should see the following display in the Command window:

```
Name    Size    Bytes    Class
A       1x1         8    double array
B       1x4        32    double array
C       3x4        96    double array
ans     1x1         8    double array
Grand total is 18 elements using 144 bytes
```

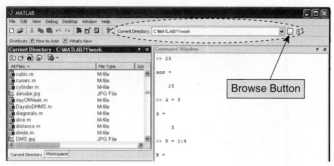

Figure 2.7 *The current directory*

computer files using the browse button located to the right of the drop-down list (circled in Figure 2.7).

2.3.5 Variable Editor

Double-clicking on any variable listed in the Workspace window automatically launches a Variable Editor window. Values stored in the variable are displayed in a spreadsheet-like format. You can change values in the Variable editor, or you can add new values.

2.3.6 Figure Window

A Figure window is created automatically when a MATLAB command requests a graph. Exercise 2.12 guides you through creating a graph. The MATLAB window opens automatically (see Figure 2.8). Any additional graphs you create will overwrite the plot in the current Figure window unless you specifically command MATLAB to open a new Figure window with the `figure` command. If you are using MATLAB version R2008a or newer, the first time you open a Figure window, a pop-up window appears with links to information about brushing and linking. As with the use of the Variable Editor, this

Hint 2.4

It is generally considered to be poor practice to edit the values of data by hand. A more rigorous approach would be to change the script that generated the data, thereby making the data changes repeatable.

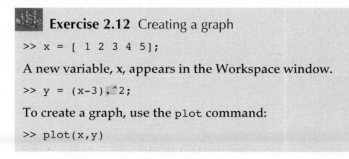

Exercise 2.12 Creating a graph

```
>> x = [ 1 2 3 4 5];
```

A new variable, x, appears in the Workspace window.

```
>> y = (x-3).^2;
```

To create a graph, use the `plot` command:

```
>> plot(x,y)
```

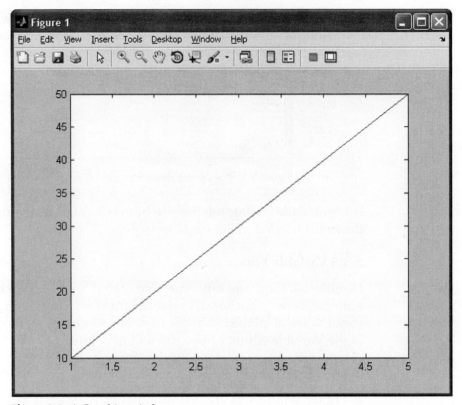

Figure 2.8 *A Graphics window*

is not the best way to modify data. See Hint 2.4. You can permanently hide this window by clicking the X at its right side.

MATLAB makes it easy to modify graphs by adding titles, x and y labels, multiple lines, and more with MATLAB built-in commands. Details of these commands will be presented in Chapter 11.

2.3.7 Editor Window

MATLAB provides a text editor, enabling you to create or modify text files that run in the Editor window. The Editor window is opened by choosing File > New > M-File. This window lets you type and save a series of commands without executing them. You can also open the Editor window by double-clicking a file name in the Current Directory window or by typing:

```
>> edit <file_name>
```

in the Command window, where `<file_name>` is the name of the file you want to open. You can open multiple files at the same time, using the tabbed overlays to identify the files. An asterisk appears on the tab with the file name to indicate that the file has been modified since it was saved. Options under the Window menu let you organize the multiple files in various ways that make more than one file visible at once. When closing the Editor window, MATLAB displays a dialog asking if you need to save any changed files.

2.4 Scripts

This section describes the basic mechanism for creating, saving, and executing scripts as m-files. Building script files lets you save and reuse program statements without retyping them in the Command window.

2.4.1 Text Files

MATLAB uses text files as a permanent means of saving scripts (sets of instructions) rather than just entering commands in the Command window. As you will see in Chapter 8, text files are streams of characters stored sequentially with "markers" that indicate the end of each line of text. For now, think of a script much like writing an e-mail message—a number of lines of text written in a "smart" editor. The MATLAB Editor uses various techniques to help you format commands in these files.

2.4.2 Creating Scripts

A MATLAB script consists of a combination of executable instructions that MATLAB interprets and comment statements that help readers understand the script. You create **comments** by putting a percent sign (%) in the text file. MATLAB will ignore all text from that mark to the end of the current line. The MATLAB Editor colors all such comments green to distinguish them from the executable instructions. Most applications that use files specify a particular file name extension (the characters after the period in the file name) to identify how the text files will be used. MATLAB uses the extension .m, and the script files are often referred to as **m-files**. You create a new script file either by choosing File > New > M-File or by clicking the new file icon on the far left of the tool bar. The MATLAB Editor will then open a blank file in which you can enter the commands and comments of your script.

Import Note: Because MATLAB treats the names of .m files much like variable names, the names of your files must follow the same rules as those for variables in Section 2.2.2 above.

Hint 2.5

We began this first script with two commands: clear and clc. Every script should have these two commands (and later, also close all) before its first executable instruction. However, to avoid repetition, we will not include these commands in subsequent listings in this test.

Exercise 2.13 Creating a script

In this exercise, you will create a script derived from the Pythagorean theorem to compute the hypotenuse of a right triangle:

$$H^2 = A^2 + B^2$$

where A and B are the sides adjacent to the right angle, and H is the hypotenuse opposite. Open a new script file and type the commands shown in Listing 2.1 (don't type the accompanying line numbers—they will be automatically displayed).

Try creating the script described in Exercise 2.13 and shown in Listing 2.1.

Listing 2.1 Script to solve for the hypotenuse

```
1. clear
2. clc
3. A = 3;    % the first side of a triangle
4. B = 4;    % the second side of a triangle
5. hypSq = A^2 + B^2;   % the square of the
                        % hypotenuse
6. H = sqrt(hypSq)      % the answer
```

In Listing 2.1:

Line 1: Instructs MATLAB to delete all variables in your working directory.

Line 2: Instructs MATLAB to clear the Command window. Any text that now appears in the Command window will be the result of running this script, not the result of previous activities.

Lines 3–4: Assign values to A and B. The semicolons prevent MATLAB from displaying the result in the Command window; the percent sign begins the legible comment. Lines may contain nothing but a comment.

Line 5: Intermediate results with suitable names sometimes improve the legibility of the algorithm.

Line 6: Invokes the built-in library function `sqrt(...)` to compute the final result.

2.4.3 The Current Directory

After you have entered a script, you must name it and save it in a directory. MATLAB will need to find that directory—its working directory—in order to run the script. By default, MATLAB expects scripts to be stored in the working directory, displayed in the tool bar at the top of the MATLAB main window. The specific path will vary with your version of MATLAB. However, the Current Directory window circled in Figure 2.7 always shows the default location when MATLAB starts. If you decide to store your scripts elsewhere, you will need to redirect MATLAB to that directory by typing it into the Current Directory window or using the browse button to the right of the display.

Once script files are saved in your working directory, you can edit them again by selecting and opening them with the MATLAB Editor. To open them, either use the File > Open menu command or double-click the file name in the Current Directory window. Before you close MATLAB, you should save the file created in Exercise 2.13.

2.4.4 Running Scripts

After you have built and saved a script, you can run it using any of the following methods:

- Type the name of the script in the Command window.
- Choose the Debug > Run menu item in the MATLAB Editor window.
- Press the F5 key when the script is visible in the editor. Doing this saves the script automatically before executing it.

The latest versions of MATLAB will echo the file name in the Command window when you invoke the script by the latter two methods. After you execute the script, the trace output is written to the Command window as if you had typed the script instructions there one at a time. For practice, run the script created in Exercise 2.13.

2.4.5 Punctuating Scripts

Many programming languages put a semicolon (;) at the end of a line to indicate the end of a command. Since the MATLAB language uses the end of a line to indicate the end of a command, it does not require an end-of-command character. If a long command needs to be extended to the next line for convenience in viewing the program, three periods, frequently referred to as **ellipses**, must be placed at the end of the line to continue the script.

The MATLAB language uses the semicolon for a different purpose. By default, all assignment commands display their results in the Command window in text form. For complex programs, the volume of this output can become too large. Whenever you really don't want to see all that output, putting a semicolon character at the end of a line will prevent the results of that assignment from displaying in the Command window.

Style Points 2.2

1. When writing scripts, you should invest some time to add comments. Comments make the scripts easier to understand as you are developing them, and make it more likely that you will be able to reuse the script later. Note: The listings included in this text will not have an appropriate level of commenting a. to save space and b. because they are explained in detail in the text.

2. Scripts should be written incrementally—build a little, test a little—rather than writing a whole script and then trying to find out where in that pile of code you made the mistake(s).

Common Pitfalls 2.1

You will quickly become accustomed to understanding the general flow of your script by observing the assignment statements reported in the Interactions window. However, especially if you have programmed in a language that requires semicolons at the end of a command, you may inadvertently put semicolons in your script. These will suppress the presentation of results and could mislead you into believing that a specific set of instructions has not been executed.

2.4.6 Debugging Scripts

MATLAB provides extensive debugging capabilities based on the use of **break points**, which are places in your program where you want to stop and verify that the code is doing what you expect. You insert break points as you edit a code segment by clicking the small dash between the line number and the start of the text. If the program is ready to run, a red dot appears in place of the dash where you clicked. If the file has been changed and hasn't been saved, the dot will be gray, in which case you should save the file. You can set any number of break points throughout your code.

After you start running a program, when MATLAB reaches a break point, execution stops, an arrow overwrites the break point symbol, and you can examine the contents of the variables either in the Workspace window or by passing the mouse slowly over the variable in the Editor window. A Debugging tool bar is available with icons that let you:

- Continue executing the logic from this point (other break points may come into effect)
- Step over the logic in this line to the next line in this code block
- Step into any modules referenced by this line of code
- Step out of this current code block

Use the script from Exercise 2.13 to practice inserting break points.

2.5 Engineering Example—Spacecraft Launch

In 1996, the Ansari X Prize was offered for the first time for a private venture: a reusable spacecraft. The requirements were for the same vehicle to carry three people into outer space twice in a two-week time period. The competition was won in 2004 by Tier 1, a company led by Burt Rutan. Their concept was to have a mother ship take off and land on a conventional runway carrying Space Ship One (see Figure 2.9). The spacecraft would be launched at 25,000 feet altitude and would reach outer space (an altitude of 100 km), then glide back and land on the same runway. They repeated this within a week, and they won the prize.

Figure 2.9 *Space Ship One*

Problem:

Assuming that the spacecraft uses all its fuel to achieve a vertical velocity u at 25,000 feet, what is the value of u for the spacecraft to reach outer space?

Style Points 2.3
Notice that when presented in this manner, the "inner values" like cm and inch cancel to ensure that the conversions are consistent.

Solution:

There are two parts to this problem: converting units to the metric system, and choosing and solving an equation for motion under constant acceleration (the rocket motor is no longer burning).

1. **Convert the launch altitude from feet to meters.** I like to remember as few numbers as possible. I do remember that 1 inch = 2.54 cm, so we will use this in a MATLAB script to find the conversion from feet to meters. The appropriate chain of calculations is this:

$$meters = feet \times \frac{meters}{cm} \times \frac{cm}{inch} \times \frac{inch}{feet}$$

Listing 2.2 shows the beginning of the script to solve this problem.

In Listing 2.2:

Lines 1–3: Define general knowledge with meaningful variable names to enable subsequent use of these values without ambiguity.

Listing 2.2 Script to compute the spacecraft's velocity (Part 1)

```
1. cmPerInch = 2.54;     % general knowledge
2. inchesPerFt = 12;     % general knowledge
3. metersPerCm = 1/100; % general knowledge
4. MetersPerFt = metersPerCm * cmPerInch * inchesPerFt;
5. startFt = 25000; % ft - given
6. startM = startFt * MetersPerFt;
```

Line 4: The conversion factor we need. Notice that because the variable names are consistent with the logic, they help to avoid errors.

Lines 5–6: Develop the initial conditions with suitable units.

2.   ***Find and solve the equation.*** Given the following:

- Initial and final altitudes from which you can compute the distance traveled: *s*
- The motion is under constant acceleration, the force of gravity: *g*
- To just reach outer space, the final velocity, *v*, is 0
- The initial velocity, *u*, is needed

So after some diligent head scratching, we remember the equation of motion under constant acceleration connecting *u, v, s,* and *a* is:

$$v^2 = u^2 + 2as$$

However, this is not yet in a useful form. For computers to be able to solve an equation, you need the unknown quantity on the left of the equation and everything known on the right. Since *u* is the unknown, we move this to the left side of the assignment, and organize the known quantities to the right. These are the final velocity, *v* (i.e., 0) the given distance, *s*, and the acceleration, *a*. Since the positive direction for *u* and *s* is upward, but gravity is downward, we must use *a* = −*g*, and the equation can be transformed to:

$$u = \sqrt{2gs}$$

With this information, you can now solve this problem. Listing 2.3 shows the rest of Listing 2.2 to complete this calculation.

Listing 2.3 Script to complete the computation of the spacecraft's velocity

```
1. g = 9.81; % m/sec^2
2. top = 100; % km - given
3. s = (top*1000) - startM; % m
4. initialV = (2*g*s)^0.5 % the final answer
```

In Listing 2.3:

> Line 1: The standard value for the acceleration due to gravity.
>
> Line 2: The altitude of outer space is given in the problem statement.
>
> Line 3: Computes the distance traveled, including the unit conversion from kilometers to meters. Note the optional, and in this case unnecessary, use of parentheses to define the order of operations.
>
> Line 4: The final computation. The operator $\wedge$ is the MATLAB expression for exponentiation; x^y in MATLAB results in computing x^y. Notice that the parentheses are required here to force the multiplication to happen before the exponentiation.

Although most modern computing environments, including MATLAB, have tools that actually solve symbolic equations, these tools are not appropriate for an introduction to programming and will not be discussed in this book.

Chapter Summary

This chapter presented some fundamental notions of computing and introduced you to the nature of MATLAB, its user interface, and the fundamental tools for making programs work.

- Abstraction lets you refer to collections of data or instructions as a whole
- An algorithm is a set of instructions at an appropriate level of abstraction for solving a specific problem
- A data class describes the type of data and the nature of operations that can be performed on that data
- An object is a specific instance of a class with specific values that can be assigned to a variable
- The Command window lets you experiment with ideas by entering commands line-by-line and seeing immediate results
- The Command History window lets you review and recall previous commands
- The Workspace window lists the names, values, and class of your local variables.
- The Current Directory window lists the current files in the directory to which MATLAB is currently pointed
- A Document window opens when a variable in the Workspace window is selected, to let you view and edit data items
- A Figure window presents data and/or images when invoked by programs
- The Editor window lets you view and modify text files
- Scripts provide the basic mechanism for implementing solutions to problems

Special Characters, Reserved Words, and Functions

Special Characters, Reserved Words, and Functions	Description	Discussed in This Section
`'abc'`	Single quotes enclose a literal character string	2.2.3
`%`	A percent sign indicates a comment in an M-file	2.4.2
`;`	A semicolon suppresses output from assignment statements	2.4.5
`...`	Ellipses continue a MATLAB command to the next line	2.4.5
`=`	The assignment operator assigns a value to a memory location; this is not the same as an equality test	2.2.2
`ans`	The default variable name for results of MATLAB calculations	2.3.1
`clc`	Clears the Command window	2.3.2
`clear`	Clears the Workspace window	2.4.2
`sqrt(x)`	Calculates the square root of x	2.4.2

Self Test

Use the following questions to check your understanding of the material in this chapter:

True or False

T 1. A bag of groceries is an example of abstraction.

F 2. An algorithm is a series of logical steps that solves one specific problem.

T 3. It is impossible to write a complete, practical program in any paradigm other than procedural.

T 4. To be useful to an algorithm, the result of every computation must be assigned to a variable.

F 5. In programming, if you know the values of z and x in the expression z = x + y, you can derive the value of y.

F 6. Untyped languages are free to ignore the nature of the data in variables.

T 7. Anything assigned to be the value of a variable is an object.

F 8. Class is a concept restricted to object-oriented programming.

F 9. You can permanently save the commands entered in the Command window.

T 10. Double-clicking an entry in the Command History window lets you rerun that command.

T 11. You can manually change the values of variables displayed in the Workspace window.

F 12. You double-click a file name in the Current Directory window to ~~run~~ *open* that script.

T 13. A Document window lets you view and edit data items.

T 14. MATLAB permits multiple Figure windows to be open simultaneously.

F 15. An asterisk on the File Name tab in the Editor window indicates that this is a script that can be executed.

F 16. MATLAB echoes comments entered in a script in the Command window.

F 17. When the name of script is typed in the Command window, it will be saved if necessary before it is executed.

Fill in the Blanks

1. *abstraction* means expressing a quality apart from a particular implementation.

2. *algorithm* is a sequence of instructions for solving a problem.

3. Without *side effects*, a programming solution can be mathematically proven to be correct.

4. Variable names must not begin with *number (numeric character)*

5. Armed with both the *name* and *type* of a variable, a compiler can do a better job of ensuring that the programmer isn't misinterpreting data.

6. An instance of a *class* is a(n) *object* that is usually stored in a variable of that *class*.

7. You can *calculations* (perform) in the Command window in a manner similar to the way you *calculations* (perform) on a scientific calculator.

8. You *double-click* an entry in the Command History window to *repeat the execution* that command.

9. The columns in the Workspace window show the *name* of the variable, its *current* (value), and its *data type*

10. You *click* (double) the name of a file in the Current Directory window to edit that file.

11. A Document window opens automatically when you ___click___ a(n)
    ___variable name___ in the Workspace window.   *[handwritten: double (above click); variable name (below, under blank)]*

12. Graphics windows are created when a(n) ___command___ requests a graph.   *[handwritten: automatically, MATLAB above]*

13. You create comments by putting a(n) ___sign (%)___ in the text file.   *[handwritten: percent]*

14. MATLAB will ___ignore___ all text from the comment mark to ___the end of the current line___   *[handwritten]*

Programming Projects

1. You are given two sides of a triangle, a = 4.5 and b = 6. The angle between them is 35 degrees. Write a script to find the length of the third side and the area of the triangle.

2. In the bottom of the ninth inning, the bases are loaded and the Braves are down by three runs. Chipper Jones steps to the plate. Twice he swings and misses. The crowd heads for the exits. The next pitch is a fast ball down the middle. He swings and makes perfect contact with the ball, sending it up at a 45-degree angle toward the fence 400 ft away.
   a. Write a script to determine how fast he must hit the ball to land at the base of the fence, neglecting the air resistance.
   b. Perform a brief experiment to determine whether there was a better angle at which to hit the ball so that it could clear a 12 ft fence.

3. If an ice cream cone is 6 inches tall, and its rim has a diameter of 2 inches, write a script to determine the weight of the ice cream that can fit in the cone, assuming that the ice cream above the cone is a perfect hemisphere. You may neglect the thickness of the cone material. Assume that a gallon of ice cream weighs 8 lb and occupies 7.5 cubic feet.

4. Write a script that validates the relationship between sin θ, cos θ, and tan θ by evaluating these functions at suitably chosen values of θ.

5. I like my shower to remain hot for hours at 100°F, but am too cheap to buy one of those on-demand hot water systems. I don't care how slowly the water runs. The water supply is at 50°F, and the water heater is rated at 50,000 BTU/hour. Write a script to compute the maximum flow rate of my shower (in cubic feet per minute) that keeps the water temperature above 100°F.

6. It takes an average of 45 horsepower to run an electric car at an average speed of 35 mph. Write a script to compute the electrical

storage capacity of the battery system that would make this car practical for a 25-mile commute, recharging the batteries only at home at night when the electricity is cheap. How many D cell alkaline batteries would be needed for this?

7. You want to buy a $300,000 home with 20% down payment. The current compound interest rate is 4.5%.
    a. Write a script to determine:
        - the monthly payments for a 30-year loan,
        - the equivalent simple interest rate,
        - the total interest paid over the life of the loan.
    b. Now, repeat the computation for a 15-year loan at 5%. Is this a better deal?

8. The distance from my house to my office is 1.5 miles. Every morning, I have to decide whether to take the bus that averages (once it arrives) 25 mph, or to walk. I can walk at 4 mph. Write a script to determine how frequently the buses should run to give them a 50% chance of getting me to the office faster than walking.

9. A glass has the shape of a truncated cone of height 5 inches. Its top diameter is 3.5 inches, and its base diameter is 2 inches. If water is poured into the glass at 2 gallons per minute, write a script to calculate how long it takes to fill the glass to the brim. One gallon is 7.5 cubic feet.

10. You can calculate the aerodynamic drag on an object by the formula:

$$\text{Drag} = \tfrac{1}{2}\, \rho\, V^2\, C_d\, S$$

The air density, ρ, is 1.3 kg/m3 and the value of the drag area, $C_d S$, is a measure of the resistance of the object as it moves through the air. An object falling through air reaches terminal velocity when the aerodynamic drag equals the object's weight.

A sky diver weighing 80 kg has a $C_d\, S$ value of 0.7 when horizontal with arms and legs extended, and 0.15 when head down with arms and legs in line. One diver jumps from a plane at an altitude of 5,000 m in the horizontal position. After 20 sec, another diver jumps. Write a script to determine how much time the second diver must spend head down in order to catch up to the first diver. Also compute the height above the ground where they first meet. For simplicity, you may assume that the sky divers immediately reach their terminal velocity when jumping.

11. You are given a circle with radius 5 centered at $x = 1$, $y = 2$. You want to calculate the intersection of some lines with that circle. Write a script to find the x and y coordinates of both points of intersection. You should test this code at least with these lines:

$$y = 2x - 1$$
$$y = -2x - 10$$
$$y = x + 5.9054$$

Vectors and Arrays

Chapter Objectives

This chapter discusses the basic calculations involving rectangular collections of numbers in the form of arrays. For each of these collections, you will learn how to:

- Create them

- Manipulate them

- Access their elements

- Perform mathematical and logical operations on them

This study of arrays will introduce the first of many language characteristics that sets MATLAB apart from other languages: its ability to perform arithmetic and logical operations on collections of numbers as a whole. You need to understand how to create these collections, access the data in them, and manipulate the values in the collections with mathematical and logical operators. First, however, we need to understand the idea of functions built into the language.

3.1 Concept: Using Built-in Functions

We are familiar with the use of a trigonometric function like cos(θ) that consumes an angle in radians and produces the cosine of that angle. In general, a function is a named collection of instructions that operates on the data provided to produce a result according to the specifications of that function. In Chapter 5, we will see how to write our own functions. In this chapter, we will see the use of some of the functions built into MATLAB. At the end of each chapter that uses built-in functions, you will find a summary table listing the function specifications. For help on a specific function, you can either select the Help menu and look up the function or type the following in the Interactions window:

```
>> help <function name>
```

where `<function name>` is the name of a MATLAB function. This will produce a detailed discussion of the capabilities of that function.

3.2 Concept: Data Collections

Chapter 2 showed how to perform mathematical operations on single data items. This section considers the concept of grouping data items in general, and then specifically considers two very common ways to group data: in arrays and in vectors, which are a powerful subset of arrays.

3.2.1 Data Abstraction

It is frequently convenient to refer to groups of data collectively, for example, "all the temperature readings for May" or "all the purchases from Wal-Mart." This allows us not only to move these items around as a group, but also to consider mathematical or logical operations on these groups. For example, we could discuss the average, maximum, or minimum temperatures for a month, or that the cost of the Wal-Mart purchases had gone up 3%.

3.2.2 Homogeneous Collection

ex)
[double double ···]
[logical logical ···]

In Chapter 7, we will encounter more general collection implementations that allow items in a collection to be of different data types. The collections discussed in this chapter, however, will be constrained to accept only items of the same data type. Collections with this constraint are called **homogeneous collections.**

3.3 Vectors   *l × n*

A vector is an array with only one row of elements. It is the simplest means of grouping a collection of like data items. Initially we will consider vectors of numbers or logical values. Some languages refer to vectors as *linear arrays* or *linear matrices*. As these names suggest, a vector is a one-dimensional grouping of data, as shown in Figure 3.1. Individual items in a vector are usually referred to as its **elements.** Vector elements have two separate and distinct attributes that make them unique in a specific vector: their *numerical value* and their *position* in that vector. For example, the individual number 66 is in the third position in the vector in Figure 3.1. Its value is 66 and its index is 3. There may be other items in the vector with the value of 66, but no other item will be located in this vector at position 3. Experienced programmers should note that due to its FORTRAN roots, indices in the MATLAB language start from 1 and not 0.

[handwritten left margin: position = index / positions = indices]

3.3.1 Creating a Vector

There are seven ways to create vectors that are directly analogous to the techniques for creating individual data items and fall into two broad categories:

- Creating vectors from constant values
- Producing new vectors with special-purpose functions

The following shows how you can create vectors from constant values:

- Entering the values directly, for example, A = [2, 5, 7, 1, 3] (the commas are optional and are frequently omitted)
- Entering the values as a range of numbers using the colon operator, for example, B = 1:3:20, where the first number is the starting value, the second number is the increment, and the third number is the ending value (you may omit the increment if the desired increment is 1)

[handwritten left margin: ∴ B = [1,4,7,10,13,16,19]]

The following introduces the most common MATLAB functions that create vectors from scratch:

- The linspace(...) function creates a fixed number of values between two limits, for example, c = linspace (0, 20, 11), where the first parameter is the lower limit, the second parameter is the upper limit, and the third parameter is the number of values in the vector
- The functions zeros(1,n), ones(1,n), rand(1,n) (uniformly distributed random numbers), and randn(1,n) (random numbers with normal distribution) create vectors filled with 0, 1, or random values between 0 and 1.

[handwritten left margin: ∴ C = [0 2 4 6 8 10 / 12 14 16 18 20]]

Try working with vectors in Exercise 3.1.

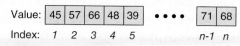

Value: | 45 | 57 | 66 | 48 | 39 | •••• | 71 | 68 |

Index: 1 2 3 4 5 $n-1$ n

Figure 3.1 *A vector*

Exercise 3.1 Working with vectors

```
>> A = [2 5 7 1 3]
A =
     2 5 7 1 3
>> B = 1:3:20
B =
     1  4  7  10 13 16 19
>> C = linspace(0, 20, 11)
C =
     0  2  4   6  8 10 12 14 16 18 20
>> D = [4]
D =
     4
>> E = zeros(1,4)
E =
     0   0   0   0
```

Now, open the Variables tab and study the contents.

The Workspace window gives you three pieces of information about each of the variables you created: the name, the value, and the "class," which for now you can equate to "data type." Notice that if the size of the vector is small enough, the value field shows its actual contents; otherwise, you see a description of its attributes, like `<1 x 11 double>`. Exercise 3.1 deliberately created the vector D with only one element, and perhaps the result surprised you. D was presented in both the Interactions window and the Workspace window as if it were a scalar quantity. This is generally true in the MATLAB language—all scalar quantities are considered vectors of unit length.

3.3.2 Size of a Vector

$V = [1 \ 4 \ 3 \ 9]$

$size(V) =$

$1 \quad 4$

(row) (column)

$length(V) =$

4

A vector also has a specific attribute: its length (n in Figure 3.1). In most implementations, this length is fixed when the vector is created. However, as you will see shortly, the MATLAB language provides the ability to increase or decrease the size of a vector by inserting or selecting certain elements. MATLAB provides two functions to determine the size of arrays in general, and of vectors in particular. The function `size(V)` when applied to the vector V returns another vector containing two quantities: the number of rows in the vector (always 1) and the number of columns (the length of the vector). The function `length(V)` returns the maximum value in the size of an array—for a vector, this is a number indicating its length.

3.3.3 Indexing a Vector

As mentioned earlier, each element in a vector has two attributes: its value and its position in the vector. You can access the elements in a vector in either of two ways: using a numerical vector or a logical vector. We refer to the process of accessing array elements by their position as "indexing."

Numerical Indexing The elements of a vector can be accessed individually or in groups by enclosing the index of zero or more elements in parentheses. Continuing Exercise 3.1, A(3) would return the third element of the vector A, 7. If you attempt to read beyond the length of the vector or below index 1, an error will result.

You can also change the values of a vector element by using an assignment statement where the left-hand side indexes that specific element (try Exercise 3.2).

A feature unique to the MATLAB language is its behavior when attempting to write beyond the bounds of a vector. While it is still illegal to write below the index 1, MATLAB will automatically extend the vector if you write beyond its current end. If there are missing elements between the current vector elements and the index at which you attempt to store a new value, MATLAB will zero-fill the missing elements. Try Exercise 3.3 to see how this works.

In Exercise 3.3 we asked to store a value in the eighth element of a vector with length 5. Rather than complaining, MATLAB was able to complete the instruction by doing two things automatically. It extended the length to 8 and stored the value 0 in the as yet unassigned elements. In these simple examples, we used a single number as the index. However, in general, we can use a vector of index values to index another vector. Furthermore, the size of the index vector does not need to match the size of the vector being indexed—it can be either shorter or longer. However, all values in an index vector must be positive; and if they are being used to extract values

> **Notes:**
>
> 1. The key word end in an indexing context represents the index of the last element in that vector.
>
> 2. The vector generated by the colon operator does not necessarily include the ending value. In this case, since there are 8 values in the vector, end takes the value 8, but since that is not odd, the index vector is [1 3 5 7]

 Exercise 3.2 Changing elements of a vector

Extending the exercise above:

```
>> A(5) = 42
A =
        2       5       7       1       42
```

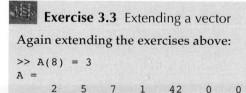 **Exercise 3.3** Extending a vector

Again extending the exercises above:

```
>> A(8) = 3
A =
        2     5     7     1     42     0     0     3
```

from a vector, the values must not exceed the length of that vector. Again continuing from Exercise 3.3, if we asked for B = A(1:2:end), we would see the value of B to be [2 7 42 0], the values of A in odd index positions. Later, we will see how to find the elements in A that have odd values.

Logical Indexing So far, the only type of data we have used has been numerical values of type double. The result of a logical operation, however, is data of a different type, with values either true or false. Such data are called **Boolean** or **logical** values. Like numbers, logical values can be assembled into arrays by specifying true or false values. For example, we might enter the following line in MATLAB to specify the variable mask:

```
>> mask = [true false false true]
mask =
     t    f    f    t[1]
```

We can index any vector with a logical vector as follows:

```
>> A = [2 4 6 8 10];
>> A(mask)
ans =
     2 8
```

When indexing with a logical vector, the result will contain the elements of the original vector corresponding in position to the true values in the logical index vector. The logical index vector can be either shorter or longer than the source vector; but if it is longer, all the values beyond the length of the source vector must be false.

3.3.4 Shortening a Vector

There are times when we need to remove elements from a vector. For example, if we had a vector of measurements from an instrument, and it was known that the setup for the third reading was incorrect, we would want to remove that erroneous reading before processing the data. To accomplish this, we make a rather strange use of the empty vector, []. The empty vector, as its name and symbol suggest, is a vector with no elements in it. When you assign the empty vector to an element in another vector—say, A—that element is removed from A, and A is shortened by one element. Try Exercise 3.4.

> **Exercise 3.4** Shortening a vector
>
> Using the vector A from Exercise 3.3:
>
> ```
> >> A(4) = []
> A =
>      2    5    7    42    0    0    3
> ```

---

[1]If you are using MATLAB, logical vectors are presented with values 0 or 1, but they are not numerical values and should not be used as such

As you can see, we asked for the fourth element to be removed from a vector initially with eight elements. The resulting vector has only seven elements, and the fourth element, originally with value 1, has been removed.

3.3.5 Operating on Vectors

The essential core of the MATLAB language is a rich collection of tools for manipulating vectors and arrays. This section first shows how these tools operate on vectors, and then generalizes to how they apply to arrays (multi-dimensional vectors) and, later, matrices. Three techniques extend directly from operations on scalar values:

- Arithmetic operations
- Logical operations
- Applying library functions

Two techniques are unique to arrays in general, and to vectors in particular:

- Concatenation
- Slicing (generalized indexing)

Arithmetic Operations Arithmetic operations can be performed collectively on the individual components of two vectors as long as both vectors are the same length, or one of the vectors is a scalar (i.e., a vector of length 1). Addition and subtraction have exactly the syntax you would expect, as illustrated in Exercise 3.5. Multiplication, division, and exponentiation, however, have a small syntactic idiosyncrasy related to the fact that these are element-by-element operations, not matrix operations. We will discuss matrix operations in Chapter 12. When the MATLAB language was designed, the ordinary symbols (*,/, and ^) were reserved for matrix operations. However, since element-by-element multiplicative operations are fundamentally different from matrix operations, a new set of operators is required to specify these operations. The symbols .*, ./, and .^ (the dots are part of the operators, but the commas are not) are used respectively for element-by-element multiplication, division, and exponentiation. Note that because matrix and element-by-element addition and subtraction are identical, no special operation symbols are required for + and –.

> **Common Pitfalls 3.1**
>
> Shortening a vector is very rarely the right solution to a problem and can lead to logical difficulties. Wherever possible, you should use indexing to copy the elements you want to keep rather than using **[ ]** to erase elements you want to remove.

Here, we first see the addition and multiplication of a vector by a scalar quantity, and then element-by-element multiplication of A and B. The first error is generated because we omitted the '.' on the multiply

size (A) =
| 5
row col

size (B) =
| 5

> **Exercise 3.5** Using vector mathematics

```
>> A = [2 5 7 1 3];
>> A + 5
ans =
       7        10        12        6        8
>> A .* 2
ans =
       4        10        14        2        6
>> B = -1:1:3
B =
      -1         0         1        2        3
>> A .* B % element-by-element multiplication
ans =
      -2         0         7        2        9
>> A * B % matrix multiplication!!
??? Error using ==> mtimes
Inner matrix dimensions must agree.
>> C = [1 2 3]
C =
       1         2         3
>> A .* C % A and C must have the same length
??? Error using ==> times
Matrix dimensions must agree.
```

symbol, thereby invoking matrix multiplication, which is improper with the vector A and B. The second error occurs because two vectors involved in arithmetic operations must have the same size. Notice, incidentally, the use of the % sign indicating that the rest of the line is a comment.

You can change the signs of all the values of a vector with the unary minus (-) operator.

Logical Operations In the earlier discussion about logical indexing, you might have wondered why you would ever use that. In this section, we will see that logical operations on vectors produce vectors of logical results. We can then use these logical result vectors to index vectors in a style that makes the logic of complex expressions very clear. As with arithmetic operations, logical operations can be performed element-by-element on two vectors as long as both vectors are the same length, or if one of the vectors is a scalar (i.e., a vector of length 1). The result will be a vector of logical values with the same length as the longer of the original vector(s).

Try Exercise 3.6 to see how vector logical expressions work.

First we built the vectors A and B, and then we performed two legal logical operations: finding where A is not less than 5, and where each

Exercise 3.6 Working with vector logical expressions

```
>> A = [2 5 7 1 3];
>> B = [0 6 5 3 2];
>> A >= 5
ans =
     0    1    1    0    0
>> A >= B
ans =
     1    0    1    0  |
>> C = [1 2 3]
>> A > C
??? Error using ==> gt
Matrix dimensions must agree.
```

Exercise 3.7 Working with logical vectors

```
>> A = [true true false false];
>> B = [true false true false];
>> A & B
ans =
     1    0    0    0
>> A | B
ans =
     1    1    1    0
>> C = [1 0 0]
>> A & C
??? Error using ==> and
Matrix dimensions must agree.
```

element of A is not less than the corresponding element of B. As with arithmetic operations, an error occurs if you attempt a logical operation with vectors of different sizes (neither size being 1).

Logical operators can be assembled into more complex operations using logical and (&) and or (|) operators. These operators actually come in two flavors: &/| and && / ||. The single operators operate on logical arrays of matching size to perform element-wise matches of the individual logical values. The doubled operators combine individual logical results and are usually associated with conditional statements (see Chapter 4). Try Exercise 3.7 to see how logical operators work.

In Exercise 3.7, we combine two logical vectors of the same length successfully, but fail, as with arithmetic operations, to combine vectors of different lengths. If you need the indices in a vector where the elements of a logical vector are true, the function find(...) accomplishes this by consuming an array of logical values and producing a vector of the positions of the true elements.

Exercise 3.8 Using the find(...) function

```
>> A = [2 5 7 1 3];
>> A > 4
ans =
     0 1 1 0 0
>> find(A > 4)
ans =
     2 3
```

Try Exercise 3.8 to see how this function works.

You can invert the values of all elements of a logical vector (changing true to false and false to true) using the unary not operator, ~. For example:

```
>> na = ~[true true false true]
na = 0 0 1 0
```

As you can see, each element of na is the logical inverse of the corresponding original element. As is usual with arithmetic and logical operations, the precedence of operators governs the order in which operations are performed. Table 3.1 shows the operator precedence in the MATLAB language. Operations listed on the same row of the table are performed from left to right. The normal precedence of operators can be overruled by enclosing preferred operations in parentheses: (...).

Applying Library Functions The MATLAB language defines a rich collection of mathematical functions that cover mathematical, trigonometric, and statistics capabilities. A partial list is provided in Appendix A. For a complete

Table 3.1 Operator precedence

Operators	Description
.', .^	Scalar transpose and power
', ^	Matrix transpose and power
+, -, ~	Unary operators
.*, ./, .\, *, /, \	Multiplication, division, left division
+, -	Addition and subtraction
:	Colon operator
<, <=, >=, >, ==, ~=	Comparison
&	Element-wise AND
		Element-wise OR
&&	Logical AND
||	Logical OR

list of those implemented in MATLAB, refer to the Help menu option in the MATLAB tool bar. With few exceptions, all functions defined in the MATLAB language accept vectors of numbers rather than single values and return a vector of the same length. The following functions deserve special mention because they provide specific capabilities that are frequently useful:

- `sum(v)` and `mean(v)` consume a vector and return the sum and mean of all the elements of the vector respectively.

- `min(v)` and `max(v)` return two quantities: the minimum or maximum value in a vector, as well as the position in that vector where that value occurred. For example:

  ```
  > [value where] = max([2 7 42 9 -4])
  value = 42
  where = 3
  ```

indicates that the largest value is `42`, and it occurs in the third element of the vector. You will see in Chapter 5 how to implement returning multiple results from a function.

- `round(v)`, `ceil(v)`, `floor(v)`, and `fix(v)` *[rounding toward zero]* remove the fractional part of the numbers in a vector by conventional rounding, rounding up, rounding down, and rounding toward zero, respectively.

Concatenation In Section 3.3.1, we saw the technique for creating a vector by assembling numbers between square brackets:

```
A = [2 5 7 1 3]
```

This is in fact a special case of concatenation. The MATLAB language lets you construct a new vector by concatenating other vectors:

```
A = [B C D ... X Y Z]
```

where the individual items in the brackets may be any vector defined as a constant or variable, and the length of A will be the sum of the lengths of the individual vectors. The simple vector constructor in Section 3.3.1 is a special case of this rule because each number is implicitly a 1×1 vector. The result is therefore a $1 \times N$ vector, where N is the number of values in the brackets. Try concatenating the vectors in Exercise 3.9.

Exercise 3.9 Concatenating vectors

```
>> A = [2 5 7];
>> B = [1 3];
>> [A B]
ans =
2 5 7 1 3
```

Notice that the resulting vector is not nested like [[2 5 7], [1 3]] but is completely "flat."

Slicing is the name given to complex operations where elements are copied from specified locations in one vector to different locations in another vector. As we saw earlier, the basic operation of extracting and replacing the elements of a vector is called indexing. Furthermore, we saw that indexing is not confined to single elements in a vector; you can also use **vectors of indices.** These index vectors either can be the values of previously named variables, or they can be created anonymously as they are needed. When you index a single element in a vector—for example, A(4)—you are actually creating an anonymous 1 × 1 index vector, 4, and then using it to access the specified element(s) from the array A.

Creating anonymous index vectors as needed makes some additional features of the colon operator available. The general form for generating a vector of numbers is: <start> : <increment> : <end>. We already know that by omitting the <increment> portion, the default increment is 1. When used anonymously while indexing a vector, the following features are also available:

- The key word end is defined as the length of the vector
- The operator : by itself is short for 1:end

Finally, as you saw earlier, it is legal to index with a vector of logical values. For example, if A is defined as:

```
A = [2 5 7 1 3];
```

then A([false true false true]) returns:

```
ans =
        5        1
```

yielding a new vector containing only those values of the original vector where the corresponding logical index is true. This is extremely useful, as you will see later in this chapter, for indexing items in a vector that match a specific test.

The general form of statements for slicing vectors is:

```
B(<rangeB>) = A(<rangeA>)
```

where <rangeA> and <rangeB> are both index vectors, A is an existing array, and B can be an existing array or a new array. The values in B at the indices in rangeB are assigned the values of A from rangeA. The rules for use of this template are as follows:

- Either the size of rangeB must be equal to the size of rangeA or rangeA must be of size 1
- If B did not exist before this statement was implemented, it is zero filled where assignments were not explicitly made

■ If B did exist before this statement, the values not directly assigned in rangeB remain unchanged

Study the comments in Listing 3.1 and do Exercise 3.10.

Listing 3.1 Vector indexing script

```
1.  A = [2 5 7 1 3 4];
2.  odds = 1:2:length(A);
3.  disp('odd values of A using predefined indices')
4.  A(odds)
5.  disp('odd values of A using anonymous indices')
6.  A(1:2:end)
7.  disp('put evens into odd values in a new array')
8.  B(odds) = A(2:2:end)
9.  disp('set the even values in B to 99')
10. B(2:2:end) = 99
11. disp('find the small values in A')
12. small = A < 4
13. disp('add 10 to the small values')
14. A(small) = A(small) + 10
15. disp('this can be done in one ugly operation')
16. A(A < 10) = A(A < 10) + 10
```

Exercise 3.10 Running the vector indexing script

Execute the script in Listing 3.1. You should see the following output:

```
odd values of A using predefined indices
ans =
     2     7     3
odd values of A using anonymous indices
ans =
     2     7     3
put even values into odd values in a new array
B =
     5     0     1     0     4
set the even values in B to 99
B =
     5    99     1    99     4
find the small values in A
small =
     1     0     0     1     1     0
add 10 to the small values
A =
    12     5     7    11    13     4
this can be done in one ugly operation
A =
    12     5     7    11    13     4
>>
```

In Listing 3.1:

Line 1: Creates a vector A with five elements.

Line 2: When predefining an index vector, if you want to refer to the size of a vector, you must use either the `length(...)` function or the `size(...)` function.

Line 3: The `disp(...)` function shows the contents of its parameter in the Interactions window, in this case: `'odd values of A using predefined indices'`. We use `disp(...)` rather than comments because comments are visible only in the script itself, not in the program output, which we need here.

Line 4: Using a predefined index vector to access elements in vector A. Since no assignment is made, the variable `ans` takes on the value of a three-element vector containing the odd-numbered elements of A. Notice that these are the odd-numbered elements, not the elements with odd values.

Line 6: The anonymous version of the command given in Line 4. Notice that the anonymous version allows you to use the word `end` within the vector meaning the index of its last element.

Line 8: Since B did not previously exist (a good reason to run the `clear` command at the beginning of a script is to be sure this is true), a new vector is created with five elements (the largest index assigned in B). Elements in B at positions less than five that were not assigned are zero filled.

Line 10: If you assign a scalar quantity to a range of indices in a vector, all values at those indices are assigned the scalar value.

Line 12: Logical operations on a vector produce a vector of Boolean results. This is not the same as typing `small = [1 0 0 1 1 0]`. If you want to create a logical vector, you must use `true` and `false`, for example:

```
small = [true false false true true false]
```

Line 14: This is actually performing the scalar arithmetic operation `+ 10` on an anonymous vector of three elements, and then assigning those values to the range of elements in A.

Line 16: Not only is this unnecessarily complex, but it is also less efficient because it is applying the logical operator to A twice. It is better to use the form in Line 14.

3.4 Engineering Example—Forces and Moments

Vectors are ideal representations of the concept of a vector used in physics. Consider two forces acting on an object at a point P, as shown in Figure 3.2. Calculate the resultant force at P, the unit vector in the direction of that resultant, and the moment of that force about the point M. We can represent each of the vectors in this problem as a MATLAB vector with three components: the x, y, and z values of the vector. The solution to this problem for specific vectors is shown in Listing 3.2.

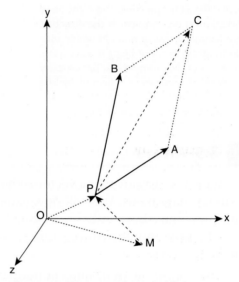

Figure 3.2 *Vector analysis problem*

Listing 3.2 Script to solve vector problems

```
1. PA = [0 1 1]
2. PB = [1 1 0]
3. P = [2 1 1]
4. M = [4 0 1]
   % find the resultant of PA and PB
5. PC = PA + PB
   % find the unit vector in the direction of PC
6. mag = sqrt(sum(PC.^2))
7. unit_vector = PC/mag
   % find the moment of the force PC about M
   % this is the cross product of MP and PC
8. MP = P - M
9. moment = cross( MP, PC )
```

In Listing 3.2:

Common Pitfalls 3.2

After any nontrivial computation, a good engineer will always perform a sanity check on the answers. When you run the code for this problem, the answers returned are:

```
PC = [  1  2  1]
unit_vector = [0.4082    0.8165    0.4082]
moment = [  1    2    -5]
```

To check the moment result, visualize the rotation of PC about M and apply the right-hand rule to find the axis of rotation of the moment. Roughly speaking, the right-hand rule states that the direction of the moment is the direction in which a normal, right-handed screw at point M would turn under the influence of this force. Without being too accurate, we can conclude that the axis of the moment is approximately along the negative z-axis, an estimate confirmed by the result shown.

Lines 1–4: Typical initial values for the problem.

Line 5: PC is the sum of the vectors PA and PB.

Lines 6–7: The unit vector along PC is PC divided by its magnitude. The magnitude is the square root of the sum of the squares of the individual components.

Line 8: The vector PM is the vector difference between P and M.

Line 9: There is a built-in function, cross(..), to compute the cross product of two vectors.

 ## 3.5 Arrays

In Section 3.2, we saw that a vector is the simplest way to group a collection of similar data items. We will now extend these ideas to include arrays of multiple dimensions, initially confined to two dimensions. Each row will have the same number of columns, and each column will have the same number of rows.

At this point, we will refer to these collections as *arrays* to distinguish them from the *matrices* discussed in Chapter 12. While arrays and matrices are stored in the same way, they differ in their multiplication, division, and exponentiation operations. Figure 3.3 illustrates a typical two-dimensional array A with m rows and n columns, commonly referred to as an m × n array.

$$A_{(m \times n)} = \begin{bmatrix} a_{11} & a_{12} & \cdots & a_{1n} \\ a_{21} & a_{22} & \cdots & a_{2n} \\ \vdots & & \ddots & \\ a_{m1} & a_{m2} & \cdots & a_{mn} \end{bmatrix}$$

Figure 3.3 *An array*

3.5.1 Properties of an Array

As with vectors, individual items in an array are referred to as its *elements*. These elements also have the unique attributes combining their value and their position. In a two-dimensional array, the position will be the row and column (in that order) of the element. In general, in an n-dimensional array, the element position will be a vector of *n* index values.

When applied to an array A with n dimensions, the function `size(...)` will return the information in one of two forms.

- If called with a single return value like `sz = size(A)`, it will return a vector of length n containing the size of each dimension of the array.
- If called with multiple return values like `[rows, cols] = size(A)`, it returns the individual array dimension up to the number of values requested. To avoid erroneous results, you should always provide as many variables as there are dimensions of the array.

The `length(...)` function returns the maximum dimension of the array. So if we created an array A dimensioned $2 \times 8 \times 3$, `size(A)` would return `[2 8 3]` and `length(A)` would return 8.

The transpose of an $m \times n$ array, indicated by the apostrophe character (') placed after the array identifier, returns an $n \times m$ array with the values in the rows and columns interchanged. Figure 3.4 shows a transposed array.

A number of special cases arise that are worthy of note:

- When a 2-D matrix has the same number of rows and columns, it is called **square.**
- When the only nonzero values in an array occur when the row and column indices are the same, the array is called **diagonal.**
- When there is only one row, the array is a row vector, or just a *vector* as you saw earlier.
- When there is only one column, the array is a **column vector,** the transpose of a row vector.

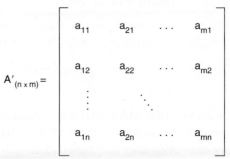

$$A'_{(n \times m)} = \begin{bmatrix} a_{11} & a_{21} & \cdots & a_{m1} \\ a_{12} & a_{22} & \cdots & a_{m2} \\ \vdots & & \ddots & \\ a_{1n} & a_{2n} & \cdots & a_{mn} \end{bmatrix}$$

Figure 3.4 *Transpose of an array*

3.5.2 Creating an Array

Arrays can be created either by entering values directly or by using one of a number of built-in functions that create arrays with specific characteristics.

- As with vectors, you can directly enter the values in an array using either a semicolon (;) or a new line to indicate the end of a row, for example: A = [2, 5, 7; 1, 3, 42].
- The functions zeros(m, n) and ones(m, n) create arrays with m rows and n columns filled with zeros and ones, respectively.
- The function rand(m, n) fills an array with random numbers in the range 0 .. 1.
- The function randn(m, n) fills an array with random numbers normally distributed about 0 with a standard deviation of 1.
- The function diag(...) takes several forms, the most useful of which are diag(A), where A is an array, that returns its diagonal as a vector, and diag(V), where V is a vector, that returns a square matrix with that diagonal. Type help diag in the Command window for a full description of the capabilities of diag(...)
- The MATLAB language also defines the function magic(m), which fills a square matrix with the numbers 1 to m^2 organized in such a way that its rows, columns, and diagonals all add up to the same value.

Try Exercise 3.11 to practice working with arrays.

3.5.3 Accessing Elements of an Array

The elements of an array may be addressed by enclosing the indices of the required element in parentheses, with the first index being the row index and the second index the column index. Considering the values produced by Exercise 3.11, A(2, 3) would return the element in the second row, third column: 42. If you were to attempt to read outside the length of the rows or columns, an error would result.

We can also store values that are elements of an array. For example, continuing Example 3.11, A(2, 3) = 0 would result in this answer:

```
A =
        2       5       7
        1       3       0
```

As with vectors, MATLAB will automatically extend the array if you write beyond its boundaries. If there are missing elements between the current array elements and the index at which you attempt to store a new value,

Exercise 3.11 Creating arrays

```
>> A = [2, 5, 7; 1, 3, 42]
A =
     2     5     7
     1     3    42
>> z = zeros(3,2)
z =
     0     0
     0     0
     0     0
>> [z ones(3, 4)]   % concatenating arrays
ans =
     0     0     1     1     1     1
     0     0     1     1     1     1
     0     0     1     1     1     1
>> rand(3,4)
ans =
   0.9501    0.4860    0.4565    0.4447
   0.2311    0.8913    0.0185    0.6154
   0.6068    0.7621    0.8214    0.7919
>> rand(size(A))
ans =
   0.9218    0.1763    0.9355
   0.7382    0.4057    0.9169
>> diag(A)
ans =
     2
     3
>> diag(diag(A))
ans =
     2     0
     0     3
>> magic(4)
ans =
    16     2     3    13
     5    11    10     8
     9     7     6    12
     4    14    15     1
>>
```

the missing elements will be zero filled. For example, again continuing Example 3.11, A(4, 1) = 3 would result in this answer:

```
A =
     2     5     7
     1     3     0
     0     0     0
     3     0     0
```

3.5.4 Removing Elements of an Array

You can remove elements from arrays in the same way that you remove elements from a vector. However, since the arrays must remain rectangular, elements have to be removed as complete rows or columns. For example, for the array A in the previous section, entering A(3, :) = [] would remove all elements from the third row, and the result would be:

A =

2	5	7
1	3	0
3	0	0

Similarly, if A(:, 3) = [] was then entered, the result would be:

A =

2	5
1	3
3	0

3.5.5 Operating on Arrays

This section discusses how array operations extend directly from vector operations: arithmetic and logical operations, the application of functions, concatenation, and slicing. This section will also discuss two topics peculiar to arrays: reshaping and linearizing arrays.

Common Pitfalls 3.3

Removing rows or columns from an array is very rarely the right solution to a problem and can lead to logical difficulties. Wherever possible, use indexing to copy the rows and columns you want to keep.

Common Pitfalls 3.4

Performing array multiplication, division, or exponentiation without appending a dot operator requests one of the specialized matrix operations that will be covered in Chapter 12. The error message when this occurs is quite obscure if you are not expecting it:

```
??? Error using ==> mtimes
Inner matrix dimensions must agree.
```

Even more obscure is the case where the dimensions of the arrays happen to be consistent (when multiplying square arrays), but the results are not the scalar products of the two arrays.

Array Arithmetic Operations Arithmetic operations can be performed collectively on the individual components of two arrays as long as both arrays have the same dimensions or one of them is a scalar (i.e., has a vector of length 1). Addition and subtraction have exactly the syntax you would expect, as shown in Exercise 3.12. Multiplication, division, and exponentiation, however, *must* use the "dot operator" symbols: .*, ./, and .^ (the dot is part of the symbol, but the commas are not) for scalar multiplication, division, and exponentiation.

Array Logical Operations As with vectors, logical array operations can be performed collectively on the individual components of two arrays as long as both arrays have the same dimensions or one of the arrays is a scalar (i.e., has a vector of length 1). The result will be an array of logical values with the same size as the original array(s). Do Exercise 3.13 to see how array logical operations work. Here, we successfully compare the array A to a scalar value, and to the array B that has the same dimensions as A. However, comparing to the array C that has the same number of elements but the wrong shape produces an error.

Exercise 3.12 Working with array mathematics

```
>> A = [2 5 7
     1 3 2]
A =
     2     5     7
     1     3     2
>> A + 5
ans =
     7    10    12
     6     8     7
B = ones(2, 3)
B =
     1     1     1
     1     1     1
>> B = B * 2
B =
     2     2     2
     2     2     2
>> A.*B % scalar multiplication
ans =
     4    10    14
     2     6     4
>> A*B % matrix multiplication does not work here
??? Error using ==> mtimes
Inner matrix dimensions must agree.
```

Exercise 3.13 Working with array logical operations

```
>> A = [2 5; 1 3]
A =
     2     5
     1     3
>> B = [0 6; 3 2];
>> A >= 4
ans =
     0     1
     0     0
>> A >= B
ans =
     1     0
     0     1
>> C = [1 2 3 4]
>> A > C
??? Error using ==> gt
Matrix dimensions must agree.
```

Applying Library Functions In addition to being able to consume vectors, most mathematical functions in the MATLAB language can consume an array of numbers and return an array of the same shape. The following functions deserve special mention because they are exceptions to this rule and provide specific capabilities that are frequently useful:

- `sum(v)` and `mean(v)` when applied to a 2-D array return a row vector containing the sum and mean of each column of the array, respectively. If you want the sum of the whole array, use `sum(sum(v))`.

- `min(v)` and `max(v)` return two row vectors: the minimum or maximum value in each column and also the row in that column where that value occurred. For example:

```
>> [values rows] = max([2   7  42;
                         9  14   8;
                        10  12  -6])
values = [10 14 42]
rows = [3 2 1]
```

This indicates that the maximum values in each column are 10, 14, and 42, respectively, and they occur in rows 3, 2, and 1. If you really need the row and column containing, say, the maximum value of the whole array, continue the preceding example with the following lines:

```
>> [value col] = max(values)
value = 42
col = 3
```

This finds the maximum value in the whole array and determines that it occurs in column 3. So to determine the row in which that maximum occurred, we index the vector of row maximum locations, `rows`, with the column in which the maximum occurred.

```
>> row = rows(col)
row = 1
```

Therefore, we correctly conclude that the maximum number in this array is 42, and it occurs at row 1, column 3.

Array Concatenation The MATLAB language permits programmers to construct a new array by concatenating other arrays in the following ways:

- Horizontally, as long as each component has the same number of rows:

  ```
  A = [B C D ... X Y Z]
  ```

- Vertically, as long as each has the same number of columns:

  ```
  A = [B; C; D; ... X; Y; Z]
  ```

The result will be an array with that number of rows and a number of columns equaling the sum of the number of columns in each individual item.

Exercise 3.14 gives you the opportunity to concatenate an array.

> **Exercise 3.14** Concatenating an array

```
>> A = [2 5; 1 7];
>> B = [1 3]';    % makes a column vector
>> [A B]
ans =
2 5 1
1 7 3
```

Style Points 3.1

The MATLAB language does not encourage concatenating data of different classes. However, it tolerates such concatenation with sometimes odd results. If you really want to achieve this in an unambiguous manner, you should explicitly cast the data to the same class.

Slicing Arrays The general form of statements for moving sections of one array into sections of another is as follows:

```
B(<rangeBR>, <rangeBC>) =
A(<rangeAR>,<rangeAC>)
```

where each <range..> is an index vector, A is an existing array, and B can be an existing array or a new array. The values in B at the specified indices are all assigned the corresponding values copied from A. The rules for using this template are as follows:

- Either each dimension of each sliced array must be equal, or the size of the slice from A must be 1 × 1.
- If B did not exist before this statement was implemented, it would be zero filled where assignments were not explicitly made.
- If B did exist before this statement, the values not directly assigned would remain unchanged.

Reshaping Arrays Occasionally, it is useful to take an array with one set of dimensions and reshape it to another set. The function reshape(...) accomplishes this. The command reshape(A, rows, cols, ...) will take the array A, whatever its dimensions, and reform it into an array sized (rows × cols × ...) out to as many dimensions as desired. However, reshape(...) neither discards excess data nor pads the data to fill any empty space. The product of all the original dimensions of A must equal the product of the new dimensions. Try Exercise 3.15 to see how to reshape an array.

Here, we first take a 1 × 10 array, A, and attempt to reshape it to 4 × 3. Since the element count does not match, an error results. When we concatenate two zeros to the array A, it has the right element count and the reshape succeeds.

Linearized Arrays A discussion of arrays would not be complete without revealing an infamous secret of the MATLAB language: multi-dimensional arrays are not stored in some nice, rectangular chunk of memory. Like all other blocks of memory, the block allocated for an array is sequential, and the array is stored in that space in column order. Normally, if MATLAB behaved as we "have a right to expect," we would not care how an array is

> **Exercise 3.15** Reshaping an array

```
>> A = 1:10
A =
    1    2    3    4    5    6    7    8    9    10
>> reshape(A, 4, 3)
??? Error using ==> reshape
To RESHAPE the number of elements must not change.
>> reshape([A 0 0], 4, 3)
ans =
        1    5    9
        2    6   10
        3    7    0
        4    8    0
```

stored. However, there are circumstances under which the designers of MATLAB needed to expose this secret. The primary situation in which array linearization becomes evident is the mechanization of the `find(...)` function. If we perform a logical operation on an array, the result is an array of logical values of the same size as the original array. In general, the `true` values would be scattered randomly about that result array. If we wanted to convert this to a collection of indices, what would we expect to see? The `find(...)` function has two modes of operation: we can give it separate variables in which to store the rows and columns by saying `[rows cols] = find(...)` or we can receive back just one result by calling `ndx = find(...)`. Indexing with this result exposes the linearized nature of arrays. The way this feature manifests itself is shown in Exercise 3.16.

Here, we build a 4 × 3 array `A` and calculate the logical array where `A` is greater than 5. When we save the result of finding these locations in the variable `ix`, we see that this is a vector of values. If we count down the columns from the top left, we see that the second, seventh, eighth, and eleventh values in the linearized version of `A` are indeed `true`. We also see that it is legal to use this linearized index vector to access the values in the original array—in this case, to add 3 to each one. Finally, we would expect a loud complaint when trying to reference the eleventh element of an array with only three rows. In fact MATLAB "unwinds" the storage of the array, counts down to the eleventh entry—3 for column 1, 3 for column 2, and 3 for column 3—and then extracts the second element of column 4.

To understand all these array manipulation ideas fully, you should work carefully through the script in Listing 3.3, study the explanatory notes that follow, and do Exercise 3.17.

> **Style Points 3.2**
>
> **I.** It is best not to expose the detailed steps of finding logical results in arrays, but to use an integrated approach:
>
> ```
> A(A>5) = A(A>5) + 3
> ```
>
> This produces the expected answers without exposing the nasty secrets underneath.
>
> **2.** Never use an array linearization as part of your program logic. It makes the code hideous to look at and/or understand, and it is never the "only way to do" anything.

Exercise 3.16 Linearizing an array

```
>> A = [2 5 7 3
        8 0 9 42
        1 3 4 2]
A =
     2    5    7    3
     8    0    9   42
     1    3    4    2
>> A > 5
ans =
     0    0    1    0
     1    0    1    1
     0    0    0    0
>> ix = find(A > 5)
ix =
     2    7    8   11
>> A(ix) = A(ix) + 3
A =
     2    5   10    3
    11    0   12   45
     1    3    4    2
>> A(11)
ans =
    42          % (sigh!)
```

Listing 3.3 Array manipulation script

```
1.  A = [2 5 7 3
2.       1 3 4 2]
3.  [rows, cols] = size(A)
4.  odds = 1:2:cols
5.  disp('odd columns of A using predefined indices')
6.  A(:, odds)
7.  disp('odd columns of A using anonymous indices')
8.  A(end, 1:2:end)
9.  disp('put evens into odd values in a new array')
10. B(:, odds) = A(:, 2:2:end)
11. disp('set the even values in B to 99')
12. B(1, 2:2:end) = 99
13. disp('find the small values in A')
14. small = A < 4
15. disp('add 10 to the small values')
16. A(small) = A(small) + 10
17. disp('this can be done in one ugly operation')
18. A(A < 4) = A(A < 4) + 10
19. small_index = find(small)
20. A(small_index) = A(small_index) + 100
```

In Listing 3.3:

Lines 1 and 2: Create a 2 × 4 array A.

Line 3: Determines the number of rows and columns.

Exercise 3.17　Running the array manipulation script

Run the script in Listing 3.3 and observe the results:

```
odds =
       1       3
odd columns of A using predefined indices
ans = 2       7
       1       4
odd columns of A using anonymous indices
ans =
       1       4
put evens into odd values in a new array
B =
       5       0       3
       3       0       2
set the even values in B to 99
B =
       5      99       3
       3       0       2
find the small values in A
small =
     1 0 0 1
     1 1 0 1
add 10 to the small values
A =
      12       5       7      13
      11      13       4      12
this can be done in one ugly operation
A =
      12       5       7      13
      11      13       4      12
do the same thing with indices
small_index =
       1
       2
       4
       7
       8
A =
     112       5       7     113
     111     113       4     112
```

Line 4: Builds a vector odds containing the indices of the odd numbered columns.

Line 6: Uses odds to access the columns in A. The : specifies that this is using all the rows.

Line 8: The anonymous version of the command in Line 6. Notice that you can use the keyword end in any dimension of the array to represent the last index on that dimension.

Line 10: Because B did not previously exist (a good reason to have clear at the beginning of the script to be sure this is true), a new array is created. Elements in B that were not assigned are zero filled.

1. Do not forget to begin all scripts with the two commands `clear` and `clc`.

    a. `clear` empties the current Workspace window of all variables and prevents the values of old variables from causing strange behavior in this script.

    b. `clc` clears the Command window to prevent confusion about whether a display was caused by this script or some earlier activity.

2. It is better to enter a few lines at a time and run each version of the script incrementally, rather than editing one huge script and running the whole thing for the first time. When you have added only a few lines to a previously working script, it is easy to locate the source of logic problems that arise.

3. It is very tempting to build large, complex vector operation expressions that solve messy problems "in one line of code." While this might be an interesting mental exercise, the code is much more maintainable if the solution is expressed one step at a time using intermediate variables.

Line 12: Puts `99` into selected locations in B.

Line 14: Logical operations on arrays produce an array of logical results.

Line 16: Adds `10` to the values in A that are small.

Line 18: Not only is this unnecessarily complex, but it is also less efficient because it is applying the logical operator to A twice.

Line 19: The function `find(...)` actually returns a column vector of the index values in the linearized version of the original array, as shown in Exercise 3.16

Line 20: As illustrated in Line 18, it is not necessary to use `find(...)` before indexing an array. However, this command does work.

Notice that all the results are consistent with our expectations.

3.6 Engineering Example—Computing Soil Volume

When digging the foundations for a building, it is necessary to estimate the amount of soil that must be removed. The first step is to survey the land on which the building is to be built, which results in a rectangular grid defining the height of each grid point as shown in Figure 3.5.

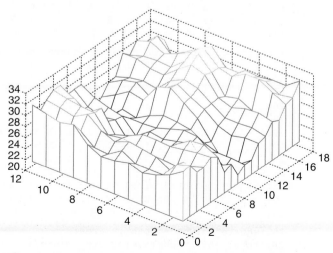

Figure 3.5 *Landscape survey*

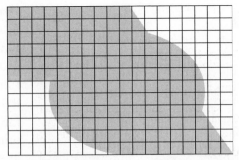

Figure 3.6 *Calculating soil volume*

The next step is to consider an architectural drawing of the basement of the building as shown in Figure 3.6. The shaded areas indicate those places where the soil really must be removed to make the building foundation. We can estimate from this figure the fraction of each surveyed square (for our purposes, a number between 0 and 1) where the soil must actually be removed.

The total amount of soil to move is then the sum of the individual square depths multiplied by the area in each square to be removed. The code in Listing 3.4 solves this problem.

Listing 3.4 Script to compute total soil

```
    % soil depth data for each square produced by the survey
 1. dpth = [8  8  9  8  8  8  8  8  7  8  7  7  7  7  8  8  8  7
 2.          8  8  8  8  8  8  8  7  7  7  7  7  8  7  8  8  8  7
 3.          8  8  8  8  7  7  8  7  8  8  8  8  8  7  8  8  8  8
 4.          7  7  7  8  7  8  8  8  8  8  8  8  7  6  7  7  7  7
 5.          8  8  8  8  8  8  8  8  7  7  7  7  7  6  6  7  7  8
 6.          8  7  7  8  7  7  8  7  7  7  7  7  7  7  7  7  7  8
 7.          9  8  8  9  8  7  8  7  7  7  7  7  6  7  6  7  7  8
 8.          8  8  8  9  9  8  8  8  7  6  6  6  6  7  7  8  7  8
 9.          9  8  8  7  7  7  7  7  7  6  6  7  7  7  8  8  7  8
10.          9  8  8  7  7  7  6  7  7  6  6  8  8  8  9  9  7  8
11.          9  9  8  8  8  8  7  7  7  7  7  8  8  9  9  9  8  8
12.          9  8  8  7  7  8  7  7  7  7  8  8  9  9  9  8  7  8];

    % estimated proportion of each square that should be excavated
13. area = [1  1  1  1  1  1  1  1  1  1 .3  0  0  0  0  0  0  0
14.         1  1  1  1  1  1  1  1  1  1 .7  0  0  0  0  0  0  0
15.         1  1  1  1  1  1  1  1  1  1  1 .8 .4  0  0  0  0  0
16.         1  1  1  1  1  1  1  1  1  1  1  1  1 .8 .3  0  0  0
17.         1  1  1  1  1  1  1  1  1  1  1  1  1  1 .7 .2  0  0
18.         1  1  1  1  1  1  1  1  1  1  1  1  1  1  1 .6  0  0
19.         0  0  0 .7  1  1  1  1  1  1  1  1  1  1  1 .8  0  0
20.         0  0  0 .7  1  1  1  1  1  1  1  1  1  1  1 .7  0  0
21.         0  0  0 .4  1  1  1  1  1  1  1  1  1  1  1 .6  0  0
22.         0  0  0 .1 .8  1  1  1  1  1  1  1  1  1  1  1 .4  0
23.         0  0  0  0 .2 .7  1  1  1  1  1  1  1  1  1  1 .9 .1
24.         0  0  0  0  0  0 .4 .8 .9  1  1  1  1  1  1  1  1 .6];

25. square_volume = dpth .* area;
26. total_soil = sum(sum(square_volume))
```

When you run this script, it produces the answer: 1,117.5 cubic units.

Common Pitfalls 3.5

The code in Listing 3.4 produces an answer around 1,120, and we should ask whether this is reasonable. There are 12 × 18 squares, each with area 1 unit, about 80% of which are to be excavated, giving a surface area of about 180 square units. The average depth of soil is about 7 units, so the answer ought to be about 180 × 7 ≅ 1,300 cubic units. This is reasonably close to the computed result.

Chapter Summary

This chapter introduced you to vectors and arrays. For each collection, you saw how to:

- Create a vectors and arrays by concatenation and a variety of special-purpose functions
- Access and remove elements, rows, or columns
- Perform mathematical and logical operations on them
- Apply library functions, including those that summarize whole columns or rows
- Move arbitrary selected rows and columns from one array to another
- Reshape and linearize arrays

Special Characters, Reserved Words, and Functions

Special Characters, Reserved Words, and Functions	Description	Discussed in This Section
[ ]	The empty vector	3.3.4
[...]	Concatenates data, vectors, and arrays	3.2.1
:	Specifies a vector as `from:incr:to`	3.2.1
:	Used in slicing vectors and arrays	3.3.5
( )	Used with an array name to identify specific elements	3.3.3
'	Transposes an array	3.5.1
;	Separates rows in an array definition	3.5.2
+	Scalar and array addition	3.3.5
−	Scalar and array subtraction or unary negation	3.3.5

Special Characters, Reserved Words, and Functions	Description	Discussed in This Section
.*	Array multiplication	3.3.5
./	Array division	3.3.5
.^	Array exponentiation	3.3.5
<	Less than	3.3.5
<=	Less than or equal to	3.3.5
>	Greater than	3.3.5
>=	Greater than or equal to	3.3.5
==	Equal to	3.3.5
≅	Not equal to	3.3.5
&	Element-wise logical AND (vectors)	3.3.5
&&	Short-circuit logical AND (scalar)	3.3.5
		Element-wise logical OR (vectors)	3.3.5
||	Short-circuit logical OR (scalar)	3.3.5
~	Unary not	3.3.5
end	Last element in a vector	3.3.5
false	Logical false	3.2.2
true	Logical true	3.2.2
ceil(x)	Rounds x to the nearest integer toward positive infinity	3.3.5
cross(a, b)	Vector cross product	3.3
diag(a)	Extracts the diagonal from an array or, if provided with a vector, constructs an array with the given diagonal	3.5.2
disp(value)	Displays an array or text	3.3.5
find()	Computes a vector of the locations of the true values in a logical array	3.3.5, 3.5.5
[rows cols] = find()	Computes vectors of row and column locations of the true values in a logical array	3.5.5
fix(x)	Rounds x to the nearest integer toward zero	3.3.5
floor(x)	Rounds x to the nearest integer toward minus infinity	3.3.5
length(a)	Determines the largest dimension of an array	3.2.2, 3.5.1
linspace(fr,to,n)	Defines a linearly spaced vector	3.2.1

Special Characters, Reserved Words, and Functions	Description	Discussed in This Section
magic(n)	Generates a magic square	3.5.2
[v,in] = max(a)	Finds the maximum value and its position in a	3.3.5
mean(a)	Computes the average of the elements in a	3.3.5
[v,in] = min(a)	Finds the minimum value and its position in a	3.3.5
ones(r, c)	Generates an array filled with the value 1	3.2.1
rand(r, c)	Calculates an r × c array of evenly distributed random numbers in the range 0…1	3.2.1
randn(r, c)	Calculates an r × c array of normally distributed random numbers	3.2.1
round(x)	Rounds x to the nearest integer	3.3.5
size(a)	Determines the dimensions of an array	3.2.2, 3.5.1
sum(a)	Totals the values in a	3.3.5

Self Test

Use the following questions to check your understanding of the material in this chapter:

True or False

F 1. A homogeneous collection must consist entirely of numbers.

T 2. The function linspace(...) can create only vectors, whereas the functions zeros(...), ones(...), and rand(...) produce either vectors or arrays of any dimension.

F 3. The length(...) function applied to a column vector gives you the number of rows.

T 4. You can access any element(s) of an array of any dimension using a single index vector.

F 5. Mathematical or logical operators are allowed only between two arrays of the same shape (rows and columns).

T 6. You can access data in a vector A with an index vector that is longer than A.

F 7. You can access data in a vector A with a logical vector that is longer than A.

T 8.   When moving a block of data in the form of specified rows and
        columns from array A to array B, the shape of the block in A must
        match the shape of the block in B.

Fill in the Blanks

1.   Vector elements have two attributes that make them unique: their
     numerical value and their _position in the vector_

2.   Vectors can be created using the colon operator, for example,
     B = 1:3:20, where the first number is the _starting value_, the second
     number is the _increment_, and the third number is the
     ending value.

3.   When indexing a source vector with a logical vector, the result will
     contain the _elements_ of the source vector corresponding in
     position to the _true values_ in the logical vector.

4.   The normal precedence of operators can be overruled by the use of
     parentheses.

5.   Arithmetic operations can be performed collectively on the
     individual components of two arrays as long as both arrays
     have the same dimensions or one of them is _scalar_.

6.   To remove elements from arrays, you write _the empty vector, []_, in
     complete rows or columns.

7.   Removing rows or columns from an array is _bad_, and
     can lead to _logical difficulties_ Wherever possible, use _indexing_
     to _copy the rows and columns you want to keep_

Programming Projects

1.   For these exercises, do not use the direct entry method to construct
     the vectors. Write a script that does the following:
     a. Construct a vector containing all of the even numbers between 6
         and 33, inclusive of the end points. Store your answer in the
         variable evens. (*Note:* 33 is not an even number)
     b. Construct a vector, threes, containing every third number
         starting with 8 and ending at 38.
     c. Construct a vector, reverse, containing numbers starting at 20
         and counting backward by 1 to 10.
     d. Construct a vector, theta, containing 100 evenly spaced values
         between 0 and 2π.
     e. Construct a vector, myZeros, containing 15 elements, all of which
         are zeros.
     f. Construct a vector, random, containing 15 randomly generated
         numbers between 1 and 12.

2.   Write a script that performs the following exercises on vectors:
      a. You are given a vector vec, defined as: vec = [45 8 2 6 98 55 45
         -48 75]. You decide that you don't want the numbers with even
         values. Write as script to remove all of the even numbers (i.e., 8, 2,
         6, 98, and −48) from vec. You should alter the vector vec rather
         than storing your answer in a new variable. Since your
         commands must work for any vector of any length, you must not
         use direct entry.
      b. Create a variable called vLength that holds the length of the
         vector vec modified in part a. You should use a built-in function
         to calculate the value based on the vector itself.
      c. Create a variable called vSum that holds the sum of the elements
         in vector vec. Do not just enter the value. You should use a
         built-in function to calculate the value based on the vector
         itself.
      d. Calculate the average of the values in the vector vec two ways.
         First, use a built-in function to find the average of vec. Then,
         use the results from parts b and c to calculate the average
         of vec.
      e. Create a variable called vProd that holds the product of the
         elements in vector vec. You should use a built-in function to
         calculate the value based on the vector itself.

3.   Write a script to solve the following problems using only vector
      operations:
      a. Assume that you have two vectors named A1 and B1 of equal
         length, and create a vector C1 that combines A1 and B1 such that
         C1 = [A1(1) B1(1) A1(2) B1(2) ... . A1(end) B1(end)]. For
         example, if A1 = [2, 4, 8] and B1 = [3, 9, 27], C1 should
         contain [2, 3, 4, 9, 8, 27]
      b. Assume that you have two vectors named A2 and B2 of different
         lengths. Create a vector C2 that combines A2 and B2 in a manner
         similar to part a. However, if you run out of elements in one of
         the vectors, C2 also contains the elements remaining from the
         longer vector. For example, if A2 = [1, 2, 3, 4, 5, 6] and B2 =
         [10, 20, 30], then C2 = [1, 10, 2, 20, 3, 30, 4, 5, 6]; if
         A2 = [1, 2, 3] and B2 = [10, 20, 30, 40, 50], then C2 = [1, 10,
         2, 20, 3, 30, 40, 50]

4.   Write a script that, when given a vector of numbers, nums, creates a
      vector newNums containing every other element of the original vector,
      starting with the first element. For example, if nums = [6 3 56 7 8 9
      445 6 7 437 357 5 4 3], newNums should be [6 56 8 445 7 357 4].
      Note: You must not simply hard-code the numbers into your
      answer; your script should work with any vector of numbers.

5.   You are given a vector, tests, of test scores and wish to normalize these scores by computing a new vector, normTests, that will contain the test scores on linear scale from 0 to 100. A zero still corresponds to a zero, and the highest test score will correspond to 100. For example, if tests = [90 45 76 21 85 97 91 84 79 67 76 72 89 95 55], normTests should be

        [92.78 46.39 78.35 21.65 87.63 100 93.81 86.6 ...
        81.44 69.07 78.35 74.23 91.75 97.94 56.7];

6.   Write a script that takes a vector of numbers, A, and return a new vector B, containing the cubes of the positive numbers in A. If a particular entry is negative, replace its cube with 0. For example, if A = [1 2 -1 5 6 7 -4 3 -2 0], B should be [1 8 0 125 216 343 0 27 0 0]

7.   Great news! You have just been selected to appear on Jeopardy this fall. You decide that it might be to your advantage to generate an array representing the values of the questions on the board.
      a. Write a script to generate the matrix jeopardy that consists of six columns and five rows. The columns are all identical, but the values of the rows range from 200 to 1,000 in equal increments.
      b. Next, generate the matrix doubleJeopardy, which has the same dimensions as jeopardy but whose values range from 400 to 2,000.
      c. You've decided to go even one step further and practice for a round that doesn't even exist yet. Generate the matrix squaredJeopardy that contains each entry of the original jeopardy matrix squared.

8.   Write a script named arrayCollide that will combine two arrays, sort them, and then return a new array of a specified size. Your script should process the following data:
      • A: a 2-D array of any size
      • B: another 2-D array that may be a different size from A
      • N: a number specifying the number of rows for the new array
      • M: a number specifying the number of columns for the new array.

      Your script should produce an array, res, of size N × M that contains the first N × M elements of A and B and is sorted columnwise. If N × M is larger than the total number of elements in A and B, you should fill empty spots with 0.

      Test this script by writing another script that repeatedly sets the values of A, B, M, and N and then invokes your arrayCollide script.

You can then create as many test cases as you wish. For example, if
A = [1 2 3; 5 4 6], B = [7 8; 9 10; 12 11], N = 3 and M = 4, res
will be

```
                    [1  4  7  10
                     2  5  8  11
                     3  6  9  12]
```

Change N to 4, and res will be

```
                    [1  5   9  0
                     2  6  10  0
                     3  7  11  0
                     4  8  12  0]
```

Execution Control

Chapter Objectives

This chapter discusses techniques for changing the flow of control in a program, which may be necessary for two reasons:

- You may want to execute some parts of the code under certain circumstances only
- You may want to repeat a section of code a certain number of times

In Chapter 3 we used the array notation to gather numbers into a form where they could be processed collectively rather than individually. This chapter deals with *code blocks* (collections of one or more lines of code) that solve a particular segment of a problem in the same way. We will see how to define a code block, how to decide to execute a code block under certain conditions only, and how to repeat execution of a code block.

4.1 Concept: Code Blocks

Some languages identify code blocks by enclosing them in braces ({. . .});
others identify them by the level of indentation of the text. The MATLAB
language uses the occurrence of key command words in the text to define
the extent of code blocks. Keywords like `if`, `switch`, `while`, `for`, `case`,
`otherwise`, `else`, `elseif`, and `end` are identified with blue coloring by the
MATLAB text editor. They are not part of the code block, but they serve as
instructions on what to do with the code block and as delimiters that define
the extent of the code block.

4.2 Conditional Execution in General

To this point, the statements written in our scripts (single code blocks)
have been executed in sequence from the instruction at the top to the
instruction at the bottom. However, it is frequently necessary to make
choices about how to process a set of data based on some characteristic of
that data. We have seen logical expressions that result in a Boolean result—
`true` or `false`. This section discusses the code that implements the idea
shown in Figure 4.1.

In the flowchart shown in Figure 4.1, a set of statements (the code block
to be executed) is shown as a rectangle, a decision point is shown as a
diamond, and the flow of program control is indicated by arrows. When
decision points are drawn, there will be at least two arrows leaving that
symbol, each labeled with the reason one would take that path. This
concept makes the execution of a code block conditional upon some test. If
the result of the test is `true`, the code block is executed. Otherwise, the code
block is omitted, and the instruction(s) after the end of that code block is
executed next.

An important generalization of this concept is shown in Figure 4.2.
Here the solution is generalized to permit the first code block to be
implemented under the first condition as before. Now, however, if that

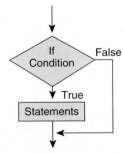

Figure 4.1 *Simple if statement*

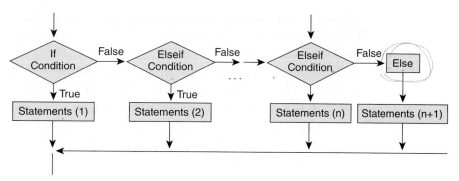

Figure 4.2 *Compound if statement*

first logical test returns `false`, a second test is performed to determine whether the second code block should be executed. If that test returns `false`, as many further tests as necessary may be performed, each with the appropriate code block to be implemented when the result is `true`. Finally, if none of these tests return true, the last code block, usually identified by the `else` keyword—(n + 1) in the figure—is executed. As the flowchart shows, as soon as one of the code blocks is executed, the next instruction to execute is the one that follows the conditional code after the `end` statement. In particular, if there is no else clause, it is possible that no code at all is executed in this conditional statement.

There are two common styles in which to implement this conditional behavior. First we will discuss the most general form, the `if` statement, and then we will discuss the more restrictive but tidier, `switch` statement. Both implementations are found in most modern languages, albeit with slightly different syntax. In each case, the code block to be implemented is all the statements between the key words colored blue by the MATLAB editor.

4.3 if Statements

Here we introduce the concept of a programming template. Many programming texts still use the idea of **flowcharts**, such as those illustrated in Figures 4.1 and 4.2, to describe the design of a solution in a manner independent of the code implementation. However, since this graphical form cannot be maintained with a text editor, if the design of the solution changes, it is difficult to maintain any design description that is separate from the code itself.

Throughout the remainder of this text, we will describe the overall design of a code module using a **design template**. Design templates are a textual form of flowchart consisting of the key words that control program flow and placeholders that identify the code blocks and expressions that are necessary to implement the solution logic. Design templates are powerful tools for the novice programmer to overcome the "blank sheet of paper" problem—"how do I start solving this problem?" All programmers need to do is recognize the nature of the solution and write down the appropriate template. Then solving a particular problem becomes the relatively simple task of writing the code blocks identified by the template.

To discuss the `if` statement, first we consider its general, language independent template and then its MATLAB implementation.

4.3.1 General Template

Template 4.1 shows the general template for the `if` statement. Note the following:

- The only essential ingredients are the first `if` statement, one code block, and the `end` statement. All other features may be added as the logic requires.
- The code blocks may contain any sequence of legal MATLAB statements, including other `if` statements (nested `ifs`), `switch` statements, or iterations (see Section 4.5).
- Nested `if` statements with a code block are an alternative implementation of a logical AND statement.
- Recall that logical operations can be applied to a vector, resulting in a vector of Boolean values. This vector may be used as a logical expression. The `if` statement will accept this expression as `true` if all of the elements are `true`.

4.3.2 MATLAB Implementation

Listing 4.1 shows the MATLAB solution to a typical logical problem: determining whether a day is a weekday or a weekend day. It is assumed that the variable `day` is a number containing integer values from 1 to 7.

Template 4.1 General template for the `if` statement

```
if <logical expression 1>
     <code block 1>
elseif <logical expression 2>
     <code block 2>
     .
     .
     .
elseif <logical expression n>
     <code block n>
else
     <default code block>
End
```

Listing 4.1 if statement example

```
1. if day == 7          % Saturday
2. state = 'weekend'
3. elseif day == 1      % Sunday
4. state = 'weekend'
5. else
6. state = 'weekday'
7. end
```

In Listing 4.1:

Line 1: The first logical expression determines whether day is 7.

Line 2: The corresponding code block sets the value of the variable state to the string 'weekend'. In general, there can be as many statements within a code block as necessary.

Line 3: The second logical expression determines whether day is 1.

Line 4: The corresponding code block also sets the value of the variable state to the string 'weekend'.

Line 5: The key word else introduces the default code block executed when none of the previous tests pass.

Line 6: The default code block sets the value of the variable state to the string 'weekday'.

Exercise 4.1 gives you the opportunity to practice using if statements, and Listing 4.2 shows a script that will satisfy Exercise 4.1.

Exercise 4.1 Using if statements

Write a script that uses input(...) to request a numerical grade in percentage and uses if statements to convert that grade to a letter grade according to the following table:

90% and better: A

80%–90%: B

70%–80%: C

60%–70%: D

Below 60%: F

Test your script by running it repeatedly for legal and illegal values of the grade percentage.

Check your work against the script shown in Listing 4.2.

Listing 4.2 Script with `if` statements

```
1. grade = input('what grade? ');
2. if grade >= 90
3.     letter = 'A'
4. elseif grade >= 80
5.     letter = 'B'
6. elseif grade >= 70
7.     letter = 'C'
8. elseif grade >= 60
9.     letter = 'D'
10. else
11.     letter = 'F'
12. end
```

In Listing 4.2:

> Line 1: Requests a grade value from the user with the `input(...)` function. The prompt appears in the Command window, and the system waits for a line of text from the user and converts that line as it would any other Command window line, returning the result to the variable `grade`.
>
> Line 2: The first logical expression looks for the grade that earns an A.
>
> Line 3: The corresponding code block sets the value of the variable `letter` to `'A'`.
>
> Lines 4–9: The corresponding logic for letter grades B, C, and D.
>
> Lines 10–12: The default logic setting the variable `letter` to `'F'`.

4.3.3 Important Ideas

There are two important ideas that are necessary for the successful implementation of `if` statements: the general form of the logical expressions and short-circuit analysis.

Logical Expressions The `if` statement requires a logical expression for its condition. A logical expression is any collection of constants, variables, and operators whose result is a Boolean `true` or `false` value.

> **Common Pitfalls 4.1**
>
> The MATLAB Command window echoes logical results as 1 (true) or 0 (false). In spite of this appearance, logical values are **not** numeric and should never be treated as if they were.

Logical expressions can be created in the following ways:

- The value of a Boolean constant (e.g., `true` or `false`)
- The value of a variable containing a Boolean result (e.g., `found`)
- The result of a logical operation on two scalar quantities (e.g., `A > 5`)

- The result of logically negating a Boolean quantity using the unary negation operator (e.g., `~found`)
- The result of combining multiple scalar logical expressions with the operators `&&` or `||` (e.g., `A && B` or `A || B`)
- The results of the functions that are the logical equivalent of the `&&`, `||`, and `~` operators: `and(A, B)` `or(A, B)` and `not(A)`
- The results of other functions that operate on Boolean vectors: `any(...)` and `all(...)`

The result from `any(...)` will be `true` if any logical value in the vector is `true`. The result from `all(...)` will be `true` only if all logical values in the vector are `true`. The function `all(...)` is implicitly called if you supply a vector of logical values to the `if` statement, as shown in Listing 4.3.

In Listing 4.3:

> Line 1: Makes the variable `A` a logical vector.
>
> Line 2: Using this as a logical expression, internally converts this expression to `all(A)`.
>
> Line 3: All the values of `A` are not true; therefore, the above code body does not execute.
>
> Line 4: Now, all the elements of `A` are true.
>
> Lines 5–6: If we repeat the test, the code body will now execute.

Short-Circuit Evaluation When evaluating a sequence of logical `&&` or `||`, MATLAB will stop processing when it finds the first result that makes all subsequent processing irrelevant. This concept is best illustrated by an example. Assume that `A` and `B` are logical results and you want to evaluate `A && B`. Since the result of this is `true` only if both `A` and `B` are `true`, if you evaluate `A` and the result is `false`, no value of `B` can change the outcome `A && B`. Therefore, there is no reason to evaluate any more components of a logical and expression once a `false` result has been found. Similarly, if you want `A || B`, if `A` is found to be true, you do not need to evaluate `B`. For example, suppose you want to test the *n*th element of a vector `v` using a variable `n`, and you are concerned that `n` might not be a legal index value.

Listing 4.3 The `if` statement with a logical vector

```
1. A = [true true false]
2. if A
      % will not execute
3. end
4. A(3) = true;
5. if A
      % will execute
6. end
```

The following code could be used:

```
if (n <= length(v)) && (v(n) > 0)
    % success!
end
```

If n were not a legal index, the indexed accessor v(n) would cause an error for attempting to reach beyond the end of the vector. However, by putting the test of n first, the short-circuit logic would not process the second part of the expression if the test of n failed.

4.4 switch Statements

A switch statement implements the logic shown in Figure 4.2 in a different programming style by allowing the programmer to consider a number of different cases for the value of one variable. First we consider the general, language-independent template for switch statements, and then its MATLAB implementation.

4.4.1 General Template

Template 4.2 shows the general template for the switch statement.

Note the following:

- All tests refer to the value of the same parameter
- case specifications may be either a single value or a set of parameters enclosed in braces { ... }
- otherwise specifies the code block to be executed when none of the case values apply
- The code blocks may contain any sequence of legal MATLAB statements, including other if statements (nested ifs), switch statements, or iterations

Template 4.2 General template for the switch statement

```
switch <parameter>
   case <case specification 1>
      <code block 1>
   case <case specification 2>
      <code block 2>
   .
   .
   case <case specification n>
      <code block n>
   otherwise
      <default code block>
end
```

4.4.2 MATLAB Implementation

Listing 4.4 shows the MATLAB implementation of a typical logical problem: determining the number of days in a month. It assumes that the value of month is 1 . . . 12, and leapYear is a logical variable identifying the current year as a leap year.

Style Points 4.1

The usual description of the logic suggests that the last case in Listing 4.4 could be the otherwise clause. However, that would prevent you from being able to <u>detect bad month</u> number values, as this code does.

Hint 4.1

The second parameter to the input(...) statement prevents MATLAB from attempting to parse the data provided, returning a string instead. Without that activity suppressed, if you enter the string 'yes', MATLAB will rush off looking for a variable by that name.

Style Points 4.2

The use of indentation is not required in the MATLAB language, and it has no significance with regard to syntax. However, the appropriate use of indentation greatly improves the legibility of code and you should use it. You have probably already noted that in addition to colorizing control statements, the text editor automatically places the control statements in the indented positions illustrated in Listings 4.3 and 4.4.

In Listing 4.4:

Line 1: All tests refer to the value of the variable month.

Line 2: This case specification is a cell array (See Chapter 7 for specifics) containing the indices of the months with 30 days.

Line 3: The code block extends from the case statement to the next control statement (case, otherwise, or end).

Line 5: This code block contains an if statement to deal with the February case. It presumes that a Boolean variable leapYear has been created to indicate whether this month is in a leap year.

Lines 10–11: Deal with the remaining months.

Line 13: A built-in MATLAB function that announces the error and terminates the script.

Listing 4.4 Example of a switch statement

```
1. switch month
2.     case {9, 4, 6, 11}
            % Sept, Apr, June, Nov
3.            days = 30;
4.     case 2              % Feb
5.        if leapYear
6.                days = 29;
7.            else
8.                days = 28;
9.            end
10.    case {1, 3, 5, 7, 8, 10, 12}
            % other months
11.              days = 31;
12.    otherwise
13.                error('bad month index')
14. end
```

Exercise 4.2 Using the `switch` statement

Write and test the script in Listing 4.4 using `input(...)` to request a numerical month value.

You will need to preset a value for `leapYear`.

Test your script by running it repeatedly for legal and illegal values of the month.

Modify your script to ask whether the current year is a leap year. (It's best to ask only for February.) You could use code like the following:

```
ans = input('leap year (yes/no)', 's');
leapYear = (ans(1) == 'y');
```

Test this new script thoroughly.

Try this script without the second parameter to `input(...)`. Can you explain what is happening?

Modify the script again to accept the year rather than yes/no, and implement the logic to determine whether that year is a leap year.

Try using the `switch` statement in Exercise 4.2.

 ## 4.5 Iteration in General

Iteration allows controlled repetition of a code block. Control statements at the beginning of the code block specify the manner and extent of the repetition:

- The `for` loop is designed to repeat its code block a fixed number of times and largely automates the process of managing the iteration.
- The `while` loop is more flexible in character. In contrast to the fixed repetition of the `for` loop, its code block can be repeated a variable number of times, depending on the values of data being processed. It is much more of a "do-it-yourself" iteration kit.

The `if` and `switch` statements allow us to decide to skip code blocks based on conditions in the data. The `for` and `while` constructs allow us to repeat code blocks. Note, however, that the MATLAB language is designed to avoid iteration. Under most circumstances of processing numbers, the array processing operations built into the language make do-it-yourself loop constructs unnecessary.

 ## 4.6 `for` Loops

Figure 4.3 shows a simple `for` loop. The hexagonal shape illustrates the control of repetition. The repeated execution of the code block is performed under the control of a loop-control variable. It is first set to an initial value

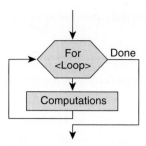

Figure 4.3 *Structure of a* for *loop*

that is tested against a terminating condition. If the terminating test succeeds, the program leaves the for loop. Otherwise, the computations in the code block are performed using the current value of that variable. When one pass through the code block is finished, the variable is updated to its next value, and control returns to the termination test.

4.6.1 General for Loop Template

The general template for implementing for loops is shown in Template 4.3. All of the mechanics of iteration control are handled automatically in the variable specification section. In some languages—especially those with their origins in C—the variable specification is a formidable collection of statements that provide great generality of loop management. The designers of the MATLAB language, with its origins in matrix processing, chose a much simpler approach for specifying the variable range, as shown in the general template. The repetition of the code block is managed completely by the specification of the loop control variable.

4.6.2 MATLAB Implementation

The core concept in the MATLAB for loop implementation is in the style of the variable specification, which is accomplished as follows:

<variable specification>: <variable> = <vector>

where <variable> is the name of the loop control variable and <vector> is any vector that can be created by the techniques discussed in Chapter 3. If

Template 4.3 General template for the for statement

```
for <variable specification>
        <code block>
end
```

we were to use the variable specification x = A, MATLAB would proceed as follows:

1. Set an invisible index to 1.
2. Repeat steps 3 to 5 as long as that index is less than or equal to the length of A.
3. Set the value of x to A(index)
4. Evaluate the code block with that value of x
5. Increment the index

For a simple example of for loops, the code shown in Listing 4.5 solves a problem that should be done in a single MATLAB instruction: max(A) where A is a vector of integers. However, by expanding this into a for loop, we see the basic structure of the for loop at work.

In Listing 4.5:

Line 1: Creates a vector A with six elements.

Line 2: The tidiest way to find limits of a collection of numbers is to seed the result, theMax, with the first number.

Line 3: Iterates across the values of A.

Lines 4–6: The code block extends from the for statement to the associated end statement. The code will be executed the same number of times as the length of A *even if you change the value of x within the code block*. At each iteration, the value of x will be set to the next element from the array A.

> **Common Pitfalls 4.2**
>
> By setting the default answer to the first value, we avoid the problem of seeding the result with a value that could be already outside the range of the vector values. For example, we might think that theMax = 0; would be a satisfactory seed. However, this would not do well if all the elements of A were negative.

Line 8: The fprintf(...)function is a very flexible means of formatting output to the Command window. See the discussion in Chapter 8, or enter the following in the Command window:

```
> help fprintf
```

Listing 4.5 Example of a for statement

```
1. A = [6 12 6 91 13 6]  % initial vector
2. theMax = A(1);        % set initial max value
3. for x = A             % iterate through A
4.      if x > theMax     % test each element
5.          theMax = x;
6.      end
7. end
8. fprintf('max(A) is %d\n', theMax);
```

4.6.3 Indexing Implementation

The above for loop implementation may seem very strange to those with a C-based language background, in which the loop-control variable is usually an index into the array being traversed rather than an element from that array. In order to illustrate the difference, we will adapt the code from Listing 4.5 to solve a slightly different problem that approximates the behavior of max(A). This time we need to know not only the maximum value in the array, but also its index. This requires that we resort to indexing the array in a more conventional style, as shown in Listing 4.6.

In Listing 4.6:

> Line 1: Generalizes the creation of the vector A using the rand(...) function to create a vector with 10 elements each between 0 and 100. The ceil(...) function rounds each value up to the next higher integer.

> Lines 2 and 3: Initialize theMax and theIndex.

> Line 4: Creates an anonymous vector of indices from 1 to the length of A and uses it to define the loop-control variable, index.

> Line 5: Extracts the appropriate element from A to operate with as before.

> Lines 6 and 7: The same comparison logic as shown in Listing 4.5.

> Line 8: In addition to saving the new max value, we save the index where it occurs.

> Line 11: This is our first occurrence where a logical line of code extends beyond the physical limitations of a single line. Since MATLAB normally uses the end of the line to indicate the end of an operation, we use ellipses (...) to specify that the logic is continued onto the next line.

You can enter and run these scripts by following Exercise 4.3.

Listing 4.6 for statement using indexing

```
 1. A = floor(rand(1,10)*100)
 2. theMax = A(1);
 3. theIndex = 1;
 4. for index = 1:length(A)
 5.     x = A(index);
 6.     if x > theMax
 7.         theMax = x;
 8.         theIndex = index;
 9.     end
10. end
11. fprintf('the max value in A is %d at %d\n', ...
12.             theMax, theIndex);
```

Exercise 4.3 Producing `for` statement results

Enter and run the scripts in Listings 4.5 and 4.6. They should each produce the following results:

```
A =
   6 12 6 91 13 61 26 22 71 54
the max value in A is 91 at 4
>>
```

4.6.4 Breaking out of a `for` Loop

If you are in a `for` loop and find a circumstance where you really do not want to continue iterating, the `break` statement will skip immediately out of the innermost containing loop. If you want to continue iterating but omit all further steps of the current iteration, you can use the `continue` statement.

 ## 4.7 `while` Loops

We use `while` loops in general to obtain more control over the number of times the iteration is repeated. Figure 4.4 illustrates the control flow for a `while` loop. Since the termination test is performed before the loop is entered, the loop control expression must be initialized to a state that will normally permit loop entry. It is possible that the code block is not executed at all—for example—if there is no data to process.

4.7.1 General `while` Template

Template 4.4 shows the general template for implementing `while` loops. The logical expression controlling the iteration is testing some state of the workspace; therefore, two things that were automatic in the `for` loop must be manually accomplished with the `while` loop: initializing the test and updating the workspace in the code block so that the test will eventually fail and the iteration will stop.

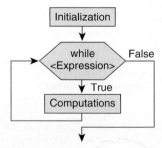

Figure 4.4 *Structure of a* `while` *loop*

Template 4.4 General template for the while statement

```
<initialization>
while <logical expression>
      <code block>    % must make some changes
            % to enable the loop to terminate
end
```

4.7.2 MATLAB while Loop Implementation

For the sake of consistency, Listing 4.7 shows you how to solve the same problem using the while syntax.

In Listing 4.7:

> Lines 1–3: Create a test vector and initialize the answers as before.
>
> Line 4: Initializes the index value since this is manually updated.
>
> Line 5: This test will fail immediately if the vector A is empty.
>
> Line 6: Extracts the item x from the array (good practice in general to clarify your code).
>
> Lines 7–9: The same test as before to update the maximum value.
>
> Line 11: "Manually" updates the index to move the loop closer to finishing.

Enter and run the script as described in Exercise 4.4.

Listing 4.7 while statement example

```
1. A = floor(rand(1,10)*100)
2. theMax = A(1);
3. theIndex = 1;
4. index = 1;
5. while index <= length(A)
6.     x = A(index);
7.     if x > theMax
8.         theMax = x;
9.         theIndex = index;
10.    end
11.    index = index + 1;
12. end
13. fprintf('the max value in A is %d at %d\n', ...
14.             theMax, theIndex);
```

Exercise 4.4 Producing while statement results

Enter and run the script in Listing 4.7. It should produce the following results:

```
A =
  6 12 6 91 13 61 26 22 71 54
the max value in A is 91 at 4
>>
```

4.7.3 Loop-and-a-Half Implementation

Listing 4.8 illustrates the implementation of the loop-and-a-half iteration style, in which we must enter the loop and perform some computation before realizing that we do not need to continue. Here we continually ask the user for the radius of a circle until an illegal radius is entered, which is our cue to terminate the iteration. For each radius entered, we want to display the area and circumference of the circle with that radius.

> **Style Points 4.3**
>
> We wrote the `for` loop examples in two styles: the direct access style and the indexing style. Many people code in the indexing style even when the index value is not explicitly required. This is slightly tacky and demonstrates a lack of appreciation for the full power of the MATLAB language.

> **Style Points 4.4**
>
> The use of `break` and `continue` statements is frowned upon in programming circles for the same reason that the `goto` statement has fallen into disrepute—they make it more difficult to understand the flow of control through a complex program. It is preferable to express the logic for remaining in a `while` loop explicitly in its controlling logical expression, combined with `if` statements inside the loop to skip blocks of code. However, sometimes this latter approach causes code to be more complex than would be the case with judicious use of `break` or `continue`.

In Listing 4.8:

Line 1: Initializes the radius value to allow the loop to be entered the first time.

Line 2: We will remain in this loop until the user enters an illegal radius.

Line 3: The `input(...)` function shows the user the text string, parses what is typed, and stores the result in the variable provided. This is described fully in Chapter 8.

Line 4: We want to present the area and circumference only if the radius has a legal value. Since this test occurs in the middle of the `while` loop, we call this "loop-and-a-half" processing.

Lines 5–8: Compute and display the area and circumference of a circle.

Try this script in Exercise 4.5.

Listing 4.8 Loop-and-a-half example

```
1. clear
2. clc
3. close all
   % Listing 04.08 Loop-and-a-half example
4. R = 1;
5. while R > 0
6.     R = input('Enter a radius: ');
7.     if R > 0
8.         area = pi * R^2;
9.         circum = 2 * pi * R;
10.        fprintf('area = %f; circum = %f\n', ...
11.            area, circum);
12.    end
13. end
```

Exercise 4.5 Producing loop-and-a-half test results

Enter and run the script in Listing 4.8. It should produce the following results:

```
Enter a radius: 4
area = 50.265482; circum = 25.132741
Enter a radius: 3
area = 28.274334; circum = 18.849556
Enter a radius: 100
area = 31415.926536; circum = 628.318531
Enter a radius: 0
>>
```

4.7.4 Breaking a `while` Loop

As with the `for` loop, `break` will exit the innermost `while` loop, and `continue` will skip to the end of the loop but remain within it.

4.8 Engineering Example—Computing Liquid Levels

Figure 4.5 shows a cylindrical tank of height H and radius r with a spherical cap on each end (also of radius, r). If the height of the liquid is h, what is the volume of liquid in the tank? Clearly, the calculation of the volume of liquid in the tank depends upon the relationship between h, H, and r:

- If h is less than r, we need the volume, v, of a partially filled sphere given by:

$$v = \frac{1}{3}\pi h^2(3r - h)$$

- If h is greater than r but less than $H - r$, we need the volume of a fully filled hemisphere plus the volume of a cylinder of height $h - r$:

$$v = \frac{2}{3}\pi r^3 + \pi r^2(h - r)$$

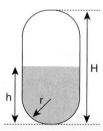

Figure 4.5 *A tank containing liquid*

- If h is greater than $H + r$, we need the volume of a fully filled sphere plus the volume of a cylinder of height $H + 2r$ minus the partially empty upper hemisphere of height $H + h$:

$$v = \frac{4}{3}\pi r^3 + \pi r^2(H - 2r) - \frac{1}{3}\pi(H - h)^2(3r - H + h)$$

The script to perform this calculation is shown in Listing 4.9. Rather than performing the computations for one liquid level only, we should write the script so that we continue to consider tanks of different dimensions and different liquid heights for each tank until the user indicates that he needs no more results.

In Listing 4.9:

Line 1: Initializes the value to keep it in the first `while` loop.

Lines 3 and 4: Get the tank sizes.

Line 5: Initializes the value to keep it in the inner `while` loop.

Line 7: Gets the liquid height.

Lines 8–14: Calculations for legal values of h. Notice that no dot operators are required here, because these conditional computations will not work correctly with vectors of H, r, or h.

Listing 4.9 Script to compute liquid levels

```
 1. another_tank = true;
 2. while another_tank
 3.      H = input('Overall tank height: ');
 4.      r = input('tank radius: ');
 5.      more_heights = true;
 6.      while more_heights
 7.          h = input('liquid height: ');
 8.          if h < r
 9.              v = (1/3)*pi*h.^2.*(3*r-h);
10.          elseif h < H-r
11.              v = (2/3)*pi*r^3 + pi*r^2*(h-r);
12.          elseif h <= H
13.              v = (4/3)*pi*r^3 + pi*r^2*(H-2*r) ...
14.                     - (1/3)*pi*(H-h)^2*(3*r-H+h);
15.          else
16.              disp('liquid level too high')
17.              continue
18.          end
19.          fprintf( ...
20.          'rad %0.2f ht %0.2f level %0.2f vol %0.2f\n', ...
21.                   r,          H,          h,        v);
22.          more_heights = input('more levels? (y/n)','s')=='y';
23.      end
24.      another_tank = input('another tank? (y/n)','s')=='y';
25. end
```

Table 4.1 Results for liquid levels
Overall tank height: 10
tank radius: 2
liquid height: 1
radius 2.00 height 10.00 level 1.00 vol 5.24
more levels? (y/n)y
liquid height: 8
radius 4.00 height 8.00 level 8.00 vol 268.08
more levels? (y/n)
another tank? (y/n)

Lines 15 and 16: Illegal *h* values end up here.

Line 17: Goes to the end of the inner loop, skipping the printout.

Lines 19–21: Print the result.

Line 22: More levels when "y" is entered.

Line 24: Another tank when "y" is entered.

Table 4.1 shows some typical results.

Chapter Summary

This chapter presented techniques for changing the flow of control of a program for condition execution and repetitive execution:

- The most general conditional form is the `if` statement, with or without the accompanying `elseif` and `else` statements
- The `switch` statement considers different cases of the values of a countable variable
- A `for` loop in its most basic form executes a code block for each of the elements of a vector
- A `while` loop repeats a code block a variable number of times, as long as the conditions specified for continuing the repetition remain true

Special Characters, Reserved Words, and Functions

Special Characters, Reserved Words, and Functions	Description	Discussed in This Section
false	Logical false	4.2
true	Logical true	4.2
break	A command within a loop module that forces control to the statement following the innermost loop	4.6.4, 4.7.4
case	A specific value within a switch statement	4.1, 4.4.1
continue	Skips to the end of the innermost loop, but remains inside it	4.6.4, 4.7.4
else	Within an if statement, begins the code block executed when the condition is false	4.1, 4.3.2
elseif	Within an if statement, begins a second test when the first condition is false	4.1, 4.3.2
end	Terminates an if, switch, for, or while module	4.1, 4.3.2
for var = v	A code module repeats as many times as there are elements in the vector v	4.1, 4.6
if <exp>	Begins a conditional module; the following code block is executed if the logical expression <exp> is true	4.1, 4.3.2
input(str)	Requests and parses input from the user	4.3.2
otherwise	Catch-all code block at the end of a switch statement	4.1, 4.4.1
switch(variable)	Begins a code module selecting specific values of the variable (must be countable)	4.1, 4.4.1
while <exp>	A code module repeats as long as the logical expression <exp> is true	4.1
all(a)	True if all the values in a, a logical vector, a, are true	4.3.3
and(a, b)	True if both a and b are true (can be vectors)	4.3.3
any(a)	True if any of the values in a, a logical vector, is true	4.3.3
not(a)	True if a is false; false if a is true (can be vectors)	4.3.3
or(a, b)	True if either a or b is true (can be vectors)	4.3.3

Self Test

Use the following questions to check your understanding of the material in this chapter:

True or False

F   1.   MATLAB keywords are colored ~~green~~ blue by the editor.

F   2.   Indentation is required in MATLAB to define code blocks.

T   3.   It is possible that no code at all is executed by `if` or `switch` constructs.

T   4.   The word `true` is a valid logical expression.

F   5.   When evaluating a sequence of logical `&&` expressions, MATLAB will stop processing when it finds the first `true` result.

T   6.   The `for` loop repeats the enclosed code block a fixed number of times even if you modify the index variable within the code block.

F   7.   Using a `break` statement is illegal in a `while` loop.

F   8.   The logical expression used in a `while` loop specifies the conditions for ~~exiting~~ staying the loop.

Fill in the Blanks

1.   MATLAB uses __words__ key command in the text to define the extent of code blocks.

2.   The function __all(...)__ is implicitly called by MATLAB if you supply a vector of logical values to the `if` statement.

3.   It is good practice to include _otherwise_ in a `switch` statement to trap illegal values entering the `switch`.

4.   There is no reason to evaluate any more components of a logical or expression once a(n) _true_ result has been found.

5.   A `while` loop can be repeated a number of times, depending on the _variable_ values of data being processed.

6.   If you are in a(n) _for/while_ loop, you can use the `break` statement to skip immediately out of the _innermost_ containing loop.

Programming Projects

1.   Write a script to solve this problem. Assume that you have a vector named D. Using iteration (`for` and/or `while`) and conditionals (`if` and/or `switch`), separate vector D into four vectors `posEven`, `negEven`, `posOdd`, and `negOdd`.
     - `posEven` contains all of the positive even numbers in D.
     - `negEven` contains all of the negative even numbers in D.
     - `posOdd` contains all of the positive odd numbers in D.
     - `negOdd` contains all of the negative odd numbers in D.

For example:

```
if D = [-4,-3,-2,-1,0,1,2,3,4],
posEven=[2,4], negEven=[-4,-2],
posOdd=[1,3] and negOdd=[-3,-1]
```

2. You must use either `for` or `while` to solve the following problems.
   a. Iterate through a vector, A, using a `for` loop, and create a new vector, B, containing `logical` values. The new vector should contain `true` for positive values and `false` for all other values. For example, if A = `[-300 2 5 -63 4 0 -46]`, the result should be B = `[false true true false true true false]`
   b. Iterate through the vector, A, using a `while` loop, and return a new vector, B, containing `true` for positive values and `false` for all other values.
   c. Iterate through a logical array, N, using a `for` loop, and return a new vector, M, containing the value 2 wherever an element of N is `true` and the value −1 (not a logical value) wherever N is `false`. For example, if N = `[true false false true true false true]`, the result should be M = `[2 -1 -1 2 2 -1 2]`
   d. Iterate through an array, Z, using a `while` loop. Replace every element with the number 3 until you reach a number larger than 50. Leave the rest unchanged. For example, if Z = `[4 3 2 5 7 9 0 64 34 43]`, after running your script, Z = `[3 3 3 3 3 3 3 3 34 43]`

3. You are hiring grad students to work for your company, which you have recently started. The Human Resources department has asked you to write a script that will help them determine the chances of an individual applicant getting a job after interviewing. The following table outlines the rules for determining the chances for the applicant to get a job:

GPA Value	Chance of Being Hired
GPA>= 3.5	90%
3.0<= GPA < 3.5	80%
2.5 <= GPA < 3.0	70%
2.0 <= GPA < 2.5	60%
1.5 <= GPA < 2.0	40%
GPA < 1.5	30%

Your script should repeatedly ask the user for a GPA value and compute the student's chances of being hired. It should continue asking for GPA values until a negative number is entered. For example:

- GPA input: 4 should give the answer 0.9
- GPA input: 3.5 should give the answer 0.9
- GPA input: 3.4 should give the answer 0.8

4. You were just hired for a summer internship with one of the area's best software companies; however, on your first day of work you learn that for the next three months, the only job you will have is to convert binary (base 2) numbers into decimal numbers (base 10). You decide to write a script that will repetitively ask the user for a binary number and return its decimal equivalent until an illegal number (one containing digits other than 0 or 1) is entered. The number entered should contain only the digits 0 and 1. The rightmost digit has the value 2^0 and the digit N places to the left of that has the value 2^N. For example, entering `110101` returns

    $$53 = 2^5 + 2^4 + 2^3 + 2^0$$

    You must use iteration to solve this problem. Note: The `input (...)` function prompts the user for a value, parses the characters entered according to normal MATLAB rules, and returns the result.

5. You have a friend who has too many clothes to store in his or her tiny wardrobe. Being a good friend, you offer to help to decide whether each piece of clothing is worth saving. You decide to write a script that will compute the value of each piece of clothing. A piece of clothing has five attributes that can be used to determine its value. The attributes are: condition, color, price, number of matches, and comfort. Each attribute will be rated on a scale of 1 to 5. Write a script called `clothes` that will ask the user for the ratings for each attribute and store the result in a vector. The order of attributes in the vector is: `[condition color price matches comfort]`

    The script should compute a value between 0 and 100; 100 represents a good piece of clothing, while 0 represents a bad piece of clothing. The points that should be given for each attribute are shown below:

Condition:	1=>0; 2=>5; 3=>10; 4=>15; 5=>20
Color:	1 => blue => 12;
	2 => red => 2;
	3 => pink => 15;
	4 => yellow => 20;
	5 => white => 12
Price:	1 => 8, 2–3 => 16, 4–5 => 20
Matches:	1–2 => 8, 3–5 => 19
Comfort:	1 => 6, 2–3 => 13, 4–5 =>18

    Note: If a number other than 1–5 is assigned for one of the attributes, no points should be given.

6. A "yard" is a traditional English container. It is 36 inches long, and can be approximated by a 4-inch diameter glass sphere attached to a conical section whose narrow end is 1 inch in diameter, and

whose wide end is 6 inches in diameter. Write a script to do the following:

a. ask the user for the height of the liquid in the yard, and
b. calculate the volume of liquid needed to fill the yard to that level.

7.   Now that you're comfortable with iteration, you're going to have to solve an interesting problem. It seems that the Math department at a rival university has once again dropped the ball, and forgotten the value of pi. You are to write a function called mypi, which consumes a number that specifies the required accuracy and then approximates the value of pi to that accuracy. You are going to use the following algorithm based on geometric probability.

Think about a quarter circle inside of a unit square (the quarter circle has area $\pi/4$). You pick a random point inside the square. If it is in the quarter circle, you get a "hit"; and if not, you get a "miss." The approximate area of the quarter circle will be given by the number of hits divided by the number of points you chose.

Hint

you could use the function rand (...) in this problem.

Your function should repeat the process of counting hits and misses until at least 10,000 tries have been made, and the successive estimates of pi are within the prescribed accuracy. It should return the estimated value of pi.

CHAPTER 5

Functions

Chapter Objectives

This chapter discusses the nature, implementation, and behavior of user-defined functions in MATLAB:

- How to define a function

- How data are passed into a function

- How to return data, including multiple results

- How to include other functions not needed except as helpers to your own function

Writing a user-defined function allows you to isolate and package together a code block, so that you can apply that code block to different sets of input data. We have already made use of some built-in functions like `sin(...)` and `plot(...)` by calling them; this chapter will deal with creating and using your own functions.

5.1 Concepts: Abstraction and Encapsulation

A **function** is an implementation of procedural abstraction and encapsulation. **Procedural abstraction** is the concept that permits a code block that solves a particular sub-problem to be packaged and applied to different data inputs. This is exactly analogous to the concept of data abstraction we discussed in Chapter 3 where individual data items are gathered to form a collection. We have already used a number of built-in procedural abstractions in the form of functions. All the mathematical functions that compute—for example, the sine of a collection of angles or the maximum value of a vector—are examples of procedural abstraction. They allow us to apply a code block about which we know nothing to data sets that we provide. To make use of a built-in function, all we have to do is provide data in the form the function expects and interpret the results according to the function's specification.

Encapsulation is the concept of putting a wrapper around a collection that you wish to protect from outside influence. Functions encapsulate the code they contain in two ways: the variables declared within the function are not visible from elsewhere, and the function's ability to change the values of variables (otherwise known as causing side effects) is restricted to its own code body.

5.2 Black Box View of a Function

The most abstract view of a function can be seen in Figure 5.1. It consists of two parts: the definition of the interface by which the user passes data items to and from the function, and the code block that produces the results required by that interface. A function definition consists of the following components:

- A name that follows the same syntactic rules as a variable name
- A set of 0 or more parameters provided to the function
- Zero or more results to be returned to the caller of the function

The basic operation of a function begins before execution of the function actually starts. If the function definition requires n parameters, the calling instructions first prepare n items of data from its workspace to be provided

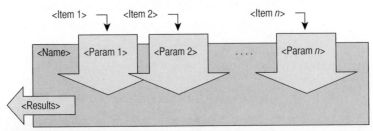

Figure 5.1 *Black box view of a function*

to the function. These data are then passed to the function, the code body is executed, and the results are returned to the caller.

 ## 5.3 MATLAB Implementation

In this section, first we consider the general template for implementing functions and then the MATLAB implementation of that template.

5.3.1 General Template

The general layout of a function definition is shown in Template 5.1. The `<return info>` section for most functions involves providing the name(s) of the results returned followed by an = sign. If more than one result is to be returned, they are defined in a vector-like container. If nothing is to be returned from this function, both the result list and the = sign are omitted. The `<function name>` is a name with the same syntactic rules as a variable name and will be used to invoke the code body. The `<parameters>` section is a comma-separated list of the names of the data to be provided to the function. The `<documentation>` section is one or more lines of comments that describe what the function does and how to call it. These lines will appear in two situations:

- All the documentation lines up to the first non-document line are printed in the Command window when you type the following:
  ```
  >> help <function name>
  ```
- The first line is listed next to the file name in the Current Directory listing

5.3.2 Function Definition

In the MATLAB language, functions must be stored in a separate file located in a directory accessible to any script or function that calls it. The file containing the definition of a function named `function_name` must be `<function_name>.m`. For the general user, the Current Directory is the normal place to store it. Listing 5.1 illustrates a typical MATLAB function called `cylinder` that consumes two parameters, the `height` and `radius` of a cylinder, and produces the return variable `volume`.

In Listing 5.1:

Line 1: The MATLAB function definition is introduced by the key word `function`, followed by the name of the return variable (if any)

Template 5.1 General template for a function

```
function <return info> <function name> (<parameters>)
<documentation>
<code body> % must return the results
```

Listing 5.1 Cylinder function

```
1. function volume = cylinder(height, radius)
   % function to compute the volume of a cylinder
   % volume = cylinder(height, radius)
2.     base = pi * radius^2
3.     volume = base * height
4. end
```

and the = sign, then the name of the function and the names of the formal parameters in parentheses. All comments written immediately after the function header are available to the MATLAB Command window when you enter:

```
>>help <function_name>
```

The first comment line also appears in the Current Directory window as an indication of the basic purpose of the function. It is a good idea to include in the comments a usage statement showing copy of the function header line, sometimes referred to as the Application Programmer Interface (API), to remind a user exactly how to use this function.

Line 3: Although encapsulation rules forbid access to the caller's variables, the code body still has access to all built-in MATLAB variables and functions (e.g., `pi`, as used here).

Line 5: You must make at least one assignment to the result variable.

Line 6: Regrettably, the `end` statement is not required if there is only one function in the file; without it, the code body terminates at the end of the file. However, it must be present if there are other function definitions in the same file.

Try saving and testing the cylinder function in Exercise 5.1.

  Exercise 5.1 Saving and testing the `cylinder` function

Enter the function definition from Listing 5.1 in the Text Editor and save it as `cylinder.m` in your Current Directory. Then enter the following experiments in the Interactions window. Notice that the first help line appears next to this file name in the Current Directory.

```
>> help cylinder
  function to compute the volume of a cylinder
    volume = cylinder(height, radius)
>> cylinder(1, 1)
ans =
    3.1416
>>
```

5.3.3 Storing and Using Functions

All user-defined MATLAB functions must be created like scripts in an m-file. When the file is first created, it must be saved in an m-file with the same file name as the function. For example, the function in Listing 5.1 named `cylinder` must be saved in a file named `cylinder.m`. Once the file has been saved, you may invoke the function by entering its name and parameters of the right type and number in the Command window, in a script, or in other function definitions. If you do not specify an assignment for the result of the function call, it will be assigned to the variable `ans`.

5.3.4 Calling Functions

When a function is defined, the user provides a list of the names of each data item expected to be provided by the caller. These are called the **formal parameters.** When this function is called, the caller must provide the same number of data values expected by the function definition. These are the **actual parameters** and can be generated in the following ways:

- Constants
- Variables that have been defined
- The result of some mathematical operation(s)
- The result returned from other functions

When the actual parameters have been computed, *copies of* their values are assigned as the values of the formal parameters the function is expecting. Values are assigned to parameters by position in the calling statement and function definition.

The process of copying the actual parameters into the formal parameters is referred to as "passing by value"—the only technique defined in the MATLAB language for passing data into a function.

Once the parameter names have been defined in the function's workspace, the function's code body

Style Point 5.1 Parameter Passing

Some languages provide an alternative technique—"passing by reference"—whereby the memory location for the parameters is passed to the function while the values remain in the caller's workspace. Syntactically, this is usually a bad thing, allowing deliberate or accidental assignments to "reach back" into the scope of the calling code and thereby perhaps causing undesirable side effects. However, restricting parameter access to passing by value can result in poor program performance. When a function needs access to large sets of data, consider improving the efficiency by using global variables.

is executed, beginning with the first instruction. If return variables have been defined for the function, every exit from the code body must assign valid values for the results.

5.3.5 Variable Numbers of Parameters

Although the number of parameters is usually fixed, most languages, including MATLAB, provide the ability to deal with a variable number of parameters, both incoming and returning. The built-in function `nargin` computes the actual number of parameters provided by the user in the current function call. If the function is designed to make use of `nargin`, the user calling this function can provide any values he deems important and allow the function to set default values for the unnecessary parameters.

Similarly, the function `nargout` computes the number of storage variables actually provided by the user. So if one or more of the results requires extensive computation or user interaction and the caller has not asked for that data, that computation can be omitted.

5.3.6 Returning Multiple Results

The MATLAB language is unique among programming languages in providing the ability to return more than one result from a function by name. The multiple results are specified as a "vector" of variable names, for example, `[area, volume]`, as shown in Listing 5.2. Assignments must be made to each of the result variables. However, the calling program is not required to make use of all the return values.

In Listing 5.2:

Line 1: Multiple results to be returned are specified as a "vector" of variable names, each of which must be assigned from the code body.
Lines 2–3: Same as Listing 5.1
Line 4: Added to set the value of the second result.

Exercise 5.2 shows how to invoke a function that can return multiple results. Notice that the normal method to access the multiple answers is to put the names of the variable to receive the results in a vector. The names may be any legal variable name, and the values are returned in the order of the results defined. If you choose less than the full number of results (or none at all), the answers that are specified are allocated from left to right from the available results. As with parameter assignment, the results are allocated by position in these vectors. Although we called the variable `v` in the last test, it still receives the value of the first result, `area`. If you really only want

---

Listing 5.2 `cylinder` function with multiple results

```
1. function [area, volume] = cylinder(height, radius)
     % function to compute the area and volume of a cylinder
     % usage: [area, volume]=cylinder(height, radius)
2.      base = pi .* radius.^2;
3.      volume = base .* height;
4.      area = 2 * pi * radius .* height + 2 * base;
5. end
```

Exercise 5.2 Testing multiple returns

Adapt the original `cylinder` function as shown in Listing 5.2 and perform the following tests in the Command window:

```
>> [a, v] = cylinder(1, 1)
a =
    6.2832
v =
    3.1416
>> cylinder(1, 1)
ans =
    6.2832
>> a = cylinder(1, 1)
a =
    6.2832
>> v = cylinder(1, 1)
v =
    6.2832
>>
```

the second result value, you must put either a '~' marker or a dummy variable name like 'junk' in the place of any variable you wish to ignore. So this call:

```
[~, v] = cylinder(1, 1);
```

will put the volume in the variable v.

5.3.7 Auxiliary Local Functions

Since the MATLAB language uses the name of the file to identify a function, every function should normally be saved in its own m-file. However, there are times when auxiliary functions (sometimes called "helper functions") are needed to implement the algorithm contained in the main function in a file. If this auxiliary function is only used in the main function or its helpers, it can be written in the same file as its calling function after the definition of the main function. By convention, some people append the word `local_` to the name of local functions.

Scripts or functions that use the code in an m-file can reach only the first function. Other functions in the m-file, the auxiliary functions, can only be called from the first function or other auxiliary functions in the same file.

5.3.8 Encapsulation in MATLAB Functions

Encapsulation is accomplished in most modern languages, including MATLAB, by implementing the concept of variable scoping. In practice, this is achieved by allocating a separate workspace to each function. When

MATLAB is first started, a default workspace is created in which variables created in the Command window or by running scripts are stored. When a function is called, a fresh workspace is created (see Section 9.1.2 for details), and the actual parameter values are copied into the formal parameter names in that new workspace. When the function finishes, this operation is reversed. The returning parameters are copied into the variables provided by the caller in the previous workspace, and the function's workspace is released. The Variables window always shows you the contents of the current workspace.

Variable scoping defines the places within your Command window, MATLAB system, and m-files to which instructions have access. It is related to the Variables window, which shows you your current workspace. When using the Command window or running a script and you access the value of a variable, the system will reach into your current workspace and then into the MATLAB system libraries to find its current value. This is referred to as **Global Scope.** When you run a function, its local variables, including the internal names of its parameters, are not included in your current workspace, and it does not look into your current workspace for values of variables it needs. This is referred to as **Local Scope,** wherein the variables within a function are not visible from outside and the function is unable to cause side effects by making assignments to variables in other workspaces except by returning results.

To illustrate variable scoping, do Exercise 5.3.

5.3.9 Global Variables

Because MATLAB always copies the input data into the function's workspace, there are occasions when it is very inefficient to pass large data sets into and out of a function. To avoid passing large amounts of data, we can use global variables. Global variables must be defined in both the calling script and the function using the key word `global`. For example, suppose we collect a large volume of data in a variable `buffer` and do not want to copy the whole buffer into and out of a function that processes that data. In this case, we declare the variable to be global in both the calling space and the called function by placing the following line of code before the variable is first used in both places:

```
global buffer
```

The function will then be able to access and modify the values in `buffer` without having to pass it in and out as a parameter. This feature must be used with caution, however, because

---

Style Points 5.2

1. Before you include a function in a complex algorithm, you should always test its behavior in isolation in a script. This test script should validate not only the normal operation of the function, but also its response to erroneous input data it might receive.

2. Although any legal MATLAB instruction is permitted within the code body of a function, it is considered bad form (except temporarily for debugging purposes) to display values in the Interactions window.

3. We also actively discourage the use of the `input(...)` function within the code body. If you need to input some values to test a function, do so from the Interactions window or a test script.

Exercise 5.3 Observing variable scoping

Put a break point at Line 6 of your version of the code in Listing 5.2, and then rerun the function by entering:

```
>> [a, v] = cylinder(1, 1)
```

Notice that the logic stops at that break point and the Text Editor displays an arrow. The Workspace window shows you the values of height, radius, and base but none of the variables you left in the workspace for the Interactions window. The function has no access to other workspaces.

Observe that as you step through the function, the variables appear in the Variables window and are updated. When you return from the cylinder function to display the results, the workspace for the function disappears. The calling environment has no access to the variables within the function.

any function with global access to data is empowered to change that data. In other words, the use of global data circumvents the natural MATLAB language's encapsulation mechanisms.

5.4 Engineering Example—Measuring a Solid Object

Problem:

Consider the disk shown in Figure 5.2. It has a radius *R*, height *h*, and eight cylindrical holes each of radius *r* bored in it. This might be a component of a machine that must be painted and then assembled with other components. During the process of designing this machine, we may need to know the weight of this disk and the amount of paint required to finish it. The weight and the amount of paint for the machine is the sum of the values for each component. Since the weight of our disk is proportional to its volume and the amount of paint is proportional to its "wetted area," we need the volume and area of this disk.

Write a script to compute the volume of the disk and its wetted area.

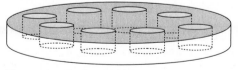

Figure 5.2 *Disk with holes*

Solution:

Listing 5.3 shows the code that solves this problem.

In Listing 5.3:

Lines 1–3: Set up the disk sizes. Notice that the script works fine with a vector of disk thicknesses to check the behavior as thickness varies.

Listing 5.3 Volume and area of a disk

```
1. h = 1:5;      % set a range of disk thicknesses
2. R = 25;
3. r = 3;

4. [Area Vol] = cylinder(h, R) % dimensions of large disk
5. [area vol] = cylinder(h, r) % dimensions of the hole

   % compute remaining volume
6. Vol = Vol - 8*vol
   % the wetted area is a little messier. If we total the
   % large disk area and the areas of the holes, we get the
   % wetted area of the curved edges inside and out.
   % However, for each hole, the top and bottom areas have
   % been included not only in the top and bottom of the big
   % disk, but also as the contributions of each hole.
   % From the sum of the top areas, we therefore have to
   % remove 32 times the hole top area

7. Area = Area + 8*(area - 2*2*pi*r.^2)
```

Line 4: Area and volume of the large disk.

Line 5: Area and volume of one hole.

Line 6: Volume computation.

Line 7: The area computation.

Table 5.1 shows the results when this code is run. Notice that for thin disks, the area is smaller with the holes. However, as the thickness increases, the area with the holes is larger than without, as one would expect.

Table 5.1 Volume and area results

Area = 4,084 4,241 4,398 4,555 4,712
Vol = 1,963 3,927 5,890 7,854 9,817
area = 75 94 113 132 151
vol = 28 57 85 113 141
Vol = 1,737 3,474 5,212 6,949 8,687
Area = 3,782 4,090 4,398 4,706 5,014

Chapter Summary

This chapter showed you how to encapsulate a code block to allow it to be reused:

- Functions are defined in a file of the same name using the key word `function` to distinguish them from scripts
- Parameters are copied in sequence into the function and given the names of the formal parameters
- Results are returned to the caller by assigning value(s) to the return variable(s)
- Variables within the function can be accessed only in the function's code block unless they are declared global
- Helper functions accessible only to functions within the same file may be added below the main function and otherwise obey the same rules as the main function

Special Characters, Reserved Words, and Functions

Special Characters, Reserved Words, and Functions	Description	Discussed in This Section
( )	Used to identify the formal and actual parameters of a function	5.3.2, 5.3.4
help	Invokes help utility	5.3.1
function	Identifies an m-file as a function	5.3.2
nargin	Determines the number of input parameters actually supplied by a function's caller	5.3.4
nargout	Determines the number of output parameters actually requested by a function's caller	5.3.4
global <var>	Defines the scope of the variable <var> as globally accessible	5.3.8

Self Test

Use the following questions to check your understanding of the material in this chapter:

True or False

F 1. All data used by a function must be passed in as parameters to the function.

F 2. The name of the first function in an m-file must match the name of the file containing its definition.

T 3. The first documentation line appears in the Current Directory listing.

F 4.   Functions must consume at least one parameter.

F 5.   The calling code must provide assignments for every result returned from a function.

F 6.   The names of auxiliary functions must begin with `local_`.

Fill in the Blanks

1.   *Procedural* _abstraction_ permits a code block to be packaged and referred to collectively rather than individually.

2.   Values of the __actual__ parameters are copied to define the __formal__ parameters inside the function.

3.   If more than one result is to be returned from a function, they are defined in a(n) _vector-like container of variable names_

4.   *Local* __scope__ describes the situation where the variables within a function are not visible from outside, and the function is unable to cause side effects by making assignments to outside variables.

5.   Calling code can only reach the __first__ function in an m-file. Other functions in the m-file can only be called from the _first function_ or _other auxiliary functions in the same file_.

Programming Projects

1.   Write a function called `checkFactor` that takes in two numbers and checks if they are divisible, that is, if the first is divisible by the second. You may assume that both numbers are positive. Your function should return a logical value, `true` or `false`.

Hint:

`mod(x, y)` gives the remainder when x is divided by y.

For example:

`checkFactor(25,6)` should return `false`.
`checkFactor (9,3)` should return `true`.
`checkFactor (3,9)` should return `false`.

2.   Write and test the code for the function `mysteryFunction` that consumes a vector, `v`, and produces a new vector, `w`, of the same length where each element of `w` is the sum of the corresponding element in `v` and the previous element of `v`. Consider the previous element of `v(1)` to be 0.

For example:

```
mysteryFunction( 1:8 ) should return
      [1  3  5  7  9 11 13 15]
mysteryFunction([1:6].^2) should return
      [1  5 13 25 41 61]
```

3.   Coming off a respectable 7–6 record last year, your football team is looking to improve on that this season. They have contacted you and asked for your help projecting some of the scenarios for their

win–loss record. They want you to write a function called
teamRecord that takes in two parameters—wins, and losses, and
returns two values—season and wPercentage. Season should be a
logical result that is true for a winning season. wPercentage is the
percentage of games won (ranging from 0 to 100).

For example:

```
        [season wPercentage] = teamRecord(3, 9)
    should return season = false, wPercentage = 25
        [season wPercentage] = teamRecord(10, 2)
    should return season = true, wPercentage = 83.3
```

4. Write a function called classAverage that takes in an array of
    numbers and, after normalizing the grades in such a way that the
    highest corresponds to 100 (see Chapter 3, Problem 5), returns the
    letter grade of the class average. The grade ranges are as follows:

```
average>90 =>      A
80<=average<90 => B
70<=average<80 => C
60<=average<70 => D
average<60      => F
```

For example:

```
classAverage( [70 87 95 80 80 78 85 90 66
                   89 89 100] ) should return B
classAverage( [50 90 61 82 75 92 81 76 87 41
                   31 98] ) should return C
classAverage( [10 10 11 32 53 12 34 74 31 30
                   26 22] ) should return F
```

5. Write a function called myMin4 that will take in four numbers and
    returns the minimum value and an index showing which parameter
    it was. You may not use the built-in min() function.

For example:

```
myMin4(1,3,5,7) should return 1 and 1
myMin4(8,9,2,4) should return 2 and 3
```

6. Write the function meansAndMedian that takes in a vector of numbers
    and returns the arithmetic and geometric means, as well as the
    median. You may not use the built-in
    functions mean(), median(), or geomean().
    However, you could type "help geomean"
    to familiarize yourself with computing the
    geometric mean of a group of numbers.

Hint:

The built-in function sort() might help to compute
the median of the vector.

7. Given an array of numbers that could be negative, write a function
    posavg(a) to calculate and return the average (mean) of the non-
    negative numbers in the single dimensional array, a. One such
    solution is mean(a(find(a>0))). In order to test your understanding

of class concepts, re-implement the `posavg(a)` function using iteration. You may not use the built-in functions `sum(...)`, `find(...)`, or `mean(...)` in your solution.

8. Write a function called `sumAndAverage`. It should take in an array of numbers and return the sum and average of the array in that order.

   For example:

   ```
   sumAndAverage([3 2 3 2]) should return 10 and 2.5
   sumAndAverage([5 -5 2 8 0]) should return 10 and 2
   sumAndAverage([]) should return 0 and 0
   ```

9. You are already familiar with the logical operators `&&` (and) and `||` (or), as well as the unary negation operator `~`(not). In a weakly typed language such as MATLAB, the binary states `true` and `false` could be equivalently expressed as a `1` or a `0`, respectively. Let us now consider a ternary number system, consisting of the states `true(1)`, `maybe(2)`, and `false(0)`. The truth table for such a system is shown below. Implement the truth table by writing the functions `f=tnot(x)`, `f=tand(x,y)`, and `f=tor(x,y)`. You may not assume that only valid input numbers will be entered.

x	y	tnot(x)	tand(x,y)	tor(x,y)
1	1	0	1	1
1	0	0	0	1
1	2	0	2	1
0	1	1	0	1
0	0	1	0	0
0	2	1	2	0
2	1	2	2	1
2	0	2	2	0
2	2	2	2	2

10. Write a function called `multiSum(A)`. This particular function should take in a N × M array, A, and return four results:

    ```
    A 1 × M vector with the sum of the columns,
    A N × 1 vector with the sum of the rows, and
    Two numbers containing the sums of the two diagonals, the
    major diagonal first.
    ```

    For example:

    ```
    columnSum([1 2 3; 4 5 6; 7 8 9]) should return
            [12 15 18], [6 15 24]', 15 and 15
    columnSum([0 2 3; 4 0 6; 7 8 0]) should return
            [11 10 9], [5 10 15]', 0 and 10
    columnSum(eye[5,5]) should return
    [1 1 1 1 1], [1 1 1 1 1]', 5 and 1
            columnSum([]) should return [], [], 0 and 0
    ```

11. You are playing a game where you roll a die 10 times. If you roll a 5 or 6 seven or more times, you win 2 dollars; four or more times, you win 1 dollar; and if you roll a 5 or 6 three or less times, you win no money. Write a function called `diceGame` that takes in a vector representing the die values and returns the amount of money won.

For example:

```
diceGame([5 1 4 6 5 5 6 6 5 2]) should return 2
diceGame([2 4 1 3 6 6 6 4 5 3]) should return 1
diceGame([1 4 3 2 5 3 4 2 6 5]) should return 0
```

Note: This function should work for any length vector.

Character Strings

Chapter Objectives

This chapter discusses the nature, implementation, and behavior of character strings in the MATLAB language:

- The internal workings of character strings as vectors

- Operations on character strings

- Converting between numeric and character string representations

- Input and output functions

- The construction and uses for arrays of strings

To this point in the text, we have seen the use of character strings that we can store in variables and display in the Command window. In reality, we have already seen a significant amount of character manipulation that we have taken for granted. The m-files we use to store scripts and functions contain lines of legible characters separated by an invisible "new-line" character.

Introduction

This chapter presents the underlying concept of character storage and the tools MATLAB provides for operating on character strings. We need to distinguish two different relationships between characters and numbers:

1. Individual characters have an internal numerical representation: the visible character shapes we see in windows are created as a collection of white and black dots by special software called a **character generator**. Character generators allow us to take the underlying concept of a character—say, "w"— and "draw" that character on screen or paper in accordance with the rules defined by the current font. A complete study of fonts is beyond the scope of this discussion, but we need to understand how computers in general and the MATLAB language in particular represent that "underlying concept" of a

121

character. This is achieved by representing each individual character by its numerical equivalent. Not long ago, there were many different representations. Today, the dominant representation is the one defined by the American Standard Code for Information Interchange (ASCII). In this representation, the most common uppercase and lowercase characters, numbers, and many punctuation marks are represented by numbers between 0 and 127. A complete listing of the first 255 values is included in Appendix B.

2. Strings of characters represent numerical values to the user: numerical values are stored in a special, internal representation for efficient numerical computation as described in Appendix C. However, whenever we need to see the value of that number in the Command window, that internal representation is automatically converted by MATLAB into a character string representing its value in a form we can read. For example, if the variable a contained the integer value 124, internally that number could be stored in a single byte (8 bits) with a binary value of 011111100—not a very meaningful representation, but efficient internally for performing arithmetic and logical operations. For the user to understand that value, internal MATLAB logic must convert it to the three printable characters: '124'. Similarly, when we type in the Command window or use the `input(...)` function, the set of characters that we enter is automatically translated from a character string into the internal number representation.

6.1 Character String Concepts: Mapping Casting, Tokens, and Delimiting

Here we see the MATLAB language tools that deal with the first relationship between characters and numbers: the numerical representation of individual characters.

The basic idea of **mapping** is that it defines a relationship between two entities. The most obvious example of mapping is the idea that the function $f(x) = x^2$ defines the mapping between the value of x and the value of $f(x)$. We will apply that concept to the process of translating a character (like "A") from its graphical form to a numerical internal code. **Character mapping** allows each individual graphic character to be uniquely represented by a numerical value.

Casting is the process of changing the way a language views a piece of data without actually changing the data value. Under normal circumstances, a language like MATLAB automatically presents a set of data in the "right" form. However, there are times when we wish to force the language to treat a data item in a specific way. For example, if we create a variable containing a character string, MATLAB will consistently display it as a character string. However, we might want to view the underlying numerical representation as a number, in which case we have to cast the variable containing the characters to a numerical data type. MATLAB implements casting as a function with the name of the data type expected. In essence, these functions implement the mapping from one character representation to another.

A **token** is a collection of characters to which we may wish to attach meaning. Obvious examples of tokens are the name of a MATLAB variable or the characters representing the values of a number to be used in an expression.

A **delimiter** is a character used to separate tokens. The space character, for example, can delimit words in a sentence; punctuation marks provide additional delimiters with specific meanings.

6.2 MATLAB Implementation

When you enter a string in the Command window or the editor, MATLAB requires that you delimit the characters of a string with a single quote mark (`'`). Note that you can include a single quote mark within the string by doubling the character. For example, if you entered the following in the Command window:

```
>>refusal = 'I can''t do that!'
```

The result displayed would be

```
refusal = I can't do that
```

Exercise 6.1 illustrates the concept of casting between data types `char` and `double`.

In Exercise 6.1 the casting function `uint8(...)` takes a character or character string and changes its representation to a vector of the same length as the original string. Then the casting function `char(...)` takes a number or vector and causes it to be presented as a string. The casting function `double(...)` appears to act in the same way as `uint8(...)`, but it actually uses 64 bits to store the values. Single quotes delimit a string to be assigned to the variable `fred`. Notice that when a string is presented as a result, the delimiters are omitted. When you apply arithmetic operations to a string, the operation is illegal on characters; therefore, an implicit casting to the numerical equivalent occurs.

You can perform any mathematical operation on the vector and use the cast, `char(...)`, to cast it back to a string.

Exercise 6.1 Character casting

Enter the following in the Command window and study the results:

```
>> uint8('A') % uint8 is an integer data type
              % with values 0 - 255
ans =
    65
>> char(100) % char is the character class
ans =
d
>> char([97 98 99 100 101])
ans =
abcde
>> double('fred')
ans =
    102 114 101 100
>> fred = 'Fred'
fred =
Fred
>> next = fred + 1
next =
    71 115 102 101
>> a = uint8(fred)
a =
    70 114 101 100
>> name = char(a + 1)
name =
Gsfe
```

6.2.1 Slicing and Concatenating Strings

Strings are internally represented as vectors; therefore, we can perform all the usual vector operations on strings. Try it in Exercise 6.2.

Exercise 6.2 Character strings

```
>> first = 'Fred'
first =
Fred
>> last = 'Jones'
last =
Jones
>> name = [first, ' ', last]
name =
Fred Jones
>> name(1:2:end)
ans =
Fe oe
>> name(end:-1:1)
ans =
senoJ derF
```

Exercise 6.3 Character string logic

```
>> n = 'fred'
n =
fred
>> n > 'g'
ans =
   0   1   0   0
```

6.2.2 Arithmetic and Logical Operations

Mathematical operations can be performed on the numerical mapping of a character string. If you do not explicitly perform that casting first, MATLAB will do the cast for you and create a result of type double (not usually suitable for character values). Note that char('a' + 1) returning 'b' is an accident of the character type mapping.

Logical operations on character strings are also exactly equivalent to logical operations on vectors, with the same automatic casting. Exercise 6.3 gives you an opportunity to try it yourself.

6.2.3 Useful Functions

The following functions are useful in analyzing character strings:

- ischar(a) returns true if a is a character string
- isspace(ch) returns true if the character ch is the space character

6.3 Format Conversion Functions

Now we turn to the second relationship between characters and numbers: using character strings to represent individual number values. We need two separate capabilities: converting numbers from the efficient, internal form to legible strings and converting strings provided by users of MATLAB into the internal number representation. MATLAB provides a number of functions that transform data between string format and numerical format.

6.3.1 Conversion from Numbers to Strings

Use the following built-in MATLAB functions for a simple conversion of a single number, x, to its string representation:

- int2str(x) if you want it displayed as an integer value
- num2str(x, n) to see the decimal parts; the parameter n represents the number of decimal places required—if not specified, its default value is 3

Frequently you need better control over the data conversion, and the function sprintf(...) provides fine-grained control. The MATLAB version of sprintf(...) is very similar to the C / C++ implementation of this capability. The first parameter to sprintf is a **format control string** that defines exactly how the resulting string should be formatted. A variable number of **value parameters** follow the format string, providing data items as necessary to satisfy the formatting.

Basically the format string contains characters to be copied to the result string; however, it also contains two types of special entry introduced by the following two special characters:

- The '%' character introduces a conversion specification, indicating how one of the value parameters should be represented. The most common conversions are %d (integer), %f (real), %g (general), %c (character), and %s (string). A number may be placed immediately after the % character to specify the minimum number of characters in the conversion. If more characters than the specified minimum ' are required to represent the data, they will be added. In addition, the %f and %g conversions can include '.n' to indicate the number of decimal places required. If you actually want a '%' character, it must be doubled, for example, '%%'. MATLAB processes each of the value parameters in turn, inserting them in the result string according to the corresponding conversion specification. If there are more parameters than conversion specifications in the format control string, the format control string is repeated.

- The '\' character introduces format control information, the most common of which are \n (new line) and \t (tab). If the '\' character is actually wanted in the result string, it should be doubled, for example, '\\'.

Consider the following statements:

```
A = [4.7 1321454.47 4.8];
index = 1;
v = 'values';
str = sprintf('%8s of A(%d) are \t%8.3f\t%12.4g\t%f\n'...
    v, index, A(index,1), A(index,2), A(index,3))
str =
    values of A(1) are   4.700      1.321e+006      4.800000
```

The first conversion, '%8s', took the value of the first parameter, v, allowed eight spaces for its conversion, and copied its contents to the result. Since this was a string conversion, the characters were merely copied. The characters ' of A(' were then appended to the output string. The second conversion, '%d', took the value of the second parameter, index, and converted it as an integer with the minimum space allocated. The characters ') are' were then appended to the output string, followed by a tab character that inserted enough spaces to bring the next characters to a column that is an even multiple of eight. The following three conversions appended the next three value parameters converted with three decimal places, a general conversion with at least 12 spaces and 4 decimal places, and the default numerical conversion. Finally, a new line character was inserted into the string.

6.3.2 Conversion from Strings to Numbers

Conversion from strings to numbers is much messier, and it should be avoided if possible. When possible, allow MATLAB's built-in function `input(...)` to do the conversion for you. If you have to do the conversion yourself, you can either split a string into tokens and then convert each token with the `str2num(str)` function or, if you are really desperate and using licensed MATLAB software, you can use the function `sscanf(...)`.

The function `input(str)` presents the string parameter to the user in the Command window and waits for the user to type some characters and the Enter key, all of which are echoed in the Command window. Then it parses the input string according to the following rules:

- If the string begins with a numerical character, MATLAB converts the string to a number
- If it begins with a non-numeric character, MATLAB constructs a variable name and looks for its current value
- If it begins with an open bracket, '[', a vector is constructed
- If it begins with the single quote character, MATLAB creates a string
- If a format error occurs, MATLAB repeats the prompt

This behavior can be modified if 's' is provided as the second parameter, `input(str, 's')`, in which case the complete input character sequence is saved as a string. Exercise 6.4 demonstrates a number of capabilities of the `input(...)` function.

In Exercise 6.4, first we define the variable `fred`. Then MATLAB attempts to interpret the result either as a number or as the name of an existing variable. Since the variable `fred` was defined (although not a number), it was assigned correctly to the variable n. MATLAB will distinguish between a variable and a number input by the first digit. Here, the information entered was an illegal variable name beginning with a number. When `input(...)` detects an error parsing the text entered, it automatically resets and requests a new entry.

On the second attempt, although this is a correctly formed variable name, its value is not known. On the third attempt, the `input(...)` function actually treats the string entered as an expression, to be evaluated by the same process as MATLAB parses the Command window entries.

Exercise 6.4 The input(...) function

```
>> fred = 'Fred';
>> n = input('Enter a number: ')
Enter a number: 5
n =
     5
>> n = input('Enter a number: ')
Enter a number: fred
n =
Fred
>> n = input('Enter a number: ')
Enter a number: 1sdf
??? 1sdf
Error: Missing MATLAB operator.
Enter a number: s1df
??? Error using ==> input
Undefined function or variable 's1df'.
Enter a number: char(fred - 2)
n =
Dpcb
>> n = input('Enter a number: ')
Enter a number: 'ABCD'
n =
ABCD
>> n = input('Enter a number: ', 's' )
Enter a number: ABCD
n =
ABCD
```

If you actually want a string literal entered, it must be enclosed in the string delimiters. If you are sure you want a string literal entered, the second parameter, 's', forces MATLAB to return the string entered without attempting to parse it.

The function str2num(str) consumes a token (string) representing a single numerical value and returns the numerical equivalent. Do Exercise 6.5 to understand this function.

Exercise 6.5 Converting strings to numbers

```
>> value = str2num('3.14159')
value =
      3.1416
Now, to check the class of the variable value, either look in the
Variables window or enter the whos command:
>> whos
   Name       Size            Bytes Class      Attributes
   value      1x1                 8 double
>>
```

We observe that the function has indeed interpreted the string as its numerical value.

The function `sscanf(...)` was designed to extract the values of variables from a string, but is really difficult to use. The author recommends the use of `strtok(...)` followed by `str2num(...)` as necessary to accomplish the same goal in a more controlled manner.

6.4 Character String Operations

As with the string-to-number conversions, input and output in the Command window can be accomplished with simple functions that have little flexibility or with complex functions that have better control.

6.4.1 Simple Data Output: The `disp(. . .)` Function

We have already seen the use of the `disp(...)` function to present data in readable form in the Intractions window. As the exercises indicate, it can present the values of any variable, regardless of type, or of strings constructed by concatenation. Note, however, that an explicit number conversion is required to concatenate variables with strings. Try Exercise 6.6.

Note that although you can concatenate strings for output, conversion from the ASCII code is not automatic; the second result produced a character whose ASCII code is 4. You must use the simple string conversion functions to enforce consistent information for concatenation.

6.4.2 Complex Output

The function `fprintf(...)` is similar to `sprintf(...)`, except that it prints its results to the Command window instead of returning a string. `fprintf(...)` returns the number of characters actually printed. Exercise 6.7 demonstrates this.

6.4.3 Comparing Strings

Since strings are readily translated into vectors of numbers, they may be compared in the obvious way with the logical operators we used on numbers. However, there is the restriction that either the strings must be

Exercise 6.6 The `disp(...)` function

```
>> a = 4;
>> disp(a)
     4
>> disp(['the answer is ', a])
the answer is
>> disp(['the answer is ', int2str(a)])
the answer is 4
```

Exercise 6.7 `fprintf(...)` and `sprintf(...)`

```
>> a = 42;
>> b = 'fried okra';
>> n = fprintf('the answer is %d\n cooking %s', ...
                               a,              b);
the answer is 42
cooking fried okra
n =
    37
>> s = sprintf('the answer is %d\n cooking %s\n', ...
                               a,              b)
s =
the answer is 42
 cooking fried Okra
>> str = input('Enter the data: ', 's');
Enter the data: 42 3.14159 -1
A = sscanf( str,'%f')
A =
    42.0000
     3.1416
    -1.0000
>>
```

of the same length or one of them must be of length 1 before it is legal to compare them with these operators. To avoid this restriction, MATLAB provides the C-style function `strcmp(<s1>, <s2>)` that returns `true` if the strings are identical and `false` if they are not.

Unfortunately, this is not quite the same behavior as the C version, which does a more rigorous comparison returning –1, 0, or 1. You can try a character string comparison in Exercise 6.8.

Exercise 6.8 Character string comparison

```
>> 'abcd' == 'abcd'
      1     1     1     1
>> 'abcd' == 'abcde'
??? Error using ==> eq
Array dimensions must match for binary array op.
>> strcmp('abcd', 'abcde')
ans =
      0   false
>> strcmp('abcd', 'abcd')
ans =
      1   true
>> 'abc' == 'a'
ans =
      1     0     0
>> strcmpi('ABcd', 'abcd')
ans =
      1
```

Common Pitfalls 6.1

The `if` statement uses a logical expression as its controlling test; therefore, it is bound by the same comparison rules as those applied to vectors. Two strings being compared must be of the same length, and all of the comparisons must match to result in a logical `true`. Frequently, we expect the `if` statement to compare strings of unequal length. However, this will cause an error whenever two strings of unequal length are compared (unless one string is just one character). You should use the `switch` statement, which will correctly compare strings of unequal length in the case tests.

In Exercise 6.8, we see that strings of the same length compare exactly to vectors returning a logical vector result. You cannot use the equality test on strings of unequal length. `strcmp(...)` deals gracefully with strings of unequal length. As with vectors, the equality test works if one of the inputs is a single character. For case-independent testing, use `strcmpi(...)`.

6.5 Arrays of Strings

Since a single character string is stored as a vector, it seems natural to consider storing a collection of strings as an array. The most obvious way to do this, as shown in previous examples, has some limitations, for which there are nice, tidy cures built into the MATLAB language. Consider the example shown in Exercise 6.9. Character arrays can be constructed by either of the following:

- As a vertical vector of strings, all of which must be the same length

Exercise 6.9 Character string arrays

```
>> v = ['Character strings having more than'
         'one row must have the same number '
         'of columns just like arrays!      ']
v =
Character strings having more than
one row must have the same number
of columns just like arrays!
>> v = ['MATLAB gets upset'
         'when rows have'
         'different lengths']
??? Error using ==> vertcat
All rows in the bracketed expression must have the
same number of columns.

>>eng=char('Timoshenko','Maxwell','Mach','von Braun')
eng =
Timoshenko
Maxwell
Mach
von Braun
>> size(eng)
ans =
     4    10
```

- By using a special version of the char(&) cast function that accepts a variable number of strings with different lengths, pads them with blanks to make all rows the same length, and stores them in an array of characters

 6.6 Engineering Example—Encryption

The Problem

As public access to information becomes more pervasive, there is increasing interest in the use of encryption to protect intellectual property and private communications from unauthorized access. The following discussion is based on no direct knowledge of the latest encryption technology. However, it illustrates a very simple approach to developing an algorithm that is immune to all but the most obvious, brute-force code-breaking techniques.

Background

Historically, simple encryption has been accomplished by substituting one character for another in the message, so that 'Fred' becomes 'Iuhg' when substituting the letter three places down the alphabet for each letter in the message. More advanced techniques use a random letter selection to substitute new letters. However, any constant letter substitution is vulnerable to elementary code-cracking techniques based on the frequency of letters in the alphabet, for example.

The Solution

We propose a simple algorithm where a predetermined random series is used to select the replacement letters. Since the same letter in the original message is never replaced by the same substitute, no simple language analysis will crack the code. The rand(...) function is an excellent source for an appropriate random sequence. If the encryption and decryption processes use the same value to seed the generator, the same sequence of apparently random **(pseudo-random)** values will be generated.

Since the seed can take on 2^{31}–2 values, it is virtually impossible to determine the decryption without knowing the seed value. The seed (i.e., the decryption key) can be transmitted to anyone authorized to decrypt the message by any number of ways. Furthermore, since there are abundant different techniques for generating pseudo-random sequences, the specific generation technique must be known in addition to the seed value for successful decryption. Listing 6.1 shows the code for encrypting and

Listing 6.1 Encryption exercise

```
1. disp('original text')
2. txt = ['For example, consider the following:' 13 ...
3.    'A = [4.7 1321454.47 4.8];' 13 ...
4.    'index = 1;' 13 ...
5.    'v = ''values'';' 13 ...
6.    'str = sprintf(''%8s of A(%d) are \t%8.3f ' 13 ...
7.    ' v, index, A(index,1) ' 13 ...
8.    'str = ' 13 ...
9.    ' values of A(1) are 4.700' 13 ...
10.   'The first conversion, ''%8s'', took the value' ...
11.   ' of the first ' ...
12.   'parameter, v, allowed 8 spaces. ' 13 ]
      % % encryption section
13. rand('state', 123456)
14. loch = 33;
15. hich = 126;
16. range = hich+1-loch;
17. rn = floor( range * rand(1, length(txt) ) );
18. change = (txt>=loch) & (txt<=hich);
19. enc = txt;
20. enc(change) = enc(change) + rn(change);
21. enc(enc > hich) = enc(enc > hich) - range;
22. disp('encrypted text')
23. encrypt = char(enc)

      % % good decryption
24. rand('state', 123456);
25. rn = floor( range * rand(1, length(txt) ) );
26. change = (encrypt>=loch) & (encrypt<=hich);
27. dec = encrypt;
28. dec(change) = dec(change) - rn(change) + range;
29. dec(dec > hich) = dec(dec > hich) - range;
30. disp('good decrypt');
31. decrypt = char(dec)

      % % bad seed
32. rand('seed', 123457);
33. rn = floor( range * rand(1, length(txt) ) );
34. change = (encrypt>=loch) & (encrypt<=hich);
35. dec = encrypt;
36. dec(change) = dec(change) - rn(change) + range;
37. dec(dec > hich) = dec(dec > hich) - range;
38. disp('decrypt with bad seed')
39. decrypt = char(dec)

      % % different generator
40. rand('seed', 123456)
41. rn = mod(floor( range * abs(randn(1, length(txt) ))/10 ),  ...
42.      range);
43. change = (encrypt>=loch) & (encrypt<=hich);
44. dec = encrypt;
45. dec(change) = dec(change) - rn(change) + range;
46. dec(dec > hich) = dec(dec > hich) - range;
47. disp('decrypt with wrong generator')
48. decrypt = char(dec)
```

decrypting by this technique and two attempts to decrypt—once with the wrong key and once with the wrong generator.

In Listing 6.1:

Lines 2–12: This is the original text taken from earlier in this chapter. Multiple lines of characters can be concatenated as shown. The number 13 inserted in the string is the numerical equivalent of the new line escape sequence, '\n'.

Line 13: Seeds the random generator with a known value.

Lines 14–16: Set the upper and lower bounds and the range of the characters we will convert. This range excludes 32, the space character, and 13, the new line character. This choice was deliberate—it leaves the encrypted text with the appearance of a character substitution algorithm since all the characters are printable, and seem to be grouped in words.

Line 17: Generates the random values between 0 and `range-1`.

Line 18: Identifies the indices of the printable characters.

Line 19: Makes a copy of the original text.

Line 20: Adds the random offsets to those characters we intend to change.

Line 21: If the addition pushes a character value above the maximum printable character, this brings it back within range.

Lines 22–23: Display the encrypted text. Notice that no two characters of the original text are replaced by the same character.

Lines 24–27: Begin the decryption by seeding the generator with the same value, creating the same random sequence, finding the printable characters, and copying the original file to the decrypt string.

Lines 28–29: We must subtract the random sequence from the encrypted string and correct for the underflow. However, there are some numerical issues involved. It is best to add the `range` value to all the letters while subtracting the random offsets, and then bring back those values that remain above the highest printable character.

Lines 30–31: Display the decrypted values.

Lines 32–39: Attempt to decrypt with the same code but a bad seed.

Lines 40–48: Attempt to decrypt with the right seed but a different generator—in this case, MATLAB's normal random generator limited to positive values within the letter range of interest.

Table 6.1 shows the output from this encryption exercise.

Table 6.1 Encryption exercise results

original text
txt =
For example, consider the following:
A = [4.7 1321454.47 4.8];
encrypted text encrypt =
@;J _a,Q/V_Q X/|IW?*q %;{ $Ctr:$&r3>
5 - v$zh uvqzmE@P(N Bh}.H
good decrypt
decrypt =
For example, consider the following:
A = [4.7 1321454.47 4.8];
decrypt with bad seed
decrypt =
tDQ <6VfMiS^ }1FI92/P c'@ eYrW%Q^2t+
6 L 4x5> B$rQ4XHpG# G;*<r
decrypt with wrong generator
decrypt =
>1E o-P:'P=p :xLjV+bi {!d 3)[Az$~c7<
' l fny& tHWB Vve6o

Chapter Summary

This chapter discussed the nature, implementation, and behavior of character strings. We learned the following:

- Character strings are merely vectors of numbers that are presented to the user as single characters
- We can perform on strings the same operations that can be performed on vectors; if mathematical operations are performed, MATLAB first converts the characters to double values
- We can convert between string representations of numbers and the numbers themselves using built-in functions
- MATLAB provides functions that convert numbers to text strings for presentation in the Command window
- Arrays of strings can be assembled using the char(...) function

Special Characters, Reserved Words, and Functions

Special Characters, Reserved Words, and Functions	Description	Discussed in This Section
`'...'`	Encloses a literal character string	6.2
`char(...)`	Casts to a character type	6.2, 6.5
`disp(...)`	Displays matrix or text	6.4.1
`double(a)`	Casts to type `double`	6.2
`fprintf(...)`	Prints formatted information	6.4.2
`input(...)`	Prompts the user to enter a value	6.3.2
`int2str(a)`	Converts an integer to its numerical representation	6.3.1
`ischar(ch)`	Determines whether the given object is of type `char`	6.2.3
`isspace(a)`	Tests for the space character	6.2.3
`num2str(a,n)`	Converts a number to its numerical representation with n decimal places	6.3.1
`sscanf(...)`	Formatted input conversion	6.3.2
`sprintf(...)`	Formats a string result	6.3.1
`str2num(...)`	Convert a string to its numerical equivalent	6.3.2
`strcmp(s1, s2)`	Compares two strings; returns `true` if equal	6.4.3
`strcmpi(s1, s2)`	Compares two strings without regard to case; returns `true` if equal	6.4.3
`uint8(...)`	Casts to unsigned integer type with 8 bits	6.2

Self Test

Use the following questions to check your understanding of the material in this chapter:

True or False

F 1. Casting changes the value of a piece of data.

T 2. The ASCII code maps individual characters to their internal numerical representation.

F 3. Because the single quote mark (') delimits strings, you cannot use it within a string.

F 4. If you attempt mathematical operations on a character string, MATLAB will throw an error.

T 5. The function disp(...) can display multiple values to the
        Command window.

F 6. The function strcmp(...) throws an error if the two strings are of
        unequal length, unless one of them is a single character.

T 7. The switch statement will correctly compare strings of unequal
        length in the case tests.

Fill in the Blanks

1. Numerical values are stored in MATLAB in _a special internal representation_ for
    efficient numerical computation.

2. Most common _characters_ , _numbers_ , and many
    punctuation marks are represented in ASCII by the numbers
    _0–127_ .

3. The function _uint8(...)_ casts a string to a vector of the same
    length as the string containing the numerical mapping of
    each letter .

4. The function fprintf(...) requires a(n) _format control string_ that defines
    exactly how the resulting string should be formatted and a variable
    number of _value parameters_

5. Since the _if_ statement tests a logical expression, it
    cannot test strings of unequal length.

6. A special version of the cast function accepts _char(...)_
    strings with different lengths, _pads them_ , and stores them in an
    array of characters. _with blanks_

Programming Projects

1. Solve the following introductory problems on strings.
    a. Write a function dayName that consumes a parameter, day,
        containing the numerical value of a day in the month of
        September 2008. Your function should return the name of that
        day as a string. For example:

        ```
        dayName( 8 ) should return 'Monday'
        ```

    b. You are now given a variable named days, a vector that contains
        the numeric values of days in the month of
        September 2008. Write a script that will
        convert each numeric value in the vector
        days into a string named daysofWeek with
        the day names separated by a comma and

Hint

You should probably be concatenating the day names
and the delimiters.

a space. For example, if days = [8, 9, 10], daysOfWeek should be 'Monday, Tuesday, Wednesday'

Notice that there is no separator before the first day name or after the last one.

2. Consider the problem the MATLAB system has in parsing the string:

'V=[1 2 3 4; 5,6, 7;8; 9 10]'

Your task is to use strtok to parse this line and construct the array it represents. You will write a function arrayParse that consumes a string and returns two variables: a string that is the variable name and an array.

a. Tokenize the string first using '=' as the delimiter to isolate the variable name and the expression to be evaluated. Return the variable name to the user and save the rest of the line as the variable str1 for further processing. You may assume that there are no spaces outside the characters '[...]'.

b. Tokenize str1 with '[' and ']' to remove the concatenation operators and save the first token as str2.

c. Tokenize str2 using ';' as the delimiter. This will produce 0 or more strings that represent the rows of the array. Save each in the variable rowString. You may assume for now that the first row is the longest one.

d. Using nested while loops, tokenize each rowString with ',' and ' ' as delimiters and use str2num(...) to extract the numerical value of each array entry. Save it as rowEntry.

e. Concatenate the rowEntry elements horizontally to produce each row of the array. If the row is too short, pad it with zeros.

f. Concatenate each row vertically to produce the resulting array and return that array to the caller.

g. Test the function with cases like:
```
empty=[]
row=[1 2 3 4]
diag=[0 0 0 1; 0 0 1; 0 1; 1]
```

3. Write a function called DNAcomplement that consumes a set of letters as a character array that forms a DNA sequence such as 'gattaca'. The function will produce the complement of the sequence so that a's become t's, g's become c's, and vice versa. The string 'gattaca' would therefore become 'ctaatgt'. You may assume that all the letters in the sequence will be lowercase and that they will all be either a, t, g, or c.

Note: You may be tempted to use iteration for this problem, but you don't need it.

4. The function rot(s, n) is a simple Caesar cipher encryption algorithm that replaces each English letter in places forward or

backward along the alphabet in the strings. For example, the result of rot('Baz!',3) is 'Edc!'. An encrypted string can be deciphered by simply performing the inverse rotation on it, that is, rot('Edc!',3), which rotates each English letter in the strings three places to the left. Numbers, symbols, and non-letters are not transformed. Implement the following function:

```
function rotatedText=rot(text,n)
```

To assist you as you solve this problem, you could write several functions as local functions in the rot.m file: isUppercaseLetter(letter), getUppercaseLetter(n), getLowercaseLetter(n), and getPosition(letter). You may also wish to use the built-in functions isletter (...), find (...), and mod (...).

5. You have a big problem. In one of your CS courses, your professor decides that the only way you will pass the class is if you write a function to get him out of a mess. All the grades in his class have been accidentally stored into one long string of characters containing only the letters A, B, C, D, F, and Y.

   a. Your job is to write a function called CrazyGrade that will take in the string and flip the grades according to the following specifications:

   A becomes F
   B becomes D
   C remains unchanged
   D becomes B
   F becomes A
   Y becomes W

   Your function should take in a string and return an inverted string. You may assume that the string will only consist of valid letter grades. For example,

   ```
   CrazyGrade('BADDAD') should return 'DFBBFB'
   CrazyGrade('BAYBAY') should return 'DFWDFW'
   ```

   b. To make matters worse, he wants you to organize this modified grade set. Write a function called GradeDist to bunch together all the similar grades (put all the A's next to each other, B's next to each other, etc.) Then, calculate and return the professor's grade distribution. Your function should take in a string and return a string with all similar grades grouped together, along with an array containing percentage values from A's all the way to F's. For example, if there are 15% A's, 16% B's, 33% C's, 16% D's, 16% F's, and 4% W's, GradeDist should return [15 16 33 16 16 4].

Cell Arrays and Structures

Chapter Objectives

This chapter discusses the nature, implementation, and behavior of collections that may contain data items of any class, size, or shape. We will deal with two different heterogeneous storage mechanisms:

- Those accessed by index (cell arrays)
- Those accessed by field name (structures)

In addition, we will consider collecting structures into arrays of structures.

Introduction

This chapter covers data collections that are more general and flexible than the arrays we have considered so far. Heterogeneous collections may contain objects of any type, rather than just numbers. Consequently, none of the collective operations defined for numerical arrays can be applied to cell arrays or structures. To perform most operations on their contents, the items must be extracted one at a time and replaced if necessary. We will consider three different mechanisms for building heterogeneous collections: you access components of a cell array with a numerical index; you access components of a structure with a symbolic field name; and you access components of a structure array by way of a numerical index to reach a specific structure, and then a symbolic field name.

7.1 Concept: Collecting Dissimilar Objects

Heterogeneous collections permit objects of different data types to be grouped in a collection. They allow data abstraction to apply to a much broader range of content. However, the fact that the contents of these collections may be of any data type severely restricts the operations that can be performed on the collections as a whole. Whereas a significant number of arithmetic and logical operations can be performed on whole number arrays, algorithms that process heterogeneous collections almost always deal with the data contents one item at a time.

 ## 7.2 Cell Arrays

Cell arrays, as the name suggests, have the general form of arrays and can be indexed numerically as arrays. However, each element of a cell array should be considered as a container in which one data object of any class can be stored.[1] They can be treated as arrays of containers for the purpose of concatenation and slicing. However, if you wish to access or modify the contents of the containers, the cells must be accessed individually.

7.2.1 Creating Cell Arrays

Cell arrays may be constructed in the following ways:

- By assigning values individually to a variable indexed with braces:

```
>> A{1} = 42
A =
    [42]
```

- By assigning containers individually to a variable indexed with brackets:

```
>> B[1] = {[4 6]};
B =
    [1x2 double]
```

- By concatenating cell contents using braces {. . .}:

```
C = {3, [1,2,3], 'abcde'}
C =
    [3] [1x3 double] 'abcde'
```

- By concatenating cell containers:

```
>> D = [A B C {'xyz'}]
D =
    [42] [1x2 double] [3] [1x3 double] 'abcde' 'xyz'
```

---

[1]Java programmers might recognize a cell array as an array of Objects.

Based on these examples, we observe the following:

- A cell array can contain any legal MATLAB object
- Just as with number arrays, cell arrays can be created "on the fly" by assigning values to an indexed variable

When the values from a cell array are displayed, their appearance is different from that of the contents of a number array. Individual numbers are shown in brackets, for example, [3]; larger numerical arrays display their size, for example, [1x3 double]; and character strings are displayed with the enclosing quotes, for example, 'abcde'.

7.2.2 Accessing Cell Arrays

Since cell arrays can be considered as conventional arrays of containers, the containers can be accessed and manipulated normally. For example, continuing the previous examples, we have the following:

```
>> E = D(2) % parentheses - a container
E =
    [4 6]
```

However, braces are used to access the contents of the containers as follows:

```
>> D{2} % braces - the contents
ans =
    4 6
```

If the right-hand side of an assignment statement results in multiple cell arrays, the assignment must be to the same number of variables. The built-in function deal(...) is used to make these allocations. Exercise 7.1 shows its use.

Notice the following observations:

- When we extract the contents of multiple cells using A{1:2}, this results in multiple assignments being made. These multiple assignments must go to separate variables. This is the fundamental mechanism behind returning multiple results from a function.
- These multiple assignments cannot be made to a single variable; sufficient storage must be provided either as a collection of variables or explicitly as a vector.
- Cell arrays can be "sliced" with normal vector indexing assignments as long as the sizes match on the left and right sides of the assignment. Any unassigned array elements are filled with an empty vector.
- The assignment B{[1 3]} = A{[1 2]} that produced an error needs some thought. Since A{[1 2]} produces two separate assignments, MATLAB will not assign the answers, even to the right number of places in another cell array. The deal(...) function is provided to capture these multiple results in different variables. Notice the difference between A{:} and A as a parameter to deal(...). When

Exercise 7.1 Cell arrays

```
>> A = { 3, [1,2,3] 'abcde'}
 A =
     [3] [1x3 double] 'abcde'
>> A{1:2}
 ans =
     3
 ans =
     1    2    3
>> [x y] = A{1:2}
x =
     3
y =
     1    2    3
>> B = A{1:2}
 ??? Illegal right-hand side in assignment.
          Too many elements.
>> B([1 3]) = A([1 2])
 B =
   [3]       []     [1x3 double]
>> B{[1 3]} = A{[1 2]}
 ??? Illegal right-hand side in assignment.
          Too many elements.
>> [a, b, c] = deal(A{:})
 a =
     3
 b =
     1    2    3
 c =
 abcde
>> [a, b] = deal(A)
 a =
     [3]     [1x3 double]     'abcde'
 b =
     [3]     [1x3 double]     'abcde'
>> B = A(1:2)
 B =
     [3]     [1x3 double]
>> for i = 1:2
          s(i) = sum(A{i})
       end
s =
     3
s =
     3    6
>> F{2} = 42
F =
     []       [42]
>> F{3} = {42}
F =
     []       [42]     {1x1 cell}
```

deal(...) is provided with a parameter other than a collection of cells, it copies that parameter to each variable.

- Assignments work normally if cell arrays are treated as vectors and the extraction of items can be indexed—s is a vector of the sums of the elements in A.
- Finally, notice that when accessing cell arrays, it is normal to have braces on one side or the other of an assignment; it is rarely appropriate to have braces on both sides of an assignment. The result here is that a cell array is loaded into the third container in the cell array.

7.2.3 Using Cell Arrays

There are a number of uses for cell arrays, some of which will be evident in upcoming chapters. For now, the following examples will suffice:

- Containing lists of possible values for switch/case statements, as we saw in Chapter 4
- Substituting for parameter lists in function calls

For example, suppose you have a function largest(a, b, c) that consumes three variables and produces the largest of the three values provided. It can be used in the following styles, as shown in Listing 7.1.

In Listing 7.1:

Lines 1–3: Set the values of A, B, and c.
Line 4: A conventional function call that results in a value of 6 for N.
Lines 5–6: The same function call implemented as a cell array, returning the same answer.

7.2.4 Processing Cell Arrays

The general template for processing cell arrays is shown in Template 7.1.

Checking the class of the element can be achieved in one of two ways:

- The function class(item) returns a string specifying the item type that can be used in a switch statement

Listing 7.1 Using cell arrays of parameters

```
1. A = 4;
2. B = 6;
3. C = 5;
4. N = largest(A, B, C)
5. params = { 4, 6, 5 };
6. N = largest(params{1:3})
```

Template 7.1 General template for processing cell arrays

```
<initialize result>
for <index specification>
      <extract an element>
      <check the element accordingly>
      <process the element accordingly>
end
<finalize result>
```

Listing 7.2 Cell array processing example

```
1. function ans = totalNums(ca)
   % count the numbers in a cell array
2.     ans = 0 ;
3.     for in = 1 :length(ca)
4.         item = ca{i} ;      % extract the item
5.         if isnumeric(item) % check if a vector
6.             ans = ans + prod(size(item));
7.         end
8.     end
```

■ Individual test functions can be used in an `if... elseif` construct; examples of the individual test functions are `isa(item, 'class')`, `iscell(...)`, `ischar(...)`, `islogical(...)`, `isnumeric(...)`, and `isstruct(...)`.

For example, suppose you are provided with a cell array and have been asked for a function that finds the total length of all the vectors it contains. The function might look like that shown in Listing 7.2.

In Listing 7.2:

Line 1: Typical function header accepting a cell array as input.

Line 2: Initializes the result.

Line 3: Traverses the whole cell array.

Line 4: Extracts each item in turn.

Line 5: Determines whether this item is of type `double`. If so, it proceeds to line 6.

Line 6: Accumulates the number of items in this array. Recall that the `size(...)` function returns a vector of the sizes of each dimension. The total number of numbers is therefore the product of these values.

7.3 Structures

Where cell arrays implemented the concept of homogeneous collections as indexed collections, structures allow items in the collection to be indexed by field name. Most modern languages implement the concept of a structure in a similar style. The data contained in a structure are referenced by field name, for example, `item1`. The rules for making a field name are the same as those for a variable. Fields of a structure, like the elements of a cell array, are heterogeneous—they can contain any MATLAB object. First, we will see how to construct and manipulate one structure, and then how to aggregate individual structures into an array of structures.

7.3.1 Constructing and Accessing One Structure

To set the value of items in a structure `A`, the syntax is as follows:

```
>> A.item1 = 'abcde'
 A =
      item1: 'abcde'
>> A.item2 = 42
A =
      item1: 'abcde'
      item2: 42
```

Notice that MATLAB displays the elements of an emerging structure by name. Fields in a structure are accessed in the same way—by using the dotted notation.

```
>> A.item2 = A.item2 ./ 2
 A =
      item1: 'abcde'
      item2: 21
```

You can determine the names of the fields in a structure using the built-in function `fieldnames(...)`. It returns a cell array containing the field names as strings.

```
>> names = fieldnames(A)
 names =
      'item1'
      'item2'
```

Fields can also be accessed "indirectly" by setting a variable to the name of the field, and then by using parentheses to indicate that the variable contents should be used as the field name:

```
>> fn = names{1};
 >> A.(fn) = [A.(fn) 'fg']
A =
        item1: 'abcdefg'
        item2: 21
```

Common Pitfalls 7.1

Be careful. `rmfield(...)` returns a new structure with the requested field removed. It does not remove that field from your original structure. If you want the field removed from the original, you must assign the result from `rmfield(...)` to replace the original structure:

```
>> A = rmfield(A, 'item1')
 A =
      item2: 21
```

You can also remove a field from a structure using the built-in function `rmfield(...)`. Exercise 7.2 gives you an opportunity to understand how to build structures. Here we build a typical structure that could be used as one entry in a telephone book. Since phone numbers usually contain punctuation, we could store

Exercise 7.2 Building structures

Suppose that you want to use structures to maintain your address book. In the Command window, enter the following commands:

```
>> entry.first = 'Fred'
entry =
    first: 'Fred'
>> entry.last = 'Jones';
>> entry.phone = '(123) 555-1212'
entry =
    first: 'Fred"
     last: 'Jones'
    phone: '(123) 555-1212'
>> entry.phone
ans =
 (123) 555-1212
>> date.day = 31;
>> date.month = 'February';
>> date.year = 1965
date =
      day: 31
    month:'February'
     year: 1965
>> entry.birth = date
entry =
    first: 'Fred'
     last: 'Jones'
    phone: '(123) 555-1212'
    birth: [1x1 struct]
>> entry.birth
ans =
      day: 31
    month: 'February'
     year: '1965'
>> entry.birth.year
ans =
  1965
```

them as strings. Notice that since a structure may contain any object, it is quite legal to make a structure containing a date and insert that structure in the date field of the entry. The structure display function, however, does not display the contents of the structures.

7.3.2 Constructor Functions

This section discusses functions that assign their parameters to the fields of a structure and then return that structure. You do this, as opposed to "manually" entering data into structures, for the following reasons:

- Manual entry can result in strange behavior due to typographical errors or having fields in the wrong order

- The resulting code is generally more compact and easier to understand
- When constructing collections of structures, it enforces consistency across the collections

There are two approaches to the use of constructor functions: using built-in capabilities and writing your own constructor. There is a built-in function, `struct(...)`, that consumes pairs of entries (each consisting of a field name as a string and a cell array of field contents) and produces a structure. If all the cell arrays have more than one entry, this actually creates a structure array, as discussed in Section 7.4.1.

The following command would construct the address book entry created in the previous section. Note the use of ellipses `(...)` to indicate to the MATLAB machinery that the logic is continued onto the next line.

```
>> struct('first','Fred', ...
'last','Jones', ...
'phone','(123) 555-1212', ...
'birth', struct( 'day', 31,
                 'month', 'February',
                 'year', 1965 ))
ans =
    first: 'Fred'
     last: 'Jones'
    phone: '(123) 555-1212'
    birth: [1x1 struct]
```

This is useful in general to create structures, but the need to repeat the field names makes this general-purpose approach a little annoying. We can create a special-purpose function that "knows" the necessary field names to create multiple structures in an organized way.

Listing 7.3 shows the code for a function that consumes parameters that describe a CD and assembles a structure containing those attributes by name.

In Exercise 7.3, you can try your hand at using this function to construct a CD structure and then verify the structure contents.

Listing 7.3 Constructor for a CD structure

```
1. function ans = makeCD(gn, ar, ti, yr, st, pr)
      % integrate CD data into a structure
2.      ans.genre = gn ;
3.      ans.artist = ar ;
4.      ans.title = ti;
5.      ans.year = yr;
6.      ans.stars = st;
7.      ans.price = pr;
```

Exercise 7.3 A CD structure

Create one entry of CD information:

```
>> CD = makeCD('Blues', 'Charles, Ray', ...
'Genius Loves Company', 2004, 4.5, 15.35 )
CD =
     genre: 'Blues'
    artist: 'Charles, Ray'
     title: 'Genius Loves Company'
      year: 2004
     stars: 4.5000
     price: 15.3500
>> flds = fieldnames(CD)
flds =
    'genre'
    'artist'
    'title'
    'year'
    'stars'
    'price'
>> field = flds{2}
field =
artist
>> CD.(field)
ans =
    Charles, Ray
```

7.4 Structure Arrays

To be useful, collections like address books or CD collections require multiple structure entries with the same fields. This is accomplished by forming an array of data items, each of which contains the same fields of information.

MATLAB implements the concept of structure arrays with the properties described in the following paragraphs.

7.4.1 Constructing Structure Arrays

Structure arrays can be created either by creating values for individual fields, as shown in Exercise 7.4; by using MATLAB's struct(...) function to build the whole structure array, as shown in Listing 7.4; or by using a custom function to create each individual structure, as shown in Listing 7.5. This latter listing illustrates these concepts by implementing a collection of CDs as a structure array using the function makeCD(...) from Listing 7.3.

Exercise 7.4 Building a structure array "by hand"

```
>> entry(1).first = 'Fred';
>> entry(1).last = 'Jones';
>> entry(1).age = 37;
>> entry(1).phone = ' (123) 555-1212';
>> entry(2).first = 'Sally';
>> entry(2).last = 'Smith';
>> entry(2).age = 29;
>> entry(2).phone = '(000) 555-1212'
entry =
1x2 structure array with fields:
    first
    last
    age
    phone
```

Listing 7.4 Building a structure array using `struct(...)`

```
1. genres = {'Blues', 'Classical', 'Country' };
2. artists = {'Clapton, Eric', 'Bocelli, Andrea', 'Twain, Shania' };
3. years = { 2004, 2004, 2004 };
4. stars = { 2, 4.6, 3.9 };
5. prices = { 18.95, 14.89, 13.49 };
6. cds = struct( 'genre', genres, ...
7.                'artist', artists, ...
8.                'year', years, ...
9.                'stars', stars, ...
10.               'price', prices)
```

In Listing 7.4:

> Lines 1–5: Build cell arrays containing field values for five CDs.
>
> Line 6: Uses the built-in `struct(...)` function to create the CD collection. The function consumes a variable number of pairs of parameters. The first parameter of the pair is a string containing the name of a field to be created. The second parameter is the content of that field expressed as either a cell array or any other data type. If the field content is a cell array, the structure to be created becomes a structure array whose length is the length of that cell array. Each field of the structure array receives the corresponding value from the cell array. If the field content is anything other than a cell array, the content of each structure array field becomes a copy of that item.

Listing 7.5 Building a structure array using a custom constructor

```
      % extracts from http://www.cduniverse.com/   12/30/04
 1. cds(1) = makeCD('Blues', 'Clapton, Eric', ...
 2. 'Sessions For Robert J', 2004, 2, 18.95 );
 3. cds(2) = makeCD('Classical', ...
 4. 'Bocelli, Andrea', 'Andrea', 2004, 4.6, 14.89 );
 5. cds(3) = makeCD( 'Country', 'Twain, Shania', ...
 6. 'Greatest Hits', 2004, 3.9, 13.49 );
 7. cds(4) = makeCD('Latin', 'Trevi, Gloria', ...
 8. 'Como Nace El Universo', 2004, 5, 12.15 );
 9. cds(5) = makeCD('Rock/Pop', 'Ludacris', ...
10. 'The Red Light District', 2004, 4, 13.49 );
11. cds(6) = makeCD('R & B', '2Pac', ...
12. 'Loyal To The Game', 2004, 3.9, 13.49 );
13. cds(7) = makeCD('Rap', 'Eminem', ...
14. 'Encore', 2004, 3.5, 15.75 );
15. cds(8) = makeCD( 'Heavy Metal', 'Rammstein', ...
16. 'Reise, Reise', 2004, 4.2, 12.65 )
```

In Listing 7.5:

> Lines 1–2: Call the `makeCD(...)` function defined in Listing 7.3 to generate the description of the first CD.
>
> Lines 3–16: Repeat the process for seven more CDs, each of which is added to the collection.

7.4.2 Accessing Structure Elements

Like normal arrays or cell arrays, items can be stored and retrieved by their index in the array. As structures are added to the array, MATLAB forces all elements in the structure array to implement the same field names in the same order. Elements can be accessed either manually (not recommended) or by creating new structures with a constructor and adding them (recommended).

If you elect to manipulate them manually, you merely identify the array element by indexing and use the `.field` operator. For example, for the CD collection `cds`, we could change the price of one of them as follows:

```
>> cds(3).price = 11.95
 cds =
1x31 struct array with fields:
    genre,
    artist,
    title,
    year,
    stars,
    price
```

This is a little hazardous when making manual additions to a structure array. A typographical error while entering a field name results in all the structures having that bad field name. For example, consider this error:

```
>> cds(3).prce = 11.95
 cds =
1x31 struct array with fields:
    genre,
    artist,
    title,
    year,
    stars,
    price,
    prce
```

You have accidentally added a new field to the whole collection. You can check this by looking at one entry:

```
>> cds(1)
 ans =
    genre: 'Blues'
    artist: 'Sessions For Robert J'
    title: 'Clapton, Eric'
     year: 2004
    stars: 2
    price: 18.95
     prce: []
```

If this happens, you can use the `fieldnames(...)` function to determine the situation and then the `rmfield(...)` function to remove the offending entry.

```
>> fieldnames(cds)
 ans =

    'genre'
    'artist'
    'title'
    'year'
    'stars'
    'price'
    'prce'
>> cds = rmfield(cds,'prce')
cds =
1x32 struct array with fields:
    genre,
    artist,
    title,
    year,
    stars,
    price
```

It is best to construct a complete structure and then insert it into the structure array. For example:

```
>> newCD = makeCD( 'Oldies', 'Greatest Hits', ...
 'Ricky Nelson', 2005, 5, 15.79 );
>> cds(8) = newCD
```

```
cds =
1x8 struct array with fields:
    genre,
    artist,
    title,
    year,
    stars,
    price
```

If you insert that new CD beyond the end of the array, as one might expect, MATLAB fills out the array with empty structures:

```
>> cds(50) = newCD
 cds =
1x50 struct array with fields:
    genre,
    artist,
    title,
    year,
    stars,
    price
>> cds(49)
ans =
      genre: []
     artist: []
      title: []
       year: []
      stars: []
      price: []
```

7.4.3 Manipulating Structures

Structures and structure arrays can be manipulated in the following ways:

I.   Single values can be changed using the "." (dot) notation directly with a field name:

```
>> cds(5).price = 19.95;
```

II. or indirectly using the "." (dot) notation with a variable containing the field name:

```
>> fld = 'price';
>> cds(5).(fld) = 19.95;
```

or by using built-in functions:

III. nms = fieldnames(str) returns a cell array containing the names of the fields in a structure or structure array.

```
>> flds = fieldnames(cds)
```

> ### Common Pitfalls 7.2
>
> A few very understandable but sneaky errors occur when adding structures that have been created "manually" rather than by means of a standardized constructor function. If the new structure has fields not in the original structure, or extra fields, you see a slightly obscure error: "Subscripted assignment between dissimilar structures."
>
> Perhaps more puzzling, if you are using an older version of MATLAB, this same error occurs if all the fields are present, but are in the wrong order.

IV. `it = isfield(str, <fldname>)` determines whether the given name is a field in this structure or structure array.

```
>> if isfield(cds, 'price') ...
```

V. `str = setfield(str, <fldname>, <value>)` returns a new structure array with the specified field set to the specified value.

```
>> cds(1) = setfield(cds(1), 'price', 19.95);
```

VI. `val = getfield(str, <fldname>)` returns the value of the specified field.

```
>> disp(getfield(cds(1), 'price') );
```

VII. `str = rmfield(str, <fldname>)` returns a new structure array with the specified field removed.

```
>> noprice = rmfield(cds, 'price');
```

VIII. Values across the whole array can be retrieved using the "." notation by accumulating them into arrays either into cell arrays:

```
>> titles = {cds.title};
>> [alpha order] = sort(titles);
```

IX. or, if the values are all numeric, into a vector:

```
>> prices = [cds.price];
>> total = sum(prices);
```

Notice that after extracting the price values into a cell array or vector, all the normal operations—in this case, `sort(...)` and `sum(...)`—can be utilized.

Exercise 7.5 provides some practice in manipulating structure arrays using the above CD collection as an example.

Exercise 7.5 The CD collection

Retrieve and run the script named `buildCDs.m` from the Companion Web site. Then, in the Interactions window, enter the following commands to create your collection of CD information:

```
>> cds(5)
ans =
     genre: 'Rock/Pop'
    artist: 'Ludacris'
     title: 'The Red Light District'
      year: 2004
     stars: 4
     price: 13.49
>> flds = fieldnames(collection)
flds =
    'genre'
    'artist'
    'title'
    'year'
    'stars'
    'price'
```

continued on next page

```
cds(5).strs = 0.5;
>> cds(5)
ans =
      genre: 'Rock/Pop'
     artist: 'Ludacris'
      title: 'The Red Light District'
       year: 2004
      stars: 4
      price: 13.4900
       strs: 0.5
>> cds(1)
ans =
      genre: 'Blues'
     artist: 'Clapton, Eric'
      title: 'Sessions For Robert J'
       year: 2004
      stars: 2
      price: 18.9500
       strs: []
>> cds = rmfield(cds, 'strs');
>> cds(1)
ans =
      genre: 'Blues'
     artist: 'Clapton, Eric'
      title: 'Sessions For Robert J'
       year: 2004
      stars: 2
      price: 18.9500
>> sum([cds.price])
ans =
  409.1100
```

7.5 Engineering Example—Assembling a Physical Structure

Many large buildings today have steel frames as their basic structure. Engineers perform the analysis and design work for each steel component and deliver these designs to the steel company. The steel company manufactures all the components, and prepares them for delivery to the building site. At this point, each component is identified only by a unique identifier string stamped and/or chalked onto that component. For even a modest-sized building, this transportation may require a significant number of truckloads of components. The question we address here is how to decide the sequence in which the components are delivered to the building site so that components are available when needed, but not piled up waiting to be used.

Consider the relatively simple structure shown in Figure 7.1. The components have individual labels, and we can obtain from the architect the identities of the components that are connected together. The

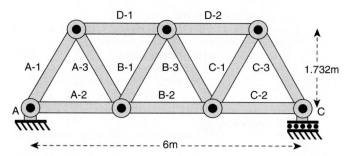

Figure 7.1 *Simple structure assembly*

construction needs to start from the fixed point A. We need to analyze this information and compute the order in which the components would be used to assemble the structure.

The data will be organized as a structure array with one entry for each component. One of the fields in that structure will be a cell array of the names of the components to which this component is connected.

The code in Listing 7.6 shows the solution to this problem.

Listing 7.6 Connectivity of a structure

```
 1. data(1) = beam('A-1', 0.866, 0.5, ...
 2.                {'A','A-2','A-3','D-1'} );
 3. data(2) = beam('A-2', 0, 1, ...
 4.                {'A', 'A-3', 'B-1', 'B-2'} );
 5. data(3) = beam('A-3', 0.866, 1.5, ...
 6.                {'A-1', 'A-2', 'B-1', 'D-1'} );
 7. data(4) = beam('B-1', 0.866, 2.5, ...
 8.                {'A-2', 'A-3', 'B-2', 'B-3', 'D-1', 'D-2'} );
 9. data(5) = beam('B-2', 0, 3, ...
10.                {'A-2', 'A-3', 'B-1', 'B-3', 'C-1', 'C-2'} );
11. data(6) = beam('B-3', 0.866, 3.5, ...
12.                {'B-1', 'B-2', 'C-1', 'C-2', 'D-1', 'D-2'} );
13. data(7) = beam('C-1', 0.866, 4.5, ...
14.                {'B-2', 'B-3', 'C-2', 'C-3', 'D-2'} );
15. data(8) = beam('C-2', 0, 5, ...
16.                {'B-2', 'B-3', 'C-1', 'C-3', 'C'} );
17. data(9) = beam('C-3', 0.866, 5.5, ...
18.                {'C-1', 'C-2', 'D-2', 'C'} );
19. data(10) = beam('D-1', 1.732, 2, ...
20.                {'A-1', 'A-3', 'B-1', 'B-3', 'D-2'} );
21. data(11) = beam( 'D-2', 1.732, 4, ...
22.                {'B-1', 'B-3', 'C-1', 'C-3', 'D-1'} )
23. conn = 'A';
24. clist = {conn};
25. while true
```

continued on next page

```
26.        index = 0;
           % find all the beams connected to conn
27.        for in = 1:length(data)
28.            str = data(in);
29.            if touches(str, conn)
30.                index = index + 1;
31.                found(index) = str;
32.            end
33.        end
           % eliminate those already connected
34.        for jn = index:-1:1
35.            if ison(found(jn).name, clist)
36.                found(jn) = [];
37.            else
38.                clist = [clist {found(jn).name}];
39.            end
40.        end
41.        if length(found) > 0
42.            conn = nextconn( found, clist );
43.        else
44.            break;
45.        end
46. end
47. disp('the order of assembly is:')
48. disp(clist)
```

In Listing 7.6:

> Lines 1–22: Construct the structure array using the `beam( ... )` constructor function below.
>
> Line 23: The current connection point, `conn`—originally, the point A.
>
> Line 24: Initializes the connection list, a cell array of names.
>
> Line 25: An infinite loop to be exited with break statements.
>
> Lines 26–33: Traverse the components to make a structure array, `found`, containing all the components connected to the current connection point, `conn`.
>
> Lines 34–40: Go through the `found` array, removing any component already on the connected list and appending the names of those not removed to the connected list.
>
> Lines 41–45: We will exit the `while` loop when there are no new components found; until then, choose the next component to connect.

The support functions for this script are assembled for convenience into Listing 7.7. They should be in separate files with the appropriate file names to be accessible by MATLAB.

Listing 7.7 Support functions

```
1. function ans = beam( nm, xp, yp, conn )
   % construct a beam structure with fields:
   % name - beam name
   % xp, yp - coordinates of its centroid
   % conn - cell array - names of adjacent beams
   % useage: ans = beam( nm, xp, yp, conn )
2.     ans.name = nm;
3.     ans.pos = [xp, yp];
4.     ans.connect = conn;
5. end
6. function res = touches(beam, conn)
   % does the beam touch this connecting point?
   % usage: res = touches(beam, conn)
7.     res = false;
8.     for in = 1:length(beam.connect)
9.         item = beam.connect{in};
10.        if strcmp(item,conn)
11.            res = true; break;
12.        end
13.    end
14. end
15. function res = ison( nm, cl )
    % is this beam on the connection list,
    % a cell array of beam names
    % usage: res = ison( beam, cl )
16.    res = false;
17.    for in = 1:length(cl)
18.        item = cl{in};
19.        if strcmp(item, nm)
20.            res = true; break;
21.        end
22.    end
23. end
24. function nm = nextconn( fnd, cl )
    % find a connection name among
    % those found not already connected
    % usage: nm = nextconn( fnd, cl )
25.    for in = 1:length(fnd)
26.        item = fnd(in);
27.        cn = item.connect;
28.        for jn = 1:length(cn)
29.            nm = cn{jn};
30.            if ~ison(nm, cl)
31.                break;
32.            end
33.        end
34.    end
35. end
```

In Listing 7.7:

Lines 1–5: Constructor for one structure defining one component.

Lines 6–14: A function to determine whether a beam touches this connecting point.

Lines 15–23: A similar function to determine whether a particular string is on the connection list, a cell array of strings.

Lines 24–35: Function to find the next connection to use based on the latest components found—the "outer edges" of the emerging structure—and its not being already on the connected list.

Here is the resulting output:

```
data =

1x11 struct array with fields:
    name,
    pos,
    connect

the order of assembly is:
'A' 'A-2' 'A-1' 'D-1' 'A-3' 'B-2' 'B-1' 'D-2' 'B-3' 'C-2' 'C-1' 'C-3'
```

Chapter Summary

This chapter covered the nature, implementation, and behavior of two heterogeneous collections:

- Cell arrays are vectors of containers; their elements can be manipulated either as vectors of containers, or individually by inserting or extracting the contents of the container using braces in place of parentheses
- The elements of a structure are accessed by name rather than by indexing, using the dot operator, '.', to specify the field name to be used
- Structures can be collected into structure arrays whose elements are structures all with the same field names. These elements can then be indexed and manipulated in the same manner as the cells in a cell array

Special Characters, Reserved Words, and Functions

Special Characters, Reserved Words, and Functions	Description	Discussed in This Section
{ ... }	Defines a cell array	7.2
.<field>	Used to access fields of a structure	7.3.1
.(<variable>)	Allows a variable to be used as a structure field	7.3.1
class(<object>)	Determines the data type of an object	7.2.4
deal(...)	Distributes cell array results among variables	7.2.2
getfield (<str>, <fld>)	Extracts the value of the field <fld> from a structure	7.4.3

Special Characters, Reserved Words, and Functions	Description	Discussed in This Section
isa(<object>, <class>)	Determines whether the <object> is of the given data type, <class>	7.2.4
iscell(<object>)	Determines whether <object> is of type cell	7.2.4
ischar(<object>)	Determines whether <object> is of type char	7.2.4
isfield(<str>, <fld>)	true if the string <fld> is a field in the structure <str>	7.4.3
islogical (<object>)	Determines whether <object> is of type logical	7.2.4
isnumeric (<object>)	Determines whether <object> is of type double	7.2.4
isstruct (<object>)	Determines whether <object> is of type struct	7.2.4
str = setfield(<str>, <fld>, <value>)	Constructs a new structure that is a copy of <str> in which the value of the field <fld> has been changed to <value>	7.4.3
[values order] = sort(<object>)	Sorts either vectors (increasing numerical order) or cell arrays of strings (alphabetically) returning the sorted data and the index order for the sort	7.4.3
struct(...)	Constructs a structure from <fieldname> <value> pairs of parameters	7.3.2

Self Test

Use the following questions to check your understanding of the material in this chapter:

True or False

F 1. Of all the collective operations defined for numerical arrays, only logical operations can be applied to a whole cell array.

T 2. A cell array or a structure can contain any legal MATLAB object.

T 3. You gain access to the contents of a cell by using braces, {...}.

T 4. Since the contents of a structure are heterogeneous, we can store other structures in any structure.

F 5. The statement rmfield(str, 'price') removes the field 'price' and its value from the structure str.

T 6. The statement getfield(str, <fldname>) returns the value of the specified field.

F   7.   You cannot extract and process all of the values of a field in a
         structure array.

Fill in the Blanks

1.   To perform any operations on the contents of a heterogeneous
     collection, the items must be _extracted_ and if necessary,
     replaced .   *one at a time*

2.   Cell arrays can be treated for the purpose of concatenation and
     slicing as _arrays_ of _containers_

3.   The assignment B{3} = {42} results in the third entry in the cell
     array B being a(n) _cell containing_ 42

4.   If a variable called `field` contains the name of a field in a structure
     `str`, the expression _str.(field)=42_ will set the value of that field to
     42.

5.   MATLAB has a built-in function _struct(...)_ that consumes pairs of
     entries, each consisting of a(n) _field name_ and a(n) _cell array_ , and
     produces a structure array.   *as a string*   *of field contents*

Programming Projects

1.   Write a function named `cellParse` that takes in a cell array with
     each element being either a string (character array), or a vector
     (containing numbers), or a boolean value (logical array of length 1).

     Your function should return the following:

     - `nStr`: the number of strings
     - `nVec`: the number of vectors
     - `nBool`: the number of boolean values
     - `cString`: a cell array of all the strings in alphabetical order
     - `vecLength`: the average length of all the vectors
     - `allTrue`: true if all the boolean values are `true` and `false`
       otherwise

     For example,

     ```
     [a b c d e f] =
     cellParse( { [1 2 3], true, 'hi there!',
                     42, false, 'abc'} )
     should return a = 2, b = 2, c = 2, d = {'abc','hi there!},
                    e = 2, and f = false.
     ```

2.   It turns out that since you have become an expert on rating clothing
     (Chapter 4, Problem 5), Acme Clothing Company has hired you to

rate its clothes. Clothes are now represented as structures instead of vectors with the fields (all of which are numbers between 0 and 5):

Condition, Color, Price, Matches, and Comfort

Acme has a much simpler way of rating its clothes than you used before:

Rating = 5 * Condition + 3 * Color + 2 * Price + Matches + 9 * Comfort

You have a script called makeClothes.m that will create a structure array called acmeClothes that contains clothes structures. You are to write a script called rateClothes that will add a Rating field and a Quality field to each of the structures in the acmeClothes array. The Rating field in each structure should contain the rating of that particular article of clothing. The Quality field is a string that is 'premium' if the Rating is over 80, 'good' over 60, 'poor' over 20, and 'liquidated' for anything else.

Note:

a. You MUST use iteration to solve this problem.

b. To make things easy, just place the line makeClothes at the top of your script, so you're guaranteed to have the correct acmeClothes array to work with.

c. The fields are case sensitive, so make sure that you capitalize them.

3. You have been hired by a used-car dealership to modify the price of cars that are up for sale. You will get the information about a car, and then change its price tag depending on a number of factors.

Write a function called usedCar that takes in a structure with the following fields:

Make: A string that represents the make of the car (e.g., 'Toyota Corolla')

Year: A number that corresponds to the year of the car (e.g., 1997)

Cost : A number that holds the marked price of the car (e.g., 7,000)

Miles : The number of miles clocked (e.g., 85,000)

Accidents: The number of accidents the car has been in (e.g., 1)

Your function should return a structure with all the above fields, with *exactly* the same names. It should have the same make, year, accidents, and miles. Here are the changes you must make:

1. Add 5,000 to the cost if the car has clocked less than 20,000 miles.

2. Subtract 5,000 if it has clocked more than 100,000 miles.

3. Reduce the price by 10,000 for every accident.

4. This problem deals with structures that represent dates.

   a. First, write a MATLAB function called `createDate` that will take in three numeric parameters. The first parameter represents the `month`, the second the `day`, and the third the `year`. The function should return a structure with the following fields:

   > `Day`: a number
   > `Month`: a 3 character string containing the first three characters of the month name
   > `Year`: a number containing the year.

   For example,

   `it = createDate(3,30,2008)` should return a structure containing:

   > ```
   > Day: 30
   > Month: Mar
   > Year: 2008
   > ```

   b. Write a function called `printDate` that displays a date in the form `Mar 30, 2007`

   c. Write a function `inBetween` that will take in three date structures. The function should return `true` if the second date is between the first and third dates, otherwise the function should return `false`.

   d. Write a function called `isSorted` that takes in a single parameter, an array of date structures. This function should return `true` if all the dates in the array are in a chronological order (regardless of whether they are in ascending or descending order), otherwise the function should return `false`.

   e. Write a test script that creates an array of date structures, prints out each date, and then states whether or not the dates are in order.

Hints

- It might help to add a field to the date class.
- The third date does not have to be chronologically later than the first date.

5. Your university has added a new award for students who were "almost there" last semester and just missed getting into the Dean's List. Write a function called `almost` that consumes an array of student structures, and produces an array of names of those who have a semester GPA between 2.9 and 2.99 (inclusive). The student structure has the following fields:

   ```
   Name - string (e.g., 'George P. Burdell')
   Semester_GPA - decimal number (e.g., 2.97)
   Cumulative_GPA - decimal number (e.g., 3.01)
   ```

6. The MATLAB language has the built-in ability to perform mathematical operations on complex numbers. However, there are times when it is useful to treat complex numbers as a structure. Write a set of functions with the following capability and a script to verify that they work correctly:

    ```
    cmplx = makeComplex(real, imag)
    res = cmplxAdd( cmpxa, cmpxb )
    res = cmplxMult( cmpxa, cmpxb )
    ```

7. In terms of atomic physics, every electron has four numbers associated with it, called the quantum numbers. These are `'principal'` (energy), `'azimuthal'` (angular momentum), `'magnetic'` (orientation of angular momentum), and `'spin'` (particle spin) quantum numbers. Wolfgang Pauli hypothesized (correctly) that no two electrons in an atom can have the same set of four quantum numbers; that is, if the `Principal`, `Azimuthal`, and `Magnetic` numbers are the same for two electrons, then it is necessary for the electrons to have different `spin` numbers.

    You need to write a function called `spinSwitch` that takes in two structures and returns both structures. Each structure represents an electron in a hydrogen atom and has the following fields:

    ```
    principal (this is always > 0)
    azimuthal (a number)
    magnetic (a number)
    spin (a string with value 'up' or 'down')
    ```

    Your function will compare the values in the two structures and check if they all have the same values for the four fields. If true, you are required to switch the spin of the second structure. You also have to add a field called "energy" to both structures. The value stored in this field must be $(-2.18*(10^{18}))/(n^2)$, where n is the value of the principal quantum number for that electron. You have to return both the structures with the energy field added to both, so that the one with the higher energy is first. If the energies are equal, return the one with the 'up' spin first. If both have the same spin and the same energy, the order does not matter.

File Input and Output

Chapter Objectives

This chapter discusses three levels of capability for reading and writing files in MATLAB, each including a discussion of the circumstances under which they are appropriate:

■ Saving and restoring the workspace

■ High-level functions for accessing files in specific formats

■ Low-level file access programs for general-purpose file processing

Reading and writing data in data files are fundamental to the utility of programming languages in general, and MATLAB in particular. In addition to the obvious need to save and restore scripts and functions (covered in Chapter 2), here we consider three types of activities that read and write data files.

■ The MATLAB language provides for the basic ability to save your workspace (or parts of your workspace) to a file and restore it later for further processing.

■ There are high-level functions that consume the name of a file whose contents are in any one of a number of popular formats and produce an internal representation of the data from that file in a form ready for processing.

■ Almost all these functions have an equivalent write function that will write a new file in the same format after you have manipulated the data.

■ However, we also need to deal with lower-level capabilities for manipulating text files that do not contain recognizable structures.

Introduction

This chapter discusses files that contain workspace variables, spreadsheet data, and text files containing delimited numbers and plain text. Subsequent chapters will discuss image files and sound files. For information on the other file formats, consult the help documentation for details of their usage.

The MATLAB language also provides the ability to access binary files—files whose data are not in text form—but the interpretation of binary data is beyond the scope of this text, and we will not consider binary files here. Refer to MATLAB documentation for information about binary files.

8.1 Concept: Serial Input and Output (I/O)

We frequently refer to the process of reading and writing data files as Input/Output (I/O). We have already seen and used examples of file I/O to store and retrieve data and programs. Your script and function files are stored in your current directory and could be invoked from there by name from the Command window. In general, any computer file system saves and retrieves data as a sequential (serial) stream of characters, as shown in Figure 8.1. Mixed in with the characters that represent the data are special characters ("delimiters") that specify the organization of the data.

When a program opens a file by name for reading, it continually requests blocks of data from the file data stream until the end of the file is reached. As the data are received, the program must identify the delimiting characters and reformat the data to reconstruct the organization of the data as represented in the file. Similarly, when writing data to a file, the program must serialize the data, as shown in Figure 8.2. To preserve the organization of the data, the appropriate delimiting characters must be inserted into the serial character stream.

The purpose of the file I/O functions discussed in this chapter is to encapsulate these fundamental operations into a single system function, or at least into a manageable collection of functions.

8.2 Workspace I/O

The MATLAB language defines the tools to save your complete workspace to a file with the `save` command and reload it with the `load` command. If you provide a file name with the save command, a file of that name will be

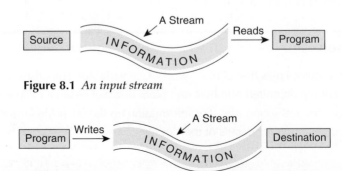

Figure 8.1 *An input stream*

Figure 8.2 *An output stream*

written into your current directory in such a form that a subsequent load command with that file name will restore the saved workspace. By convention, these files will have a `.mat` extension. If you do not provide a file name, the workspace is saved as `matlab.mat`.

If you are using MATLAB, you can also identify specific variables that you want to save—either by listing them explicitly or by providing logical expressions to indicate the variable names. For example:

```
>> save mydata.mat a b c*
```

would save the variables `a` and `b` and any variable beginning with the letter `c`. For more details, consult the MATLAB help documentation.

8.3 High-Level I/O Functions

We turn to the general case of file I/O in which we expect to load data from external sources, process that data, and perhaps save data back to the file system with enhancements created by your program. When you try to process data from some unknown source, it is difficult to write code to process the data without some initial exploration of the nature and organization of that data. So a good habit is to explore the data in a file by whatever means you have available and then decide how to process the data according to your observations.

Most programming languages require the programmer to write detailed programs to read and write files, especially those produced by other application programs or data acquisition packages. Fortunately for MATLAB programmers, much of this messy work has been built into special file readers and writers. Table 8.1 identifies the type of data, the name of the appropriate reader and writer, and the internal form in which MATLAB returns the data.

> **Style Points 8.1**
>
> In a practical sense, saving workspace data is very rarely an appropriate approach to saving work because it saves the results but not the code that generated the results. It is almost always better to save the scripts and raw data that created the workspace. For example, this is a good idea when you have a lengthy computation (perhaps one run overnight) to prepare data for a display. You could split that script into two halves. The first half would do the overnight calculation and save the workspace. The second part can then read the workspace quickly, and you can develop sophisticated ways to display the data without having to re-run the lengthy calculations.

8.3.1 Exploration

The types of data of immediate interest are text files and spreadsheets. In Table 8.1 notice that the delimited text files are presumed to contain numerical values, whereas the spreadsheet data may be either numerical data stored as doubles or string data stored in cell arrays. Typically, text files are delimited by a special character (comma, tab, or anything else) to designate the column divider and a new-line character to designate the

Table 8.1 File reading and writing

File	Content	Reader	Writer	Data Format	Extension
Plain text	Any	`textscan`	`fprintf`	Specified in the function calls	.txt usually
CSV	Comma separated values	`csvread`	`csvwrite`	double array	.csv
Delimited	Numbers separated by delimiters	`dlmread`	`dlmwrite`	double array	.txt usually
Excel worksheet	Microsoft specific	`xlsread`	`xlswrite`	Double array + 2 cell arrays	.xls
Image data	Various	`imread`	`imwrite`	True color, grayscale, or indexed image	various
Audio file	AU or WAV	`auread` or `wavread`	`Auwrite` or `wavwrite`	Sound data and sample rate	.au or .wav
Movie	AVI	`aviread`	`no`	movie	.avi

rows. Once the data are imported, all of our normal array and matrix processing tools can be applied. The exception to this rule is the plain text reader that must be provided with a format specifier to define the data, and the names of the variables in which the data are to be stored.

So when you are approached with a file, the file extension (the part of the file name after the dot) gives you a significant clue to the nature of the data. For example, if it is the output from a spreadsheet, you should open the data in that spreadsheet program to explore its contents and organization. [Typically, spreadsheet data will not open well in a plain text editor.] If you do not recognize the file extension as coming from a spreadsheet, try opening the file in a plain text editor such as that used for your scripts and functions and see if the data are legible. You should be able to discern the field delimiters and the content of each line if the file contains plain text.

8.3.2 Spreadsheets

Excel is a Microsoft product that implements spreadsheets. Spreadsheets are rectangular arrays containing labeled rows and columns of cells. The data in the cells may be numbers, strings, or formulae that combine the data values in other cells. Because of this computational capability, spreadsheets can be used to solve many problems, and most offer flexible plotting packages for presenting the results in colorful charts. There are occasions, however, when we need to apply the power of the MATLAB language to the data in a spreadsheet.

MATLAB provides a reader for Excel spreadsheets that gives you a significant amount of flexibility in retrieving the data from the spreadsheet. Consider the typical set of data in a spreadsheet named `grades.xls` shown in Table 8.2. The goal of your spreadsheet reader is to separate the text and numerical portions of the spreadsheet. The parameter consumed by your spreadsheet reader is the name of the file; you can ask for up to three return variables: the first will hold all the numerical values in an array of doubles; the second will hold all the text data in cell arrays; and the third, if you request it, will hold both string and numerical data in cell arrays (try Exercise 8.1).

Table 8.2 Sample spreadsheet date		
name	**age**	**grade**
fred	19	78
Joe	22	83
Sally	98	99
Charlie	21	56
Mary	23	89
Ann	19	51

Exercise 8.1 Reading Excel data

```
>> [nums txt raw] = csvread('grades.csv')
% or xlsread('grades.xls') with MATLAB
nums =
      19      78
      22      83
      98      99
      21      56
      23      89
      19      51
txt =
    'name'          'age'        'grade'
    'fred'            "             "
    'joe'             "             "
    'sally'           "             "
    'charlie'         "             "
    'mary'            "             "
    'ann'             "             "
raw =
    'name'          'age'        'grade'
    'fred'          [ 19]        [   78]
    'joe'           [ 22]        [   83]
    'sally'         [ 98]        [   99]
    'charlie'       [ 21]        [   56]
    'mary'          [ 23]        [   89]
    'ann'           [ 19]        [   51]
    'ann'           [ 19]        [   51]
```

The reader first determines the smallest rectangle on the spreadsheet containing all of the numerical data; we will refer to this as the "number rectangle." Then it produces the following results:

1. The first returned result is an array with the same number of rows and columns as the number rectangle and containing the values of all the numeric data in that rectangle. If there are non-numeric values within that rectangle, they are replaced by NaN, the built-in name for anything that is not a number.

2. The second returned result is a cell array with the same size as the original spreadsheet, containing only the string data; to ensure the consistency of this cell array, all numbers present are replaced by the empty string.

3. The third returned result is a cell array also with the same size as the original spreadsheet, containing both the strings and the numbers. Cells that are blank are presumed to be numerical, and are assigned as a cell containing an empty vector.

Frequently, after processing data, you need to write the results back to a spreadsheet. Excel spreadsheets can be written using:

```
xlswrite(<filename>, <array>, <sheet>, <range>)
```

where `<filename>` is the name of the file, `<array>` is the data source (a cell array), `<sheet>` is the sheet name, and `<range>` is the range of cells in Excel cell identity notation. The sheet name and range are optional.

8.3.3 Delimited Text Files

If information is not available specifically in spreadsheet form, it can frequently be presented in text file form. If the data in a text file are numerical values only and are organized in a reasonable form, you can read the file directly into an array. It is necessary that the data values are separated (delimited) by commas, spaces, or tab characters. Rows in the data are separated as expected by the new-line character. These values might be saved in a file named `nums.txt`. This type of numerical data (not strings) in general delimited form can be read using `dlmread(<file>,<delimiter>)`, where the delimiter parameter is a single character that can be used to specify an unusual delimiting character. However, the function can usually determine common delimiter situations without specifying the parameter.

The `dlmread(...)` function produces a numerical array containing the data values. Try reading delimited files in Exercise 8.2. Table 8.3 shows the content of the file `nums.txt`.

Notice that the array elements where data are not supplied are filled with zero.

Exercise 8.2 Reading delimited files

```
>> A = dlmread('nums.txt')
A =
        19        78        42
        22        83       100
        98        99        34
        21        56        12
        23        89         0
        19        51         0
```

Delimited data files can be written using: `dlmwrite( <filename>, <array>, <dlm>)` where `<filename>` is the name of the file, `<array>` is the data source (a numerical array), and `<dlm>` is the delimiting character. If the delimiting character is not specified, it is presumed to be a comma.

The `csvread(...)` function is a special case of `dlm read(...)` where the delimiter is presumed to be a comma, and it produces a numerical array containing the data values. As noted above, the MATLAB version of `csvread(...)` has been enhanced so that if the data contain only numerical values, it will return an array. However, if the data contain some strings, it produces the three results specified above for `xls read(...)`. The normal content of CSV files allows embedded strings to contain the comma character. This is accomplished by surrounding any such string with double quotes—for example, `"Jones, Tom"` in a CSV file would prevent the embedded comma from separating this string into the two strings: `'Jones'` and `'Tom'`.

Common Pitfalls 8.1

It is best not to provide the delimiter unless you have to. Without it, MATLAB will assume that repeated delimiters—like tabs and spaces—are single delimiters. If you do specify a delimiter, it will assume that repeated delimiter characters are separating different, absent field values.

Table 8.3 Sample delimited text file		
19	78	42
22	83	100
98	99	34
21	56	12
23	89	
19	51	

8.4 Lower-Level File I/O

Some text files contain data in mixed format that are not readable by the high-level file reading functions. The MATLAB language provides a set of lower-level I/O functions that permit general-purpose text file reading and writing. The following is a partial discussion of these functions that is sufficient for most text file processing needs. In general, the file must be opened to return a value to be used by subsequent functions to identify its data stream. We usually refer to this identifier as the "file handle." After the file contents have been manipulated, the file must be closed to complete the activity. Because these are lower-level functions used in combination to solve problems, we will need to discuss the behavior of several of them before we can show examples of their use.

8.4.1 Opening and Closing Files

To open a file for reading or writing, use `fh = fopen( <filename>, <purpose>)` where `fh` is a file handle used in subsequent function calls to identify this particular input stream, `<filename>` is the name of the file, and `<purpose>` is a string specifying the purpose for opening the file. The most common purposes are `'r'` to read the file, `'w'` to write it, or `'a'` to append to an existing file. See the help files for more complex situations. If the purpose is `'r'`, the file must already exist; if `'w'` and the file already exists, it will be overwritten; if `'a'` and the file already exists, the new data will be appended to the end. The consequence of failure to open the file is system dependent. In the standard version on a PC, this is indicated by returning a file handle of –1.

To close the file, call `fclose( fh )`.

8.4.2 Reading Text Files

To read a file, three levels of support are provided: reading whole lines with or without the new-line character, parsing into tokens with delimiters, or parsing into cell arrays using a format string.

- To read a whole line including the new-line character, use `str = fgets( fh )` that will return each line as a string until the end of the file, when the value –1 is returned instead of a string. To leave out each new-line character, use `fgetl(...)` instead (the last character is a lowercase `l`).
- To parse each line into tokens (elementary text strings) separated by white space delimiters, use a combination of `fgetl(...)` and the tokenizer function `[<tk>, <rest>] = strtok( <ln> );` where `<tk>` is a string token, `<rest>` is the remainder of the line, and `<ln>` is a string to be parsed into tokens.

- If you are using MATLAB, you could try to parse a line according to a specific format string into a cell array by using `ca = textscan( fh, <format> );` where `ca` is the resulting cell array, `fh` is the file handle, and `<format>` is a format control string such as we used for `sscanf(...)` in Chapter 6.

8.4.3 Examples of Reading Text Files

To illustrate the use of these functions for reading a text file, the script shown in Listing 8.1 shows a script that will list any text file in the Command window.

In Listing 8.1:

Line 1: Asks the user for the name of a file.

Line 2: Opens the file for reading and returns the file handle.

Line 3: Initializes the `while` loop control variable.

Line 4: When the file read reaches the end of the file, the reading function returns −1 instead of a string.

Line 5: Reads a string, including the end of line character.

Line 6: Classic loop-and-a-half logic that determines whether there is a line to process.

Line 7: Displays that line if present.

Line 10: Closes the file when finished.

As an example of the use of a tokenizer, consider the code shown in Listing 8.2, which performs the same function as Listing 8.1 but uses tokens.

Line 5: Uses `fgetl(...)` instead of `fgets(...)` because the tokenizer does not need the new-line character.

Line 7: Initializes the resulting cell array.

Line 8: The tokenizer will be finished when it leaves an empty line as the result.

Line 9: Creates a token from the remains of the line and puts the remains back into the variable `ln`.

Listing 8.1 Script to list a text file

```
1.  fn = input( 'file name: ', 's' );
2.  fh = fopen( fn, 'r' );
3.  ln = '';
4.  while ischar( ln )
5.       ln = fgets( fh );
6.       if ischar( ln )
7.            fprintf( ln );
8.       end
9.  end
10. fclose( fh );
```

Listing 8.2 Listing a file using tokens

```
1. fn = input( 'file name: ' , 's' );
2. fh = fopen( fn, 'r' );
3. ln = '';
4. while ischar( ln )
5.      ln = fgetl( fh );
6.      if ischar( ln )
7.           ca = [];
8.           while ~isempty( ln )
9.                [tk, ln] = strtok( ln );
10.               ca = [ca {tk}];
11.          end
12.          disp( ca );
13.     end
14. end
15. fclose( fh );
```

Line 10: Adds the current token to the result.

Line 12: Shows the tokens for one line.

Line 15: Closes the file.

Run the scripts in Listings 8.1 and 8.2. This will show the difference in output results between the conventional listing script and the tokenizing lister. With the tokenizer, we see each individual token (really, each word in a normal text file) separately listed.

8.4.4 Writing Text Files

Once a file has been opened for writing, the `fprintf(...)` function can be used to write to it by including its file handle as the first parameter. For example, Listing 8.3 is a minor alteration to Listing 8.1, copying a text file instead of listing it in the Command window.

Listing 8.3 Script to copy a text file

```
1. ifn = input( 'input file name: ', 's' );
2. ofn = input('output file name: ', 's' );
3. ih = fopen( ifn, 'r' );
4. oh = fopen( ofn, 'w' );
5. ln = '';
6. while ischar( ln )
7.      ln = fgets( ih );
8.      if ischar( ln )
9.           fprintf( oh, ln );
10.     end
11. end
12. fclose( ih );
13. fclose( oh );
```

In Listing 8.3:

> Line 2: Fetches the output file name.
>
> Line 4: Opens the output file for writing.
>
> Line 9: Adding `oh` as the first parameter to `fprintf(...)` redirects the output to the specified file.
>
> Line 13: Closes the output file.

8.5 Engineering Example—Spreadsheet Data

- Frequently, engineering data are provided in spreadsheets. Here we will adapt the structure assembly problem from Chapter 7. The script for that solution created the data using a constructor function. Consider the situation in which the data are provided in a spreadsheet such as that shown in Figure 8.3. We have to start by examining the layout of the data and the process necessary to extract what we need. Bearing in mind the three results returned from `xlsread(...)`, first we determine which of the three is most appropriate:

- The {`xlsread(...)`} function is going to include all the numerical cells from the spreadsheet in the numerical array. This is awkward because there are numbers in the first column; and since the primary interest in this problem is not the numerical data, we will not use the numerical array directly.

- However, this is not exclusively a text processing problem. Since we need the numerical coordinates, the second, text-only result is not what we need.

- Therefore, in this particular application, we will process the raw data provided by `csvread(...)`, giving both the string and numerical data.

The other concern is that there are a different number of connections on each row of the sheet. When a connection is present, it is a string. When it is

	A	B	C	D	E	F	G	H	I	J
1	Item	Name	X	Y	Connected to					
2	1	A-1	0.866	0.5	A	A-2	A-3	D-1		
3	2	A-2	0	1	A	A-3	B-1	B-2		
4	3	A-3	0.866	1.5	A-1	A-2	B-1	D-1		
5	4	B-1	0.866	2.5	A-2	A-3	B-2	B-3	D-1	D-2
6	5	B-2	0	3	A-2	A-3	B-1	B-3	C-1	C-2
7	6	B-3	0.866	3.5	B-1	B-2	C-1	C-2	D-1	D-2
8	7	C-1	0.866	4.5	B-2	B-3	C-2	C-3	D-2	
9	8	C-2	0	5	B-2	B-3	C-1	C-3	C	
10	9	C-3	0.866	5.5	C-1	C-2	D-2	C		
11	10	D-1	1.732	2	A-1	A-3	B-1	B-3	D-2	
12	11	D-2	1.732	4	B-1	B-3	C-1	C-3	D-1	

Figure 8.3 *Data in a spreadsheet*

not there, we refer to the behavior of the raw data to discover that the contents of empty cells appear as [] of type double.

We need a function that will read this file and produce the same model of the structure used in Chapter 7. Such a function is shown in Listing 8.4.

In Listing 8.4:

> Line 1: The function consumes the file name and produces a structure array with the fields described in the following comments.
>
> Line 2: Reads the spreadsheet and keeps only the raw data.
>
> Line 3: Gets the rows and columns in the raw data; we need to ignore the top row and left column.
>
> Line 4: Initializes the output index for the structure array.
>
> Line 5: Ignoring the first row, traverses all the remaining rows.
>
> Line 6: The component name is in the second column.
>
> Line 7: The coordinates of the component are in the third and fourth columns.

Listing 8.4 Reading structure data

```
 1. function data = readStruct(filename)
      % read a spreadsheet and produce a
      % structure array:
      % name - the second column value
      % pos - columns 3 and 4 in a vector
      % connect - cell array with the remaining
      % data on the row

 2.     [no no raw] = xlsread(filename);
 3.     [rows cols] = size(raw);
        % ignore the first row and column
 4.     out = 1;
 5.     for row = 2:rows
 6.         str.name = raw{row,2};
 7.         str.pos = [raw{row,3} raw{row,4}];
 8.         cni = 1;
 9.         conn = {};
10.         for col = 5:cols
11.             item = raw{row, col};
12.             if ~ischar(item)
13.                 break;
14.             end
15.             conn{cni} = item;
16.             cni = cni + 1;
17.         end
18.         str.connect = conn;
19.         data(out) = str;
20.         out = out + 1;
21.     end
22. end
```

Lines 8–9: Initialize the search for the connections for this component. It is important to empty the array `conn` before each pass to avoid "inheriting" data from a previous row.

Lines 10–11: Extract each item in turn from the row.

Lines 12–14: If the item is not of class `char`, this is the blank cell at the end of the row; the `break` command exits the `for` loop moving across the row.

Lines 15–16: Otherwise, it stores the connection and keeps going.

Lines 18–20: When the connections are complete, it stores them in the structure, stores the structure in the structure array, and continues to the next row.

Line 21: When the rows are completed, the data are ready to return to the calling script.

To test this function, replace the structure array construction in lines 1–22 of Listing 7.6 in Chapter 7 with the following line:

```
data = readStruct('Structure_data.xls');
```

The script should then produce the same results as before.

Chapter Summary

We have described three levels of capability for reading and writing files:

- The save and load operators allow you to save variables from the workspace and restore them to the workspace
- Specialized functions read and write spreadsheets and delimited text files
- Lower-level functions provide the ability to open and close files, and to read and write text files in any form that is required

Special Characters, Reserved Words, and Functions

Special Characters, Reserved Words, and Functions	Description	Discussed in This Section
`[nums,txt,raw] = csvread(<file>)`	Reads comma-separated text files	8.3
`csvwrite(<file>,<data>)`	Writes comma-separated text files	8.3
`dlmread(<file>,<dlm>)`	Reads text files separated by the given delimiting character	8.3
`dlmwrite (<file>, <data>, <dlm>)`	Reads text files separated by the given delimiting character	8.3

Special Characters, Reserved Words, and Functions	Description	Discussed in This Section
`fclose(fh)`	Closes a text file	8.4.1
`fgetl(fh)`	Reads a line, omitting the new-line character	8.4.2
`fgets(fh)`	Reads a line, including the new-line character	8.4.2
`fh = fopen(<file>, <why>)`	Opens a text file for reading or writing	8.4.1
`fprintf(...)`	Writes to the console, or to plain text files	8.3, 8.4.4
`load <filename>`	Loads the workspace from a file	8.2
`save <filename>`	Saves workspace variables in a file	8.2
`[tk rest] = strtok (<str>, <dlm>)`	Extracts a token from a string and returns the remainder of the string	8.4.2
`ca = textscan(fh, format)`	Acquires and scans a line of text according to a specific format	8.3, 8.4.2
`[nums, txt, raw] = xlsread(<file>)`	Reads an Excel spreadsheet	8.3.2
`xlswrite(<file>,<data>, <sheet>, <,range>)`	Writes an Excel spreadsheet in a specific row/column range	8.3.2

Self Test

Use the following questions to check your understanding of the material in this chapter:

True or False

T 1. All data files should be treated as a sequential series of characters.

F 2. When you save a workspace, you are actually saving the scripts that generate the data in the workspace.

F 3. MATLAB reads strings from tab- or comma-delimited files by recognizing the double quotes that delimit strings.

F 4. If you use `fopen(...)` to open an existing file and write to it, the original data in the file will be overwritten.

T 5. The function `fgets(fh)` does not always return a string.

Fill in the Blanks

1. In general, data files contain text that represents the _values_ of the data and control characters that specify the _organization_ of the data.

2. The MATLAB `xlsread(...)` function returns three results: the _numerical values_ in a(n) _double array,_ the _text data_ in a(n) _cell array,_ and _both string_ in a _cell array_. _and numerical data_

3. When using `dlmread(...)` to populate a(n) _numerical_, any unassigned values are _filled with_ _array_ _zero_

4. When using `fopen(...)`, the consequence of failure to open the file is _system dependent_ (-1 for PC)

Programming Projects

1. Write a script that performs the following operations:
   a. Set the value of variables `a`, `b`, `c1`, `c2`, `c3`, and `x`. The values don't matter, except you should set `c2` to `42`.
   b. Save the values of all the variable except `x` to `mydata.mat` using the save operation.
   c. Set the value of `c2` to `-99`.
   d. Load `myData.mat` and check that `c2` is now `42`.
   e. Clear all variables.
   f. Load `myData.mat` again and note that the variable `x` is not present.

2. One requirement for all freshmen classes is an issue of a `'Standing'` during the middle of the term. The results are either Satisfactory `(s)` or Unsatisfactory `(u)`. Since you are the office employee in charge of issuing these grades, you decide to write a function called `midtermGrades` to help yourself. You discover that the grades are on a spreadsheet organized like this:

   * Each student is represented by one row on the spreadsheet.
   * Unfortunately, since these sheets are created by different instructors, they are not necessarily consistent in their layout.
   * The first row will contain the following six strings in any order:

     `'name'`, `'math'`, `'science'`, `'english'`, `'history'`, and `'cs'`.

   * Under the name column will be a string with the student's name.
   * Grades in the other columns can be `'A'`, `'B'`, `'C'`, `'D'`, `'F'`, or `'W'`.
   * A student's grade is `'s'` if there are more A's, B's and C's than not.

   Your function should print out grades ready to be entered consisting of a table with headings `'Name'` and `'S/U'`

3. Write a function called `genstats` that will compute statistics for a set of class grades. The grades will be stored in a spreadsheet, and your function will compute statistics and then write the grades along with the statistics to another spreadsheet.

You may assume that the initial spreadsheet will have a format similar too:

Student Name	Exam1	Exam2	Exam3	...
student 1	100	76	45	...
student 2	34	83	89	...

The first row is the header row, and the first column is the list of student names. There may be any number of exam grades, and there may be any number of students. Although, you may assume that there will be at least one student and that there will be at least one exam.

Also, every student will have a grade for every exam.

Your function should only have one input (a string containing the file name of the grades file) and no outputs. You must write your function to perform the following steps:

a. Calculate the average grade of each student (across the rows) and store it in a new column called 'Average' (to the right of the last exam grade).

b. Calculate the deviation of each student's overall average (calculated in step a) from the maximum student average and store it in a new column called 'Deviation' (to the right of the 'Average' column). Note that deviation is just the difference between the maximum student average and a student's overall average.

c. Calculate the average of each column's data (each exam), the averages calculated in step a, and the deviations calculated in step b, then store these averages below the last row of the original data and name that row 'Total Average'.

d. Write the original data along with all of the new data to a file named 'Stats_<name_of_original_file>' (so if the inputted file name was 'Student_Grades.csv', the new data would be written to the file named 'Stats_Student_Grades.csv').

e. Construct a spreadsheet with suitable test data and use it to test your function.

4. Write a function called replaceStr. Your function should take in the following order:

filename: A string that corresponds to the name of a file

wordA: A string that is a word (contains no spaces)

wordB: Another string that is also a word (contains no spaces)

Your function should do the following:

a. Read the file a line at a time.

b. On each line, replace every occurrence of wordA with wordB.

    c. Write the modified text file with the same name as the original file, but preprended with `'new_'`. For instance, if the input filename was `'data.txt'`, the output filename would be `'new_data.txt'`.

    d. Prepare a test file by downloading a text file from the Internet. For example, the complete works of Shakespeare are accessible at http://www.william-shakespeare.info

    e. Examine the file for repeated words, and test your function by writing a script that replaces frequently repeated words.

Recursion

Chapter Objectives

This chapter discusses the following basic ideas of recursive programming:

- Three basic characteristics must be present for a recursive function to work

- Exceptions are a powerful mechanism for detecting and trapping errors

- A wrapper function is used to set up the recursion

- Other forms of recursion occur in special circumstances

Introduction

Recursion is an alternative technique by which a code block can be repeated in a controlled manner. In Chapter 4, we saw repetition achieved by inserting control statements in the code (either `for` or `while`) to determine how many times a code block would be repeated. Recursion uses the basic mechanism for invoking functions to manage the repetition of a block of code.

While some problems are naturally solved by iterative solutions, there are many problems for which a recursive solution is elegant and easily understood. Frequently, a recursive function needs a "wrapper function" to set up the recursion correctly, and to check for erroneous initial conditions that might cause errors. The actual recursive function then becomes a private helper function.

9.1 Concept: The Activation Stack

In order to understand recursive programming, we must look deeper into the mechanism by which function calls are mechanized. Calling any function depends on a special kind of data structure built into the architecture of the central processing unit (CPU). This is called the **activation stack.** It enables the CPU to determine which functions are active or suspended awaiting the completion of other function calls. To understand the activation stack, first we consider the basic concept of a stack.

9.1.1 A Stack

A stack is one of the fundamental data structures of computer science. It is best modeled by considering the trays at the front of the cafeteria line. You cannot see how many trays there are on the stack, and the only access you have to them is to take a tray off the stack or put one on. So a stack is a collection of objects of arbitrary size with a restricted number of operations we are allowed to perform on that collection (see Figure 9.1). Unlike a vector, where it is permissible to read, add, or remove items anywhere in the collection, we are only allowed the following operations with a stack:

- Push an object onto the stack
- Pop an object off the stack
- Peek at the top object without removing it
- Check whether the stack is empty

9.1.2 Activation Stack

The core concept that enables any function (especially a recursive function) to operate is the concept of an activation stack. The activation stack is the means by which the operating system allocates memory to functions for

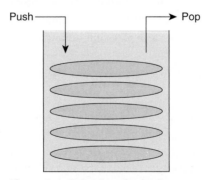

Figure 9.1 *Behavior of a stack*

local storage. Typically, local storage is required by a function for the following reasons:

- Storing the location in memory to which control must be returned when the function execution completes
- Storing copies of the function parameter values
- Providing space for the values of any local variables defined within the function

When MATLAB is initializing, the operating system allocates a block of memory to contain its activation stack and allocates the first item (usually called a "frame") on the activation stack to store variables defined in the Command window and by scripts. An astute reader might recognize this as the initial workspace for the system. When the user starts a script or makes an entry in the Command window, any variables created are stored in that **stack frame**. When that application calls a function, a new stack frame is allocated and "pushed" onto the activation stack. The calling program is then suspended, actual parameters are copied to formal parameters in the new workspace and control is passed to the function. Any new variables created are stored in its stack frame. When that function completes, its frame is popped off the stack and destroyed, and control is returned to the frame beneath, which is now the top of the stack. If an active function calls another function, this process is repeated. The calling function is suspended, a stack frame is pushed onto the activation stack for the new function, and the original function is suspended until the new function completes.

Technical Insight 9.1

In most computer languages, user programs and functions are compiled before they can be run. Part of that compilation process is defining the variable names and data types. This allows the system processes to compute the exact size of each stack frame before the program begins to run. Since the MATLAB language is interpreted and interactive, this information is not available. Consequently, every stack frame must be dynamically sized to allow for the "surprises" inherent in this style of programming.

9.1.3 Function Instances

In Chapter 2 we discussed the difference between the type of data defined by its class and an object—an instance of that class assigned to a variable. In the same way, we draw the distinction between the .m file that defines the behavior of a function and the instance(s) of that function that results when the function is called. Each new instance of a function has its own workspace that occupies a temporary stack frame allocated from the activation stack.

9.2 Recursion Defined

Following the previous line of reasoning, in principle there is no reason why a function could not in fact "call itself," and this is the logical basis for recursive programming. Of course, as with iterative programming, if there is no mechanism to stop the recursion, the process would repeat endlessly. In the case of endless recursion, since space is being consumed on the activation stack, the system will eventually terminate the process when the memory originally allocated for the activation stack is exhausted.

The canonical illustration of recursion is the computation of n factorial. We could view the calculation of `5!` in the following ways:

```
5! = 5 × 4 × 3 × 2 × 1
5! = 5 × 4!
```

The second representation is the recursive view, which warrants a closer examination as follows:

```
n! = n × (n-1)!
```

This definition would not be complete, however, without realizing that it must stop somewhere. In the original definition above, we did not continue the chain of multiplication with " `*` `0` `*` `(-1)` `*` `(-2)` `...`" for obvious reasons—multiplying by 0 makes all factorial values 0! Mathematically, we "artificially" define the terminating condition for the factorial calculation as the state where `0!` `=` `1`.

We can derive from this example the three necessary characteristics of a recursive function:

1. There must be a terminating condition to stop the process
2. The function must call a *clone* of itself
3. The parameters to that call must move the function toward the terminating condition

The word *clone* is important here—a recursive function really does not "call itself," because it requests a new stack frame and passes different parameters to the instance of the function that occupies the new frame.

 ## 9.3 Implementing a Recursive Function

Template 9.1 shows the general template for recursive functions. The following general guidelines indicate how the recursive template is implemented:

■ The `<function_name>`, like the name of any other function, may be any legal variable name

■ The variable `<result>` may be any legal variable name or a vector of variable names

■ As usual with functions, you should supply at least one line of `<documentation>` to define its purpose and implementation

Template 9.1 General template for a recursive function

```
function <result> = <function_name> (<formal_params>)
<documentation>
  if <terminating condition 1>
     <result> = <initial value 1>
  elseif <terminating condition 2>
     <result> = <initial value 2>
       ...
  else
     <result> = <operation> ...
           (<formal_params>, ...
             <function_name> (<new_params>))
  end
```

- Each exit from the function must assign values to all the result variables
- The first design decision is to determine the condition(s) under which the recursive process should stop, and how to express this as the `<terminating condition N>` tests
- The `<initial value N>` entries are the value(s) of the result(s) at the terminating condition(s)
- The second design decision is to determine the `<operation>`—the specific mathematical or logical operation that must be performed to combine the current formal parameters with the result of the recursive call to create a new value of the `<result>`
- The last design decision is to determine how to compute the `<actual_params>` of the recursive call to ensure that the process moves toward at least one of the `<terminating condition N>` states

The implementation of the factorial function is shown in Listing 9.1.

In Listing 9.1:

Before Line 2, we show a diagnostic print call that, if not commented, enables you to observe the sequence of events.

Line 2: The terminating condition.

Listing 9.1 Function to compute N factorial

```
1. function result = fact(N)
   % recursive computation of N!
   % fprintf('fact( %d )\n', N); % testing only
2.     if N == 0
3.          result = 1;
4.     else
5.          result = N * fact(N - 1);
6. end
7.     end
```

Exercise 9.1 Analyzing recursive behavior

1. Create the `fact(...)` function from Listing 9.1, remove the first '%' from Line 3 to enable the printout, and run it from the Command window:

   ```
   >> fact(4)
   fact( 4 )
   fact( 3 )
   fact( 2 )
   fact( 1 )
   fact( 0 )
   ans =
        24
   ```

2. Put a break point at Line 4 and run `fact(2)`. The function should pause in the first stack frame. Notice that the only variable in the workspace is N with a value 2.

3. Find the "step into" button and click it. Since N is not 0, the arrow should move to Line 7.

4. Click again, and the workspace should change to a new workspace with the value N = 1— you just called a clone of the original function with its own stack frame. There should be a second, transparent arrow at Line 7 to indicate that some clone of this function is waiting at that point for a result.

5. Continue stepping into functions until you return from the copy where N = 0. When this return happens, you return to the frame with N = 1, the frame "underneath," at Line 7, and are then able to compute the first result.

6. Further stepping will return from each stack frame until you finally return to your script's workspace with the final answer.

Line 5: The result at termination.

Line 7: Calls a clone of the function, which moves closer to termination by reducing N and computing the result.

Exercise 9.1 provides an analysis of recursive behavior. In particular, notice that all the mathematical operations are performed as the activation stack "unwinds."

9.4 Exceptions

We digress here to discuss how programs deal with unexpected circumstances. Exceptions are a powerful tool for gracefully managing run-time errors caused by programming errors or bad data. The general need for an exception mechanism might best be established by way of an example.

Suppose you write a program that requests some data from a user and then launches a significant number of nested function calls—perhaps even a recursive function—to perform an analysis on the data received. Somewhere in the depths of these function calls, the program divides something by a value, but in this instance that value is zero. The cause of this problem is probably bad data entered by the user in the top-level script. However, the effect is discovered deep in the activation stack in the middle of some obscure numerical computation.

9.4.1 Historical Approaches

Early programming languages attempted to deal with this problem in one of two equally unpleasant ways:

- Some languages require any mathematical function that might produce an error to return the status of that calculation to the calling function. They allow errors to be reported and processed, but they have two unpleasant consequences: using up the ability of a function to return a value and calling this function, which means choosing between testing for errors and solving the problem locally and passing the error condition back to its calling function in the hope that somewhere the error will be dealt with.

- Perhaps worse than this are the languages that use a globally accessible variable, such as `ierror`, to report status. For example, if `ierror` were normally set to `0`, an error could be announced by setting its value to something other than `0` to indicate the nature of the failure. This frees the function from needing to return status, but it does not relieve the calling function of the need to check whether the `ierror` value is bad, or solving the problem, or elevating it. Furthermore, if an error does occur within a function, since it is now still returning a value, what value should it return if it is unable to complete its assigned calculation?

9.4.2 Generic Exception Implementation

By contrast, most modern programming languages provide an exception mechanism whereby if an error occurs, regardless of how deep in the activation stack, program implementation is immediately suspended in the current stack frame. The activation stack below this frame is then searched for the frame of a program that has "volunteered" to process this type of exception. When it is found, all the stack frames above this frame are removed from the stack and the code in the exception handling mechanism is activated. If no such frame is discovered, the overall program aborts with an error code.

The following mechanisms are necessary to implement the exception mechanism effectively:

- *Throwing an exception.* Whenever a problem occurs, the operating system must suspend operations at that point in the activation stack and go looking for a function equipped to handle the specific exception. If no such function is found, the program is terminated and an exception is shown to the user (in MATLAB, it is written in red in the Command window).
- *Catching an exception.* A function that is able to deal with a specific exception uses a `try ... catch` construct to identify the suspect code and resolve the problem. Between `try` and `catch`, the programmer puts a code block that contains activities that could throw exceptions. After the `catch` statement, there is a code block that should fix the problem.

Depending on the specific language implementation, the exception-catching mechanism usually offers facilities both for determining exactly where the exception occurred and for reconstructing the activation stack with all the variable values as they were at the time of the exception.

In the previous example, the general template for successfully interacting with the user is shown in Template 9.2. The successful Boolean flag will be set only if the data are processed without error. It does not matter how deep in the data processing code the error occurs—the user interface catches the error, reports it to the user, and prompts the user for better data.

For example, you might have noticed earlier that the input(...) function has a built-in `try ... catch` mechanism to deal with erroneous user input. If something is entered that cannot be parsed, rather than throw red ink in the Command window, the exception is caught and the prompt repeated for the user.

Template 9.2 General template for processing exceptions

```
successful = false
while <not successful>
    try
        <request data from the user>
        <process the data>
        successful = true
    catch
        <announce the error to the user>
    end
end
```

9.4.3 MATLAB Implementation

MATLAB implements a simplified version of the most general form of exception processing. The `try ... catch ... end` construct is fully supported. However, unlike some languages, the MATLAB language does not distinguish between the kinds of exception that can be thrown.

- All built-in functions throw exceptions when they discover error conditions—attempting to open a nonexistent file for reading, for example—and expect the programmer to catch these exceptions if they are recoverable.

- To throw an exception manually, the program calls the `error(...)` function that takes one parameter, a string defining the error. If the exception is not caught, the string provided is displayed in red to the user. If the exception is caught, that string is ignored.

- To handle an exception, a code block we suspect might throw an exception is placed between `try` and `catch` statements. If no error occurs in the code block, the `catch` statement is ignored. If an exception is thrown from that code block, however, execution is suspended at that point. No further processing is performed, no data are returned from functions, and the code in the closest `catch` block is executed up to the associated `end` statement. To determine the cause of the exception, you can use the `lasterror` function. It returns the textual information provided at the exception and a structure array describing the activation stack.

- In more complex situations where this function may not be able to actually handle the error, a further exception can be thrown from the `catch` block. This exception will escape from this `try ... catch` block and must be caught (if at all) by another function or script deeper in the activation stack.

Listing 9.2 illustrates a simple example. The objective is to have the user define a triangle by entering a vector of three sides and to calculate the angle between the first two sides. The `acosd(...)` function computes the inverse cosine of a ratio. If that ratio is greater than one, there is something seriously wrong with the triangle, and `acosd` returns a complex number. This script detects that the answer is complex and throws an exception.

In Listing 9.2:

> Lines 1 and 2: We will repeat the attempts to compute the angle of a triangle until successful.
>
> Line 3: Begins the suspect code.
>
> Line 8: Detects the problem with the data.

Listing 9.2 MATLAB script using exception processing

```
1. OK = false;
2. while ~OK
3.     try
4.         side = input('enter a triangle: ');
5.         a = side(1); b = side(2); c = side(3);
6.         cosC = (c^2 - a^2 - b^2)/(2 * a * b);
7.         angle = acosd(cosC);
8.         if imag(angle) ~= 0
9.             error('bad triangle')
10.        end
11.    catch
12.        disp('bad triangle - try again')
13.    end
14.    OK = true;
15. end
16. fprintf('the angle is %f\n', angle)
```

Line 9: Throws the exception. In this case, the exception occurs visibly in this script. However, the `try ... catch` behavior is the same if the exception occurs deep in a set of nested function calls.

Line 11: The end of the suspect code block and the beginning of the exception handler—in this case, it's a warning to the user that the data are bad.

Line 14: This line is reached only if the suspect code block executed correctly, in which case we can exit the `while` loop.

You have an opportunity to work with exception processing in Exercise 9.2.

Style Points 9.1

1. You should allow the exception-processing mechanism to simplify the structure of your code. Rather than attempting to detect every possible data error and return error condition, perhaps from deeply nested function calls, allow the exception mechanism to return control directly to the code that can deal with the problem.

2. Exception processing is for processing events that occur outside the normal thread of execution. It may be tempting at times to use the exception mechanism as a clever means of changing the normal flow of program control, but resist that temptation. It produces ugly, untraceable code and should be avoided.

Exercise 9.2 Processing exceptions

Put the code from Listing 9.2 in a script and execute it, using the following data:

```
enter a triangle: [3 4 8]
bad triangle - try again
enter a triangle: [3 4 6]
the angle is 62.720387
```

Then, edit the script to remove the `try` statement and the `catch` block and repeat the test.

9.5 Wrapper Functions

Consider the factorial function again for a moment—specifically, ask how you would deal with a user who accidentally called for the factorial of a negative number or of a number containing a fractional part. Our original recursive `fact(...)` function is not protected from these programmer errors. There are three possible strategies for dealing with this situation:

1. *The legalist approach* ignores the bad values, lets the user's program die, and then responds to user complaints by pointing out that the documentation clearly indicates that you should not call for the factorial of a negative number. Usually this is not the best approach from the customer relations viewpoint or from the technical support effort viewpoint, especially since recursive code that hangs up typically crashes with a stack overflow—not the easiest symptom to diagnose!

2. *In-line coding* builds into the code a test for N less than zero (or fractional) and throws an exception with a meaningful error message. Although this is an improvement over the first choice because it exits gracefully, the test is in a bad place. The function is recursive; therefore, the code for that test is repeated as many times as the function is called. While modern computers are fast enough that one would probably not notice the difference, in general this is a poor implementation that punishes those who are using the function correctly with the same test each time the recursive function is called.

3. *A wrapper function* is the best solution. A wrapper function is called once to perform any tests or setup that the recursion requires and then to call the recursive function as a helper to the main function call. While there is a small computational cost to using a wrapper, it is only executed once rather than each time the recursive function is called. Template 9.3 illustrates this idea.

The first function named `<function_name>` is actually the wrapper function with the return result, parameters, and documentation expected by the caller. It makes whatever tests are necessary to validate the input data, cleans it up if necessary, and calls the helper function named `<private_name>`.

Listing 9.3 is the implementation of the factorial function with protection from bad data.

In Listing 9.3:

Line 1: To the outside world, this is the function actually called. (Ugly secret: even if the name is not the same name as the file, the first function in the file is always executed first.)

Line 2: Checks for negative and fractional inputs.

Template 9.3 General template for a wrapper function

```
function <result> = <function_name> (<formal_params>)
<documentation>
        if <bad_condition>
            <throw exception>
        else
            <result> = <private_name> (<actual_params>)
        end

function <result> = <private_name> (<formal_params>)
<documentation>
    if <terminating condition 1>
        <result> = <initial value 1>
    elseif <terminating condition 2>
        <result> = <initial value 2>
    else
        <result> = <operation>
            (<formal_params>, ...
              <private_name> (<new_params>) )
    end
```

Listing 9.3 Wrapper implementation for the factorial function

```
 1. function result = fact(N)
      % computation of N!
 2.      if (N < 0) || ((N - floor(N)) > 0)
 3.          error('bad parameter for fact');
 4.      else
 5.          result = local_fact(N);
 6.      end
 7. end
 8. function result = local_fact(N)
      % recursive computation of N!
 9.      fprintf('fact( %d )\n', N);
10.      if N == 0
11.          result = 1;
12.      else
13.          result = N * local_fact(N - 1);
14. end
15.      end
```

Line 4: Throws an exception if the data are bad.

Line 6: Calls the recursive version if the data are valid.

Line 9: Definition of the recursive function. By convention, some MATLAB users tend to give the prefix `local_` to private functions like this, but this has no significance to the system.

Line 15: Calls the local recursive function—it is not necessary to go back to the wrapper by calling `fact(..)` here.

Exercise 9.3 gives you an opportunity to work with the protected factorial.

Exercise 9.3 Writing the protected factorial

Write the `fact(...)` function as shown in Listing 9.3, and test it in the Command window:

```
>> fact(-1)
??? Error using ==> fact
bad parameter for fact
>> fact(.5)
??? Error using ==> fact
bad parameter for fact
>> fact(4)
ans =
    24
```

 ## 9.6 Examples of Recursion

We conclude this chapter with three examples of recursive programming: detecting palindromes, computing the Fibonacci series of numbers, and finding zeros of a function. The examples are followed by a practical engineering example of the use of zero finding.

9.6.1 Detecting Palindromes

We might want to determine whether a word or phrase received as a string is a palindrome, that is, whether it is spelled the same forward and backward. Of course, you could accomplish this in one line with vector operations (think about it!) but that would not be a good recursive exercise. One could design a recursive function named `isPal(<string>)` as follows:

- The function `isPal(<string>)` terminates if the `<string>` has zero or one character, returning `true`.
- It also terminates if the first and last characters are not equal, returning `false`.
- Otherwise (first and last are equal), the function returns `isPal(<shorter string>)`, where the shorter string is obtained by removing the first and last characters of the original string.
- Clearly, since the string is always being shortened, the recursive solution is approaching the terminating condition.

The MATLAB implementation of the palindrome detector is shown in Listing 9.4.

In Listing 9.4:

> Line 3: The successful terminating condition is when the length of the string is under 2.

Listing 9.4 Recursive palindrome detector

```
1. function ans = isPal(str)
   % recursive palindrome detector
2.     if length(str) < 2
3.         ans = true;
4.     elseif str(1) ~= str(end)
5.         ans = false;
6.     else
7.         ans = isPal(str(2:end-1));
8.     end
9. end
```

Line 5: The failure condition is when the first and last characters do not match.

Line 8: To move toward termination, remove the first and last characters that have already been checked.

We should observe further that a serious student of palindromes might know that real palindromes contain spaces, punctuation marks, and uppercase and lowercase characters. We leave it as an exercise for you to write a wrapper function that cleans up strings containing these issues before passing the string to the recursive palindrome detector.

9.6.2 Fibonacci Series

The Fibonacci series was originally named for the Italian mathematician Leonardo Pisano Fibonacci, who was studying the growth of rabbit populations in the eleventh century. He hypothesized that rabbits mature one month after birth, after which time each pair would produce a new pair of rabbits each month. Starting with a pair of newborn rabbits free in a field, he wanted to calculate the rabbit population after a year. Figure 9.2 illustrates the calculation for the first six months, counting rabbit pairs. It

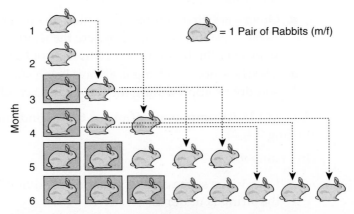

Figure 9.2 *Computing rabbit populations*

Technical Insight 9.2

Truthfulness requires pointing out that while computing the Fibonacci series recursively is a very nice, conceptually simple approach, it is a nightmare as far as the computational load on your processor. Do not try to compute beyond about 27 numbers in the series. An iterative solution, while less elegant, runs in linear time rather than exponential.

soon becomes clear that the number of rabbits in month N comprises the number in month N-1 (since in this ideal example, none of them die) plus the new rabbits born to the mature pairs (shown in boxes in the figure). Since the rabbits mature after a month, the number of mature pairs that produce a new pair is the number of rabbits in the month before, N-2. So the algorithm for computing the population of pairs after N months, fib(N), is recursive:

- There is a terminating condition: when N = 1 or N = 2, the answer is 1
- The recursive condition is: `fib(N) = fib(N-1) + fib(N-2)`
- The solution is moving toward the terminating condition, since as long as N is a positive integer, computing N-1 and N-2 will move toward 1 or 2.

The implementation of the Fibonacci function is shown in Listing 9.5.

The algorithm produces the Fibonacci series: 1, 1, 2, 3, 5, 8, 13, 21, 34, 55, 89, 144, 233, . . ., giving a population after a year of 144.

A closely related phenomenon is the golden ratio or golden number computed as the limit of the ratio of successive Fibonacci series values—approximately 1.618034—that has been found to occur in nature. To the surprise of naturalists, this series of numbers occurs in nature in a remarkable number of circumstances. Consider Figure 9.3 for example, where a set of squares placed side by side in a rotating sequence is drawn using the Fibonacci series for the size of each square. The resulting geometric figure is a close approximation to the logarithmic spiral so frequently found in nature, such as the nautilus shell pictured in the figure.

9.6.3 Zeros of a Function

Frequently we need to solve nonlinear equations by seeking the values of the independent variable that produced a zero result. There are a number of well-known numerical techniques for achieving this goal. We will examine

Listing 9.5 The Fibonacci function

```
1. function result = fib(N)
     % recursive computation the Nth Fibonacci number
2.     if N == 1 || N == 2
3.         result = 1;
4.     else
5.         result = fib(N-1) + fib(N-2);
6.     end
7. end
```

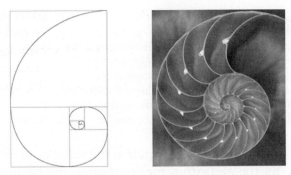

Figure 9.3 *Fibonacci in nature*

a recursive approach to determining the zeros of functions. However, especially when there are multiple zero crossings, it is very helpful to have a good initial estimate of the location(s) of the crossing(s). As an example, consider a function $f(x)$. We will use the function given by:

$$f(x) = 0.0333x^6 - 0.3x^5 - 1.3333x^4 + 16x^3 - 187.2x + 172.9$$

as plotted in Figure 9.4. However, this algorithm will work for any function of x. We assume that the continuous line describes the exact function, and the plus marks indicate locations for which we have measurements. Clearly, there are a number of zero crossings of this function, including a very messy looking crossing at around = 6.

We will find the exact value of one of the zeros of this function by first estimating the zero crossings and then by using a recursive technique for refining a better estimate to arbitrary levels of accuracy.

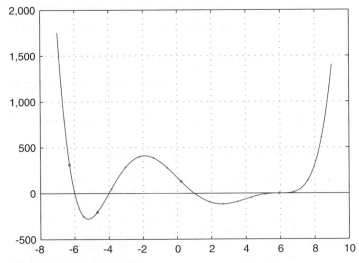

Figure 9.4 *A function f(x)*

Estimating Critical Points of a Function First, we need to compute an approximation to the roots of this equation. These approximations will be found by finding the x values at which adjacent values of the function change sign. The technique for determining where adjacent points change sign is simply to multiply adjacent values of $f(x)$ and find where that product is not positive, as shown in Listing 9.6.

In Listing 9.6:

> Line 1: Establishes samples of x.
>
> Line 2: Computes $y = f(x)$.
>
> Line 3: Detects the indices where the zero crossings occur by shifting y to the right by one and by shortening the original by one to keep the vector size equal.
>
> Lines 4 and 5: Display the zero crossing estimates.
>
> Line 6: Calls the recursive function to find the third zero crossing that estimates one root of this equation. Clearly, one could iterate here to find all of the roots.

Listing 9.6 produces the following results, which can be verified by observing the circled data points shown in Figure 9.4:

```
zeros occur just after
ans =
   -6.3000    -4.6667    0.2333    5.9500
```

Having observed these results, we decide to compute the exact value of the first positive root, occurring at the third crossing.

Recursive Refinement of the Estimate The recursive function to find the third root of $f(x)$ works on the principle of binary division. It consumes a vector of adjacent values of x that are guaranteed to have values of `f(x)` of opposite sign. The fundamental features of the recursive solution are as follows:

- The terminating condition is when the two x values are within acceptable error—in this case, 0.001
- Otherwise, we find the middle of this x range, `mx`, find its `f(mx)`, and then make the recursive call either with `[x(1) mx]` or `[mx x(2)]`, depending on the sign of `f(mx) × f(x(1))`
- This will always converge because each recursive call halves the distance between the x limits.

Listing 9.6 Initial zero crossings

```
1. px = linspace(-6.3, 8.4, 19);
2. py = f(px);
3. zeros = find(py(1:end-1) .* py(2:end) <= 0)
4. disp('zeros occur just after')
5. px(zeros)
6. root = findZero([px(zeros(3)) px(zeros(3)+1)])
```

Listing 9.7 Recursive root finding

```
 1. function pt = findZero(x)
    % x is a lower-upper pair guaranteed to have
    % y values of opposite sign
    % return the x coordinate of the root
 2.      if abs(x(1)-x(2)) < .001
 3.           pt = x(1);
 4.      else
 5.           mx = sum(x)/2;
 6.           my = f(mx);
 7.           if my*f(x(1)) <= 0
 8.                pt = findZero([x(1) mx]);
 9.           else
10.                pt = findZero([mx x(2)]);
11.           end
12.      end
13. end
```

In general, this method is a little slower than Newton's method, which uses the slope of $f(x)$ to compute the next estimate. However, it is very strong and somewhat immune from the instability suffered by Newton's method on undulating data. The function that solves this problem is shown in Listing 9.7.

In Listing 9.7:

> Line 1: The function consumes a pair of x limits and produces the x root.
>
> Lines 2–4: Check for the terminating condition and return the x root.
>
> Lines 5 and 6: Calculate the x and y values of the midpoint of the x range.
>
> Line 7: Checks the sign of the y value of the midpoint.
>
> Line 8: If different from the sign at first limit, it makes the recursive call with the first limit and the midpoint.
>
> Lines 9 and 10: Otherwise, it uses the range from the midpoint to the second limit.

This function computes the correct crossing at $x = 1.00$.

9.7 Engineering Example—Robot Arm Motion

Here we consider the problem of programming the arm of a robot to move in a straight line. Consider the arm shown in Figure 9.5. It consists of two jointed limbs of length r_1 and r_2 at angles α and β, respectively, to the horizontal.

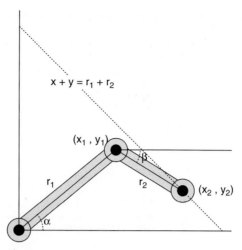

Figure 9.5 *The robot arm problem*

Overall Objective

The ultimate challenge of this situation is to calculate the sequence of values of α and β that will guide the end of the arm along the straight line:

$$x + y = r_1 + r_2 \tag{1}$$

However, this complete problem is more complex than necessary for this point in the text. First, we will address a necessary component of the problem.

Immediate Objective

The sub-problem we address here is to determine for a given value of α, the value β that will place the end of the arm at some place on the line. The algebra and trigonometry of this problem are quite simple. The position of the end of the arm, $[x_2\ y_2]$, is expressed as:

$$x_2 = r_1 \cos \alpha + r_2 \cos \beta \tag{2}$$
$$y_2 = r_1 \sin \alpha + r_2 \sin \beta \tag{3}$$

Combining these two relationships with Equation (1) gives the equation for $F(\beta)$, the difference between the end point derived from β and the straight line. We need to solve this for $F(\beta) = 0$:

$$F(\beta) = r_1 \cos \alpha + r_2 \cos \beta + r_1 \sin \alpha + r_2 \sin \beta - (r_1 + r_2) \tag{4}$$

If we are given values for r_1, r_2, and the angle α, we will use the method of Section 9.6.3 to find the value(s) of α that satisfies this equation. By inspecting Figure 9.5, we might expect two answers—one with a small negative value and one "bending backward" at an angle greater than 90°.

Figure 9.6 shows a plot of this function for $r_1 = 4$, $r_2 = 3$, and $\alpha = 30°$. The zero crossings of this function confirm our intuition that there are two values

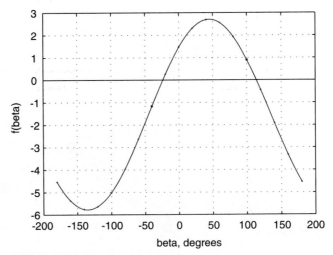

Figure 9.6 *The relationship between β and the value of F(β)*

of α that satisfy the equation for small, positive values of β: one around −30° and one around 110°.

The Solution to the Sub-problem
As before, since there is no analytical solution to this function, we will find the approximate location of the zero crossings and then use a recursive function to find the exact roots. The script that accomplishes this is shown in Listing 9.8.

In Listing 9.8:

> Lines 1–6: Establish the parameters of the problem as `global` variables to avoid the overhead cost of passing them into recursive functions.

Listing 9.8 Finding arm position

```
 1. global r1
 2. r1 = 4
 3. global r2
 4. r2 = 3
 5. global alpha
 6. alpha = pi/6 % 30 deg
 7. beta = linspace(-pi, pi, 19);
 8. pf = fab(beta);
 9. zeros = find(pf(1:end-1) .* pf(2:end) <= 0)
10. disp('zeros occur just after')
11. beta(zeros)
    %
12. zero = findZeroAB([beta(zeros(1)) ...
13.         beta(zeros(1)+1)])
```

Lines 7 and 8: Sample the possible range of β values with enough values to identify the zero crossings, and compute the corresponding values of F(β).

Lines 9–11: Estimate the zero locations by multiplying adjacent function values and display the results.

Line 12: Calls the recursive function to find the zero crossing.

Running this script produces the following:

```
r1 =
     4
r2 =
     3
alpha =
     0.5236
zeros =
     8 15
zeros occur just after
ans =
   -0.6981 1.7453
zero =
   -0.4152 -0.0009
```

The function for which we are seeking the zero is shown in Listing 9.9.

In Listing 9.9:

Lines 2–4: Gain access to the global parameters.

Lines 5–6: Compute the left-hand side of Equation (4).

The function that finds the zero crossings of `fab(beta)` is shown in Listing 9.10.

In Listing 9.10:

Line 2: Computes the y values corresponding to the x limits.

Lines 3 and 4: Check the terminating condition and return the `[x y]` coordinates of the result.

Lines 6 and 7: Find the x and y values of the midpoint.

Lines 8 and 9: If the midpoint is on the opposite side of the x-axis from the lower limit, make a recursive call using these limits.

Listing 9.9 Function for zeros

```
1. function res = fab(beta)
   % f(beta) = r1 (cos(alpha) + sin(alpha) - 1)
   %           + r2 (cos(beta) + sin(beta) - 1)
2. global r1
3. global r2
4. global alpha
5. res = r1 * (cos(alpha) + sin(alpha) - 1) ...
6.       + r2 * (cos(beta) + sin(beta) - 1);
```

Listing 9.10 Recursive zero finder

```
1. function pt = findZeroAB(x)
   % x is a lower-upper pair guaranteed to have
   % y values of opposite sign
2.     y = fab(x);
3.     if abs(x(1)-x(2)) < .001
4.         pt = [x(1) y(1)];
5.     else
6.         mx = sum(x)/2;
7.         my = fab(mx);
8.         if my*y(1) < 0
9.             pt = findZeroAB([x(1) mx]);
10.        else
11.            pt = findZeroAB([mx x(2)]);
12.        end
13.    end
14. end
```

Line 11: Otherwise, makes the recursive call using the midpoint and the upper limit.

Reflection

A modest amount of code is all that is required to create an elegant solution to a nontrivial problem. The structure of the recursive function shown in Listing 9.8 clearly reflects the standard recursive template, and that function can be used to find zeros of any continuous function defined in `fab(x)`.

 Chapter Summary

This chapter discussed the three basic principles of recursive programming that must be present for a recursive program to succeed:

- There must be a terminating condition
- The function must call a clone of itself
- The parameters of that clone must move the function toward the terminating condition

We have also seen some other important capabilities as follows:

- Exceptions are declared either within system functions or by the user using the `error(...)` function; they are trapped and perhaps remedied using `try ... catch` code blocks
- A wrapper function is used to set up a recursive solution by validating the incoming data

Special Characters, Reserved Words, and Functions

Special Characters, Reserved Words, and Functions	Description	Discussed in This Section
catch	End of a suspect code block where the exception is trapped	9.4.3
error(str)	Announces an error with the string provided	9.4.3
global <var>	Defines the variable <var> as globally accessible	9.1
lasterror	Provides a structure describing the environment from which the last exception was thrown	9.4.3
try	Begins a block of suspect code from which an exception might be thrown	9.4.3

Self Test

Use the following questions to check your understanding of the material in this chapter:

True or False

T 1. We limit the functionality of a stack in order to protect the data from corruption.

F 2. The only way to remove a stack frame from the activation stack is to exit from the function instance hosted by that frame.

F 3. All the math operations in a recursive function are performed as the activation stack unwinds.

T 4. Exception processing can be used as a clever means of changing the normal flow of program control.

F 5. The name of the first function in a function definition m-file must match the name of the file.

Fill in the Blanks

1. Recursion is ___an alternative technique___ by which a code block can be repeated in a controlled manner.

2. Very frequently, a recursive function needs a(n) ___wrapper function___ to set up the recursion correctly and to ___check for erraneous data___

3. Exceptions are a powerful tool for managing ___runtime errors___ caused by either ___programming___ or ___bad data___ .
   ___errors___

4. A wrapper function is called once to perform _any tests or setup_ that the recursion requires, and then to call the recursive function _as a helper to the main function call_

5. You can _compute_ one of the zeros of a function by first _estimating the answer_, and then using a(n) _recursive function_ for refining a better estimate to arbitrary levels of accuracy.

Programming Projects

1. For this problem, you will be required to write three functions: `recurSum`, `recurProd`, and `fibVector`. The first one will take in a vector and compute the sum of the elements of the vector. The second one will take in a vector and compute the product of the elements of the vector. The third one will take in a number, N, and return a vector containing the first N terms of the Fibonacci sequence. You must use recursion to complete these functions. You may not use `for` loops, `while` loops or the functions `sum`, `prod`, or `factorial`. Your function headers should be:

```
function ans = recurSum(arr)
function ans = recurProd(arr)
function vec = fibVector (num)
```

2. Write a recursive function called oddfact(n) that takes in a number and returns the factorial of the odd numbers between the given number and 1.

For example:

```
oddfact(4) returns 3
oddfact(9) returns 945 = 9*7*5*3*1
```

3. Consider the problem of structures with nested fields.
   a. Write a function called `tracker` that takes in a structure and returns the number of levels at which it has a field called `'Inner'`. Each of these fields can also be structures having a field called `'Inner'`, but at each level there can be only one field called `'Inner'`. The innermost structure will not contain a field called `'Inner'`. You must use recursion. Hint: use the `isfield(...)` function. Your function header should be:

```
function num = tracker(astruct)
```

   b. Create a structure with at least three levels of recurring fields, and use it to test your tracker function.

4. Create a recursive function with a wrapper to protect it from illegal values. The function name should be `recursiveFib`. It should take in

a number `n` and return the nth Fibonacci number. You should ensure that `n` is a non-negative integer, and announce an error if that is not the case.

Fibonacci numbers are defined as:

```
F(n) = 0                    if n = 0
F(n) = 1                    if n = 1
F(n) = F(n-1) + F(n-2)      otherwise.
```

This produces the following sequence of numbers:

```
0, 1, 1, 2, 3, 5, 8, 13, 21, 34, 55...
```

For example:

```
a = recursiveFib(0) should return 0
b = recursiveFib(1) should return 1
c = recursiveFib(-1) should cause an error
d = recursiveFib(8) should return 21
```

5. Create and test a function called `recursiveMin` that takes in a vector and returns the element with the minimum value and the index of that element as separate returned values, much as the standard `min(...)` function. If the input vector is of length zero, your function should return two empty vectors. If the input vector contains two minimum elements of equal value, your function should return the index of the first element. Create suitable test cases and use the built-in function `min(...)` only to test your answers.

For example:

```
[m n] = recursiveMin([]) should return [] and []
[m n] = recursiveMin([5]) should return 5 and 1
[m n] = recursiveMin([5 2]) should return 2 and 2
[m n] = recursiveMin([2 5 2]) should return 2 and 1
[m n] = recursiveMin([2 5 2 1 6 7]) should return 1 and 4
```

Principles of Problem Solving

Chapter Objectives

This chapter presents an overview of framing the solutions to problems:

- We begin with simple problems that can be solved in a single step

- We continue to strategies for solving more complex problems involving data collections by dividing the solution into the following fundamental operations that can be performed on any collection of data:
  - Inserting
  - Traversing
  - Building
  - Mapping
  - Filtering
  - Summarizing
  - Searching
  - Sorting

Then we will briefly discuss how to combine these fundamental tools to solve more complex data manipulation problems.

Introduction

Programming is really all about applying the computer as a tool to solve problems. One of the most difficult tasks facing novice programmers is the blank sheet of paper. Faced with a problem you have never seen before, how do you start to solve it? The problem-solving style recommended in this text is first to identify the basic character of the data and the basic operation(s) we are asked to perform. If these two ideas are clear, we can create a template or outline of the solution and begin to fill in the blanks.

As we gain more experience with the language, we have more computing tools to apply, and we can attack larger, more complex problems. We now have sufficient tools available to consider a more principled approach to data manipulation and problem solving. We will begin with the typical plan for solving simple problems in one step and then continue to consider assembling multiple steps to solve more complex problems.

10.1 Solving Simple Problems

In Chapter 2 we saw the basic plan for solving simple problems:

- Define the input data
- Define the output data
- Discover the underlying equations to solve the problem
- Implement the solution
- Test the results
- Repair the code until it conforms to the specifications

This plan works whenever the problem is simple enough to be able to visualize the complete solution. Typically, however, problems are more complex and require a number of steps to be assembled.

10.2 Assembling Solution Steps

Problem complexity frequently comes in the form of data collections that need to be transformed into other collections or summarized as intermediate results. Identifying the operation(s) that will create the output from the input requires some experience. The rest of this chapter provides some guidelines for identifying elementary steps whose solutions can be combined to create solutions to many complex problems.

10.3 Summary of Operations

First, we document the operations we expect to be able to perform on collections. Table 10.1 lists the generic operations, a brief description of each, and a discussion of the consequences. The following paragraphs illustrate these fundamental operations, using the array of structures from Chapter 7 as examples. The discussion of each step takes the form of a written description, a flowchart, and a template for writing the code.

> **Style Points 10.1**
>
> It is conceivable—and in fact, a common practice—to combine multiple operations into one computing module, but it is poor abstraction and leads to code that is hard to understand and/or debug.

Table 10.1 Taxonomy of solution steps

Operation	Description	Consequence
Insert	Inserts one item into a collection	Collection with one more item
Build	Creates a collection from a data source (external file or traversing another collection); usually accomplished by starting with an empty collection and inserting one item at a time	A new collection of data
Traverse	Touches each item of data in the collection—frequently used to display or copy a collection	The collection is unchanged
Map	Changes the content of some or all of the items in the collection	A new collection of the same length, but the content of some or all items is changed
Filter	Removes some items from the collection	A new collection with reduced length, but the content of the items remains unchanged
Fold	Traverses the collection, summarizing the contents with a single result (e.g., sum, max, or mean)	A single result summarizing the collection in some way; the collection is unchanged
Search	Traverses the collection until an item matches a given search criterion and then stops, returning the result	A single result or the indication that the desired match was not achieved; the collection is unchanged
Sort	Puts the collection in order by some specific criterion	A new collection of the same length

10.3.1 Basic Arithmetic Operations

The simple problem solution described in Section 10.1 frequently needs to be used as part of a larger problem solution. We include this activity in this list for completeness.

10.3.2 Inserting into a Collection

Inserting an item into a collection is a process usually used to build or maintain a collection of information. In this text, we have seen four basic data collection types to which insertion applies: vectors, arrays, cell arrays, and structure arrays. We will discuss the peculiarities of each collection and then the common processing algorithm that can be used to insert a new entry into the collection.

- **Vectors** are very flexible collections in the MATLAB language, and suffer only from the obvious limitation that one can add only numbers to a vector

- **Arrays** are as flexible as vectors, except that they require that new data be inserted a row or column at a time, and that the size of the new item must match the existing array dimensions
- **Cell arrays** can be indexed like numerical arrays and can contain any object; however, to compare one element to another usually requires a special-purpose comparison function
- **Structure arrays** as a collection behave like cell arrays, except that any structure inserted must have the same fields as those in the existing structure

In general, inserting into any of these collections involves insertion into the front of the collection, the back of the collection, or at some position in the middle in order to keep the collection in order by a specific comparison method.

Inserting into the front is accomplished by concatenating the new element before the existing collection. For example, adding `item` to the front of an existing cell array, `ca`, is accomplished as follows:

```
>> ca = [{item} ca] % note the braces needed for a cell array
```

Inserting at the back is accomplished by concatenating the new element after the existing collection. For example, adding `item` to the back of an existing cell array, `ca`, is accomplished as follows:

```
>> ca = [ca {item}] % note the braces needed for a cell array
```

Inserting in order is usually accomplished using a `while` loop. If we are inserting `item` into a collection `coll`, we will use a `while` loop to find the index of the insertion point, `ins`, and then concatenate the three parts of the new collection. Figure 10.1 shows the flowchart that applies here, and Template 10.1 shows the template for the general solution.

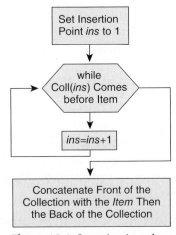

Figure 10.1 *Inserting in order*

> **Template 10.1** Template for inserting
>
> ```
> %inserting item into a collection coll
>
> <set insert point, ins, at the front>
> while <insertion point in coll and
>         item comes before coll(ins)>
>    <move insertion point forward>
> <end of the while loop>
> <concatenate coll before ins with item and
>       coll at and beyond ins>
> ```

For example, adding `item` in order to a vector, `v`, is accomplished as follows:

```
ins = 1;
while ins <= length(v) && before(item, v(ins))
      ins = ins + 1;
end
v = [v(1:ins-1) item v(ins:end)]
```

where `before(a,b)` is a generic comparator that determines whether `a` comes before `b` in the ordering scheme. Notice that this covers the cases where `item` must be the first or last item in the collection. Consequently, we could include the case of front or back insertion by having `before(a,b)` return `true` for inserting in the front and `false` for inserting at the back.

10.3.3 Traversing a Collection

Traversal involves moving across all elements of a collection and performing some step (not necessarily the same step) on each element without changing that element. Figure 10.2 and Template 10.2 illustrate the flowchart and basic template for traversing a collection. They assume that you are doing something like writing a file that needs to be initialized and finalized. These two steps may not always be required.

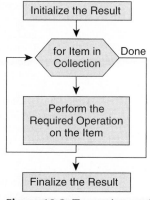

Figure 10.2 *Traversing a collection*

Template 10.2 Template for traversing

```
<initialize the result>
for item <across the whole collection>
    <operate on the item>
<end of the loop>
<finalize the result>
```

10.3.4 Building a Collection

In practice, frequently we combine traversal of one collection and building of another to copy data from one collection into another. Building a collection is the process of beginning with an empty collection and assembling data elements by inserting them one at a time into the new collection. The size of the collection increases continually until the process is finished. Figure 10.3 and Template 10.3 illustrate the algorithm for building a collection.

10.3.5 Mapping a Collection

The purpose of mapping is to transform a collection by changing the data in some or all of its elements according to some functional description without changing its length. It is distinct from traversal because its intent is to change

Template 10.3 Template for building

```
<initialize the new collection>
for item <across the data source>
    <extract the item>
    <insert item in new collection>
<end of the loop>
<finalize the new collection>
```

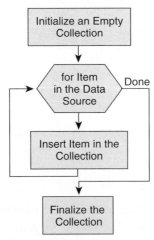

Figure 10.3 *Building a collection*

> **Template 10.4** Template for mapping
>
> ```
> <initialize the result>
> for item <across the whole collection>
>     <extract the item>
>     <modify the item>
>     <insert modified item in the result>
> <end of the loop>
> <finalize the result>
> ```

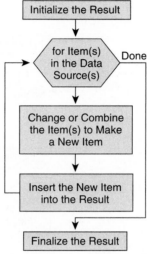

Figure 10.4 *Mapping a collection*

Style Points 10.2

A simpler example of collection building occurred when we built the CD collection initially by repeated calls to the makeCD method, as shown in Chapter 7 when we were inserting each item at the end of the collection. However, while that example seems to simplify the process of building the collection, it really did not. The data for the function calls had to be extracted from a CD listing and edited to construct the function calls—normally not an efficient or effective way to compose a collection. Such hard-wiring should generally be avoided.

the data elements. While many languages permit collections to be modified in place, the MATLAB language usually requires you to create a new collection. However, this is still considered mapping. The scalar mathematical and logical operations on vectors are good examples of mapping. Figure 10.4 and Template 10.4 illustrate the basic algorithm for mapping. As illustrated in the example of operations on vectors, mapping may involve combining two or more collections of the same length.

10.3.6 Filtering a Collection

Filtering involves removing items from a collection according to specified selection criteria. The data contents of the remaining items in the collection should not be changed, and the collection will usually be shorter than before.

Template 10.5 Template for filtering

```
<initialize the new collection>
for item <across the whole collection>
    <extract the item>
    if <keep the item>
        <insert item in new collection>
    <end if>
<end for>
<finalize the new collection>
```

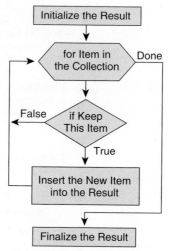

Figure 10.5 *Filtering a collection*

For example, we filter vectors by applying built-in logical operations and then indexing with the results to produce new, shorter arrays. Figure 10.5 and Template 10.5 illustrate the general algorithm for filtering a collection.

10.3.7 Summarizing a Collection

Folding is the name given to summarizing a collection. It is a special case of traversal where all of the items in the collection are summarized as a single result. The collection is not altered in size or values by the operation. Totaling, averaging, and finding the largest element in a vector are typical examples of folding. For example, we might want to find the CD with the best value in a collection. Figure 10.6 and Template 10.6 show the basic algorithm for folding a collection. The general form of a fold should be to initialize the summary value and then traverse the whole collection, updating the summary when necessary.

Template 10.6 Template for folding

```
<initialize the summary value>
for item <across the whole collection>
    <extract the item>
    <update the summary value>
<end for>
<finalize the summary value>
```

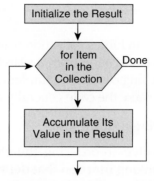

Figure 10.6 *Folding a collection*

10.3.8 Searching a Collection

Searching is the process of traversing the collection and applying a specified test to each element in turn, terminating the process as soon as the test is satisfied. This is superficially similar to filtering, except that it is not necessary to touch all the elements of the collection; the search stops as soon as one element of the collection matches the search criteria. If the criteria are extremely complex, it is sometimes advisable to perform a mapping or folding before the search is performed. Figure 10.7 and Template 10.7 illustrate one way to

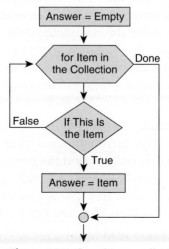

Figure 10.7 *Searching a collection*

Template 10.7 Template for searching

```
<initialize result to not succeeded>
for <item in the collection>
    if <found criteria>
        <set result to succeeded>
        <break the loop>
    <end if>
<end for>
<check for failure>
```

implement searching a collection using a `for` loop with a break exit. There are always two exit criteria from a search—finding what you seek and failing to find it. Searching can also be implemented with a `while` loop, but the multiple exit criteria make the code generally more complex.

10.3.9 Sorting a Collection

Sorting involves reordering the elements in a collection according to a specified ranking function that defines which item "comes before" another. Sorting is computationally expensive. However, if a large collection of data is stable—items are added or removed infrequently—but is frequently searched for specific items, keeping the data sorted can greatly improve the efficiency of the searches. Chapter 16 is devoted to the details of sorting algorithms, but the concept is included here to complete the list of operations we can perform on a collection.

10.4 Solving Larger Problems

Problem statements are rarely simple enough to be able to seize one of the above steps and solve the whole problem. Usually, the solution involves choosing a number of known operations and performing those operations in order to solve the complete problem. Solution steps are combined in one of two ways—in sequence or nested. When considering the overall strategy for solving a problem, one might identify steps A and B as contributing to the solution. Your logical statement might say either "do A and then B" sequential steps—or "for each part of A, do B"—nested steps.

For example, consider the baseball card problem originally proposed in Chapter 1. You have collected over the years a huge number of baseball cards, and you wish to find the names of the 10 "qualified" players with the highest lifetime batting average. To qualify, the players must have been in the league at least five years, had at least 100 plate appearances per year, and made less than 10 errors per year.

The first step is to build a collection containing the relevant information on the cards for each player, and the use of a structure array seems a good

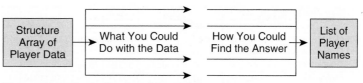

Figure 10.8 *Generalized problem solving*

choice. Next, we need to operate on this collection to solve the problem. Consider again the overall problem situation, as shown in Figure 10.8. The original data are the structure array containing all the player data. The final result is a list of 10 names of the qualified players with the highest batting averages. There may be more than one sequence of operations to solve this problem, and some may be more efficient than others.

First, we consider the operations that could be performed on the original data. Since the end result is a collection, it is unlikely that the first step would reduce the collection to one answer. This eliminates folding and searching. Since the collection is already built, we do not need to insert or build, leaving four possible operations to consider—traversal, mapping, filtering, and sorting.

Now, consider the last operation—it seems reasonable that the last thing to do is a mapping—taking the 10 selected structures and extracting the names.

Now, we must think about how to find these 10 structures. If we had a collection of qualified players sorted by their batting average, we could accomplish this with a special filter taking the first 10 from these sorted, qualified players. Backing up one more step, we can see that the sorted collection we need is just a sort of the qualified players, and we can chain these steps together to solve the whole problem.

10.5 Engineering Example—Processing Geopolitical Data

Imagine that you have decided to move your prosperous business overseas to the country with the most business-friendly environment. After considerable study, you decide that the best measure of friendliness would be to compute the rate of growth of the gross domestic product for candidate countries, subtract their rate of population growth, and use this measure to choose the best country. An Internet search provides an interesting source of data. Figure 10.9 shows an excerpt from a spreadsheet containing historical data for 154 countries from Penn World Table Version 6.1.[1] The data columns of interest to us contain the following information:

---

[1]Credit: Alan Heston, Robert Summers, and Bettina Aten, Penn World Table Version 6.1, Center for International Comparisons at the University of Pennsylvania (CICUP), October 2002.

	A	B	C	D	E	F	G	H	I	J	K	L	M	N	O	P
1	Country	Code	Year	POP	XRAT	PPP	cgdp	cc	ci	cg	P	pc	pg	pi	openc	cgnp
2	Angola	AGO	1960	4816.00	0.03	0.01	542.68	76.75	8.84	9.45	17.51	13.07	24.03	49.11	36.98	na
3	Angola	AGO	1961	4884.19	0.03	0.00	564.37	74.23	7.92	9.85	17.36	13.18	23.65	48.67	35.23	na
4	Angola	AGO	1962	4955.35	0.03	0.00	573.94	75.48	6.76	10.55	17.28	13.41	23.65	50.44	38.79	na
5	Angola	AGO	1963	5028.69	0.03	0.01	593.72	73.68	5.72	13.56	17.73	13.90	24.04	52.06	38.69	na
⋮	⋮	⋮	⋮	⋮	⋮	⋮	⋮	⋮	⋮	⋮	⋮	⋮	⋮	⋮	⋮	⋮
36	Angola	AGO	1994	10627.18	59.51	53.32	1095.94	34.66	9.09	46.75	89.59	70.34	76.84	228.63	160.87	47.86
37	Angola	AGO	1995	10972.00	2750.23	1007.53	1244.73	41.86	9.43	57.65	36.63	29.58	31.91	96.85	146.58	48.19
38	Angola	AGO	1996	11316.94	128029.20	54873.28	1362.32	37.17	8.57	56.75	42.86	34.35	37.77	113.51	134.87	52.97
39	Angola	AGO	1997	na	na	na	na	na	na	na	na	na	na	na	na	59.09
40	Angola	AGO	1998	na	na	na	na	na	na	na	na	na	na	na	na	50.08
41	Angola	AGO	1999	na	na	na	na	na	na	na	na	na	na	na	na	44.52
42	Angola	AGO	2000	na	na	na	na	na	na	na	na	na	na	na	na	53.81
43	Albania	ALB	1991	3277.00	15.63	3.13	1605.36	82.81	6.92	36.66	20.04	23.78	12.02	17.70	54.89	98.10
44	Albania	ALB	1992	3225.00	75.03	10.53	1566.99	136.94	5.11	35.08	14.03	15.59	7.88	14.42	108.94	95.94
45	Albania	ALB	1993	3179.00	102.06	19.33	2031.94	109.39	12.54	25.73	18.94	20.80	10.51	20.01	77.14	99.02
⋮	⋮	⋮	⋮	⋮	⋮	⋮	⋮	⋮	⋮	⋮	⋮	⋮	⋮	⋮	⋮	⋮
5795	Zambia	ZMB	1998	9665.71	1862.07	744.91	800.69	85.12	13.75	14.14	40.00	39.54	33.22	49.87	68.86	93.36
5796	Zambia	ZMB	1999	9881.21	2388.02	941.87	765.24	91.82	15.30	12.54	39.44	39.02	31.89	48.14	66.55	94.97
5797	Zambia	ZMB	2000	10089.00	3110.84	1157.63	840.97	86.33	15.38	12.34	37.21	37.70	29.54	40.65	70.45	95.88
5798	Zimbabwe	ZWE	1954	3011.69	0.71	0.37	400.19	66.89	41.48	4.03	50.97	60.59	135.99	29.92	77.30	na
5799	Zimbabwe	ZWE	1955	3127.52	0.71	0.36	429.04	65.87	50.95	3.47	50.40	60.80	136.52	31.10	78.43	na
5800	Zimbabwe	ZWE	1956	3264.42	0.71	0.36	471.08	63.51	54.77	3.53	50.08	62.11	136.86	30.53	74.27	na
⋮	⋮	⋮	⋮	⋮	⋮	⋮	⋮	⋮	⋮	⋮	⋮	⋮	⋮	⋮	⋮	⋮
5842	Zimbabwe	ZWE	1998	12153.85	23.68	4.06	2799.85	77.66	10.75	13.39	17.16	14.97	22.03	26.87	91.96	93.25
5843	Zimbabwe	ZWE	1999	12388.32	38.30	6.12	2770.48	76.89	10.73	12.81	15.98	14.35	19.01	24.02	92.99	93.75
5844	Zimbabwe	ZWE	2000	12627.00	44.42	9.48	2607.03	69.23	8.62	22.44	21.33	19.26	23.63	31.96	62.61	96.62

Figure 10.9 *Spreadsheet samples*

- Country—Country name
- Code—Country code
- Year—Year in which the data in this row were recorded
- POP—Population that year
- XRAT—Exchange rate versus U.S. currency that year
- PPP—Purchasing power parity over GDP that year
- CGDP —Real gross domestic product per capita that year

Figure 10.9 also illustrates one of the weaknesses of spreadsheets: they are inherently two dimensional, and the data in this case are three dimensional; each country has several sets of data as functions of the year when the information was recorded. Therefore, the data must be massaged into a form more useful to us. A careful examination of the data also reveals the following challenges:

- The years in which the data were available vary from country to country—most have data from 1950 to 2000

Listing 10.1 Country analysis

```
     % build the country array
1.   worldData = buildData('World_data.xls');
2.   best = findBest(worldData);
3.   fprintf('best country is %s\n', ...
4.       worldData(best).name)
```

- There are some places within the numerical data where the values are not available, signified by the letters "na" at those locations

Our algorithm must take into account the variable number of years and the potential presence of strings within the data. Fortunately, the `cvsread(...)` function discussed earlier[2] recognizes this situation and inserts `NaN` in the numerical data fields. To ensure clarity and reliability in our solution, we need a careful design for this data processing task as follows.

- Looking at the end result desired, eventually we need to fold a collection of data about each country and choose the friendliest one.
- The information describing each country must include not only its name, but also vectors of the population and CGDP as a function of the year. It seems that a structure array by country would be an appropriate form for the data.
- Therefore, before actually solving the problem, we have to build this structure.
- Having built the structure, the folding operation to find the friendliest country follows the folding template shown in Section 10.3.7.

Listing 10.1 shows the script that accomplishes this analysis, although most of the work is actually done in the following functions.

In Listing 10.1:

Line 1: `worldData` will be a structure array containing the relevant data from the spreadsheet.

Line 2: `best` will be the index of the friendliest country according to the criteria defined in the function `findBest(...)`.

Lines 3–4: Here we can look up and print the name of the best country.

Listing 10.2 lists the function that builds the country data. The algorithm violates the best style by taking advantage of the logical ordering of the data in the spreadsheet to traverse the data from the spreadsheets simultaneously, filter out the data for each country in turn, and then map the available data for that country into the emerging structure array.

---

[2]For MATLAB users, xlsread(...) should be used here.

Listing 10.2 Building the country data

```
1. function worldData = buildData(name)
     % read the spreadsheet into a data array
     % and a text cell array
2.      [data txt] = xlsread(name);
3.      country = ' '; % force the first data row
                       % to change the country
4.      cntry_index = 0;
        % Traverse the data and cell arrays producing
        % an array of structures,
        % one for each country
5.      for row = 1:length(data)
            % Because the text data in txt contains
            % the header row of the spreadsheet,
            % the data at a given row belongs to the country
            % whose name is at txt{row+1}.
            % if the country name changes,
            % begin a new structure.
6.          if ~strcmp(txt{row+1}, country)
7.              col = 1;
8.              country = txt{row+1};
9.              cntry_index = cntry_index + 1;
10.             cntry.year = 1;
11.             cntry.pop = 1;
12.             cntry.gdp = 1;
13.         end
14.         cntry.name = country;
15.         cntry.year(col) = data(row, 1);
16.         cntry.pop(col) = data(row, 2);
17.         cntry.gdp(col) = data(row, 5);
18.         col = col + 1;
19.         worldData(cntry_index) = cntry;
20.     end
21. end
```

In Listing 10.2:

Line 2: Reads the Excel spreadsheet—we need the numerical data and the text part for the names of the countries.

Lines 3 and 4: Initialize the results of the traversal, setting an unknown country name and the initial country count.

Lines 5–20: Traverse the rows of the numerical data.

Line 6: Since the numerical data skipped the header row, the name of the country corresponding to each row of data is in the text file at row+1. When the country changes, we step to the next country index, reset the year counter, col, for that country, and empty the structure used to accumulate the country data.

Line 7: Resets the counter that indexes the year storage for the current country.

Line 8: Saves the name of the new country to continue retrieving its data.

Line 9: Increases the country count.

Lines 10–12: Reset the structure used to store the vectors of data. This is crucial because the number of annual data items for all countries is not the same.

Lines 14–17: Add this row of data to the structure. Column 1 is the year, column 2 is the population, and column 5 is the CGDP.

Line 18: Moves to the next year.

Line 19: Saves all this in the structure array.

Listing 10.3 Folding the country data

```
 1. function besti = findbest(worldData)
    % find the index of the best country
    % according to the criterion in the function
    % fold
 2.     best = fold(worldData(1));
 3.     besti = 1;
 4.     for ndx = 2:length(worldData)
 5.         cntry = worldData(ndx);
 6.         tryThis = fold(cntry);
 7.         if tryThis > best
 8.             best = tryThis;
 9.             besti = ndx
10.         end
11.     end
12. end
13. function ans = fold(st)
    % s1 is the rate of growth of population
14.     pop = st.pop(~isnan(st.pop));
15.     yr = st.year(~isnan(st.pop));
16.     s1 = slope(yr, pop)/mean(pop);
    % s2 is the rate of growth of the GDP
17.     gdp = st.gdp(~isnan(st.gdp));
18.     yr = st.year(~isnan(st.gdp));
19.     s2 = slope(yr, gdp)/mean(gdp);
    % Measure of merit is how much faster
    % the gdp grows than the population
20.     ans = s2 - s1;
21. end
22. function s1 = slope(x, y)
    % Estimate the slope of a curve
23.     if length(x) == 0 || x(end) == x(1)
24.         error('bad data')
25.     else
26.         s1 = (y(end) - y(1))/(x(end) - x(1));
27.     end
28. end
```

Listing 10.3 shows the function that finds the best country by folding the country structure array, together with the two supporting functions that provide the comparison criteria. Notice that the complexity of the data has forced the solution into nested folds: to fold the country data array, we have to summarize (fold) the annual data for each country.

In Listing 10.3:

> Lines 2 and 3: As with any folding function that is looking for the maximum or minimum of a collection, the best place to start is the first item in the collection. The remaining items can then be compared to this one.
>
> Lines 4–11: Loop through the remaining countries in the array.
>
> Line 5: Extracts one structure.
>
> Line 6: Computes its friendliness value.
>
> Lines 7–10: If the result is improved, these lines update the stored values. The index `besti` is returned when the loop finishes.
>
> Line 13: This function computes the measure of friendliness for each country. The goal is to subtract the rate of population growth from the rate of growth of the GDP. So first we compute the rate of population growth.
>
> Lines 14 and 15: These lines establish two local vectors containing the population value and the corresponding year without the values that are `NaN`, the places where "na" appears in the spreadsheet.
>
> Line 16: Calls the helper function for the slope of this relationship, and non-dimensionalizes the result by dividing by the mean population.
>
> Lines 17–19: Repeat the same logic for the non-dimensional rate of increase of the GDP.
>
> Line 20: Returns the difference in growth rates.
>
> Line 22: The function that estimates the rates of growth.
>
> Lines 23 and 24: We have a problem if there is no data or if the value we will subsequently use as a divisor is zero.
>
> Line 26: A very crude measure of the slope is to divide the difference between the first and last data points by the difference between the first and last x values. (We will be able to improve on this approach later.)

When we run this program, we see the following result:

```
>> best country is Equatorial Guinea
```

This may not be exactly the result we were hoping for. In Chapter 16 we will revisit this example with some better tools that will allow us to apply additional criteria to selecting countries.

Chapter Summary

This chapter presented the fundamental operations that can be applied to problem solving:

- Using normal arithmetic operations with specific input and output values
- Inserting new elements in a collection
- Traversing a collection
- Building a collection by repetitive insertion
- Mapping a collection—changing the values of the data items in the collection, but not the number of them
- Filtering a collection—reducing the number of entries, but not changing the data contents of the collection
- Folding—summarizing the values in a collection into a single quantity
- Searching for a specific match in a collection
- Sorting a collection

Then we briefly discussed how to combine these fundamental tools to solve more complex data manipulation problems.

Self Test

Use the following questions to check your understanding of the material in this chapter:

True or False

T 1. Copying the elements of a structure array into a cell array is a combination of traversal and insertion.

F 2. If you map a collection, you must change at least one of its elements.

F 3. When you filter a collection, at least one data element is changed.

F 4. The function `max(...)` is not folding because it returns two values.

T 5. You can use a `for` loop to search a collection even if you need to stop the search when you find the answer.

F 6. Sorting must involve putting the items in a collection in numerical order (ascending or descending).

Fill in the Blanks

1. The problem-solving style recommended in this text is to identify the _character_ and the _basic operations we are asked to perform of the data_.

2. Building is usually the process of _beginning with an empty collection_ and _inserting elements one at a time_.

3. Mapping may involve combining __two or more__ of the same length.
   collections

4. We __filter__ vectors by applying built-in logical operations and then indexing with the results to produce new, shorter arrays.

5. Totaling, averaging, and finding the smallest element in a vector are typical examples of __folding__.

6. There are almost always two exit criteria for a search: __finding what you seek__ or __failing to find it__

7. To save a collection to a text file, you __traverse__ the collection __writing__ it to the file.

Programming Projects

1. The purpose of this problem is to write a set of functions that calculate the volume of a slant cylinder with an irregular pentagonal cross section shown in Figure 10.10.

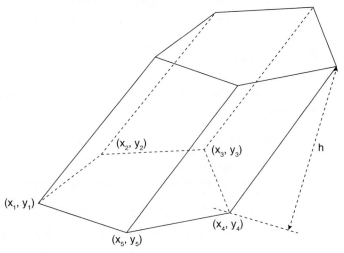

Figure 10.10 *The Slant Cylinder*

You will be given two vectors, x and y, containing the coordinates of the corners of the pentagon, and the value h, the vertical height of the cylinder. We will need to break this problem apart, writing functions to solve each part:

a. The volume of the cylinder is the area of the pentagon multiplied by the vertical height; write a function polyvol(x, y, h) to solve this.

b. The area of the pentagon is the sum of the areas of three triangles shown in Figure 10.11. So we need to write a function pent_area(x, y) that asks for the area of the three triangles and adds them together.

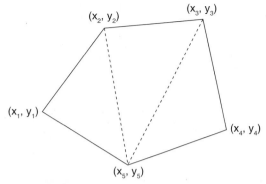

Figure 10.11 *Break down the pentagon*

c. Given the coordinates of the corners of a triangle, we need a function `tri_area(x, y)` to calculate the area of the triangle—see Figure 10.12. To compute the area of the triangle, we need the values of a, b, and c. So if we had the lengths of the lines, the area of the triangle is given by Heron's formula:

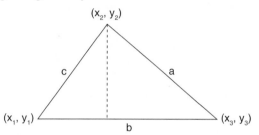

Figure 10.12 *Area of a triangle*

A = (s(s-a)(s-b)(s-c))
where s is half the sum of a, b, and c

d. So we need a function `tri_side(x, y)` that computes the length of a line when given its end points.

e. Then, we can put the pieces back together by calling the functions with the right parameters, and then build and test `polyvol` using the test cases provided.

2. This problem is about processing structure arrays. Write a function named `structSort` that sorts a structure array based on a given field that contains numerical values. Your function should take in a structure array and a string that should correspond to one of the fields of the structure array and return the original structure array sorted on the given field. It should check to be sure that the specified field name is in fact one of the fields of the structure array, and call the `error(...)` function if it is not.

   Test your function by using the `buildCDs` script from Chapter 7, using the input function to specify the sorting field.

CHAPTER 11

Plotting

Chapter Objectives

This chapter presents the principles and practice of plotting in the following forms:

- Basic two-dimensional (2-D) line plots

- 2-D parametric plots

- Three-dimensional (3-D) line and parametric plots

- Basic 3-D surface plots

- Parametric surface plots

- Bodies of rotation

There is a much-quoted expression that "a picture is worth a thousand words," and this is never more appropriate than when talking about data. In previous chapters, we used some simple plot commands to display data to illustrate its behavior. The capability of the MATLAB language to present data reaches far beyond ordinary data plotting, and far beyond the limited confines of a textbook. This chapter will present the fundamental concepts of the different forms in which data can be presented, but it leaves to the reader the challenge of exploring the full range of capabilities available. You only really discover the power inherent in the plotting capabilities of MATLAB when you have some unusual data to visualize.

11.1 Plotting in General

Before considering the details of how each plotting mode works, we should set the context. In this section, we will discuss the general container for all graphical types, the figure, and some basic operations that apply to all figures—functions that enhance them, the ability to assemble subplots into a single figure, and the advisability of making manual changes to plots.

11.1.1 A Figure—The Plot Container

The fundamental container for plotting is a figure. In a simple script, if you just start plotting data, *figure number 1* is automatically generated to present the data. You can manage the figures by asserting the `figure` command. Each time `figure` is called, a new figure is made available, with the next higher figure number. If you use the form `figure <number>`, you can select a specific figure for the next plot.

To clear the current figure, put the key word `clf` in the header of your script. To remove all the figures, put the key phrase `close all` at the beginning of your script. The listing examples below will assume that each script begins with `clear, clc, close all`.

11.1.2 Simple Functions for Enhancing Plots

We have already introduced `plot(x, y)`, the basic function that creates a simple plot of x versus y. The following functions can be used to enhance any of the plots discussed in this chapter. Note that they enhance an existing plot; they should all be called after the fundamental function that creates a plot figure.

- `axis <param>` provides a rich set of tools for managing the appearance of the axes, including the following:
  - `tight` reduces the axes to their smallest possible size
  - `equal` sets the x and y scales to the same value
  - `square` makes the plot figure of equal width and height
  - `off` does not show the axes at all
- `axis([xl xu yl yu zl zu])` overrides the automatic computation of the axis values, forcing the x-axis to reach from `xl` to `xu`, the y-axis from `yl` to `yu`, and the z-axis from `zl` to `zu`. For 2-D plots, the z values should be omitted.
- `colormap <specification>` establishes a sequence of colors, the color map, to be used under a number of circumstances to cycle through a series of colors automatically. The legal specification values are listed in Appendix A.
- `grid on` puts a grid on the plot; `grid off` (the default) removes grid lines.

- `hold on` holds the existing data on the figure to allow subsequent plotting calls to be added to the current figure without first erasing the existing plot; `hold off` (the default) redraws the current figure, erasing the previous contents.

- `legend(...)` takes a cell array of strings, one for each of the multiple plots on a single figure, and creates a legend box. By default, that box appears in the top-right corner of the figure. However, this default can be overridden by explicitly specifying the location of the legend. See the help files for a complete discussion of the legend options.

- `shading <spec>` defines the method for shading surfaces. See the help files for a complete discussion of the shading specification options.

- `text(x, y, {z,}, str)` places the text provided at the specified (x, y) location on a 2-D plot, or at the (x, y, z) location on a 3-D plot.

- `title(...)` places the text provided as the title of the current plot.

- `view(az, el)` sets the angle from which to view a plot. The parameters are `az`, the azimuth, an angle measured in the horizontal plane, and `el`, the elevation, an angle measured upward from the horizontal. Both angles are specified in degrees.

- `xlabel(...)` sets the string provided as the label for the x-axis.

- `ylabel(...)` sets the string provided as the label for the y-axis.

- `zlabel(...)` sets the string provided as the label for the z-axis. (As we will see, all plots actually have a third axis.)

11.1.3 Multiple Plots on One Figure—Subplots

Within the current figure, you can place multiple plots with the `subplot` command, as shown in Figure 11.1. The function `subplot(r, c, n)` divides the current figure into `r` rows and `c` columns of equally spaced plot areas, and then establishes the `nth` of these (counting across the rows first) as the current figure. You do not have to draw in all of the areas you specify. Figure 11.1 was generated by the code shown in Listing 11.1.

In Listing 11.1:

Line 1: `close all` closes all figures currently open. This command should always be present at the beginning of a script but will be omitted from the example listings that follow.

Line 2: Specifies a suitable range of x values.

Line 3: Sets the first subplot region.

Line 4: This is the simple version of the `plot(...)` function introduced earlier, plotting `x` against `y` and automatically

Listing 11.1 Creating a subplot

```
 1. close all
 2. x = -2*pi:.05:2*pi;
 3. subplot(3,2,1)
 4. plot(x, sin(x))
 5. title('1 - sin(x)');
 6. subplot(3,2,2)
 7. plot(x, cos(x))
 8. title('2 - cos(x)');
 9. subplot(3,2,3)
10. plot(x, tan(x))
11. title('3 - tan(x)');
12. subplot(3,2,4)
13. plot(x, x.^2)
14. title('4 - x^2');
15. subplot(3,2,5)
16. plot(x, sqrt(x))
17. title('5 - sqrt(x)');
18. subplot(3,2,6)
19. plot(x, exp(x))
20. title('4 - e^x');
```

creating the axes, creating subplot 1, the plot in the top-left corner. Note that although in the figure seen here the line is gray, when you run the script, the line will appear in its default color, blue.

Line 5: The `title(...)` function puts the specified string at the top of the plot as its title.

Lines 6–8: Create subplot 2, the second plot on the first row.

Lines 9–11: Create subplot 3, the first plot on the second row.

Lines 12–14: Create subplot 4, the second plot on the second row.

Lines 15–17: Create subplot 5, the first plot on the bottom row.

Lines 18–20: Create subplot 6, the second plot on the bottom row.

Style Points 11.1

All of these capabilities are also available to the script that creates the plots, and you are very likely to want to generate a plot more than once. Therefore, it is unwise to put a significant amount of manual effort into adjusting a plot. It is better to experiment with the manual adjustments and then find out how to make the same adjustments in the script that creates the plots. This also leaves you a permanent record of how the plot was generated.

11.1.4 Manually Editing Plots

When a figure has been created, you are free to manipulate many of its characteristics by using its menu items and tool bars. They provide the ability to resize the plot, change the view characteristics, and annotate it with legends, axis labels, lines, and text callouts.

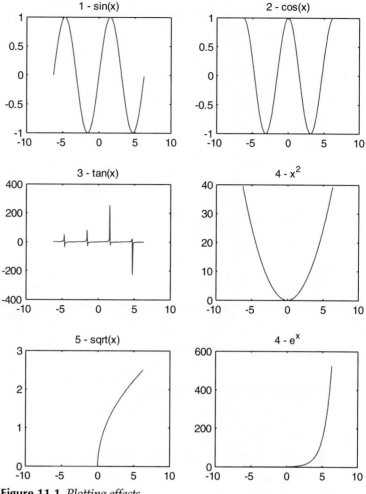

Figure 11.1 *Plotting effects*

11.2 2-D Plotting

11.2.1 Simple Plots

The basic function to use for 2-D plots is plot(...). The normal use of this function is to give it three parameters, plot(x, y, str), where x and y are vectors of the same length containing the x and y coordinates, respectively, and str is a string containing one or more optional line color and style control characters. A complete list of these control characters is included in Appendix A. If the vector x is omitted, MATLAB assumes that the x coordinates are 1:N, where N is the length of the y vector. If the str is omitted, the default line is solid blue. The MATLAB definition of this function also permits multiple (x, y, str) data sets in a single function call. It is always possible to produce the same result with multiple function calls in hold on mode.

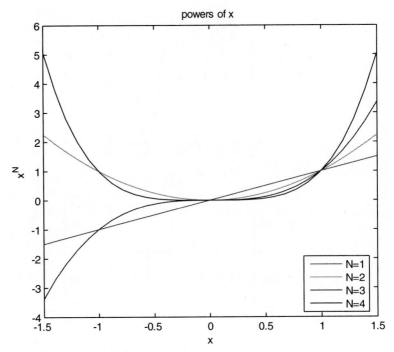

Figure 11.2 *Powers of x*

Listing 11.2 Simple 2-D plots

```
1. x = linspace(-1.5, 1.5, 30);
2. clr = 'rgbk';
3. for pwr = 1:4
4.     plot(x, x.^pwr, clr(pwr))
5.     hold on
6. end
7. xlabel('x')
8. ylabel('x^N')
9. title('powers of x')
10. legend({'N=1', 'N=2', 'N=3', 'N=4'}, ...
11.              'Location','SouthEast')
```

Since we have already seen basic 2-D plotting at work, it should be sufficient to observe and comment on the simple example seen in Figure 11.2, generated by the code shown in Listing 11.2.

In Listing 11.2:

> Line 1: Sets the range of x values.
>
> Line 2: Color specifications for the plots—red, green, blue, and black.
>
> Lines 4–7: Plot x, x^2, x^3, and x^4 with the above colors used in sequence.

Lines 7–11: Add enhancements to the plot as noted above.

Line 11: One of many possible parameters to the `legend(...)` function—this one forces its location to the lower-right corner of the figure, out of the way of the data.

11.2.2 Plot Options

In addition to the plot enhancement tools listed in Section 11.1.2, the following capabilities are available.

- Setting line styles and symbols to mark the data points (details in Appendix A)
- Using `plotyy(...)` to put a second axis on the right side of the figure
- Obtaining logarithmic plots on the x-axis (`semilogx(...)`), y-axis (`semilogy(...)`), or both axes (`loglog(...)`)

We strongly suggest that the reader experiment with these features and observe their effects.

11.2.3 Parametric Plots

Plotting is not restricted to the situation where the data along one axis are the independent variable and that along the other are dependent. Parametric plots allow the variables on each axis to be dependent on a separate, independent variable. That independent variable will define a path on the plotting surface. Consider the plot shown in Figure 11.3, which presents a simple exercise in transforming a circle into an airfoil. It was generated using the code shown in Listing 11.3.

Style Points 11.2

By convention, good engineers are expected to represent the data with appropriate line styles to avoid misleading the reader. For example, if you have some raw data that is only valid at the measurement points, it should be plotted with symbols only. Connecting the data with a line would imply that the data have some interpolated values, which may not be the case. On the other hand, if you calculate a theoretical curve that is good throughout the range of x, it should be plotted as a continuous curve, perhaps even at a better resolution (more x values) than the raw data samples.

Listing 11.3 Parametric plots

```
1. th = linspace(0, 2*pi, 40);
2. r = 1.1; g = .1;
3. cx = sqrt(r^2-g^2) - 1; cy = g;
4. x = r*cos(th) + cx;
5. y = r*sin(th) + cy;
6. plot( x, y,  'r' )
7. axis equal
8. grid on
9. hold on
10. z = complex(x, y);
11. w = z + 1./z;
12. plot( real(w), imag(w), 'k' );
```

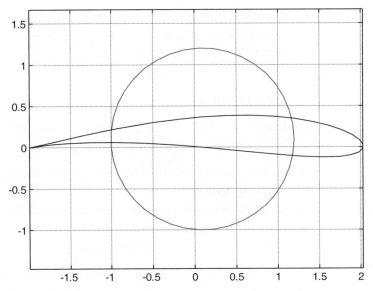

Figure 11.3 *Parametric 2-D plot*

In Listing 11.3:

> Line 1: The independent variable in this case is the angle th varying from 0 to 2π.
>
> Line 2: The particular transformation we use here requires a circle with a radius, r, slightly greater than 1 offset by a small distance, g, from the x-axis, passing through the point $(-1, 0)$.
>
> Line 3: We compute the center of the circle passing through the point $(-1, 0)$.
>
> Lines 4–5: A standard polar-to-Cartesian coordinate transformation computing the coordinates of the circle.
>
> Line 6: Plots the two dependent variables x and y with a red line.
>
> Line 7: Equalizes the axes and forces the circle to be drawn correctly.
>
> Line 8: Displays a grid on which to estimate specific values.
>
> Line 9: Here we want to add a second plot to the figure.
>
> Lines 10–11: The Joukowski transformation is easiest when expressed in complex terms: if z is the path around the required circle, w = z + 1/z traces a very credible looking airfoil shape.
>
> Line 12: Adds the plot of w, and reverts from the complex plane to plot the real and imaginary parts of the answer colored in black.

11.2.4 Other 2-D Plot Capabilities

You can also create some more exotic plots that are not necessary to understand the basic principles of plotting, but are powerful methods for visualizing real data:

- `bar(x, y)` produces a bar graph with the values in `y` positioned at the horizontal locations in `x`. The options available can be studied with >> `help bar`.
- `barh(x, y)` produces a bar graph with the values in `y` positioned at the horizontal locations in `x`. The options available can be studied with >> `help barh`.
- `fill(x,y,n)` produces a filled polygon defined by the coordinates in `x` and `y`. The fill color is specified by indexing `n` into the color map. The options available can be studied with >> `help fill`.
- `hist(y, x)` produces a histogram plot with the values in `y` counted into bins defined by `x`. The options available can be studied with >>`help hist`.
- `pie(y)` makes a pie chart of the values in `y`. For more options, see >> `help pie`.
- `polar(th, y)` makes a polar plot of the angle `th` (radians) with the radius `r` specified for each angle. For more options, see >> `help polar`.

11.3 3-D Plotting

Before attacking the details of plotting in three dimensions, it should be noted that even 2-D plots are actually 3-D plots. Consider the picture shown in Figure 11.4, which was generated originally as the 2-D plot in Figure 11.3. By selecting the Rotate 3-D icon on the tool bar and moving the mouse on your figure, it becomes apparent that what appeared to be a 2-D plot in the x-y plane is really a 3-D plot in the x-y-z plane "suspended in space" at z = 0.

11.3.1 Linear 3-D Plots

The simplest method of 3-D plotting is to extend our 2-D plots by adding a set of z values. In the same style as `plot(...)`, `plot3(x, y, z, str)` consumes three vectors of equal size and connects the points defined by those vectors in 3-D space. The optional `str` specifies the color and/or line style. If the `str` is omitted, the default line is solid blue.

Figure 11.5 shows three curves plotted in three dimensions, using the script shown in Listing 11.4. Each plot is in the z-x plane: the red curve at y = 0, the blue curve at y = 0.5, and the green curve at y = 1.

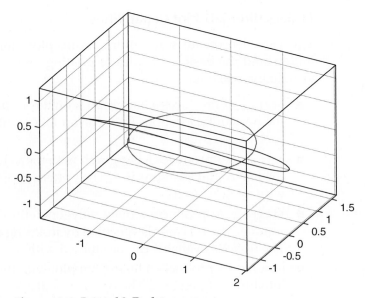

Figure 11.4 *Rotated 2-D plot*

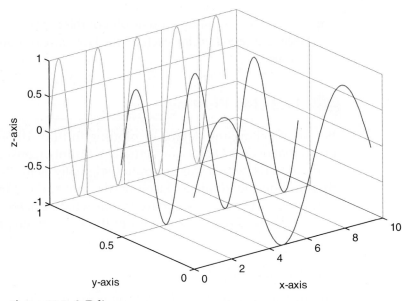

Figure 11.5 *3-D lines*

In Listing 11.4:

　　Line 1: Each plot has the same set of x values.

　　Lines 2–3: The y values for the first plot are all 0.

　　Lines 4–5: The second and third plots are sin(x) at different frequencies.

Listing 11.4 Simple 3-D line plots

```
1.  x=0:0.1:3.*pi;
2.  y1=zeros(size(x));
3.  z1=sin(x);
4.  z2=sin(2.*x);
5.  z3=sin(3.*x);
6.  y3=ones(size(x));
7.  y2=y3./2;
8.  plot3(x,y1,z1, 'r',x,y2,z2, 'b',x,y3,z3, 'g')
9.  grid on
10. xlabel('x-axis'), ylabel('y-axis'), zlabel('z-axis')
```

Lines 6–7: The y values of the second and third plots are all 0.5 and 1, respectively.

Lines 8–10: Plot and annotate the results.

11.3.2 Linear Parametric 3-D Plots

We can generalize the concept of parametric plots to 3-D, as shown in Figure 11.6, in which the x, y, and z values are mappings of some linear parameter. On the left side, the spiral is an example of a 3-D plot where two of the dimensions, x and y, are dependent on the third, independent parameter. The independent parameter in this example is the rotation angle, π, varying from 0 to 10π (five complete revolutions). The x and y

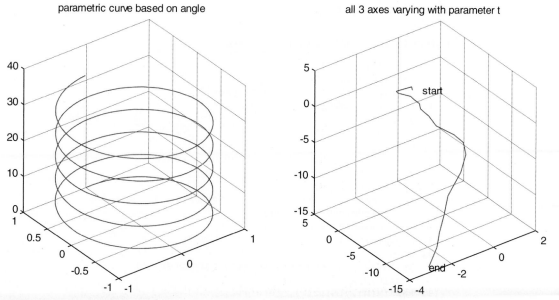

Figure 11.6 *Parametric 3-D plots*

values are mapped as sin(θ) and cos(θ)—the classic means of describing a circle. The spiral effect is accomplished by plotting θ on the z-axis.

The right half of Figure 11.6 illustrates a fully parametric plot, where the values of all three coordinates are mappings of an independent parameter, t. This particular example is a plot of the 3-D motion of a particle receiving random impulses in all three axes. Note the use of text anchored in x-y-z space to label points on the graph. The figure is drawn using Listing 11.5.

In Listing 11.5:

> Lines 2–5: Draw the spiral plot with a simple `plot3(...)` call.
>
> Lines 8–10: Define random velocity increments in x, y, and z.
>
> Lines 11–13: Integrate to compute the position in x, y, z space. There will be a full discussion of integration in Chapter 15.
>
> Lines 14–16: Plot and enhance the time history of the particle.
>
> Lines 17 and 18: Add labels to indicate the start and end of the trace.

11.3.3 Other 3-D Plot Capabilities

If you are using MATLAB, you can also create some more exotic 3-D plots that are not necessary to understand the basic principles of plotting, but are powerful methods for visualizing real data:

- `bar3(x, y)` produces a bar graph with the values in y positioned at the horizontal locations in x. The options available can be studied with >> `help bar3`.

Listing 11.5 Linear parametric 3-D plots

```
 1. subplot(1, 2, 1)
 2. theta = 0:0.1:10.*pi;
 3. plot3(sin(theta),cos(theta),theta)
 4. title('parametric curve based on angle');
 5. grid on
 6. subplot(1, 2, 2)
 7. N = 20;
 8. dvx = rand(1, N) - 0.5    % random v changes
 9. dvy = rand(1, N) - 0.5
10. dvz = rand(1, N) - 0.5
11. x = cumsum(cumsum(dvx)); % integrate to get pos
12. y = cumsum(cumsum(dvy));
13. z = cumsum(cumsum(dvz));
14. plot3(x,y,z)
15. grid on
16. title('all 3 axes varying with parameter t')
17. text(0,0,0, 'start');
18. text(x(N),y(N),z(N), 'end');
```

- `barh3(x, y)` produces a bar graph with the values in y positioned at the horizontal locations in x. The options available can be studied with >> `help barh`.
- `pie3(y)` makes a 3-D pie chart of the values in y. For more options, see >> `help pie3`.

 ## 11.4 Surface Plots

In Section 11.3.2, we saw that data can be generated for all three axes based on one linear parameter. However, more dramatic graphics are produced by a different group of 3-D graphics functions that produce images based on mapping a 2-D surface. The underlying 2-D surface is sometimes referred to as *plaid* because of its conceptual similarity to a Scottish tartan pattern. To design such a pattern, one needs only to specify the color sequence of the horizontal and vertical threads. In the same way, we specify a plaid by defining vectors of the row and column data configurations.

11.4.1 Basic Capabilities

Three fundamental functions are used to create 3-D surface plots:

- `meshgrid(x, y)` accepts the x_{1*m} and y_{1*n} vectors that bound the edges of the plaid and replicates the rows and columns appropriately to produce xx_{n*m} and yy_{n*m}, containing the x and y values (respectively) of the complete plaid. This enables us in general to compute mappings for the 3-D coordinates of the figure we want to plot.
- `mesh(xx, yy, zz)` plots the surface as white facets outlined by colored lines. The line coloring uses one of many color maps (listed in Appendix A), where the color is selected in proportion to the zz parameter. You can turn the white facets transparent with the command `hidden off`.
- `surf(xx, yy, zz)` plots the surface as colored facets outlined by black lines. The line coloring by default is selected in proportion to the zz parameter. You can remove the lines by using one of a number of `shading` commands listed in Appendix A.

11.4.2 Simple Exercises

We will consider some simple situations that illustrate many of the features of surface drawing.

Drawing a Cube In the first example, in order to understand the underlying logic, we will develop the basic concept of drawing surfaces *without* the help of the `meshgrid(...)` function. Figure 11.7 shows the coordinates of a cube of side 2 units centered at the origin. Listing 11.6 shows the code that plots a cube from scratch. Figure 11.8 shows the results from this script. To

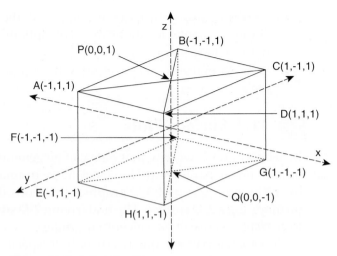

Figure 11.7 *A simple cube*

Figure 11.8 *The solid cube plot*

define the top and bottom of the cube, we must add the points P and Q. Although only one point each is required to define P and Q, the array must have the same number of columns in each row. Therefore, P and Q must be replicated five times to keep the arrays rectangular.

One could think about the way the surf(...) function works by drawing the line defined by the top row of the xx, yy, and zz arrays. Then it locates the line defined by the next row and makes a smooth surface between the two lines. Physically, this has the following effect:

- Beginning at point P, it draws expanding squares until it reaches ABCD

Listing 11.6 Simple solid cube

```
 1. xx = [  0   0   0   0   0    % P-P-P-P-P
 2.           -1  -1   1   1  -1    % A-B-C-D-A
 3.           -1  -1   1   1  -1    % E-F-G-H-E
 4.            0   0   0   0   0]   % Q-Q-Q-Q-Q
 5. yy = [  0   0   0   0   0    % P-P-P-P-P
 6.            1  -1  -1   1   1    % A-B-C-D-A
 7.            1  -1  -1   1   1    % E-F-G-H-E
 8.            0   0   0   0   0]   % Q-Q-Q-Q-Q
 9. zz = [  1   1   1   1   1    % P-P-P-P-P
10.            1   1   1   1   1    % A-B-C-D-A
11.           -1  -1  -1  -1  -1    % E-F-G-H-E
12.           -1  -1  -1  -1  -1]   % Q-Q-Q-Q-Q
13. surf(xx, yy, zz)
14. colormap bone
15. axis equal
16. shading interp
17. view(-36, 44)
18. axis off
```

- "Sliding down" the sides of the cube to EFGH
- Shrinking that square down to the point Q

In Listing 11.6:

Lines 1–12: Establish the plaid defining the point P, the A-B-C-D plane, the E-F-G-H plane, and the point Q. Notice that the first corner is repeated on each row to close the figure shape.

Lines 13–18: Plot the cube top, sides, and bottom.

A Simple Parabolic Dish The simplest surface plots are obtained by defining a z value for each point on an x-y plaid. We will continue with a simple example illustrating the use of meshgrid(...) to define the plaid. Consider how we might plot the data shown in Figure 11.9. Before we look at the code, consider what the picture represents. Clearly, the independent variables are x and y, each covering the range from –3 to 3, each having seven discrete values. As the label indicates, the z values are calculated as the sum of x^2 and y^2. There are not, however, 14 z values as the range of x and y values might suggest, but 49! In order to plot the 3-D shape of our parabolic bowl, we must have a z value for every point on the x-y surface. Each of these points has a value of x corresponding to the reading on the x-axis, and a value of y from the y-axis. Therefore, the process of creating this plot has three parts:

1. Develop the underlying plaid specifying the x-y location of every point on the x-y plane.
2. Calculate the z values from the plaid.
3. Call a plotting function that will accept the plaid and these z values to produce the required plot.

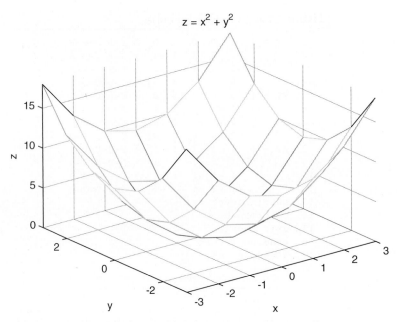

Figure 11.9 *A mesh plot*

The code to accomplish this is shown in Listing 11.7.

In Listing 11.7:

> Line 1: The x and y vectors define the edges of the plaid.
>
> Line 2: Generates the plaid.
>
> Line 3: In this particular example, we map only the z coordinate, leaving the plaid (xx and yy) as the x and y coordinates of the figure.
>
> Line 4: mesh(...) is one of the many functions that represent 3-D mappings of a plaid in different ways. Notice in the figure that the faces between line segments are solid white, and the line colors change with the z coordinate.
>
> Lines 5–7: Annotate the plot.

Listing 11.7 Simple surface plot

```
1. x=-3:3; y = x ;
2. [xx,yy]=meshgrid(x,y);
3. zz=xx.^2 + yy.^2;
4. mesh(xx,yy,zz)
5. axis tight
6. title('z = x^2 + y^2')
7. xlabel('x'),ylabel('y'),zlabel('z')
```

Exercise 11.1 Exploring the simple plot

1. run script in Listing 11.7 without the semicolon on Line 2, and observe the following:

```
xx =
    -3 -2 -1  0  1  2  3
{etc}
yy =
    -3 -3 -3 -3 -3 -3 -3
-{etc}
     3  3  3  3  3  3  3
```

Notice that in general, if x is length m and y is length n, the xx values consist of the x vector in rows replicated n times, and the yy values consist of the y vector as a column replicated m times. Together, they provide the underlying x and y values for the "floor" of the bowl plot from which the z values are computed to draw the picture.

2. Insert the line `hidden off` after `mesh(xx, yy, zz)`. Notice that the faces are now transparent.

3. Change `mesh(xx, yy, zz)` to `surf(xx, yy, zz)`. Notice that the panels are now colored and the lines are black. This form is also insensitive to the `hidden parameter`.

4. Replace `hidden off` with `shading flat`, and notice that the lines have disappeared.

5. Replace `shading flat` with `shading interp`, and notice that the surface coloring now varies smoothly.

6. Insert the line `colormap 'summer'` after `surf(xx, yy, zz)`. Look up colormap in Appendix A for details.

7. Do not forget to rotate your images and examine them from different points of view using the 3-D rotate tool bar icon.

Try Exercise 11.1 and make your observations.

Manipulating Plots Thoughtful students might develop their own tests to investigate the behavior of the following tools:

- The function `surfc(xx, yy, zz)` puts contour lines on the x-y plane base.

- The function `view(az, el)` changes the viewing angle. This is useful to capture a specific view angle after you have used the rotation tool to select a good presentation of the data.

- The command `colorbar` allows you to show how the colors are quantified on the plot.

- Adding a 4th parameter to `surf(xx, yy, zz, yy)` overrides the default color direction z with, in this case, the y direction.

- The 4th parameter can also be a function like `del2(zz)` that computes the second derivative, or curvature, of the plot, so now the coloring highlights the areas of maximum curvature.
- The 4th parameter can also be an image (see Chapter 13) that will appear to be pasted onto the plotting surface.
- For an eye-catching effect, add the line `lightangle(60, 45)` at the bottom of the script. This illuminates the surface with a light at the specified azimuth and elevation angle (degrees). The resulting faceted appearance can be alleviated by decreasing the granularity of the underlying plaid coordinates.

11.4.3 3-D Parametric Surfaces

Cylinder Consider first the construction of a cylinder as illustrated in Figure 11.10. One could consider this figure as a sheet of paper rolled up in a circular shape. We could visualize that piece of paper as a plaid of values, not of x-y in this case, but perhaps x – θ. The range of x would be from 0 to the length of the cylinder, and the range of θ would be 0 to 360°.

To plot this, one would then merely need to create a plaid in x and θ, and then decide on the mapping from θ to the y and z values of the cylinder. The resulting picture is shown in Figure 11.11, and the code is shown in Listing 11.8.

In Listing 11.8:

> Line 1: Constants to define the smoothness of the cylinder.
>
> Lines 2–4: Define a plaid in x and θ. Note that only two points are needed in the x direction because that contour is straight.
>
> Lines 5 and 6: The circular cross-section is achieved by using the parametric definition of a circle of a given radius.

Listing 11.8 Constructing a cylinder

```
 1. facets = 120; len = 2; radius = 1;
 2. thr = linspace(0, 2*pi, facets);
 3. xr = [0 len];
 4. [xx, tth] = meshgrid( xr, thr );
 5. yy = radius * cos(tth);
 6. zz = radius * sin(tth);
 7. surf(xx, yy, zz);
 8. shading interp
 9. colormap bone
10. axis equal,axis tight,axis off
11. lightangle(60, 45)
12. alpha(0.8)
13. view(-20, 35)
```

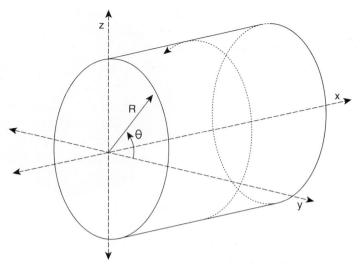

Figure 11.10 *Creating a cylinder image*

Figure 11.11 *A cylinder plot*

Line 9: Changes the color to a pleasant metallic scale.

Line 10: Squares up and removes the axes.

Line 11: Illuminates the figure.

Line 12: Sets the transparency of the surface so that a portion of the hidden details can show through.

Sphere Now, we construct a sphere as shown in Figure 11.12, starting with the cylinder. However, instead of using a constant radius in the x direction, we will calculate the radius in that direction by rotating a second angle, ψ, from 0 to 180°. Think of this as mapping or "wrapping" a plaid with two angles as the independent variables around the sphere. The coordinate in the x direction would be r cos ψ, and the radii of the y-z

Figure 11.12 *A sphere*

Listing 11.9 Constructing a sphere

```
 1. facets = 120; radius = 1;
 2. thr = linspace(0, 2*pi, facets); % range of theta
 3. phir = linspace(0, pi, facets); % range of phi
 4. [th, phi] = meshgrid( thr, phir );
 5. x = radius * cos(phi);
 6. y = radius * sin(phi) .* cos(th);
 7. z = radius * sin(phi) .* sin(th);
 8. surf(x, y, z);
 9. shading interp
10. colormap copper
11. axis equal, axis tight, axis off
12. lightangle(60, 45)
```

---

circles would be r sin ψ. The code for drawing this sphere is shown in Listing 11.9.

In Listing 11.9:

Line 1: The `radius` set here is the sphere radius.

Lines 2 and 3: Set the ranges of θ and ψ.

Line 4: Builds the plaid in θ and ψ.

Line 5: As ψ rotates, the value of x varies as its cosine.

Lines 6 and 7: The radius of rotation about the x-axis varies as the sine of ψ.

Lines 8–12: Draw and annotate the plot.

11.4.4 Bodies of Rotation

The cylinder and sphere drawn in the above section are special cases of a more general form of solid body. Bodies of rotation are created in general by rotating a general function $v = f(u)$ defined over a range of u values about the x or z axes. Note: this is perfectly general because rotating such a function about the y-axis would result merely in "smearing" the function across a flat surface in the x-z plane. We use z rather than y for the dependent variable here because in our 3-D plots, the z-axis is drawn as the vertical axis. In general, we make no claims about the nature of $f()$. It could be a rational function, or merely a "lookup table" specifying a value of v for every u.

Rotating Continuous Functions First, we consider rotating a continuous function $v = f(u)$ about the x and z axes.

- To rotate $v = f(u)$ about the x-axis, we could consider this equation as $r = f(x)$. Figure 11.13 shows the logic of this rotation. The independent variable is x, and the values of y and z are computed as the usual polar-to-Cartesian conversion:

  $$y = r \cos(\theta)$$
  $$z = r \sin(\theta)$$

  Notice that these are the two axes about which we are not rotating.

- To rotate $v = f(u)$ about the z-axis, we could consider this equation as $z = f(r)$. Figure 11.14 shows the logic of this rotation. The independent variable is now r, and the values of x and y are computed as the usual polar-to-Cartesian conversion:

  $$x = r \cos(\theta)$$
  $$y = r \sin(\theta)$$

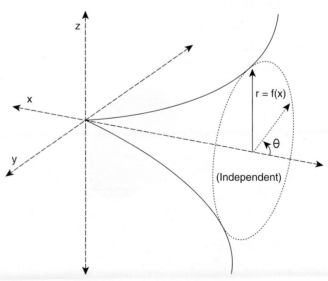

Figure 11.13 *Rotating* $v = f(u)$ *about the x-axis*

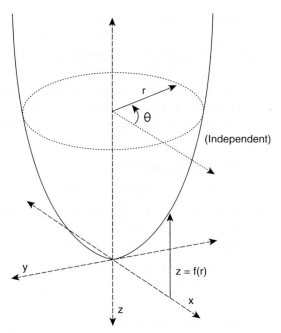

Figure 11.14 *Rotating* `v = f(u)` *about the z-axis*

Notice again that these are the two axes about which we are not rotating. Notice also a simple rule of thumb: if you rewrite `v = f(u)` correctly for each rotation, the independent variable is always the parameter of `f(...)`.

Figure 11.15 shows the result of the rotations generated by the code shown in Listing 11.10.

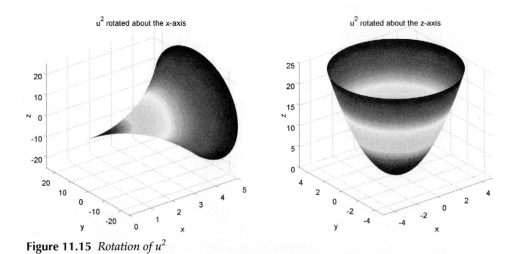

Figure 11.15 *Rotation of* u^2

Listing 11.10 Rotating $v = u^2$ about the x and z axes

```
 1. facets = 100;
 2. u = linspace(0, 5, facets);
 3. th = linspace(0, 2*pi, facets);
 4. [uu tth] = meshgrid(u, th);
    % rotate about the x-axis
 5. subplot(1, 2, 1)
 6. rr = uu.^2;
 7. xx = uu;
 8. yy = rr .* cos(tth);
 9. zz = rr .* sin(tth);
10. surf(xx, yy, zz, xx);
11. shading interp, axis tight
12. xlabel('x'), ylabel('y'), zlabel('z')
13. title('u^2 rotated about the x-axis')
    % rotate about the z-axis
14. subplot(1, 2, 2)
15. rr = uu;
16. zz = rr.^2;
17. xx = rr .* cos(tth);
18. yy = rr .* sin(tth);
19. surf(xx, yy, zz);
20. shading interp, axis tight
21. xlabel('x'), ylabel('y'), zlabel('z')
22. title('u^2 rotated about the z-axis')
```

In Listing 11.10:

> Lines 1–4: Set up the plaid of u, the independent variable for the function, and θ for the rotations.

> Lines 6–13: Compute the rotation about the x-axis. Notice that when rotating about a specific axis, that axis must be treated separately; the other two axes will always have the form of a polar-to-Cartesian transformation. In rotating about the x-axis, since u is the independent variable for our function, we only need to compute the yy and zz values.

> Line 10: We use the fourth parameter to surf(...) to set the direction of color variation.

> Lines 15–22: Compute the z-axis rotation. Some apparent sleight of hand is necessary here. In this case, the axis containing the independent variable is being rotated about the z-axis. Because the radius of the rotated surface is the original independent variable, uu, we copy uu to the variable radius. Then we define xx together with yy as the polar-to-Cartesian transformation to achieve the rotation. In this case, the z value of the surface is f(u), u^2.

Rotating Discrete Functions There is no need to restrict ourselves to continuous functions as the profiles for bodies of rotation. Figure 11.16 shows the 2-D profile of a fictitious machine part and the picture created

2-D profile

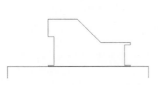

rotated object

Figure 11.16 *Rotation of an irregular shape*

when that profile is rotated about the x-axis. The figure was generated by the code shown in Listing 11.11.

In Listing 11.11:

> Lines 1–9: Define and plot the initial 2-D profile.
>
> Lines 10–22: Perform the rotation about the x-axis. The only unusual idea here is how to turn this discrete collection of points

Listing 11.11 Rotating an irregular shape

```
1. u = [0 0 3 3 1.75 1.75 2 2 1.75 1.75 3 4 ...
2.      5.25 5.25 5 5 5.25 5.25 3 3 6 6];
3. v = [0 .5 .5 .502 .502 .55 .55 1.75 1.75 ...
4.      2.5 2.5 1.5 1.5 1.4 1.4 ...
5.      .55 .55 .502 .502 .5 .5 0];
6. subplot(1, 2, 1)
7. plot(u, v, 'k')
8. axis ([-1 7 -1 3]), axis equal, axis off
9. title('2-D profile')
10. facets = 200;
11. subplot(1, 2, 2)
12. [xx tth] = meshgrid( u, linspace(0, 2*pi, facets) );
13. rr = meshgrid( v, 1:facets);
14. yy = rr .* cos(tth);
15. zz = rr .* sin(tth);
16. surf(xx, yy, zz);
17. shading interp
18. axis square, axis tight, axis off
19. colormap bone
20. lightangle(60, 45)
21. alpha(0.8)
22. title('rotated object')
```

into the equivalent of `v = f(u)`. Line 12 shows an elegant way to solve this dilemma. After going through the `meshgrid(..)` to produce a plaid of `xx` and `tth`, we run `meshgrid(...)` again, but keeping only the first result, `rr`.

Rotating about an Arbitrary Axis Bodies of rotation are not confined to rotating about the x, y, or z axes. The simplest approach to rotating `z = f(x)` about an arbitrary axis is as follows:

- Calculate the matrix that will place your axis of rotation along the x-axis (see Chapter 12)
- Transform u and v with that rotation
- Rotate the transformed u and v about the x-axis
- Invert the transformation on the resulting surface

11.4.5 Other 3-D Surface Plot Capabilities

The MATLAB language also defines special-purpose functions to enhance the quality of surface plots:

- `alpha(x)` sets the transparency of the surfaces. `0<=x<=1`, where `0` means completely transparent and `1` (the `default value`) is opaque. The options available can be studied with >> `help alpha`.
- `contour(z)` produces a contour plot of the plaid surface defined by `z`. The options available can be studied with >> `help bar3`.
- `[x,y,z] = cylinder(n)` constructs the `meshgrid` for a cylinder with n facets in each direction. For more options, see >> `help cylinder`.
- `[x,y,z] = ellipsoid(n)` constructs the `meshgrid` for an ellipsoid with n facets in each direction. For more options, see >> `help ellipsoid`.
- `[x,y,z] = sphere(n)` constructs the `meshgrid` for ansphere with n facets in each direction. For more options, see >> `help sphere`.
- `meshc(x,y,z)` makes a mesh plot with contours below. For more options, see >> `help meshc`.
- `meshz(x,y,z)` makes a mesh plot with vertical line extensions. For more options, see >> `help meshz`.
- `surfc(x,y,z)` makes a surface plot with contours below. For more options, see >> `help surfc`.
- `surfz(x,y,z)` makes a surface plot with vertical line extensions. For more options, see >> `help surfz`.
- `waterfall(x,y,z)` makes a mesh plot with vertical line extensions only in the x direction. For more options, see >> `help waterfall`.

Figure 11.17 *The Klein bottle*

11.4.6 Assembling Compound Surfaces

We can assemble more complex solid bodies by constructing simple surfaces and concatenating the data before submitting it to the rendering machine. Shapes of considerable complexity can be assembled this way. Consider, for example, the Klein bottle, a well-documented example of topological curiosity. The particular example shown in Figure 11.17 was constructed by building the individual components and then concatenating the arrays.

The code is a little too complex to be included here, but can be found on the companion Web site.

11.5 Manipulating Plotted Data

Two new features introduced with MATLAB 7.6 (R2008a) allow you to interact with the data presented in a plot. Brushing allows you to select portions of the data presented in a plot and make changes to the values presented. Linking allows you to connect the plotted data to the underlying data source, so that when you make changes to the plotted data, these changes are reflected in the data source. Whereas these tools allow the user to change the appearance of data presentations interactively, a careful user would return to the original tools that created the plots and explicitly insert the logic that changes the appearance of the results. This provides a traceable set of programs that show exactly how the data were generated.

11.6 Engineering Example—Visualizing Geographic Data

You have been given two files of data: `atlanta.txt`, which presents the streets of Atlanta in graphical form, and `ttimes.txt`, which gives the travel times between Atlanta suburbs and the city center. You have been asked to present these data sets in a manner that will help to visualize and validate the data.

11.6.1 Analyzing the Data

First, we proceed to determine the nature of the data by opening the files and examining their format and content.

1. Determine the file format: the first step is to open the data files in a plain text editor. The format appears to be consistent with that of a text file delimited by tab characters. Since there are no strings in the file, it should be suitable to be read using the built-in `dlmread(...)` function.

2. Discern the street map file content: Table 11.1 shows the first few lines of the file `atlanta.txt` simplified by omitting certain irrelevant columns. The numbers in columns 3–6 are pairs, the first of the pair being a large negative number, and the second a smaller positive number. Assuming that each row of this file is a street segment, these could be the x-y coordinates of the ends of a line. A little thought confirms this guess when we realize that the latitude of Atlanta is −84° 42′ relative to the Greenwich meridian, and its longitude is 33° 65′— clearly, the values in these columns are 1,000,000 times the latitude and longitude of points within the city, probably each end of street segments. Column 7 contains numbers mostly in the range 1–6, which could indicate the type of street. We could explore this idea by coloring each line according to that value.

3. Discern the travel time file content: Table 11.2 shows the first few lines of the file `ttimes.txt` simplified by omitting certain irrelevant columns. The

Table 11.1 Street map data

...	...	−84546100.00	33988160.00	−84556050.00	33993620.00	1.00	...
...	...	−84546080.00	33988480.00	−84558400.00	33995480.00	1.00	...
...	...	−84243880.00	33780010.00	−84249980.00	33800840.00	1.00	...

{etc}

Table 11.2 Travel time data

I	I	. . .	−84575725	33554573	14.34
I	2	. . .	−84569612	33554573	0
I	3	. . .	−84563499	33554573	0
I	4	. . .	−84557387	33554573	0

{ etc}

same latitude/longitude values occur in columns 4 and 5, but they are not repeated, suggesting that the data in this file are in a different form. Examining the first two columns, the numbers in column 2 cycle repeatedly from 1 to 75, with column 1 counting the number of cycles up to 75. Furthermore, the values in column 5 are the same whenever column 1 is the same, and the values in column 4 are the same whenever the value in column 2 matches. This seems to be much like the plaid that results from a `meshgrid(...)` function call. The values in column 6 then become evident—they would be the z values of the plaid, and it seems reasonable to assume that they represent the travel time in minutes.

11.6.2 Displaying the Data

With this much understanding of the data sources, we proceed to solve the problem of presenting the data. The script shown in Listing 11.12 shows the code used to visualize these data files.

Listing 11.12 Map data analysis

```
      % draw the streets
 1. raw = dlmread('atlanta.txt');
 2. streets = raw(:,3:7);
 3. [rows,cols] = size(streets)
 4. colors = 'rgbkcmo';
 5. for in = 1:rows
 6.      x = streets(in,[1 3])/1000000;
 7.      y = streets(in,[2 4])/1000000;
 8.      col = streets(in,5);
 9.      col(col < 1) = 7;
10.      col(col > 6) = 7;
11.      plot(x,y,colors(col));
12.      hold on
13. end
      % plot the travel times
14. tt = dlmread('ttimes.txt');
15. [rows,cols] = size(tt)
16. for in = 1:rows
17.      r = tt(in, 1); c = tt(in, 2);
18.      xc(r,c) = tt(in, 4)/1000000;
19.      yc(r,c) = tt(in, 5)/1000000;
20.      zc(r,c) = tt(in, 6);
21. end
22. surf(xc, yc, zc)
23. shading interp
24. alpha(.5)
25. grid on
26. axis tight
27. xlabel('Longitude')
28. ylabel('Latitude')
29. zlabel('Travel Time (min)')
30. view(-30, 45)
```

In Listing 11.12:

> Line 1: Reads the street map data.
>
> Lines 2–3: Extract the relevant columns and determine the size of the array.
>
> Line 4: Color symbols to use for the lines.
>
> Line 5: Traverses the rows of the file.
>
> Lines 6 and 7: Extract the longitude and latitude in degrees.
>
> Lines 8–10: Extract and limit the line colors.
>
> Lines 11 and 12: Plot the street lines on the same figure.
>
> Lines 14 and 15: Read the travel times.
>
> Line 16: Constructs the plaid by traversing the array.
>
> Line 17: Extracts the row and column numbers.
>
> Lines 18–20: Extract the plaid values.
>
> Lines 22–30: Plot and display the results.

Figure 11.18 shows the resulting plot. As a credibility check, the plot has been rotated to look straight down on the map. Rotate the plot to other view angles to understand the 3-D nature of the information. The travel time surface shows "valleys" of low travel times that follow the paths of the major expressways through the city.

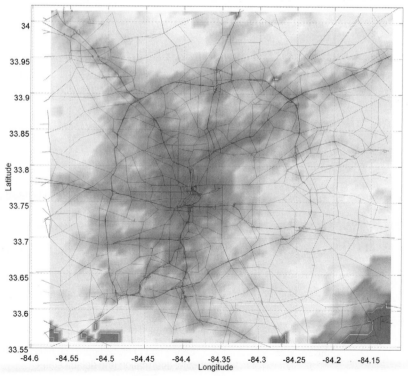

Figure 11.18 *Atlanta travel times*

Chapter Summary

This chapter presented the principles and practice of plotting:

- Basic 2-D line plots are accomplished by using `plot(x,y)`, where `x` is the independent variable and `y` the dependent variable
- 2-D parametric plots are accomplished by using `plot(x,y)`, where both `x` and `y` are dependent on another independent variable
- 3-D line and parametric plots are accomplished by using `plot3(x,y,z)`
- Basic 3-D surface plots are accomplished by building a plaid using `[xx yy] = meshgrid(x,y)`, computing the `zz` layer as a function of `xx` and `yy`, and then plotting the surface using `mesh(xx, yy, zz)` or `surf(xx, yy, zz)`
- Parametric surface plots, like parametric line plots, are achieved by building the plaid with two independent variables and making `xx`, `yy`, and `zz` functions of those independent variables
- Bodies of rotation are a special case of parametric surface plots where one of the independent variables is an angle with values between 0 and 2π.

Special Characters, Reserved Words, and Functions—2-D

Special Characters, Reserved Words, and Functions	Description	Discussed in This Section
`axis(...)`	Freezes the current axis scaling for subsequent plots or specifies the axis dimensions	11.1.2
`bar`	Generates a bar graph	11.2.4
`barh`	Generates a horizontal bar graph	11.2.4
`clf`	Clears the current figure	11.1.1
`close all`	Closes all graphics windows	11.1.1
`colormap <spec>`	Specifies a sequence of colors to be used when a cycle of color values is required	11.1.2
`figure`	Opens a new figure window	11.1.1
`fill(x,y,n)`	Fills a polygon defined by `x` and `y` with color index `n`	11.2.4
`grid off`	Turns the grid off (default is on)	11.1.2
`grid on`	Adds a grid to the current and all subsequent graphs in the current figure	11.1.2
`hist`	Generates a histogram	11.2.4
`hold off`	Sets a flag to erase figure contents before adding new information (the default state)	11.1.2

Special Characters, Reserved Words, and Functions	Description	Discussed in This Section
hold on	Sets a flag not to erase figure contents before adding new information	11.1.2
legend(ca)	Adds a legend to a graph	11.1.2
loglog	Generates an x-y plot, with both axes scaled logarithmically	11.2.4
pie	Generates a pie chart	11.2.4
plot(...)	Creates an x-y plot	11.1.2
polar	Creates a polar plot	11.2.4
semilogx	Generates an x-y plot, with the x-axis scaled logarithmically	11.2.4
semilogy	Generates an x-y plot, with the y-axis scaled logarithmically	11.2.4
shading <spec>	Shades a surface according to the specification	11.1.2
subplot(plts, n)	Divides the graphics window into sections available for plotting	11.1.1
text(x,y,{z,} str)	Adds a text string to a graph	11.1.2
title(str)	Adds a title to a plot	11.1.2
view(az,el)	Sets the angle from which to view a plot	11.1.2
xlabel(str)	Adds a label to the x-axis	11.1.2
ylabel(str)	Adds a label to the y-axis	11.1.2
zlabel(str)	Adds a label to the z-axis	11.1.2

Special Characters, Reserved Words, and Functions—3-D

Special Characters, Reserved Words, and Functions	Description	Discussed in This Section
alpha(x)	Sets the transparency of the surface	11.3.3
bar3	Generates a 3-D bar graph	11.3.3
barh3	Generates a horizontal 3-D bar graph	11.3.3
contour(xx, yy, zz)	Generates a contour plot	11.4.5
cylinder(n)	Constructs the plaid for a cylinder with n facets	11.4.5
ellipsoid(n)	Constructs the plaid for an ellipsoid with n facets	11.4.5
lightangle(az,el)	Sets the angle of a light source, angles in degrees	11.4.5
mesh(xx,yy,zz)	Generates a mesh plot of a surface	11.4.1

Special Characters, Reserved Words, and Functions	Description	Discussed in This Section
meshc(xx,yy,zz)	Generates a mesh plot of a surface with a contour below it	11.4.5
meshz(xx,yy,zz)	Generates a mesh plot of a surface with vertical line extensions	11.4.5
[rr cc] = meshgrid(r,c)	Creates a plaid for 3-D plots	11.4.1
pie3	Generates a 3-D pie chart	11.3.3
plot3(...)	Generates a 3-D line plot	11.3.1
sphere(n)	Example function used to demonstrate graphing	11.4.5
surf(xx,yy,zz)	Generates a surface plot	11.4.1
surfc(xx,yy,zz)	Generates a combination surface and contour plot	11.4.5
waterfall(xx,yy,zz)	Generates a mesh plot of a surface with vertical line extensions in the x direction only	11.4.5

Self Test

Use the following questions to check your understanding of the material in this chapter:

True or False

T 1. The plot(...) function needs only one parameter to function correctly.

F 2. Plot enhancement functions may be called before or after the function that plots the data.

F 3. You must provide plots for all the specified sub-plot areas.

T 4. meshgrid(...) accepts vectors of length m and n that bound the edges of the plaid and produces two arrays sized m × n giving the complete plaid.

F 5. To construct a parametric surface, both independent parameters must be angles.

F 6. When rotating a function about the y-axis, the variables along the x and y axes are computed from a classic polar-to-Cartesian conversion.

F 7. To compute a body of rotation, the curve must be a continuous, differentiable function.

F 8. Bodies of rotation are confined rotating about the x, y, or z axes.

Fill in the Blanks

1. Each time `figure` is called, a(n) _new figure_ is made available, with figure number _the next higher_

2. To prepare for plotting, put ___clf___ or _close all_ at the beginning of your script.

3. Parametric plots allow the variables on each axis to be _dependent_ on a(n) _separate_ , _independent_ variable.

4. The simplest surface plots are obtained by defining a(n)_z_ value for each point on _an x-y plaid_

5. We construct a sphere by wrapping a(n) _plaid_ with two _angles_ as the independent variables around the sphere.

6. Bodies of rotation are created by rotating a(n) _linear curve_ about a(n) _specified axis_

Programming Projects

1. Write a script that creates six sub-plots in two columns each with three rows. Each plot should have an appropriate title and labels on the x and y axes. The plot in the top left sub-plot should be `y = cos(θ)` for values of θ from −2π to 2π. Subsequent plots going across the rows before going down the columns should be of `y = cos(2θ)`, `y = cos(3θ)`, etc., to `y = cos(6θ)` over the same range of θ.

2. Your task is to create a script called `thisPlot`. This script should do the following:
   a. Ask the user to enter in a positive number, N, greater than 5.
   b. Calculate the factorial for each number from 1 to N. Each of these values should be stored into a vector.
   c. Display a graph titled `'Logarithmic Growth'`, where the logarithms for each of the factorials are displayed.
   d. Add to the graph a continuous linear line that follows the equation `y = x` with x values from 1 to N.
   e. Since the numbers will have different magnitudes, use `plotyy` to plot the linear values on the right hand axis.

3. Write a function called `sineGraph` that graphs a sine function four times between the interval `[start,stop]` on the same graph. The `start` and `stop` values should be parameters of the function. The number of points per interval will vary. More specifically:
   • The first time you graph the sine function, you should have two evenly spaced points, `start` and `stop`
   • The next plot should have four evenly spaced points—`start`, `stop`, and two points between them

- The third should have eight evenly spaced points and the fourth 256 points.
- Make sure to add a legend and a title—'Multiple graphs on one plot'—and to label the axes. Make sure that each line has a different color.
- The function should return the x and y values for the 256 point set.

Test your function with the following intervals [0,π/2], [0,2π], [0,4π], [0,16π]

4. This programming problem will compare the surf(...) and mesh(...) functions by putting two 3-D side-by-side plots for comparison using subplot(...). You should label all axes accordingly ('X-axis', 'Y-axis', etc.) and title your plot corresponding to the problem statement.
   a. On the left side, plot the function f(x,y)=x^2*cos(y) in the range x= -5:5 and y= -5:5 using mesh and name your plot 'Using Mesh'.
   b. On the right side, plot the same function, in the same range, but using surf. Name your plot 'Using Surf'.

5. Georgia Tech wants to tear down the Campanile and build a new one that is ridiculously tall. However, before it is built, it needs you to model it. Using the equation z = 1/(x^2 + y^2) as the model, write a script that will plot the Campanile. Your domain should be -.75 <= x <=.75 and -.75 <= y <= .75 using an increment of .05 for each range. Set your axes such that all of the x, y domain is seen and z runs from 0 to 300. Use surf(...) to plot your image.

6. You are provided the file 'data.csv', which contains two columns of numbers. Each column contains the same number of elements. The first row contains the titles of the x and y values, respectively. Create a script called spreadSheetPlot that plots the data in this file. The first column represents your x values, and the second column is your y values. Read the numbers from the file and make a plot of the x vs. y values. Title your plot 'spreadSheetPlot' and use the first row data to label the x and y axes. For example, the spreadsheet might look like:

	A	B
1	time(sec)	distance(ft)
2	0	0.84
3	0.2	0.23
4	0.4	0.77
5	0.6	1.06
6	0.8	1.28
7	1	1.48
8	1.2	1.63
9	...	...
10	...	...
11	...	...
12		

7. You just realized that February 14th has passed and you haven't gotten anything for your Valentine. Since your date is a CS major, sending the lucky person a coded heart seems like a cool and sincere thing to do. Make sure that you follow each and every instruction carefully, or your heart will end up broken. Trust us.

You are going to write a script to draw this heart using the following steps:

a. Create a plaid [xx, yy] using x values with range (0 to 2π, with an interval 0.05π) and y values with the range (0 to 1, with an interval 0.05).

b. Define the following variables:

```
c=[0.1 + 0.9*(π-abs(xx - π))/π ] .* yy

aa = c .* cos(xx)

bb = c.* sin(xx)

zz = (-2)*aa.^3 + (3/2)*c.^2 + 0.5
```

c. Plot `zz` against `aa` and `bb` using the `surf()` function with interpolated colors.

8. Write a function named `plotRotation` that takes in two vectors, x and z, and a vector th. Your function should plot three plots in the same figure by using the `subplot` command. The figure should have 1×3 plots. The plots should be as follows:

a. z vs. x, titled `'z vs. x'`. Note that you will have to use `plot3()` to correctly plot this in the x-z plane rather than the x-y plane a `plot()` would do. Also, you should use `view(0, 0)` to make the plot produced by `plot3()` show up as 2-D.

b. z vs. x rotated around the x-axis using `mesh()` with flat shading and a square axis, titled `'z vs. x about x using mesh'`.

c. z vs. x rotated around the z-axis using `surf()` with `interp` shading and a square axis, titled `'z vs. x about z using surf'`.

For plots b and c, the input vector th should be used for your independent vector theta, which is used to convert from polar-to-Cartesian coordinates. Don't forget to title and label each of the three plots.

CHAPTER 12

Matrices

Chapter Objectives

This chapter shows matrices as logical extensions of arrays. You will learn about two specialized operations performed with matrices:

- Multiplication for coordinate rotation
- Division for solving simultaneous equations

Although the matrix operations that are the subject of this chapter can be performed on pairs of vectors or arrays that meet certain criteria, when using these operations, we tend to refer to the data objects as matrices. In most mathematical discussions, the words "matrix" and "array" can be used interchangeably, and rightly so, because they store data in exactly the same form. Moreover, almost all of the operations we can perform on an array can also be performed on a matrix—logical operations, concatenation, slicing, and most of the arithmetic operations behave identically. The fact that some of the mathematical operations are defined differently gives us a chance to think about an important concept that is usually well hidden within the MATLAB language definition.

12.1 Concept: Behavioral Abstraction

Recall the following concepts:

- *Abstraction* is the ability to ignore specific details and generalize the description of an entity
- *Data abstraction* is the specific example of abstraction that we first considered whereby we could treat vectors of data (and later other collections like structures and arrays) as single entities rather than enumerating their elements individually
- *Procedural abstraction* are functions that collect multiple operations into a form; once they are developed, we can overlook the specific details and treat them as a "black box," much as we treat built-in functions

Behavioral abstraction combines data and procedural abstraction, encapsulating not only collections of data, but also the operations that are legal to perform on that data. One might argue that this is a new, irrelevant concept best ignored until "we just have to!" However, consider the rules we have had to establish for what we can and cannot do with data collections we have seen so far. For example, am I able to add two arrays together? Yes, but only if they have the same number of rows and columns, or if one of them is scalar. Can I add two character strings? Almost the same answer, except that each string is first converted to a numerical quantity and the result is a vector of numbers and not a string. Can I add two cell arrays? No.

So at least some, and maybe all, data collections also "understand" the set of operations that are permitted on the data. This encapsulation of data and operations is the essence of behavioral abstraction. Therefore, we distinguish arrays from matrices not by the data they collect, but by the operations that are legal to perform on them.

12.2 Matrix Operations

The arithmetic operations that differ between arrays and matrices are multiplication, division, and exponentiation.

12.2.1 Matrix Multiplication

Previously, when we considered multiplying two arrays, we called this scalar multiplication, and it had the following typical array operation characteristics:

- Either the two arrays must be the same size, or one of them must be scalar
- The multiplication was indicated with the .* operator

- The result was an array with the same size as the larger original array
- Each element of the result was the product of the corresponding elements in the original two arrays

This is best illustrated in Figure 12.1. Scalar division and exponentiation have the same constraints.

Matrix multiplication, on the other hand, performed using the normal `*` operator, is an entirely different logical operation, as shown in Figure 12.2. The logical characteristics of matrix multiplication are as follows:

- The two matrices do not have to be the same size. The requirements are either:
  - One of the matrices is a scalar, in which case the matrix operation reduces to a scalar multiply.
  - The number of columns in the first matrix must equal the number of rows in the second. We refer to these as the **inner dimensions.** The result is a new matrix with the column count of the first matrix and the row count of the second.
- If, as illustrated, A is an m × n matrix and B is an n × p matrix, the result of A `*` B is an m × p matrix.
- The item at (i, j) in the result matrix is the sum of the scalar product of the ith row of A and the jth column of B.

$$
A_{(mxn)} = \begin{bmatrix} a_{11} & a_{12} & \cdots & a_{1n} \\ a_{21} & a_{22} & \cdots & a_{2n} \\ \vdots & & \ddots & \\ a_{m1} & a_{m2} & \cdots & a_{mn} \end{bmatrix} \quad .* \quad B_{(mxn)} = \begin{bmatrix} b_{11} & b_{12} & \cdots & b_{1n} \\ b_{21} & b_{22} & \cdots & b_{2n} \\ \vdots & & \ddots & \\ b_{m1} & b_{m2} & \cdots & b_{mn} \end{bmatrix}
$$

$$
\longrightarrow \begin{bmatrix} a_{11} \times b_{11} & a_{12} \times b_{12} & \cdots & a_{1n} \times b_{1n} \\ a_{21} \times b_{21} & a_{22} \times b_{22} & \cdots & a_{2n} \times b_{2n} \\ \vdots & & \ddots & \\ a_{m1} \times b_{m1} & a_{m2} \times b_{m2} & \cdots & a_{mn} \times b_{mn} \end{bmatrix}
$$

Figure 12.1 *Matrix dot multiply*

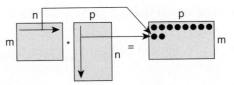

Figure 12.2 *Mechanics of matrix multiplication*

- Whereas with scalar multiplication A .* B gives the same result as B .* A, this is not the case with matrix multiplication. In fact, if A * B works, B * A will not work unless both matrices are square, and even then the results are different. (Proof of this can be derived immediately from Figure 12.3 by eliminating the third row and column and exchanging a for b. All four terms of the result of A * B are different from B * A.)

- Whereas with scalar multiplication the original array A can be recovered by dividing the result by B, this is not the case with matrix multiplication unless both matrices are square.

- The **identity matrix,** sometimes given the symbol I_n, is a square matrix with n rows and n columns that is zero everywhere except on its major diagonal, which contains the value 1. I_n has the special property that when pre-multiplied by any matrix A with n columns, or post-multiplied with any matrix A with n rows, the result is A. We will need this property to derive matrix division below. (The built-in function eye(...) generates the identity matrix.)

Figure 12.3 illustrates the mathematics for the case where a 3×2 matrix is multiplied by a 2×3 matrix, resulting in a 3×3 matrix.

$$A_{(mxn)} = \begin{bmatrix} a_{11} & a_{12} \\ a_{21} & a_{22} \\ a_{m1} & a_{m2} \end{bmatrix} * B_{(mxn)} = \begin{bmatrix} b_{11} & b_{12} & b_{13} \\ b_{21} & b_{22} & b_{23} \end{bmatrix}$$

$$\rightarrow \begin{bmatrix} (a_{11} \times b_{11} + a_{12} \times b_{21}) & (a_{11} \times b_{12} + a_{12} \times b_{22}) & (a_{11} \times b_{13} + a_{12} \times b_{23}) \\ (a_{21} \times b_{11} + a_{22} \times b_{21}) & (a_{21} \times b_{12} + a_{22} \times b_{22}) & (a_{21} \times b_{13} + a_{22} \times b_{23}) \\ (a_{31} \times b_{11} + a_{32} \times b_{21}) & (a_{31} \times b_{12} + a_{32} \times b_{22}) & (a_{31} \times b_{13} + a_{32} \times b_{23}) \end{bmatrix}$$

Figure 12.3 *Matrix multiplication*

12.2.2 Matrix Division

Matrix division is the logical process of reversing the effects of a matrix multiplication. The goal is as follows: given $A_{n \times n}$, $B_{n \times p}$, and $C_{n \times p}$, where $C = A * B$, we wish to define the mathematical equivalent of C/A that will result in B.

Since $C = A * B$, we are actually searching for some matrix $K_{n \times n}$ by which we can multiply each side of the above equation:

$$K * C = K * A * B$$

This multiplication would accomplish the division we desire if $K * A$ were to result in I_n, the identity matrix. If this were the case, pre-multiplying C by K would result in $I_n * B$, or simply B by the definition of I_n above. The matrix K is referred to as the inverse of A, or A^{-1}. The algebra for computing this inverse is messy but well defined. In fact, Gaussian Elimination to solve linear simultaneous equations accomplishes the same thing. The MATLAB language defines both functions ($inv(A)$) and operators ("back divide," \) that accomplish this. However, two things should be noted:

- This inverse does not exist for all matrices—if any two rows or columns of a matrix are linearly related, the matrix is *singular* and does not have an inverse
- Only non-singular, square matrices have an inverse (just as a set of linear equations is soluble only if there are as many equations as there are unknown variables)

12.2.3 Matrix Exponentiation

For completeness, we mention here that matrix operations include exponentiation. However, this does not suggest that one would encounter $A_{n \times n}{}^{B_{n \times n}}$ in the scope of our applications. Rather, our usage of matrix exponentiation will be confined to A^k where k is any non-zero integer value. The result for positive k is accomplished by multiplying A by itself k times (using matrix multiplication). The result for negative k is accomplished by inverting A^{-k}. (There is, in fact, meaning in matrix exponentials with non-scalar exponents, but this involves advanced concepts with eigen values and eigenvectors and is beyond the scope of this text.)

12.3 Implementation

In this section, we see how MATLAB implements matrix multiplication and division. However, since applications that require matrix exponentiation A^k where k is anything but a scalar quantity are beyond the scope of this text, we will not look at its implementation in MATLAB.

12.3.1 Matrix Multiplication

Matrix multiplication is accomplished by using the "normal" multiplication symbol, as illustrated in Exercise 12.1.

In Exercise 12.1 we make the following observations:

- Entry 1 creates a 2×3 matrix, A
- Entry 2 creates a 3×1 matrix, B, a column vector
- Entry 3 indicates that this multiplication is legal because the columns in A match the rows in B
- Entry 4 shows that, likewise, it is legal to multiply a 1×2 vector by a 2×3 matrix
- Entry 5 creates an identity matrix
- Entry 6 shows that pre-multiplying A by this is legal because the inner dimensions match

Exercise 12.1 Matrix multiply

```
1. >> A = [2 5 7; 1 3 42]
A =
     2     5     7
     1     3    42
2. >> B = [1 2 3]'
B =
     1
     2
     3
3. >> A * B
ans =
    33
   133
4. >> (1:2) * A
ans =
     4    11    91
5. >> I2 = eye(2)
I2 =
     1     0
     0     1
6. >> I2 * A
ans =
     2     5     7
     1     3    42
7. >> A*I2
??? Error using ==> mtimes
Inner matrix dimensions must agree.
8. >> A*eye(3)
ans =
     2     5     7
     1     3    42
```

- Entry 7 shows that post-multiplying A by I_2 does not work because the inner dimensions do not match
- Entry 8 uses I_3 to post-multiply legally

12.3.2 Matrix Division

Matrix division is accomplished in a number of ways, all of which appear to work, but some give the wrong answer. Returning to the division problem described in Section 12.2.2, we know that A is a square matrix of side n, and B and c have n rows, and c = A * B. If we are actually given the matrices A and B, we can compute B in one of the following ways:

- B = inv(A) * C —using the MATLAB inv(...) function to compute the inverse of B
- B = A \ C—"back dividing" B into c to produce the same result
- B = C / A—apparently performing the same operation, *but giving different answers*

Technical Insight 12.1

According to the MATLAB language help system, the third way really computes (C'\A')', which can only work if C is also square.

The order in which the matrix multiply is done affects the value of the result; therefore, care must be taken to ensure that the appropriate inversion or division is used. Study the results of Exercise 12.2 carefully.

Exercise 12.2 Matrix divide

```
>> A = magic(3)
A =
     8     1     6
     3     5     7
     4     9     2
>> B = [1 26 24; 9 22 20; 5 12 16]
B =
     1    26    24
     9    22    20
     5    12    16
>> AB = A * B
AB =
    47   302   308
    83   272   284
    95   326   308
>> BA = B * A
BA =
   182   347   236
   218   299   248
   140   209   146
```

continued on next page

```
>> AB * inv(B)
ans =
     8    1    6
     3    5    7
     4    9    2
>> AB / B
ans =
     8    1    6
     3    5    7
     4    9    2
>> B \ BA
ans =
     8    1    6
     3    5    7
     4    9    2
>> BA / B
ans =
   -4.3000   29.2000  -15.3000
   -9.9667   27.5333   -3.9667
   -5.7333   20.7667   -8.2333
```

In Exercise 12.2 we make the following observations:

Entries 1 and 2 construct two 3×3 matrices, A and B

Entries 3 and 4 pre-multiply and post-multiply B and A; recall that we expect this to produce different answers

Entry 5 shows that since we defined inv(B) as that function that produces the result B*inv(B)=I, this should produce a matrix with the same values as A

Entry 6 reveals that normal division by B should also produce a matrix with the same values as A

Entry 7 shows that back dividing B into BA should also produce a matrix equal to A

Entry 8 verifies that dividing BA by B works but does not return the matrix A

12.4 Rotating Coordinates

A common use for matrix multiplication is for rotating coordinates in two or three dimensions. Previously we have seen the ability to rotate a complete picture by changing the viewing angle. We can move and scale items on a plot by adding coordinate offsets or multiplying them by scalar quantities. However, frequently the need arises to rotate the coordinates of a graphical object by some angle. We can use matrix multiplication to rotate individual items in a picture in two or three dimensions.

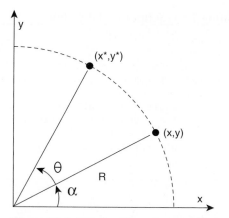

Figure 12.4 *Rotating Cartesian coordinates*

12.4.1 2-D Rotation

The mathematics implementing rotation in two dimensions is relatively straightforward, as shown in Figure 12.4. If the original point location P is (x, y) and you wish to find the point P* (x*, y*) that is the result of rotating P by the angle θ about the origin of coordinates, the mathematics are as follows:

```
x* = x cosθ - y sinθ
y* = x sinθ + y cosθ
```

which can be expressed as the matrix equation:

```
P* = A * P
```

where A is found by:

```
A = [cosθ -sinθ
     sinθ  cosθ]
```

To rotate the x-y coordinates of a graphic object in the x-y plane about some point, P, other than the origin, you would do as follows:

1. Translate the object so that P is at the origin by subtracting P from all the object's coordinates

2. Perform the rotation by multiplying each coordinate by the rotation matrix shown above

3. Translate the rotated object back to P by adding P to all the rotated coordinates

Rotating a Line Listing 12.1 illustrates a simple script to rotate a line about the origin.

Listing 12.1　Script to rotate a line

```
 1. pts =      [3, 10
 2.             1, 3];
 3. plot(pts(1,:), pts(2,:))
 4. axis ([0 10 0 10]), axis equal
 5. hold on
 6. for angle = 0.05:0.05:1
 7.     A = [ cos(angle), -sin(angle); sin(angle), cos(angle) ];
 8.     pr = A * pts;
 9.     plot(pr(1,:), pr(2,:))
10. end
```

In Listing 12.1:

> Lines 1 and 2: Considering the form of the rotation equations, we need to define the points where the x values are in the first row and the y values are in the second row.
>
> Line 3: Plots the line in its original location from (3, 1) to (10, 3).
>
> Lines 4 and 5: Fix the axes at a suitable size.
>
> Line 6: Iterates across a selection of angles (in radians).
>
> Line 7: Computes the rotation matrix.
>
> Line 8: Rotates the original line by the current angle.
>
> Line 9: Plots the rotated line.

Figure 12.5 shows the plot resulting from this script.

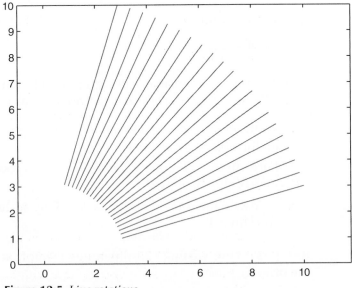

Figure 12.5　*Line rotations*

Listing 12.2 Simulating stars

```
1. nst = 20; th = 0;
2. for ndx = 1:nst
3.        pos(ndx,:) = rand(1,2)*10;
4.        scale(ndx) = rand(1,1) * .9 + .1;
5.        rate(ndx) = rand(1,1) * 3 + 1;
6. end
7. while true
8.        for str = 1:nst
9.                  star(pos(str,:), ...      % location
10.                          scale(str), ...  % scale
11.                          th, ...           % basic angle
12.                          rate(str))        % angle multiplier
13.        end
14.        colormap autumn
15.        axis equal; axis([-.5 10.5 -.5 10.5])
16.        axis off; hold off
17.        th = mod(th + .1, 20*pi);
18.        pause(0.1)
19. end
```

Twinkling Stars As a second example, consider the problem of simulating twinkling stars. One way to accomplish this is to draw two triangles for each star rotating in opposite directions. The script shown in Listing 12.2 accomplishes this.

In Listing 12.2:

> Line 1: Sets the number of stars and the initial rotation angle.
>
> Lines 2–6: Establish the location, size, and rotation speed of each star.
>
> Lines 7–19: Continue drawing until interrupted by Ctrl-C.
>
> Lines 8–13: Draw each star at the current rotation (see Listing 12.3 for the star(...) function).
>
> Line 14: Chooses a color map with yellow as the first color.
>
> Lines 15 and 16: Show the normal display environment setup.
>
> Line 17: Updates the angle of rotation.
>
> Line 18: Waits 1/10 sec for the figure to be displayed. Without this, the computation would be continuous and the user would never see the result.

In Listing 12.3:

> Line 1: Draws one star at location [pt(1), pt(2)] with scale sc, rotation speed v, and angle th.
>
> Lines 2–4: Invoke the helper function triangle(...) to draw two triangles rotating in opposite directions.
>
> Line 6: Function to draw one triangle with the following parameters: up, with values 1 for upright and -1 for point down; th, the scaled

Listing 12.3 Drawing one star

```
1. function star(pt, sc, v, th)
   % draw a star at pt(1), pt(2),
   % scaled with sc, at angle v*th
2.     triangle(1, v*th, pt, sc)
3.     hold on
4.     triangle(-1, v*th, pt, sc)
5. end
6. function triangle( up, th, pt, sc )
7.     pts = [-.5   .5     0   -.5;   % x values
8.            -.289 -.289 .577 -.289]; % y values
       % rotation matrix
9.     A = sc * [cos(th), -sin(th); sin(th), cos(th)];
10.    thePts = A * pts;
11.    fill( thePts(1,:) + pt(1), ...
12.          up*thePts(2,:) + pt(2), 1);
13. end
```

rotation angle; and `pt` and `sc`, which are passed directly through from the `star(...)` function.

Lines 7 and 8: Are coordinates of an equilateral triangle.

Line 9: Computes the rotation matrix and applies the scaling factor.

Line 10: Rotates and scales the points of the triangle.

Lines 11 and 12: Call the function `fill(...)` to fill the triangle, offsetting the `x` and `y` coordinates by the original location of the triangle, and scaling `y` by the `up` multiplier to invert the triangle if necessary.

The results of this script are shown in Figure 12.6.

12.4.2 3-D Rotation

The mathematics implementing rotation in three dimensions is a natural extension of the 2-D rotation case. We present here a simple way to make this extension. The 2-D rotation in Section 12.4.1 that rotates by the angle θ in the x-y plane is actually rotating about the z-axis. If P* and P are now 3-D coordinates, we can rotate P by an angle θ about the z-axis with the equation:

```
P* = Rz * P
```

where R_z is computed as

```
Rz =   [ cosθ,    -sinθ,    0
          sinθ,     cosθ,    0
            0,        0,     1]
```

Figure 12.6 *Stars*

Similarly, we can develop matrices R_x and R_y that rotate about the x and y axes by angles ϕ and ψ, respectively.

```
Rx  =     [    1,         0,           0
               0,       cosφ,        -sinφ
               0,       sinφ,         cosφ]
Ry  =     [  cosψ,       0,          sinψ
               0,         1,           0
            -sinψ,       0,          cosψ]
P*  =  Rx * Ry * Rz  *  P
```

An example of a script to rotate the solid cube drawn in Chapter 11 is shown in Listing 12.4. The major problem with rotating solid objects is that the coordinates of the object are defined as arrays of points. However, the rotation matrices need each set of coordinates in single rows. To accomplish this, we will use the `reshape(...)` function to transform the coordinates to and from the row vectors necessary for the coordinate rotation.

In Listing 12.4:

> Lines 1–12: Build the coordinates of the cube centered at the origin.
>
> Lines 13 and 14: Determine the length of the linearized row vector for the `reshape(...)` function.
>
> Lines 15 and 16: Set up the three rotation angle parameters—the initial values and the increments.
>
> Lines 17 and 18: Repeat the drawing loop until the variable `go` is reset.

Listing 12.4 Rotating a solid cube

```
 1. xx = [ 0   0   0   0   0;
 2.        -1  -1   1   1  -1;
 3.        -1  -1   1   1  -1;
 4.         0   0   0   0   0]
 5. yy = [ 0   0   0   0   0;
 6.        -1   1   1  -1  -1;
 7.        -1   1   1  -1  -1;
 8.         0   0   0   0   0]
 9. zz = [ 1   1   1   1   1;
10.         1   1   1   1   1;
11.        -1  -1  -1  -1  -1;
12.        -1  -1  -1  -1  -1]
13. [r c] = size(xx);
14. ln = r*c; % length of reshaped vector
15. th = 0; ph = 0; ps = 0;
16. dth = 0.05; dph = 0.03; dps = 0.01;
17. go = true
18. while go
19.     surf(xx+4, yy, zz)
20.     shading interp; colormap autumn
21.     hold on; alpha(0.5)
22.     Rz = [cos(th) -sin(th)   0
23.           sin(th)  cos(th)   0
24.              0        0      1];
25.     Ry = [cos(ph)    0    -sin(ph)
26.              0       1       0
27.           sin(ph)    0   cos(ph)];
28.     Rx = [ 1         0       0
29.            0       cos(ps) -sin(ps)
30.            0       sin(ps) cos(ps)];
31.     P(1,:) = reshape(xx, 1, ln);
32.     P(2,:) = reshape(yy, 1, ln);
33.     P(3,:) = reshape(zz, 1, ln);
34.     Q = Rx*Ry*Rz*P;
35.     qx = reshape(Q(1,:), r, c);
36.     qy = reshape(Q(2,:), r, c);
37.     qz = reshape(Q(3,:), r, c);
38.     surf(qx, qy, qz)
39.     shading interp
40.     axis equal; axis off; hold off
41.     axis([-2 6 -2 2 -2 2])
42.     lightangle(40, 65); alpha(0.5)
43.     th = th+dth; ph = ph+dph; ps = ps+dps;
44.     go = ps < pi/4
45.     pause(0.03)
46. end
```

Lines 19–21: Draw one cube not rotated four units down the x-axis.

Lines 22–30: Set up the rotation matrices.

Lines 31–33: Reshape the x, y, and z arrays into linear form.

Line 34: Performs the rotation.

Figure 12.7 *Solid cubes*

Lines 35–37: Recover the original array shapes.

Lines 38–42: Draw the rotated cube.

Line 43: Updates the rotation angles.

Line 44: Shows the terminating condition.

Line 45: Pauses to give the figure time to draw.

The results after running this script are shown in Figure 12.7. Notice that the mechanization of the top face has caused a "wrapped parcel" effect on the light reflections off that surface.

12.5 Solving Simultaneous Linear Equations

A common use for matrix division is solving simultaneous linear equations. To be solvable, simultaneous linear equations must be expressed as N independent equations involving N unknown variables, x_i. They are usually expressed in the following form:

$$A_{11} x_1 + A_{12} x_2 + ... + A_{1N} x_N = c_1$$
$$A_{21} x_1 + A_{22} x_2 + ... + A_{2N} x_N = c_2$$

$$A_{N1} x_1 + A_{N2} x_2 + ... + A_{NN} x_N = c_N$$

In matrix form, they can be expressed as follows:

$$A_{N \times N} = X_{N \times 1} = C_{N \times 1}$$

from which, since all of the values in A and C are constants, we can immediately solve for the column vector X by back division:

```
X = A\C
```

or by using the matrix inverse function:

```
X = inv(A) * C
```

12.5.1 Intersecting Lines

A typical example of a simultaneous equation problem might take the following form. Consider two straight lines on a plot with the following general form:

A_{11} x + A_{12}y = c_1
A_{21} x + A_{22}y = c_2

These lines intersect at some point P (x, y) that is the solution to both of these equations. The equations can be rewritten in matrix form as follows:

A * V = c

where c is the column vector $[c_1 \ c_2]$ ' and v is the required result, the column vector $[x \ y]$ '. The solution is obtained by matrix division as follows:

V = A \ c

Recall that back divide, like the `inv(...)` function, will fail to produce a result if the matrix is singular, that is, has two rows or columns that have a linear relationship. In the specific example of two intersecting lines, this singularity occurs when the two lines are parallel, in which case there is no

Listing 12.5 Plotting line intersections

```
      % equations are y = m1 x + c1
      % y = m2 x + c2
      % in matrix form:
      % [ -m1 1; * [xp; = [c1
      % -m2 1 ] yp] c2]
 1.  ax = [-0.5 6]; ay = [-4.5 18];
      % plot the two lines
 2.  m1 = 3; c1 = -2;
 3.  y1 = m1*ax + c1;
 4.  m2 = -2; c2 = 9;
 5.  y2 = m2*ax + c2;
 6.  plot(ax, y1)
 7.  hold on
 8.  plot(ax, y2, 'b—')
      % solve for the intersection point
 9.  A = [-m1 1; -m2 1];
10.  c = [c1; c2];
11.  P = A\c;
      % draw intersection identification lines
12.  ix = P(1); iy = P(2);
13.  plot([ix ix], [0 iy*1.2], 'r:')
14.  plot([0 ix*1.2],[iy iy], 'r:')
      % draw the axes
15.  plot(ax, [0 0], 'k');
16.  axis([ax ay])
17.  plot([0 0], ay, 'k');
18.  legend({'Line 1','Line 2','Intersect'}, ...
19.          'Location','NorthWest' )
```

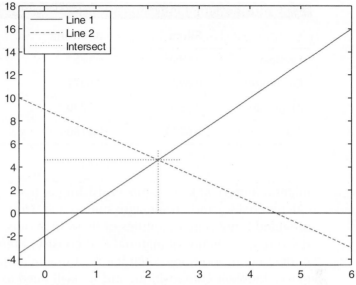

Figure 12.8 *Lines intersecting*

point of intersection. Listing 12.5 shows the solution to a pair of simultaneous equations.

In Listing 12.5:

> Line 1: Sets the x and y limits of the plot.
> Lines 2–8: Plot the original lines.
> Line 9: Sets the simultaneous equation matrix.
> Line 10: Shows the right-hand side of the equation.
> Line 11: Solves the linear equations—P(1) is the x value; P(2) is the y value.
> Lines 12–14: Plot the lines identifying the intersection point.
> Lines 15–17: Plot the axes.
> Lines 18–19: Finish the plot.

Figure 12.8 shows the result of this script.

12.6 Engineering Examples

The following examples illustrate applications of the matrix capabilities discussed in this chapter.

12.6.1 Ceramic Composition

Industrial ceramics plants require mixtures with precise formulations in order to produce products of consistent quality. For example, a factory

	Silica	**Alumina**	**CaO**	**MgO**
Feldspar	0.6950	0.1750	0.0080	0.1220
Diatomite	0.8970	0.0372	0.0035	0.0623
Magnesite	0.0670	0.0230	0.0600	0.8500
Talc	0.6920	0.0160	0.0250	0.2670

Table 12.1 Compound compositions

might require 100 kg of a mix consisting of 67% silica, 5% alumina, 2% calcium oxide, and 26% magnesium oxide. However, the raw material provided is not pure quantities of these materials. Rather, they are delivered as batches of material that consist of the required components in different proportions. Each batch of raw materials is analyzed to determine their composition, and we will need to do the analysis to determine the proportions of the raw materials to mix in order to accomplish the appropriate formulation. The raw materials we will use here are feldspar, diatomite, magnesite, and talc. Table 12.1 illustrates a typical analysis of the composition of these compounds.

For example, if we mixed W_f kg of feldspar, W_d kg of diatomite, W_m kg of magnesite, and W_t kg of talc, the amount of silica would be 0.695 W_f + 0.897 W_d + 0.067 W_m + 0.692 W_t. Repeating this equation for the other components produces a matrix equation that reduces to:

```
C = A * W
```

where C is the required composition of the resulting mix, A is a 4 × 4 matrix showing the results of analyzing the four raw materials, and W is the proportions in which should we mix the raw material to produce the desired result. We find the appropriate amounts of the raw material by solving these equations:

```
W = A\B
```

A script that works this problem is shown in Listing 12.6.

Listing 12.6 Analyzing ceramic composition

```
1. A = [0.6950  0.8970  0.0670  0.6920
2.        0.1750  0.0372  0.0230  0.0160
3.        0.0080  0.0035  0.0600  0.0250
4.        0.1220  0.0623  0.8500  0.2670]
5. B = [67 5 2 26]'
6. W = (inv(A) * B)'
```

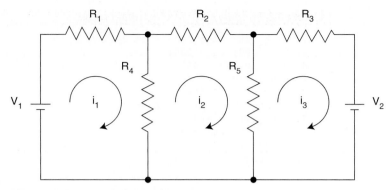

Figure 12.9 *Typical electrical circuit*

In Listing 12.6:

> Lines 1–4: Matrix A is the transpose of the original data table.
>
> Line 5: Shows the required composition in kg.
>
> Line 6: Shows the computed weights of the raw materials in kg, which produces the following result:

```
W =
    16.0083  35.3043  15.1766  33.5108
```

12.6.2 Analyzing an Electrical Circuit

Figure 12.9 illustrates a typical electrical circuit with two voltage sources connected to five resistors with three closed loops. The voltages and resistances are given. We are asked to determine the voltage drop across R_1. Solution techniques apply Ohm's Law to the voltage drops around each closed circuit. When this technique is applied, the equations are as follows:

```
V₁ = i₁ * R₁ + (i₁ - i₂) * R₄
0 = i₂ * R₂ + (i₂ - i₃) * R₅ + (i₂ - i₁) * R₄
-V₂ = i₃ * R₃ + (i₃ - i₂) * R₅
```

When these three equations are manipulated to isolate the three currents, we have the following matrix equation:

```
V = A * I
```

which can be solved as usual by:

```
I = A \ V
```

The script to accomplish this is shown in Listing 12.7.

Listing 12.7 Analyzing an electrical circuit

```
1. R1 = 100; R2 = 200; R3 = 300;
2. R4 = 400; R5 = 500;
3. V1 = 10; V2 = 5;
4. A = [R1+R4    -R4       0
5.       -R4     R2+R4+R5 -R5
6.        0      -R5       R3+R5];
7. B = [V1; 0; -V2];
8. curr = inv(A) * B
9. fprintf('drop across R1 is %6.2f volts\n', ...
10.     curr(1) * R1 );
```

In Listing 12.7:

> Lines 1–3: Set up the parameters of the problem.
>
> Lines 4–7: Set up the coefficient matrices.
>
> Lines 8–10: Compute and display the answers.

Running this script produces the following printout:

```
curr =    0.0283
          0.0104
          0.0003
   drop across R1 is 2.83 volts
```

Chapter Summary

This chapter presented two specialized operations performed with matrices:

- Matrix multiplication can be used for 2-D and 3-D coordinate rotations by building the appropriate rotation matrices
- Matrix division can be used for solving simultaneous equations by setting up the equations in the general form B = A * x, where the known matrix A is n × n and the known column vector B is n × 1; the unknown vector x is then found by x = A\B or x = inv(A) * B

Special Characters, Reserved Words, and Functions—2 -D

Special Characters, Reserved Words, and Functions	Description	Discussed in This Section
*	Matrix multiplication	12.2.1
/	Matrix division	12.2.2
\	Matrix back division	12.2.2
^	Matrix exponentiation	12.2.3
eye(n)	Computes the identity matrix	12.2.1
inv(a)	Computes the inverse of a matrix	12.2.3
reshape(a,r,c)	Changes the row/column configuration of the array a	12.4.2

Self Test

Use the following questions to check your understanding of the material in this chapter:

True or False

T   1.   All MATLAB classes exhibit some form of behavioral abstraction.

F   2.   Matrix multiplication requires that the inner dimensions match.

T   3.   The results of A * B and B * A are identical.

T   4.   Both A * A^{-1} and A^{-1} * A return the identity matrix.

F   5.   Multiplying inv(A) * B is logically equivalent to B ✗ A.   A \ B

T   6.   All sets of simultaneous linear equations can be solved by matrix inversion.

Fill in the Blanks

1.   Behavioral abstraction combines ___data___ abstraction and ___procedural___ abstraction.

2.   The result of a matrix multiplication is a new matrix with the ___column___ count of the first matrix and the ___row___ count of the second.

3.   To rotate a graphic object in the x-y plane about some point, P, other than the origin, you first ___translate___, then ___perform___, and then ___translate the rotated___   ___the object___   ___the rotation___   ___object back to P___

4.   To be soluble, simultaneous linear equations must be expressed as N ___independent___ equations involving N ___unknown___ variables, x$_i$, and ___N*(N+1)___ values.   ___constant___

Programming Projects

1.   This is a set of simple matrix manipulations.
   a. Create a five by six matrix, A, that contains random numbers between 0 and 10.
   b. Create a six by five matrix, B, that contains random numbers between 0 and 10.
   c. Find the inverse of matrix A*B and store it in the variable, C.
   d. Without iteration, create a new matrix D that is the same as A except that all values less than 5 are replaced by zero.
   e. Using iteration, create a new matrix F that is the same as A except that all values less than 5 are replaced by zero.
   f. Create a new matrix G that is the matrix A with the columns reversed.

For example:

if A is [1 2 3; 3 2 5; 1 7 4], G should be
[3 2 1; 5 2 3; 4 7 1]

g. Find the minimum value among all the elements in A and store your answer in the variable H.

2. Imagine that world leaders have decided to come up with a single currency for the world. This new currency, called the Eullar, is defined by the following:

Seven dollars and 3 Euros make 71 Eullars.
One dollar and 2 Euros make 20 Eullars.

You are a reputed economist, and your job is to find out the value of a dollar in terms of Eullars.

3. As an enthusiastic and motivated student, you decided to go out and buy plenty of pens for all your classes this semester. This spending spree unfortunately occurred before you realized your engineering classes seldom required the use of "ink." So now, you're left with four different types of pens and no receipt—you only remember the total amount you spent, and not the price of each type of pen. You decide to get together with three of your friends who coincidentally did the same thing as you, buying the same four types of pens and knowing only the total amount. Write a script to find the prices of each type of pen.

> **Hint:**
>
> In order to find the price of each individual pen, you could create a matrix called "pens," where each column represents a different type of pen and each row represents a different person and a column vector totals that contains the amount of money each of you spent on the pens.

4. Write a function called rotateLine that takes in two vectors, x and y, of the same length that represent a set or ordered pairs that could be used to plot a line. Your function should also take in a third parameter, theta, representing an angle in degrees. Your function should return xprime and yprime where xprime and yprime represent the line that is x and y rotated about the origin by the angle theta.

For example:

```
x = [ 7 7 11 11 7];
y = [-5 -9 -9 -5 -5];
[xprime yprime] = rotateLine(x, y, 90) returns
xprime = [5      9       9      5      5]
yprime = [7      7      11     11      7]
```

5. Write a function named solveSystem that has three inputs: two vectors consisting of the coefficients [a b c] of two line equations of the form ax + by = c and a vector of x values
   a. The function should output a vector giving the x and y values of the point of intersection between the two lines. If the lines are parallel, return the empty vector.
   b. Your function should also plot the two lines using the inputted vector of x values as x. In addition, on the same graph, plot the intersection point of the two lines. Make the first line blue, the second line red, and the intersection point a magenta diamond. Make sure that you label your plot appropriately.

Images

Chapter Objectives

This chapter covers:

- The basic representation of images

- How to read, display, and write JPEG image files

- Some basic operations on images

- Some advanced image processing techniques

Introduction

The graphical techniques we have seen so far have been 2-D and 3-D plots, whose basic concept is to write in places on the screen where data are required and to leave the rest of the screen blank. These presentations are easily generated when we have a mathematical model of the data and wish to represent it graphically. However, many sensors observing the world do not have that underlying model of the data. Rather, they passively generate 2-D representations that we see as images, leaving the interpretation of those images to a human observer. This kind of presentation is exemplified by a digital photograph but includes images from many other sources like radar or X-ray machines.

This chapter discusses some of the elementary processes that can be applied to images in order to begin to extract meaning from them.

13.1 Nature of an Image

Before we confine ourselves to practical, computational reality, we need to understand the general nature of an image. The easiest answer would be that an image is a 2-D sheet on which the color at any point can have essentially infinite variability. However, since we live in a digital world, we will immediately confine ourselves to the conventional representation of images required for most digital display processors, as shown in Figure 13.1. We can represent any image as a 2-D, M × N array of points usually referred to as picture elements, or **pixels,** where M and N are the number of rows and columns, respectively. Each pixel is "painted" by blending variable amounts of the three primary colors: red, green, and blue. (Notice that this is not the same blending process used in painting with oils or water colors, where the second primary color is yellow and the combination process is reversed—increasing amounts of the primary colors tends toward black, not white.)

The resolution of a picture is measured by the number of pixels per unit of picture width and height. This governs the fuzziness of its appearance in print, and controls the maximum size of good-quality photo printing. The color resolution is measured by the number of bits in the words containing the red, green, and blue (RGB) components. Since one value generally exists for each of the M × N pixels in the array, increasing the number of bits for each pixel color will have a significant effect on the stored size of the image. Typically, 8 bits (values 0–255) are assigned to each color.

The MATLAB language has a data type, `uint8`, which uses 8 bits to store an unsigned integer in the range 0–255. It is unsigned because we are not interested in negative color values, and to specify the sign value would cost a data bit and reduce the resolution of the data to 0–127. By combining the three color values, there are actually 2^{24} different combinations of color available to a true-color image—many more possible combinations than the human eye can distinguish.

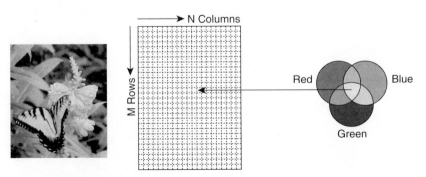

Figure 13.1 *The nature of images*

13.2 Image Types

Our sources for images to process are data files captured by imaging devices such as cameras, scanners, and graphic arts systems, and these image files are provided in a wide variety of formats. According to the MATLAB documentation, it recognizes files in TIFF, PNG, HDF, BMP, JPEG (JPG), GIF, PCX, XWD, CUR, and ICO formats. The various file formats are usually identified by their file extensions. While this seems a bewildering collection of formats, MATLAB provides one image reading function that converts these file formats to one of three internal representations: true color, gray scale, or color mapped images. In the MATLAB implementation, we will confine our interests to two formats: .png files when absolute color fidelity is required and .jpg files that offer better compression ratios to give a smaller file size for a given image.

13.2.1 True Color Images

True color images are stored according to the scheme shown in Figure 13.2 as an M × N × 3 array where every pixel is directly stored as `uint8` values in three layers of the 3-D array. The first layer contains the red value, the second layer the green value, and the third layer the blue value. The advantage of this approach, as the name suggests, is that every pixel can be represented as its true color value without compromise. The only disadvantage is the size of the image in memory because there are three color values for every pixel.

13.2.2 Gray Scale Images

Gray scale images are also directly stored, but save the black-to-white intensity value for each pixel as a single `uint8` value rather than three values.

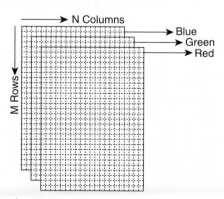

Figure 13.2 *A true color image*

13.2.3 Color Mapped Images

Color mapped, or indexed, images keep a separate color map either 256 items long (for maximum economy of memory) or up to 32,768 items long. Each item in the color map contains the red, blue, and green values of a color, respectively. As illustrated in Figure 13.3, the image itself is stored as an M × N array of indices into the color map. So, for example, a certain pixel index might contain the value 143. The color to be shown at that pixel location would be the 143rd color set (RGB) on the color map.

If the color map is restricted to 256 colors, each pixel can be drawn at the same color resolution as a true color image, as three 8-bit values, but the choice of colors is very restricted, and normal pictures of scenery—sky, for instance—take on a "layered color" appearance. Color mapped images can be used effectively, however, to store "cartoon pictures" economically where limited color choices are not a problem. Using a larger color map provides a larger, but still sometimes restrictive, range of color choices; but since the indices in the picture array must be 16-bit values and the color map is larger, the memory size advantages of this method of storage are diminished. Computationally, it is possible to convert a color mapped image to true color, but true color or black-and-white images cannot normally be converted to color mapped format without loss of fidelity in the color representation.

13.2.4 Preferred Image Format

In order to avoid confusion in the format of images, we will confine our discussions to one specific image file format that is prevalent at the time of writing and that provides a nice compromise between economy of storage as an image file and accessibility within MATLAB. We will discuss files compressed according to a standard algorithm originally proposed by the Joint Photographic Experts Group (JPEG). When MATLAB reads JPEG images, they are decoded as true color images; when MATLAB writes them, they are again encoded in compressed form. The file size for a typical JPEG file is 30 times less than the size you would need to store the M × N × 3

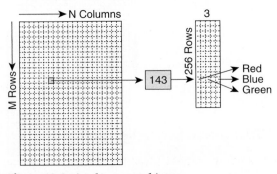

Figure 13.3 *A color mapped image*

bytes of the image. As we will see later, however, this compression does not come without cost.

 ## 13.3 Reading, Displaying, and Writing Images

MATLAB uses one image reading function, `imread(...)`, for all image file types. To read a file named `myPicture.jpg`, we use the following command:

```
>> pic = imread('myPicture.jpg', 'jpg')
```

where the result, `pic`, is an M × N × 3 `uint8` array of pixel color values, and the second parameter, `'jpg'`, provides the format of the file explicitly. This parameter is optional; MATLAB usually infers the file format correctly from the file contents.

Once the picture has been read, you can display it in a figure window with fixed size and axes visible by using the following command:

```
>> image(pic)
```

This actually stretches or shrinks the image to fit the size of the normal plot figure, a behavior you normally desire; however, occasionally, you want the plot figure to match the actual image size (or at least, preserving its aspect ratio). Releases of MATLAB after R20008a provide the `imshow(...)` function, which presents the image without stretching, shrinking, or axes (unless the figure window is too small).

Similarly, there is one function for writing files: `imwrite(...)`, which can be used to write most common file formats. If we have made some changes to `pic`, the internal representation of the image, we could write a new version to the disk by using the following:

```
>> imwrite( pic, 'newPicture.jpg', 'jpg')
```

where the third parameter, `'jpg'`, is required to specify the output format of the file.

 ## 13.4 Operating on Images

Since images are stored as arrays, it is not surprising that we can employ the normal operations of creation, manipulation, slicing, and concatenation. We will note one particular matrix operation that will be of great value before examining some applications of array manipulation related to image processing.

13.4.1 Stretching or Shrinking Images

In earlier chapters we have seen the basic ability to use index vectors to extract rows and columns from an array. Now we extend these ideas to understand how to uniformly shrink or stretch an array to match an exact size. Consider, for example, A, a rows × cols array. Assume for a moment that the vertical size is good, but we want to stretch or shrink the image horizontally to newRows—a number that might be larger or smaller than rows. We use linspace(...) to create an index vector as follows:

```
>> rowVector = linspace(1, rows, newRows)
```

where the third parameter is the desired size of the new array. In general, this index vector will contain fractional values, but MATLAB will truncate the index values. We can round the results as follows:

```
>> rowVector = round(rowVector)
```

Then we can use this vector to shrink or stretch the picture pic as follows:

```
>> newPic = pic(rowVector, cols, :)
```

Clearly, this can be applied to both dimensions simultaneously, as shown in Exercise 13.1.

In this exercise, first we read an image and determine its size. Note that with 3-D images, you must give to the size(...) function three variables. Then we illustrate the "normal" slicing operations by reducing the image to the even rows, and every third column. Next, we generalize this image slicing by stretching the number of rows by a factor 1.43 and shrinking the number of columns by a factor 0.75. This is accomplished by building a row index vector, rowVec, and a column index vector, colVec, according to the algorithm above. The stretching is achieved by repeating selected values in the index vector, and shrinking is achieved by omitting some.

13.4.2 Color Masking

As an example of image manipulation, consider the image shown in Figure 13.4. This is a 2400 × 1600 JPEG image that can be taken with any good digital camera. However, the appearance of the Vienna garden is somewhat

---

Exercise 13.1 Working with image stretching

```
>> pic = imread(<your favorite image>);
>> [rows cols clrs] = size(pic)
>> imshow( pic(2:2:end, 3:3:end, :);
>> RFactor = 1.43; CFactor = 0.75; % shrink / stretch factors
>> rowVec = round(linspace(1, rows, Rfactor*rows));
>> colVec = round(linspace(1, cols, Cfactor*cols));
>> imshow(pic(rowVec, colVec,:)); % shrunk / stretched image
>> imshow(pic(:, :, [2 3 1])); % re-ordering the color layers
```

Figure 13.4 *A garden in Vienna*

Figure 13.5 *A cottage in Oxfordshire*

marred by the fact that the sky is gray, not blue. Fortunately, we have a picture of a cottage, as shown in Figure 13.5, with a nice, clear blue sky. So our goal is to replace the gray sky in the Vienna garden with the blue sky from the cottage picture.

Initial Exploration Before we can do this, however, we need to explore the Vienna picture to determine how to distinguish the gray sky from the rest of the picture. In particular, there are patches of sky visible between the tree

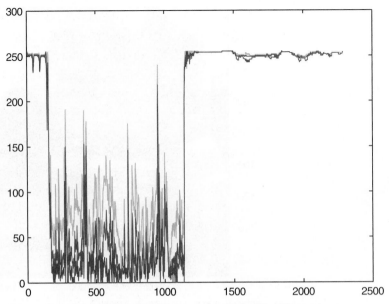

Figure 13.6 *Plot of the color values on one row of the Vienna image*

branches that must be changed as well as the open sky. Listing 13.1 illustrates a good way to accomplish this. Here we display the image in one figure; choose a representative row in the image that includes some sky showing through the tree (we chose row 350); and then plot the red, blue, and green values of the pixels across that row. Figure 13.6 shows the resulting plot.

In Listing 13.1:

Line 1: Reads the image.

Line 2: Displays the image.

Listing 13.1 Exploring the sky situation

```
 1. v = imread('Vienna.jpg');
 2. image(v)
 3. figure
 4. row = 400;
 5. red = v(row, :, 1);
 6. gr = v(row, :, 2);
 7. bl = v(row, :, 3);
 8. plot(red, 'r');
 9. hold on
10. plot(gr,  'g');
11. plot(bl, 'b');
```

Line 3: Creates a new figure window for the next plots.

Line 4: Determines a suitable row (350 is a good choice).

Lines 5–7: Extract the three color layers for the chosen row.

Lines 8–11: Plot the three colors. Since we omitted one of the axis values, we make the assumption that the x values are the integers `1:length(y)`, which give us the horizontal pixel number across the row.

Analysis As we examine Figure 13.6, we see that the red, green, and blue values for the open sky are all around 250 because the sky is almost white. However, the color "spikes" that correspond to the color values of the sky elements that show through the tree are actually lower. We could decide, for example, to define the sky as all those pixels where the red, blue, and green values are all above a chosen threshold, and we could comfortably set that threshold at 160.

There is one more important consideration. It would be unfortunate to turn the hair of the lady (the author's wife) blue, and there are fountains and walkways that might also logically appear to be "sky." We can prevent this embarrassment by limiting the color replacement to the upper portion of the picture above row 700.

Final Computation So we are ready to create the code that will replace the gray sky with blue. The code in Listing 13.2 accomplishes this, and Figure 13.7 shows the resulting image.

Figure 13.7 *The Vienna garden with a blue sky*

Listing 13.2 Replacing the gray sky

```
 1. v = imread('Vienna.jpg');
 2. w = imread('Witney.jpg');
 3. image(w)
 4. figure
 5. thres = 160;
 6. layer = (v(:,:,1) > thres) ...
 7.         & (v(:,:,2) > thres) ...
 8.         & (v(:,:,3) > thres);
 9. mask(:,:,1) = layer;
10. mask(:,:,2) = layer;
11. mask(:,:,3) = layer;
12. mask(700:end,:,:) = false;
13. nv = v;
14. nv(mask) = w(mask);
15. image(nv);
16. imwrite(nv, 'newVienna.jpg', 'jpg')
```

In Listing 13.2:

Lines 1 and 2: Read the two images.

Line 3: Draws the cottage picture.

Line 4: Makes a new figure window.

Line 5: Sets the arbitrary threshold.

Lines 6–8: Define a 2-D layer containing logic that separates the Vienna sky from the rest of the picture.

Lines 9–11: Build a logical mask to replace the appropriate pixels from the cottage picture into the Vienna picture by populating each color layer of the mask with that layer.

Line 12: Refuses to replace any pixels below row 700.

Line 13: Copies the original image.

Line 14: Replaces the sky.

Line 15: Shows the image.

Line 16: Saves the JPEG result.

Post-operative Analysis We realize that this is not quite the end of the story, because a wire has suddenly become evident in the picture. Furthermore, if we take a close look at the wire (Figure 13.8), we see a number of disturbing things:

- The sky is by no means uniform in color—justifying the assertion that color mapped images do not have enough different colors to draw a true sky effectively
- The color of the wire is not far removed from the color of some parts of the blue sky—so replacing slightly darker blue would be problematic

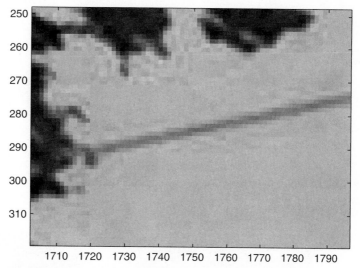

Figure 13.8 *Magnified image of the wire*

- There is a light colored "halo" around the wire that is actually a result of the original JPEG compression of the image so that even if we did replace the darker colors, the "ghost" of the wire would still be visible

Common Pitfalls 13.1

Be careful requesting the size of 3-D (and more) arrays. If you leave off variables—as here, you might be tempted not to ask for the number of colors because you know it's three—the `size(...)` function multiplies together the remaining dimension sizes. So if `img` is sized 1200 * 1600, `[r,c] = size(img)` would return r = 1200 and c = 4800! If you provide to only one variable, it returns a vector of the sizes of each dimension of the array. So `v = size(img)` returns [1200 1600 3].

So pixel replacement will probably not solve our wire problem. We will take a different approach to solve this problem in Chapter 15.

13.4.3 Creating a Kaleidoscope

Originally, a kaleidoscope was a cardboard tube in which a number of mirrors were arranged in such a manner that one image—usually, a collection of colored beads—was reflected to produce a symmetrical collection of images. We will replicate that general idea using MATLAB. Figure 13.9 illustrates the geometric manipulation necessary to create one particular kaleidoscope picture. We start with an arbitrary image and use shrinking or stretching to generate a square picture—the 'F' in the figure. We then mirror it horizontally and concatenate it horizontally with the original image. We then mirror these two images vertically and concatenate them vertically. Finally, we take that compound image and repeat the process to produce the 4 × 4 image on the right side.

Figure 13.10 shows the original image and the results. The overall logic flow of the solution matches that shown in Figure 13.9.

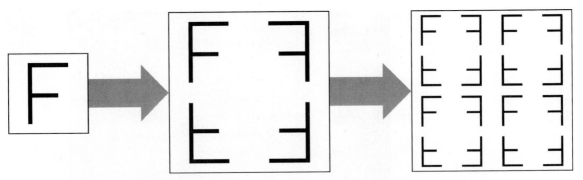

Figure 13.9 *Logic for the kaleidoscope*

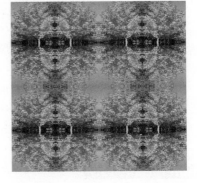

Figure 13.10 *The kaleidoscope*

Listing 13.3 shows the code that makes the kaleidoscope.

In Listing 13.3:

Line 2: Reads the original image.

Lines 2–3: Draw it on the left subplot.

Listing 13.3 Making a kaleidoscope

```
1. function kaleidoscope(name)
   % Making a kaleidoscope
   % usage: kaleidoscope(file_name)
       %read the image
2.     picture = imread(name);
3.     subplot(1,2,1); imshow(picture(ceil(1:1.5:end),:,:))
       % resize it to 128*128
4.     [rows cols ~] = size(picture);
5.     n = 128;
6.     rndx = ceil(linspace(1,rows, n));
7.     cndx = ceil(linspace(1,cols, n));
```

```
 8.       pic = picture(rndx, cndx, :);
          % build the kaleidoscope
 9.       img = buildIt(buildIt(pic));
10.       subplot(1,2,2); imshow(img)
11. end
12. function img = buildIt(img)
       % helper function to do the manipulations
       %             top left          top right
       %             bottom left       bottom right
13.       img = [img                   img(:,end:-1:1,:)
14.              img(end:-1:1,:,:) img(end:-1:1,end:-1:1,:)];
15. end
```

Lines 4–8: Make it square.

Line 9: Calls the helper function to build the first set of 4, and then immediately call it again to build the 4 × 4 compound image.

Line 10: Draws it on the right panel.

Lines 12–15: Helper function to build four mirrored images from the original.

13.4.4 Images on a Surface

In Chapter 11 we saw how to create a surface representing solid objects and, in particular, how to create a spherical image that rotates with lighting.

Spectacular effects can be created by "pasting" images onto these surfaces, as will be illustrated in this last example. Here, we are given an image of the surface of the earth using Mercator projection, shown in Figure 13.11.[1] It is important to use the Mercator projection, named for the sixteenth-century Flemish cartographer Gerardus Mercator, because this projection keeps the lines of latitude and longitude on a rectangular grid. This allows a correct representation of the map as it is pasted onto the spherical surface. However, it also presents a challenge because in this projection, the north and south poles would be stretched to infinite length across the top and bottom of the map. This map, therefore, leaves off the region near the poles, and we have to replace those regions.

The objective of this exercise is to paste this image onto a rotating globe. The trick to accomplishing this is to use a feature of the surf(...) function, whereby the image is supplied in a specific form as the fourth parameter, as follows:

```
surf(xx, yy, zz, img)
```

---

[1]The file *earth_s.jpg* is provided as part of the MATLAB system.

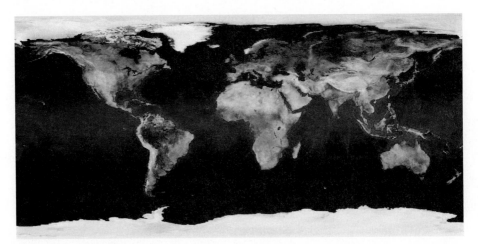

Figure 13.11 *Map projection*

It will replace the normal coloring scheme of the surface with the image under the following conditions:

- The rows and columns of the image match the rows and columns of the xx, yy, zz plaid
- The image supplies the red, green, and blue layers in the same form as true color images
- The color values, however, must be of type `double` in the range `0..1`

In the following code, rather than stretching the image to the size of the plaid, we choose to size the plaid to the image, thereby preserving all the image resolution. Clearly, in different circumstances where the size of the plaid is specified, the image can be stretched to suit those dimensions. The code to accomplish all this is shown in Listing 13.4.

In Listing 13.4:

Line 1: Reads the JPEG image.

Line 2: Enables good closure at the image edge by copying the first column of the map beyond the last column.

Line 3: Computes the mean image intensity of the snow on the top edge of the image. This will be used to fill the circles at the north and south poles.

Line 4: Fetches the size of the map.

Line 5: To calculate the size of the circles at the poles, we assume that the map takes us to ±85° of latitude, so we need the equivalent of 5° at the top and bottom of the map. This line calculates how many rows represent 1° of latitude.

Listing 13.4 Rotating a globe

```
1.  WM = imread('earthmap_s.jpg');
2.  WM(:,end+1,:) = WM(:,1,:);
3.  snow = mean( mean(WM(1,:,:)));
4.  [WMr, WMc, clr] = size(WM);
5.  rowsperdeglat = WMr/170
6.  add = floor(rowsperdeglat * 5)
7.  addlayer = uint8(ones(add, WMc) * snow);
8.  toAdd(:,:,1) = addlayer;
9.  toAdd(:,:,2) = addlayer;
10. toAdd(:,:,3) = addlayer;
11. worldMap = [toAdd; WM; toAdd];
12. [nlat nlong clr] = size(worldMap)
13. lat = double(0:nlat-1) * pi / nlat;
14. long = double(0:nlong-1) * 2 * pi / (nlong-1);
15. [th phi] = meshgrid(long, lat);
16. radius = 10;
17. zz = radius * cos(phi);
18. xx = radius * sin(phi) .* cos(th);
19. yy = radius * sin(phi) .* sin(th);
20. wM = double(worldMap) / 256;
21. surf(xx, yy, zz, wM);
22. shading interp
23. axis equal, axis off, axis tight
24. material dull
25. th = 0;
26. handle = light('Color',[int,int,int]); % a custom light source
27. while true
28.     th = th - 1;
29.     view([th 20]);
30.     lightangle(handle, th+50, 20)
31.     pause(.001)
32. end
```

Line 6: Shows the number of rows to add to the map.

Line 7: Computes the values of a single color layer by making an array with ones(...) using the number of rows to add and the number of map columns, and multiplying by the snow intensity.

Lines 8–10: Build the strips to add to the globe map by copying this layer to the red, green, and blue layers of a new image array.

Line 11: Prepares the complete map by concatenating this image to the top and bottom of the map.

Line 12: Retrieves the size of this map.

Lines 13 and 14: Prepare the vectors defining the plaid by spreading the map dimensions across π radians in latitude and 2π radians in longitude.

Lines 15–19: Prepare the sphere.

Figure 13.12 *Globe*

Line 20: Scales the image to double values between 0 and 1 as required by `surf(...)`.

Lines 21–23: Draw the surface as usual, using the image as the color distribution.

Lines 24–26: Special preparation of the surface luminosity and light characteristics to prevent glare spots.

Lines 27–32: The perpetual rotation with the angle `th` moving backward one degree at a time.

Line 30: This keeps the light in the same position relative to the observer.

Line 31: The usual `pause` to allow the drawing to take place for each iteration.

A snapshot of the globe as it is rotating is shown in Figure 13.12.

13.5 Engineering Example—Detecting Edges

While images are powerful methods of delivering information to the human eye, they have limitations when being used by computer programs. Our eyes have an astonishing ability to interpret the content of an image, such as the one shown in Figure 13.13. Even a novice observer would have no difficulty seeing that it is a picture of an aircraft in flight. An experienced observer would be able to identify the type of aircraft as a Lockheed C-130 and perhaps some other characteristics of the aircraft.

Figure 13.13 *C-130 in flight*

Figure 13.14 *Result of edge detection*

While our eyes are excellent at interpreting images, computer programs need a lot of help. One operation commonly performed to reduce the complexity of an image is edge detection, in which the complete image is replaced by a very small number of points that mark the edges of "interesting artifacts." Figure 13.14 shows the results from a simple program attempting to paint the outline of the aircraft in black by putting a black pixel at an identified edge. The key element of the algorithm is the ability to determine unambiguously whether a pixel is part of the object of interest or not. An edge is then defined as a pixel where some of the surrounding pixels are on the object and some are not. The image selected for this exercise makes

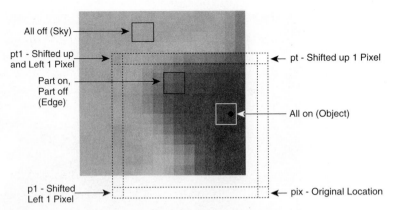

Figure 13.15 *Overlapping picture layers*

edge detection simple since the aircraft is everywhere darker than the surrounding sky.

The script used to generate this picture is shown in Listing 13.5. The basic approach of the algorithm is to use simple array processing tools to detect

Listing 13.5 Edge detection

```
1. pic = imread('C-130.jpg');
2. imshow(pic)
3. figure
4. [rows, cols, cl] = size(pic);
5. amps = uint16(pic(:,:,1))...
6.        + uint16(pic(:,:,2))...
7.        + uint16(pic(:,:,3));
8. up = max(max(amps))
9. dn = min(min(amps))
10. fact = .5
11. thresh = uint16(dn + fact * (up - dn))
12. pix = amps(2:end, 2:end);
13. ptl = amps(1:end-1, 1:end-1);
14.  pt = amps(1:end-1, 2:end);
15.  pl = amps(2:end, 1:end-1);
16. alloff= and(and((pix > thresh), ( pt  > thresh)),...
17.             and(( pl > thresh), (ptl > thresh)));
18. allon = and(and((pix <= thresh), ( pt <= thresh)),...
19.             and(( pl <= thresh), (ptl <= thresh)));
20. edges = and(not(allon), not(alloff));
21. layer = uint8(ones(rows-1, cols-1) *255);
22. layer(edges) = 0;
23. outline(:,:,1) = layer;
24. outline(:,:,2) = layer;
25. outline(:,:,3) = layer;
26. image(outline)
27. imwrite(outline, 'c-130 edges.jpg', 'jpg')
```

the edges across the whole image at once. To accomplish this, we create four arrays, each one row and one column less than the original image and each offset by one pixel, as illustrated in Figure 13.15. The array pix is in the original location, pt is one row up from that location, pl is one row left, and ptl is one row left and up. If we now collapse these arrays on top of each other, we are simultaneously comparing the values of a square of four pixels across the whole image (less one row and one column).

In Listing 13.5:

> Lines 1–4: Read the original image, display it, and determine its size.
> Lines 5–7: Construct an array of size rows × cols containing the total color intensity of each pixel. The class uint16, using two bytes instead of one, is big enough for the sum of three unit8s.
> Lines 8–11: Rather than guess an amplitude threshold, we compute a threshold halfway between the maximum and minimum intensities across the picture.
> Lines 12–15: Set up the four overlapping arrays offset by a pixel each.
> Lines 16–17: The logical array alloff will be true wherever all four adjacent pixels have an intensity above the threshold—these are on the sky.
> Lines 18–19: The logical array allon will be true wherever all four adjacent pixels have an intensity below the threshold—these are on the aircraft.
> Line 20: The pixels we are looking for are those where the pixel is neither completely sky nor completely aircraft.
> Line 21: Makes a white image the same size as the logical arrays.
> Line 22: Sets the edges to black.
> Lines 23–27: Put that layer into the RGB layers, show the image, and write it to the disk.

Observation Clearly, while there is much more to be done with this data for it to be useful, the complexity of this image has been reduced from 12 million uint8 values with no real meaning to a small number of data values that outline an object of interest. Algorithms beyond the scope of this text could be used to convert these outlining points to polynomial shapes. These shapes could then be matched against projections of 3-D models to actually identify the object in the picture.

Chapter Summary

This chapter covered the following:

■ Images represented internally in bit-mapped, gray scale, or true color form

- Image files that come in a large variety of formats; MATLAB provides a single reader function and a single writer function to manipulate all the common image types
- Common operations on images, including cropping, stretching or shrinking, and concatenating and pasting an image onto a surface
- An engineering example showing how edge detection begins the process of extracting meaning from an image

Special Characters, Reserved Words, and Functions

Special Characters, Reserved Words, and Functions	Description	Discussed in This Section
image(<picture>)	Displays an image in a figure of fixed dimensions with axes	13.3
imread(<file_name>)	Reads an image file	13.3
imshow(<picture>)	Displays an image in a figure of variable dimensions without axes	13.3
imwrite(data, file, format)	Writes an image file	13.3
linspace(from, to, n)	Defines a linearly spaced vector	13.2.1, 13.4.1
rot90(A,n)	Rotates A by 90° clockwise n times	13.4.4
tril(A)	Reduces A to its lower triangular half with zeros in the upper triangle	13.4.4
uint8/16	Unsigned integer type with the specified number of bits	13.1

Self Test

Use the following questions to check your understanding of the material in this chapter:

True or False

F 1. An image whose color values are all 0 will be all white [black] on the screen.

T 2. The MATLAB language defines one image reader for all image file types.

T 3. The normal operations of creation, slicing, and concatenation can be used to manipulate images.

F 4. rot90(A) rotates a 3-D array by 90° clockwise.

T 5.   Edge detection dramatically reduces the amount of data to be processed by image identification software.

Fill in the Blanks

1.   Each pixel of a true color image is stored as __three__ values of type __uint8__ containing values __0 - 255__.

2.   Gray scale images store the black-to-white intensity value for each __pixel__ as a(n) __uint8__.

3.   When you read JPEG files, they are __decoded__ as __true color__ images containing __three color__ layers.

4.   Once a picture has been read, you can display it in a(n) __figure window__ with the function __image(...)__.

5.   The operator __transpose__ mirrors an array about its __major diagonal__.

Programming Projects

1.   As an introduction to image problems, perform the following manipulations:
     a. Find a suitable JPEG image file. Read it, display it, and store the result in A.
     b. Create a copy of A, flip the image from left to right, and display it in a new figure.
     c. Create a copy of A, swap the values for red and blue, and display it in a new figure.
     d. Create a copy of A, stretch the image to four times its original size (twice as many rows and twice as many columns), and display it in a new figure.
     e. Create a copy of A and then shrink the image to 0.7 its original size in each dimension and display it in a new figure.

2.   An image could be scrambled by doing the following in order:
     a. multiple quadrant flips:
         • top left quadrant becomes bottom right quadrant
         • top right quadrant becomes bottom left quadrant
         • bottom right quadrant becomes top left quadrant
         • bottom left quadrant becomes top right quadrant
     b. The image is flipped upside down.
     c. The red values are swapped with the green values.
     d. The blue values are flipped left to right.

     Write a function called imageScrambler that takes in an image array and a string. If the string is equal to 'scramble', your function should scramble the image according to the above method and return the modified image in array form. If the string is equal to `'unscramble'`, your function should unscramble the image by reversing the above method and return the modified array. Otherwise, your function should return the array untouched. You may assume that the image array provided will always contain an even number of rows and columns.

Test your solution by writing a script that reads a selected image, A, ensures that there is an even number of rows and columns, and tests the scrambling and unscrambling the image.

3. You are provided an image, and your job is to convert the full-sized image to a smaller one. Normally when image processing software is required to resize an image, a complex resizing algorithm is used to accomplish the conversion. We will attempt to duplicate this conversion. Write a function called `resizeMe` that takes in a string as an input corresponding to an image file name. The function should then resize the image to 1.414 times its original size in each dimension and display it. Additionally, your function should use the built-in function `imwrite(...)` to write the new image to a file. The name of the new file will be the original file name preceded by `'LG'`. For example, if the original filename is called `'yellow_bird.jpg'`, the new file should be called `'LGyellow_bird.jpg'`.

4. Write a function called `rotate` that takes in an image array and a number. The number represents the number of times the function will rotate the image clockwise by 90 degrees. A negative number signifies counter-clockwise rotation and a positive one signifies clockwise rotation.

5. We have obtained new intelligence that the Housing Department has plans to renovate all the rooms in the dorms with a new prototype. However, the prototype has been encoded into three separate images to avoid rival students finding out about it and thus seeking refuge here. Each image only contains one layer of color (e.g., `roomScrambledRed.jpg` only contains the Red layer). As a loyal student, it is your job to reconstruct a new image out of these three images.
    a. Create a script called `room`, and read the three layers using `'imread'`. Create the new matrix `ReconImage` with the three layers, and display it using `'imshow'`.
    b. After detailed analysis of the image, you find that it is also scrambled. Using advanced crytography and whizbang mathematical formulas, you have come to the conclusion that the four quadrants of the image have been re-arranged. Manipulate the composite image from part a. and re-arrange the pieces to

form the proper image. Display it using `subplot(...)`, below the first image.

6. For this exercise, you will visit—at least in MATLAB—a place you have always wanted to go.

    a. Find or take a picture of yourself with a plain background such as a green screen, using the JPEG image format. It would be a good idea not to wear the color of the background.

    b. Find a JPEG image of the place you want to go and decide on the rectangle in that scene where your image should appear. Save the width and height of the rectangle and the row and column of its top left corner.

    c. Re-size your image to be the width and height of the rectangle.

    d. Use the color masking technique of section 13.4.2 to copy your image without the green screen into the selected rectangle of your dream scene.

Hint

The trick to this is to move each pixel from its current location (in polar coordinates, $r - \theta$) to a new location on the new image. The new location is found by adding the rotation angle provided to the angular value, θ, of each pixel. Those pixels in the new image not occupied by a pixel will be black.

7. Write a function called `adjustImage` that consumes the name of an image file and an angle in degrees and produces a new image rotated counter-clockwise by that number of degrees about the center of the original image. Your new image will be larger than the original image.

Processing Sound

Chapter Objectives

This chapter discusses the following:

- How sound is physically recorded and played back and our internal storage of sound

- Operations that can be performed with the original time trace

- The ability to transform the data into the frequency domain and the physical significance of the transformed data

- Operations that can be performed in the frequency domain

14.1 The Physics of Sound

Any sound source produces sound in the form of pressure fluctuations in the air. While the air molecules move infinitesimal distances in order to propagate the sound, the important part of sound propagation is that pressure waves move rapidly through the air by causing air molecules to "jostle" each other. These pressure fluctuations can be viewed as analog signals—data that have a continuous range of values. These signals have two attributes: their amplitude and their frequency characteristics.

In absolute terms, sound is measured as the **amplitude** of pressure fluctuations on a surface like an eardrum or a microphone. However, the challenging characteristic of these data is their dynamic range. Our ears are able to detect small sounds with amplitudes around 10^{10} (10 billion) times smaller than the loudest comfortable sound. Sound intensity is therefore usually reported logarithmically, measured in decibels where the intensity of a sound in decibels is calculated as follows:

$$I_{DB} = 10 \; \log_{10}(I \; / \; I_0)$$

where I is the measured pressure fluctuation and I_0 is a reference pressure usually established as the lowest pressure fluctuation a really good ear can detect, 2×10^{-4} dynes/cm^2.

Also, sounds are pressure fluctuations at certain **frequencies**. The human ear can hear sounds as low as 50 Hz and as high as 20 kHz. Voices on the telephone sound odd because the upper frequency is limited by the telephone equipment to 4 kHz. Typically, hearing damage due to aging or exposure to excessive sound levels causes an ear to lose sensitivity to high and/or low frequencies.

14.2 Recording and Playback

Early attempts at sound recording concentrated first on mechanical, and later magnetic, methods for storing and reproducing sound. The phonograph/record player depended on the motion of a needle in a groove as a cylinder or disk rotated at constant speed under the playback head. Not surprisingly, when you see the incredible dynamic range required, even the best stereos could not reproduce high-quality sound. Later, analog magnetic tape in various forms replaced the phonograph, offering less wear on the recording and better, but still limited, dynamic range. Digital recording has almost completely supplanted analog recording and will be the subject of this chapter.

Of course, sound amplitude in analog form is unintelligible to a computer—it must be turned into an electrical signal by a microphone, amplified to suitable voltage levels, digitized, and stored, as shown in

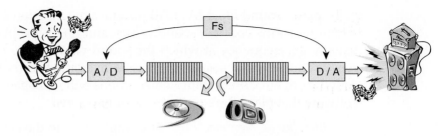

Figure 14.1 *Mechanics of sound recording and playback*

Figure 14.1. The key to successful digital recording and playback—whether by digital tape machines, compact disks, or computer files—is the design of the analog-to-digital (A/D) and digital-to-analog (D/A) devices. The reader should remember that this is still low-level data. Each word coming out of the A/D or going into the D/A merely represents the pressure on the microphone at a point in time.

The primary parameter governing the sound quality is the recording rate—how quickly the mechanism records samples of the sound (the sampling rate). Basic sampling theory suggests that we should use a sampling rate twice the highest frequency you are interested in reproducing, usually around 20,000 samples per second for good music, 5,000 samples per second for speech.

The other parameter, the resolution of the recorded data, has remarkably little effect on the quality of the recording to an untrained ear. The resolution is usually either 8 bits (−128 to 127) or 16 bits (−32,768 to 32767). While 8-bit resolution ought to offer very limited dynamic range, and theoretically should be used only for recording speech, in practice it results in a quality of reproduction for music that is, to an untrained ear, indistinguishable from that provided by 16-bit resolution.

Technical Insight 14.1

The background theory of sampling is beyond the scope of this text. Interested readers should research Nyquist on a good search engine.

These parameters must be stored with any digital sound recording medium and retrieved by the tools that play those sounds. To be able to play such a file, we must receive not only the data stream, but also information indicating the sample frequency, Fs, and the word size.

14.3 Implementation

MATLAB offers a number of tools for reading sound files: `wavread(...)` for `wav` files and `auread(...)` for `.au` files, for example. Both return three variables: a vector of sound values, the sampling frequency in Hz (samples per second), and the number of bits used to record the data (8 or 16).

To play a sound file, MATLAB provides the function `sound(data, rate)` where `data` is the vector of sound values, and `rate` is the playback frequency, usually the frequency at which the sound values were recorded. We will see that the function `sound(...)` passes the data directly to the computer's sound card, but different implementations will manage the behavior of the software that plays the sound in one of two ways.

> *Blocking vs. Non-blocking:* "Blocking" refers to the behavior of your system after you have called the `sound(...)` function to play a sound. Blocking players will not return control to the code playing the sound until the sound has completed. This will allow only one sound to be played from an application at a time. Non-blocking players will not wait for the sound card to finish playing the sound, so multiple calls to the `sound(...)` function will overlay different sounds. You will need to experiment with your particular system to determine whether it blocks or not.

A number of `.wav` files are included on the book's Companion Web site to demonstrate many aspects of sound files.

14.4 Time Domain Operations

First, we consider three kinds of operations on sound files in the time domain: slicing, playback frequency changes, and sound file frequency changes.

14.4.1 Slicing and Concatenating Sound

Consider the problem of constructing comedic sayings by choosing and assembling words from published speeches. The Companion Web site contains a sampling of speech clips selected from various Web sites. In particular, it has the *Apollo 13* speech, "Houston, we have a problem"; "Frankly, my dear . . ." from *Gone with the Wind*; and "You can't handle the truth" from *A Few Good Men*. Exercise 14.1 describes the process of assembling parts of these speeches into a semi-coherent conversation.

The first part of Exercise 14.1 reads the *Apollo 13* speech, plays the speech, and plots the data (with the data index as x-axis). The resulting plot is shown in the left half of Figure 14.2. Since the sound actually includes more than we need, the next step is to crop this file to keep only the words we

Exercise 14.1 Locating the first part of the speech

```
>> [houston, Fsh] = wavread('a13prob.wav');
>> subplot(1, 2, 1)
>> plot(houston);
>> sound(houston, Fsh);
```

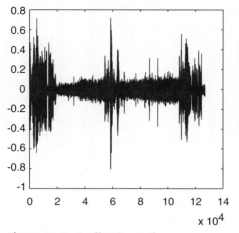 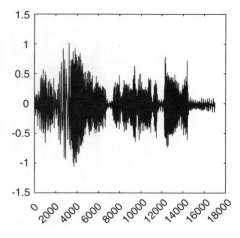

Figure 14.2 *Apollo 13 speech*

Exercise 14.2 Extracting the first part of the speech

```
>> clip = 110000;
>> prob = houston(clip:end)*2;
>> subplot(1, 2, 2)
>> plot(prob)
```

need. By listening to the speech using the function `sound(...)`, and judiciously zooming and panning the plot, it is possible to narrow down the location in the file where the problem speech starts, at about 111000. In Exercise 14.2 you will extract the first part of the speech.

In Exercise 14.2 we truncate the speech file to the words we need and also, realizing that the amplitude of these words is a little low, raise its amplitude by a factor of 2.

In Exercise 14.3, by a similar process, we remove "my dear" from the "frankly, my dear . . ." speech, reducing its amplitude by one-half, which results in Figure 14.3.

Exercise 14.3 Extracting "my dear"

```
>> figure
>> [damn, Fsd] = wavread('givdamn2.wav');
>> subplot(1, 2, 1)
>> plot(damn);
>> lo = 4500;
>> hi = 8700;
>> sdamn = [damn(1:lo); damn(hi:end) ] * .5;
>> subplot(1, 2, 2)
>> plot(sdamn);
```

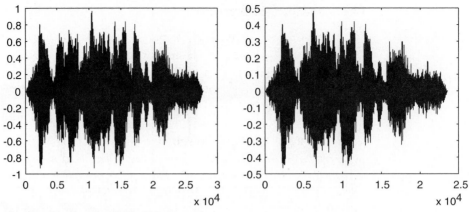

Figure 14.3 *Gone with the Wind speech*

Finally, in Exercise 14.4, we assemble the complete speech by concatenating these two fragments with the speech from *A Few Good Men*. The resulting picture is shown in Figure 14.4.

Exercise 14.4 Assemble the speech

```
>> [truth, Fst] = wavread('truth1.wav');
>> speech = [prob; sdamn; truth * .7];
>> figure
>> plot(speech);
>> sound(speech, Fst);
```

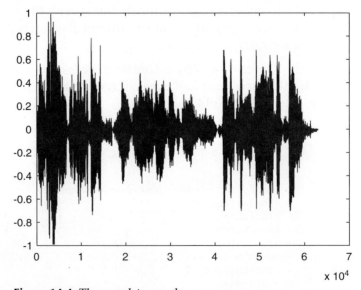

Figure 14.4 *The complete speech*

14.4.2 Musical Background

For good historical reasons, music is usually described graphically on a music score. The graphics describe for each note to be played its pitch and its duration, together with other notations indicating how to introduce expression and quality into the music. However, this graphical notation is not amenable to the simple representation of music we need for these experiments. Rather, we will use the representation illustrated in Figure 14.5. The right side of this figure shows a standard piano keyboard, the index of each white note, and the number of half steps necessary to achieve the pitch of each note. On the left side of the figure, we see the method to be used in this text to describe simple tunes. It will consist of an array with two columns and n rows, where n is the number of notes to be played for each tune. The first column is the key number to play, and the second column is the number of beats each note should be played.

The examples to follow will manipulate the file `piano.wav` to produce a snippet of music. This file is a recording of a single note played on a piano. Other files provided in the Companion Web site are the same note played on a variety of instruments. There are two ways to accomplish this, as follows:

1. Playing each note at a different playback frequency
2. Stretching or shrinking each note to match the required note pitch and playing them all at the same playback frequency

The first way is easier to understand and code, but very inflexible; the second method is a little more difficult to implement, but completely extensible. Musically speaking, if a sound is played at twice its natural frequency, it is heard as one musical octave higher. When you play a scale by playing each white key in turn from one note to the next octave, there are 8 keys to play with 7 frequency changes: 5 whole note steps (those separated by a black note) and 2 half note steps, for a total of 12 half note steps. These 12 half steps are logarithmically divided where the frequency multiplier between half note steps is $2^{1/12}$.

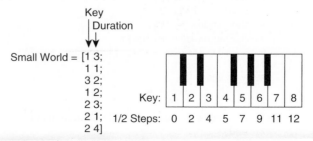

Figure 14.5 *Musical notes*

14.4.3 Changing Sound Frequency

We will leave as an exercise for the reader the question of playing a tune by changing the playback frequency of each note, which is really never a practical thing to do, and concentrate on playing all the notes of a tune with the same playback frequency. This allows the different notes to be copied into a single sound file and saved to be played back on any digital sound system.

In order to change the perceived note frequency without changing the playback frequency, we have to change the number of data samples in the original data file much as we stretched or shrunk an image in Section 13.4.1. Use Exercise 14.5 to experiment with this technique for playing notes at different pitches.

In Exercise 14.5 we first read and play the note at its natural frequency. Then we raise its pitch by removing about one-third of the samples and then lower the pitch by an octave by doubling the number of samples.

Play a Scale Listing 14.1 shows a script that uses this capability to play the C Major scale (all white notes) on the piano. It repeatedly shortens the vector newNote to increase the frequency of the note played.

In Listing 14.1:

> Lines 1–3: Read the note and set the step multipliers.
>
> Lines 4–12: Play eight notes of a major scale.

Exercise 14.5 Note pitch experiment

```
>> [note Fs] = wavread('instr_piano.wav');
>> sound(note, Fs);
>> sound(note(ceil(1:1.3:end)), Fs);
>> sound(note(ceil(1:0.5:end)), Fs);
```

Listing 14.1 Play a scale by shrinking the note

```
 1. [note, Fs] = wavread('instr_piano.wav');
 2. half = 2^(1/12);
 3. whole = half^2;
 4. for index = 1:8
 5.     sound(note, Fs);
 6.     if (index == 3) || (index == 7)
 7.         mult = half;
 8.     else
 9.         mult = whole;
10.     end
11.     note = note(ceil(1:mult:end));
12. end;
```

Line 5: Plays the note. This implementation uses a blocking `sound(...)` function. If your system does not block, you will need to insert `pause(0.3)` here to wait for most of the note to complete.

Lines 6–10: Choose the appropriate frequency multiplying factor.

Line 11: Shrinks the note file by the chosen factor.

Play a Simple Tune We now write a script to build a playable `.wav` file using the note shrinking technique. The script is shown in Listing 14.2. It uses the array `steps` to decide how many half-tone steps are necessary to reach the nth note on the scale and uses the array `doremi` to define the tune. The first column specifies the relative pitch (the note on the scale) and the second the duration in "beats." The script sets the beat time to be 0.2 seconds.

The goal of the script is to put the notes into a single sound array called `tune`, as illustrated in Figure 14.6, rather than playing the notes "on the fly." This is accomplished as follows:

- Create an empty array, `tune`, of the appropriate length (the length of the original note plus the total number of beats in the song)
- Initialize `storeAt` to store the first note at the start of the tune
- Iterate across the `tune` definition array `doremi` with the following steps:
  - Start with the original `note`
  - Get the key index to decide how many times to raise the `note` array by half a step
  - Raise the `note` to the right pitch and save it as `theNote`
  - Add that `theNote` vector to the `tune` vector, starting at `storeAt`
  - Move the `storeAt` variable down the `tune` vector a distance equivalent to the duration of that note
- When all the notes have been added to the tune file, play the tune and save it as a `.wav` file.

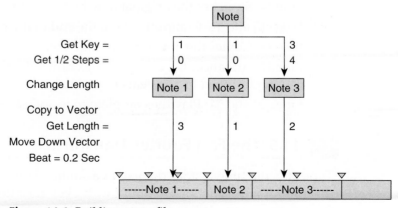

Figure 14.6 *Building a tune file*

Listing 14.2 Building a tune file

```
 1. [note, Fs] = wavread('instr_piano.wav');
 2. half = 2^(1/12);
 3. doremi = [1 3; 2 1; 3 3; 1 1; 3 2; 1 2; 3 4; 2 3;
 4.           3 1; 4 1; 4 1; 3 1; 2 1; 4 8; 3 3; 4 1;
 5.           5 3; 3 1; 5 2; 3 2; 5 4; 4 3; 5 1; 6 1;
 6.           6 1; 5 1; 4 1; 6 4 ];
 7. steps = [0 2 4 5 7 9 11 12];
 8. dt = .2;
 9. nCt = floor(dt*Fs);
10. storeAt = 1;
11. for index = 1:length(doremi)
12.     key = doremi(index,1);
13.     pow = steps(key);
14.     theNote = note(ceil(1:half^pow:end));
15.     noteLength = length(theNote);
16.     noteEnd = storeAt + noteLength - 1;
17.     tune(storeAt:noteEnd,1) = theNote;
18.     storeAt = storeAt + doremi(index,2) * nCt;
19. end
20. sound(tune, Fs)
21. wavwrite(tune, Fs, 'dohAdeer.wav')
```

In Listing 14.2:

> Lines 1–6: Read the file and set up the parameters.
>
> Line 7: A vector defining how many half steps it takes to set the frequency of notes 1–8.
>
> Line 8: The time between notes of length 1—the beat of the tune.
>
> Line 9: The number of samples to play for one beat of the tune.
>
> Line 10: Begins storing notes at the beginning of the tune.
>
> Lines 11–19: Insert each note in the song file into the tune file.
>
> Line 12: Fetches the key number.
>
> Line 13: Extracts the number of half steps required for this note.
>
> Line 14: Stretches the original note by this multiplier.
>
> Lines 15 and 16: Compute where the end of the note will be stored.
>
> Line 17: Copies the note into the tune file.
>
> Line 18: Advances the storeAt index down the tune file by the beat count multiplied by the beats required for this note.
>
> Lines 20 and 21: Play the complete tune and save it as a .wav file.

14.5 The Fast Fourier Transform

Typically, the time history display of a sound shows you the amplitude of the sound as a function of time but makes no attempt at showing the frequency content. While this works for the exercises above, we are often more interested in the frequency content of a sound file, for which we need a different presentation—a spectrum display.

14.5.1 Background

In general, a spectrum display shows the amount of sound energy in a given frequency band throughout the duration of the sound analyzed but ignores the time at which the sound at that frequency was generated. Many acoustic amplifiers (see Figure 14.7) include two features that allow you to customize the sound output:

- A spectral display that changes values as the sound is played, indicating the amount of sound energy (vertically) in different frequency bands (horizontally)
- Filter controls to change the relative amplification in different frequency bands

In the following paragraphs, we will consider only the analysis of the sound frequency content. The ability to reshape the sound frequency content as the sound plays is beyond the scope of this text.

To achieve the motion of the spectrum display, software to analyze a segment of the sound file runs periodically and updates the spectrum display. Typically, perhaps 20 times a second, 1/20th second of sound file is analyzed and transformed. The software used for this conversion is known as the Fourier transform.

While the mathematics of the Fourier transform is beyond the scope of this book, we can make use of the tools it offers without concerning ourselves with the details. There are a number of implementations of this transform; perhaps the most commonly used is the Fast Fourier Transform (FFT). The FFT uses clever matrix manipulations to optimize the

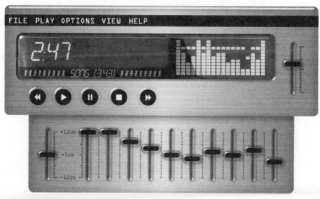

Figure 14.7 *A typical spectrum display*

mathematics needed to generate the forward (time to frequency) and reverse (frequency to time) transforms.

14.5.2 Implementation

Figure 14.8 illustrates the overall process of transforming between the time domain and frequency domain. It starts with a simple sound file, a vector of N sound values in the range (−1.0 to 1.0), which, if played back at a sample frequency Fs samples per second, reproduces the sound. The parameters of interest for characterizing the time trace are:

N	the number of samples
F_s	the sampling frequency
Δt	the time between samples, computed as $1/F_s$
Tmax	the maximum time is $N \times \Delta t$

The FFT consumes a file with these characteristics and produces a frequency spectrum with a corresponding set of characteristics. The frequency spectrum consists of the same number, N, of data points, each of which is a complex value with real and imaginary parts. (While many displays actually plot the magnitude of the spectrum values, to accomplish the inverse transform, the complex values must be retained.) The frequency

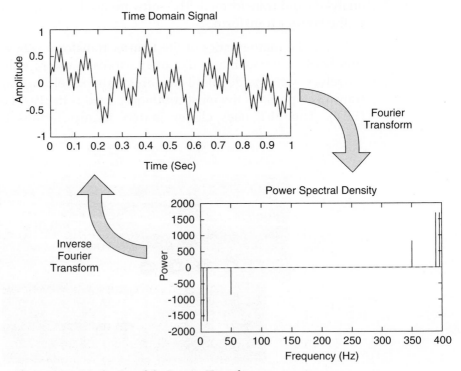

Figure 14.8 *Mechanics of the Fourier Transform*

values are "folded" on the plot so that zero frequency occurs at either end of the spectrum, and the maximum frequency occurs in the middle, at spectrum data point N/2.

The equivalent characteristics for the spectrum data are as follows:

N   the number of samples

Δf the frequency difference between samples, computed as $1/T_{max}$

F_{max},   the frequency value at the end of the plot, is N $\times$ Δf. However, since the mathematics force this frequency to actually replicate the beginning frequency, the maximum effective frequency actually occurs at the mid-point with value $F_{max}/2$.

The FFT is mechanized using the function fft(...), which consumes the time history and produces the complex spectrum file. The inverse FFT function, ifft(...), takes a spectrum array and reconstructs the time history. This pair of functions provides a powerful set of tools for manipulating sound files.

> **Technical Insight 14.2**
>
> The fact that the actual maximum frequency is half of the sampling frequency is consistent with the Nyquist criterion that the maximum frequency you can discern with digital sampling is half the sampling frequency.

14.5.3 Simple Spectral Analysis

Listing 14.3 illustrates a script that creates 10 seconds of an 8 Hz sine wave, plots the first second of it, performs the FFT, and plots the real and imaginary parts of the spectrum. Notice the following:

- A sine wave in the time domain transforms to a line in the frequency domain because all its energy is concentrated at that frequency—8 Hz in this example.

- Since the FFT is a linear process, multiple sine or cosine waves added together at different frequencies have additive effects in the spectrum.

- The resulting spectrum is complex (with real and imaginary parts) and symmetrical about its center, the point of maximum frequency. On the plot, of course, one cannot make the frequency axis labels reduce from the center to the end.

- The real part of the spectrum is mirrored about the center; the imaginary part is mirrored and inverted (the complex conjugate of the original data).

- The phase of the complex spectrum retains the position of the sine wave in the time domain—it would be totally real for a cosine wave symmetrically placed in time and totally imaginary for a sine wave in the same relationship.

Listing 14.3 FFT of a sine wave

```
 1. dt = 1/400              % sampling period (sec)
 2. pts = 10000             % number of points
 3. f = 8                   % frequency
 4. t = (1:pts) * dt;       % time array for plotting
 5. x = sin(2*pi*f*t);
 6. subplot(3, 1, 1)
 7. plot(t(1:end/25), x(1:end/25));
 8. title('Time Domain Sine Wave')
 9. ylabel('Amplitude')
10. xlabel('Time (Sec)')
11. Y = fft(x);             % perform the transform
12. df = 1 / t(end)         % the frequency interval
13. fmax = df * pts / 2
14. f = (1:pts) * 2 * fmax / pts;
                            % frequencies for plotting
15. subplot(3, 1, 2)
16. plot(f, real(Y))
17. title('Real Part')
18. xlabel('Frequency (Hz)')
19. ylabel('Energy')
20. subplot(3, 1, 3)
21. plot(f, imag(Y))
22. title('Imaginary Part')
23. xlabel('Frequency (Hz)')
24. ylabel('Energy')
```

The script in Listing 14.3 creates three sub-plots: the original sine wave and then the amplitude and phase of the spectrum.

In Listing 14.3:

> Lines 1–5: Set up the time domain signal.
>
> Lines 6–10: Plot the front part of the time trace.
>
> Line 11: Performs the FFT.
>
> Lines 12–14: Set up the frequency plots.
>
> Lines 15–19: Plot the spectrum real part.
>
> Lines 20–24: Plot the spectrum imaginary part.

Figure 14.9 shows the result from running this script. It confirms the earlier statement that the real part of the spectrum is mirrored about the center frequency, and the imaginary part is mirrored and inverted.

14.6 Frequency Domain Operations

As a typical example of operating in the frequency domain, we will consider analyzing the spectral quality of different musical instruments. The intent of this section is to develop a plot showing the spectra of a selection of different musical instruments. We will first build a function that plots the spectrum for a single instrument and then build the script to create all the

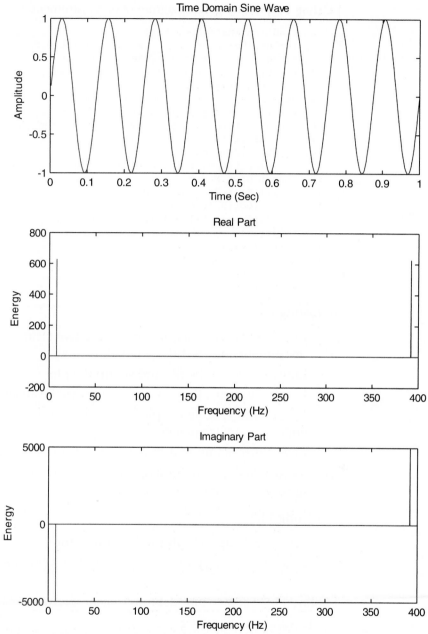

Figure 14.9 *FFT of a sine wave*

plots. Listing 14.4 shows a function that reads the `.wav` file of an instrument from the music samples in the University of Miami's Audio and Signal Processing Laboratory.[1] All the instruments are carefully playing a note at about 260 Hz.

---

[1]http://chronos.ece.miami.edu/~dasp/samples/samples.html

Listing 14.4 Plotting the spectrum of one instrument

```
 1. function inst(name, ttl)
      % plot the spectrum of the instrument with
      % the given name, with the given plot title
 2. [x, Fs] = wavread(['instr_' name '.wav']);
 3. N = length(x);
 4. dt = 1/Fs;        % sampling period (sec)
 5. t = (1:N) * dt;   % time array for plotting
 6. Y = abs(fft(x)); % perform the transform
 7. mx = max(Y);
 8. Y = Y * 100 / mx;
 9. df = 1 / t(end) ; % the frequency interval
10. fmax = df * N / 2 ;
11. f = (1:N) * 2 * fmax / N;
12. up = floor(N/10);
13. plot(f(1:up), Y(1:up) );
14. title(ttl)
15. xlabel('Frequency (Hz)')
16. ylabel('Energy')
```

In Listing 14.4:

> Line 1: Shows a function consuming two strings: the name of the instrument and the title of the plot.
>
> Lines 2–5: Read the file and set up the plot parameters.
>
> Line 6: Performs the FFT and computes the absolute value.
>
> Lines 7 and 8: Scale the plot to be a percentage of the maximum energy at any frequency.
>
> Lines 9–16: Set up and plot the first 10% of the spectrum.

The script that uses this function to plot the instrument data is shown in Listing 14.5.

In Listing 14.5:

> Line 1: Sets up the sub-plots configuration.
>
> Lines 2–17: Each pair of lines makes the sub-plots of one instrument.

Listing 14.5 Script to plot eight-instrument spectra

```
 1. rows = 4; cols = 2
 2. subplot(rows, cols, 1)
 3. inst('sax', 'Saxophone');
 4. subplot(rows, cols, 2)
 5. inst('flute', 'Flute');
 6. subplot(rows, cols, 3)
 7. inst('tbone', 'Trombone');
 8. subplot(rows, cols, 4)
 9. inst('piano', 'Piano');
10. subplot(rows, cols, 5)
11. inst('tpt', 'Trumpet');
```

continued on next page

```
12. subplot(rows, cols, 6)
13. inst('mutetpt', 'Muted Trumpet');
14. subplot(rows, cols, 7)
15. inst('violin', 'Violin');
16. subplot(rows, cols, 8)
17. inst('cello', 'Cello');
```

The results are shown in Figure 14.10. It is interesting to notice the following:

- None of the instruments produce a pure tone. The lowest frequency at which there is energy is usually called the fundamental

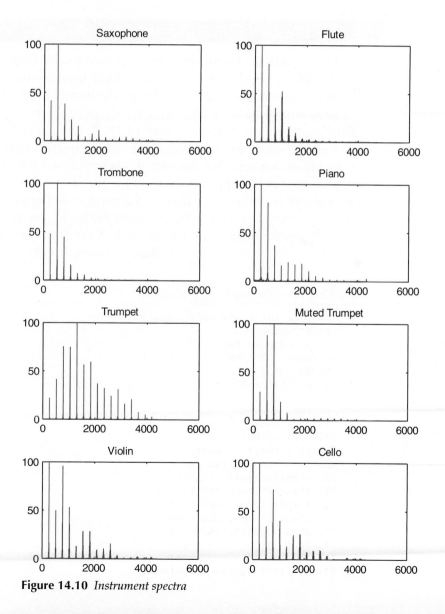

Figure 14.10 *Instrument spectra*

frequency, and successive peaks to the right at multiples of the fundamental frequency are referred to, for example, as the first, second, and third harmonics.

- Several instruments have much more energy in the harmonics than in the fundamental frequency.
- "Families" of instruments have similar spectral shapes—the strings, for example, have strong fundamental and second harmonic energy. In principle, these characteristic spectral "signatures" can be used to synthesize the sound of instruments, and even to identify individual instruments when played in groups.

14.7 Engineering Example—Music Synthesizer

A music synthesizer is an electronic instrument with a piano style keyboard that is able to simulate the sound of multiple instruments. Unlike the instrument sounds we have used so far, the instrument sounds are not stored as large time histories. Rather, they are stored as the Fourier coefficients similar to those illustrated in Figure 14.10. The sound is then reconstructed by multiplying sin or cosine waves of the right frequency by the stored coefficients. For some instruments, this is sufficient. Other instruments such as pianos need to have the amplitude of the resulting sound modified to match a typical profile. Listing 14.6 illustrates a possible technique for extracting the most important Fourier coefficients from the piano sound. The result will be a little disappointing because the sound does not fade with time. We will need some techniques from the next chapter to complete the story.

Listing 14.6 Synthesizing a piano

```
 1. [snd Fs] = wavread('instr_piano.wav');
 2. N = length(snd)
 3. sound(snd, Fs)
 4. tMax = N / Fs
 5. dt = 1 / Fs
 6. Y = fft(snd);
 7. Ns = N/4;
 8. fMax = Fs/4;
 9. df = fMax / Ns;
10. f = ((1:Ns) - 1) * df;
11. rl = real(Y(1:Ns));
12. im = imag(Y(1:Ns));
13. plot(f, abs(Y(1:Ns)))
14. xlabel('frequency (Hz)')
15. ylabel('real amplitude')
16. zlabel('imag amplitude')
17. amps = abs(Y(1:end/2));
18. Nc = 25;
19. for ndx = 1:Nc
20.    [junk where] = max(amps);
```

continued on next page

```
21.     C(ndx).freq = where;
22.     C(ndx).coeff = Y(where);
23. amps(where-25:where+25) = 0;
24. end
25. frq = [C.freq];
26. [frq order] = sort(frq);
27. sortedStr = C(order);
28. Nt = 25;
29. t = (1:2*Fs) * dt;
30. f = zeros(1, length(t));
31. for ndx = 1:Nt
32. w = frq(ndx) * df * 2 * pi;
33. ct = cos(w*t);
34. st = sin(w*t);
35. Cf = sortedStr(ndx).coeff;
36. f = f + real(Cf) * ct + imag(Cf) * st;
37. end
    % amplitude shaping goes here
38. sf = f ./ max(f);
39. sound(sf, Fs)
```

In Listing 14.6:

> Lines 1–5: Read the sound file and compute the representative parameters.
>
> Lines 6–9: Perform the FFT and compute its representative parameters and Ns, the number of samples we are interested in.
>
> Lines 10–12: Compute a vector of the frequencies and extract the real and imaginary coefficients.
>
> Lines 13–16: Plot the coefficient absolute values (see Figure 14.11).

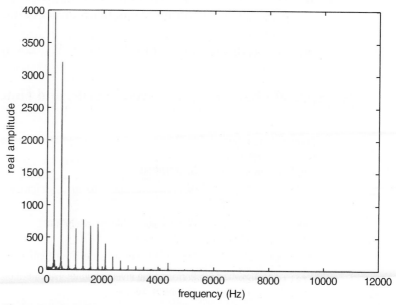

Figure 14.11 *Instrument spectrum*

Line 17: Stores the absolute values of the coefficients.

Lines 18–24: Extract the 25 largest coefficients by first finding the maximum absolute coefficient (Line 20), saving the frequency and complex amplitudes (Lines 21–22), and then removing that peak from the amplitude vector.

Lines 25–27: Sort the complex coefficients in frequency order.

Lines 29 and 30: Set up the time trace parameters and storage.

Lines 31–37: Build the sound file composed of the real coefficients times the cosine of the frequency and the imaginary coefficients times the sine of the frequency.

Lines 38–39: Scale and play the sound.

We will complete this synthesis for a piano sound in the next chapter.

 ## Chapter Summary

This chapter presented the following:

- Sounds are read with specific readers that provide a time history and sampling frequency
- Sounds can be played through the computer's sound system and saved to disk as a sound file ready for playing on any digital player
- We can slice and concatenate sounds to edit speeches and change the frequency of the sound to change its pitch
- We can analyze the frequency content of sound using the Fast Fourier Transform (FFT)
- We can modify the spectra by adding, deleting, or changing the sound levels at chosen frequencies under certain controlled conditions
- We can reconstruct a sound from the FFT coefficients.

 ## Special Characters, Reserved Words, and Functions

Special Characters, Reserved Words, and Functions	Description	Discussed in This Section
`[data Fs nb]` `= auread(file)`	Reads an `.au` sound file in `.wav` format	14.3
`auwrite((data,` `Fs, nb, file)`	Writes a sound file in `.au` format	14.3
`fft(ftime)`	Performs the Fast Fourier Transform on a sound file	14.5.2
`ifft(ffreq)`	Performs the inverse Fourier Transform on a spectrum file	14.5.2

Special Characters, Reserved Words, and Functions	Description	Discussed in This Section
`sound(data, Fs)`	Plays a sound file	14.3
`[data Fs nb] = wavread(file)`	Reads a `.wav` sound file in `.wav` format	14.3
`wavwrite(data, Fs, nb, file)`	Writes a sound file in `.wav` format	14.3

Self Test

Use the following questions to check your understanding of the material in this chapter:

True or False

T 1. Playing a sound file at double the recorded sample frequency raises its pitch by an octave.

F 2. Removing every other sample from a sound file lowers the pitch by an octave.

F 3. The resolution of the recorded data has a significant effect on the quality of the recording.

T 4. After performing an FFT, the zero frequency occurs at either end of the spectrum and the maximum frequency occurs in the middle.

T 5. Since the mathematics of the FFT are linear, the spectrum of a sound added in the time domain is also added in the frequency domain.

Fill in the Blanks

1. Sound pressure fluctuations have two attributes: their _amplitude_ and their _frequency_.

2. Each word coming out of the _A/D_ or going into the _D/A_ merely represents the _pressure_ on the microphone at a point in time.

3. The steps from one note to the next higher octave are divided into _7_ increments: _5_ whole note steps and _2_ half note steps, for a total of _12_ half note steps.

4. A spectrum display shows the amount of _sound energy_ in a given _frequency band_ throughout the duration of the sound analyzed.

Programming Projects

1. These are fundamental exercises with sound files. You should not hard-code any of the answers for this problem, and you should not need iteration.

   a. Select and read a suitable .wav file, and save the sound values and sampling frequency.

   b. Create a new sound that has double the frequency of the original sound, and store your answer in the variable sound_Double.

   c. Create a new sound that is the same as the original except that the pitch is raised by five half tones. Store your answer in the variable raised_pitch.

   d. We need a figure showing two views each of these three sounds, created using subplot. In the left column, plot the original sound, sound_Double, and raised_pitch, labeling each plot accordingly.
   In the right column, plot the first quarter of the values of the power spectrum of each sound with the proper frequency values on the horizontal axis.

   e. Play each of the sounds in the following order: original sound, sound_Double, and raised_pitch each at the original sampling frequency.

2. Write a function that will accept a string specifying a sound file and do the following:

   a. Play back the sound.

   b. Plot the sound in the time domain, titling and labeling your plot appropriately.

   c. Compute the frequency with the most energy in this file. Validate your answer by plotting the lower quarter of the frequencies of the Fourier Transform of the sound. Don't forget that the Fourier Transform is complex; you will need to reason with and plot the absolute value of the spectrum.

   d. Test this function with suitable .wav files.

3. Write a function named plotSound that takes in the name of a sound file and produces a 1 × 2 figure with two plots. The first plot should be a plot of the sound in the time domain. The second plot should be a plot of the sound in the frequency domain. Your function should not return anything. Label the first plot 'Time Domain' and label its axes appropriately. Label second plot 'Frequency Domain' and label its axes appropriately.

   The Time Domain plot should be an amplitude vs. time plot. For simplicity make sure that your time vector starts at dt (delta time) and goes to n*dt (t_{max}) where n is the number of samples.

The Frequency Domain plot should be a power vs. frequency plot where power is the absolute value of the FFT of the amplitude values. For simplicity make sure that your frequency vector starts at df (delta frequency) and goes to n*df ($2*f_{max}$).

4. In this exercise, we will write a script to create an instrument sound from scratch.
   a. Create a vector, t, of time values from 0 to 2 seconds with length 40,000 samples.
   b. Convert the frequency of middle C (261.6 Hz) to ω radians per second.
   c. Compute a sound sample as cos(ωt) over the range of t in part a.
   d. Play that sound at a sample frequency of 20,000, and verify that it sounds "about right."
   e. Perform the Fourier Transform on the sound vector, establish the correct axis values, and prove that the sound is exactly Middle C.

5. Write a function named playNote that takes in a string representing a note on the piano. Your function should return a vector representing the amplitude values of the note in addition to the correct sampling frequency to be used to play it back. You should do this by modifying the sound in the provided instr_piano.wav file which is Middle C played on the piano. Note that the returned sampling frequency should be the same as that in instr_piano..wav.

   Here is a list of all the possible note names representing notes that your function should work with and below that is the number of half steps above/below the middle C for that note:

cn	cn#	dn	dn#	en	fn	fn#	gn	gn#	a(n+1)	a(n+1)#	b(n+1)	c(n+1)
-12	-11	-10	-9	-8	-7	-6	-5	-4	-3	-2	-1	0

   where c4 is the middle C, c5 is 1 octave above it, and c3 is 1 octave below it. Similarly, f5 is 1 octave higher than f4, etc. For example, [y1 fs] = playNote('c5'); should return a vector such that sound(y1, fs) should sound like middle C

6. Finally, you will use these tools to play your favorite song.
   a. Find the music for your favorite song, and translate it into the symbology of Problem 14.5.
   b. Write a script that uses the playNote function to play your song on the piano.
   c. Modify playNote to use your synthetic instrument from Problem 14.3, and save it as playSynthetic.
   d. Write a script that uses playSynthetic to play your song in futuristic style.

Numerical Methods

Chapter Objectives

This chapter discusses the implementations of four common numerical techniques:

- Interpolating data
- Fitting polynomial curves to data
- Numerical integration
- Numerical differentiation

Introduction

Real-world data are rarely in such a form that you can use it immediately. Frequently, the data must be manipulated according to the user's actual needs:

- If the data samples have correct values but are not close enough together to be used directly, we can use interpolation to compute data points between the samples provided.

- There are occasions where the data-gathering facilities add some amount of noise to the data. To minimize the effects of the noise, we can compute the coefficients of a polynomial function that best matches the data.

- There are also times when the data must be integrated or differentiated to derive the quantities of interest.

15.1 Interpolation

If our data samples have correct values but are not close enough to be used directly, we can use either linear or cubic interpolation to compute data points between the samples provided. For example, plotting functions use linear interpolation to draw the lines between data points. In general, interpolation is a technique by which we estimate a variable's value between known values. In this section, we present the two most common types of interpolation: linear interpolation and cubic spline interpolation. In both techniques, we assume that we have a set of data points that represents x-y coordinates for which y is a function of x; that is,

$$y = f(x).$$

We then have a value of x that is not part of the data set for which we want to find the y value. Figure 15.1 illustrates the definition of the interpolation problem.

15.1.1 Linear Interpolation

Linear interpolation is one of the most common techniques for estimating data values between two given data points. With this technique, we assume that the function between the points can be represented by a straight line drawn between the points, as shown in Figure 15.2. Since we can find the equation of a straight line defined by the two known points, we can find y for any value of x. The closer the points are to each other, the more accurate our approximation is likely to be. Of course, we could use this equation to

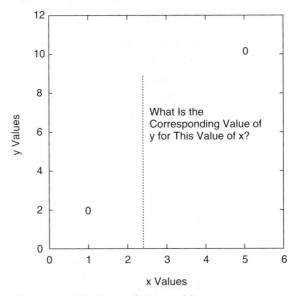

Figure 15.1 *The interpolation problem*

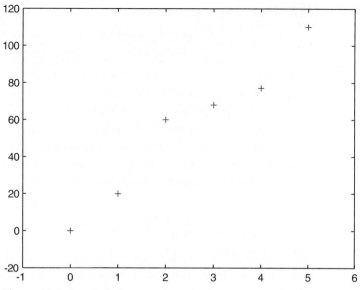

Figure 15.2 *Interpolation raw data*

extrapolate points past our collected data. This is rarely wise, however, and often leads to significant errors.

The function that performs linear interpolation is as follows:

```
new_y = interp1(x, y, new_x)
```

where the vectors x and y contain the original data values and the vector new_x contains the point(s) for which we want to compute interpolated new_y values. The x values should be in ascending order, and the new_x values should be within the range of the original x values. Note that the last character in the name interp1 is the numeric 1 (one), not a lowercase L.

The use of interp1(...) is demonstrated in Listing 15.1.

Listing 15.1 Linear interpolation

```
1. x = 0:5;
2. y = [0, 20, 60, 68, 77, 110];
3. plot(x, y, 'r+')
4. hold on
5. fprintf('value at 1.5 is %2.2f\n', interp1(x, y ,1.5));
6. new_x = 0:0.241:5;
7. new_y = interp1(x,y,new_x);
8. plot(new_x, new_y, 'o')
9. axis([-1,6,-20,120])
10. title('linear Interpolation Plot')
11. xlabel('x values') ; ylabel('y values')
12. fprintf('value at 7 is %2.2f\n', interp1(x, y ,7));
```

In Listing 15.1:

> Lines 1–3: We use the data illustrated in Figure 15.2.
>
> Line 5: We take a single interpolated reading from the data at x = 1.5.
>
> Lines 4–8: We plot points spaced 0.241 units apart on the x-axis marked with circles, as shown in Figure 15.3. Notice that the circles fall on the straight lines between the given data values.
>
> Lines 9–11: Document the plot.
>
> Line 12: Finally, we attempt to extrapolate to the point x = 7 and see that NaN (Not a Number) is returned because interp1 refuses to extrapolate outside the original range of x values. The output from running this script is:

```
value at 1.5 is 40.00
value at 7 is NaN
```

The MATLAB language allows us to provide a fourth parameter to the interp1 function that must be a string that modifies its behavior. The choices are as follows:

> 'nearest' nearest neighbor interpolation
>
> 'linear' linear interpolation—the default
>
> 'spline' piecewise cubic spline interpolation (see Section 15.1.2)
>
> 'pchip' shape-preserving piecewise cubic interpolation
>
> 'cubic' same as 'pchip'
>
> 'v5cubic' cubic interpolation that does not extrapolate, and uses 'spline' if x is not equally spaced

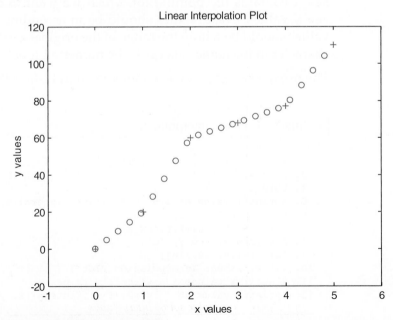

Figure 15.3 *Linear interpolation*

The MATLAB language also provides for two-dimensional (`interp2`) and three-dimensional (`interp3`) interpolation functions, which are not discussed here.

15.1.2 Cubic Spline Interpolation

A **cubic spline** is a smooth curve constructed to go through a set of points. The curve between each pair of points is a third-degree polynomial that has the general form:

$$x = a_{x0}t^3 + a_{x1}t^2 \ 1 \ a_{x2}t + a_{x3} \text{ and}$$
$$y = a_{y0}t^3 + a_{y1}t^2 + a_{y2}t + a_{y3}$$

where t is a parameter ranging from 0 to 1 between each pair of points. The coefficients are computed so that this provides a smooth curve between pairs of points and a smooth transition between the adjacent curves. Figure 15.4 shows a cubic spline smoothly connecting six points using a total of five different cubic equations.

The function that performs linear interpolation is as follows:

```
new_y = spline(x, y, new_x);
```

where the vectors x and y contain the original data values, and the vector x_new contains the point(s) for which we want to compute interpolated y_new values. The x values should be in ascending order, and while the x_new values should be within the range of the x values, this function will attempt to extrapolate outside that range.

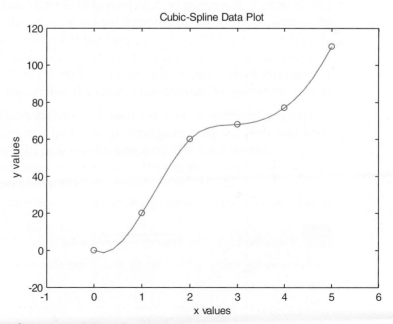

Figure 15.4 *Cubic spline interpolation*

Listing 15.2 Spline interpolation

```
1. x = 0:5;
2. y = [0, 20, 60, 68, 77, 110];
3. new_x = 0:0.2:5;
4. new_y = spline(x, y, new_x);
5. plot(x, y, 'o', new_x, new_y, '-')
6. axis([-1,6,-20,120])
7. title('Cubic-Spline Data Plot')
8. xlabel( 'x values'); ylabel('y values')
```

The curve in Figure 15.4 was created using the code shown in Listing 15.2.

Style Points 15.1

A good convention to adopt is shown in Figure 15.4:

- Use symbols to plot data points that are real values with no associated information connecting them
- Draw lines between data points only when there is an analytic relationship that connects the data points

Here, we use a circle symbol for the raw data to emphasize the original source of the information, and a smooth line for the spline curve to indicate that we are assuming a possibly erroneous but continuous relationship between data points.

In Listing 15.2:

Lines 1 and 2: Show the original x and y values.

Line 3: Shows dense x values to define the curve.

Line 4: Computes the spline function.

Lines 5–8: Plot the original data and the smooth curve.

15.1.3 Extrapolation

A note of caution about extrapolation—attempting to infer the values of data points outside the range of data provided is problematic at best and usually gives misleading results. Although logically your code may allow you to, you should never do it. The interp1 and spline functions behave differently in this respect. As we saw previously, the interp1 function refuses to supply results outside the range of the original x data. If you try, for every new_x value outside the range of the original x values, it will return NaN—not a number.

This is actually quite nice because if you accidentally request interpolated data like this, the plot programs ignore NaN values. The spline function, however, has no such scruples and allows you to request any x values you want, using the equation of the closest line segment. So considering Figure 15.4, if you asked for the value at x = -3, it would use the segment between 0 and 1, which has a violent upswing at the lower end (see Exercise 15.1).

Exercise 15.1 The evils of extrapolation

After running the script in Listing 15.1, enter this code:

```
>> spline(x, y, -3)
ans =
  813.3333
```

This might be what you want, but it looks odd! Chances are the data are not as accurate as you thought, and you probably need to fit a curve to the data, as explained in the following section.

15.2 Curve Fitting

There are occasions where the data acquisition facilities add some amount of noise to the data. To minimize the effects of the noise, we can smooth the data by computing the coefficients of a polynomial function that best match the data. The choice of the order of the polynomial must be made by the users, depending upon their understanding of the underlying physics that generated the data.

For example, assume that we have a set of data points collected from an experiment. After plotting the data points, we find that they generally fall in a straight line. However, if we were to try to draw a straight line through the points, probably only a couple of the points would fall exactly on the line. A least squares curve fitting method could be used to find the straight line that is the closest to the points, by minimizing the distance from each point to the straight line. Although this line can be considered a "best fit" to the data points, it is possible that none of the points would actually fall on the line of best fit. (Note that this method is different from interpolation, because the lines used in interpolation actually fall on all of the original data points.)

In the following section, we will discuss fitting a straight line to a set of data points, and then we will discuss fitting a polynomial of higher order.

15.2.1 Linear Regression

Linear regression is the process that determines the linear equation that is the best fit to a set of data points in terms of minimizing the sum of the squared distances between the line and the data points. To understand this process, first we consider the same set of data values used previously and attempt to "eyeball" a straight line through the data. Assume, for example, that $y = 20x$ is a good estimate of the curve. Listing 15.3 shows the code to plot the points and this estimate.

Listing 15.3 Eyeball linear estimation

```
1. x = 0:5;
2. y = [0 20 60 68 77 110];
3. y2 = 20 * x;
4. plot(x, y, 'o', x, y2);
5. axis([-1 7 -20 120])
6. title('Linear Estimate')
7. xlabel('Time (sec)')
8. ylabel('Temperature (degrees F)')
9. grid on
```

In Listing 15.3:

> Lines 1 and 2: Show the original data points.
>
> Line 3: Is our eyeball estimate.
>
> Lines 4–9: Plot the original data and the estimate.

Looking at the results in Figure 15.5, it appears that $y = 20x$ is a reasonable estimate of a line through the points. We really need the ability to compare the quality of the fit of this line to other possible estimates, so we compute the difference between the actual y value and the value calculated from the estimate:

```
>> dy = [0, 0, 20, 8, -3, 10]
```

It turns out that the best way to make this comparison is by the **least squares technique,** whereby the measure of the quality of the fit is the sum of the squared differences between the actual data points and the linear estimates. This sum can be computed with the following command:

```
>> sum_sq = sum(dy.^2)
```

For the above set of data, the value of sum_sq is 573. As we will see, MATLAB can automatically produce the best linear fit shown in Figure 15.6 whose sum of squares is 356.82, a significant improvement over our original guess. This result was achieved by running Exercise 15.2.

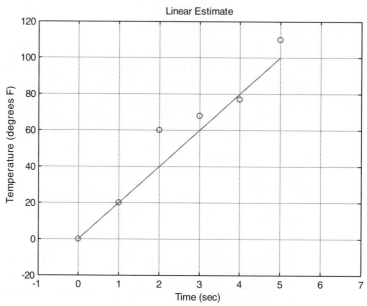

Figure 15.5 *An eyeball estimate of a linear fit*

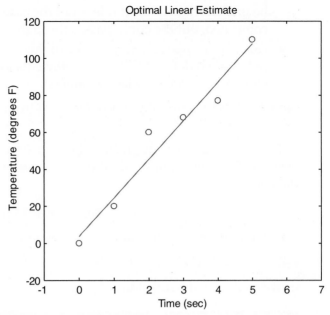

Figure 15.6 *Linear curve fit*

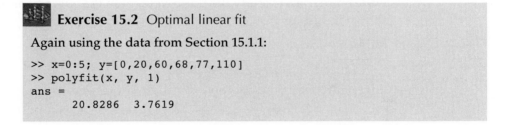

Exercise 15.2 Optimal linear fit

Again using the data from Section 15.1.1:

```
>> x=0:5; y=[0,20,60,68,77,110]
>> polyfit(x, y, 1)
ans =
     20.8286   3.7619
```

15.2.2 Polynomial Regression

Linear regression is a special case of the polynomial regression technique. Recall that a polynomial with one variable can be written by using the following formula:

$$f(x) = a_0 x^n + a_1 x^{n-1} + a_2 x^{n-2} + a_3 x^{n-3} + \ldots a_{n-1} x + a_n$$

The degree of a polynomial is equal to the largest value used as an exponent. MATLAB provides a pair of functions to compute the coefficients of the best fit to a set of data and then interpolate on those coefficients to produce the data to plot:

- `coef = polyfit(x, y, n)` computes the coefficients of the polynomial of degree `n` that best matches the given `x` and `y` values. The function returns the coefficients, `coef`, in descending powers of `x`. For the least squares calculation to work, the length of `x` should be greater than n - 1. If this is not the case, the coefficients are still computed, but the curve passes through all the data points.

- new_y = polyval(coef, new_x) can then be used to interpolate the polynomial defined by these coefficients for the new_y value(s) corresponding to any new_x value(s).

Note that there is nothing to prevent you from using these coefficients for extrapolation.

Exercise 15.2 illustrates fitting the best straight line to the data used in Section 15.1.1, indicating that the first-order polynomial that best fits our data is as follows:

$$f(x) = 20.8286x + 3.7169$$

We could interpolate the values of new_x with:

new_y = coef(1) * new_x + coef(2)

or we could use the function polyval:

new_y = polyfit(coef, new_x)

We can use our new understanding of the polyfit and polyval functions to write a program to study the improvement in the curve fit as n increases, as shown in Listing 15.4.

In Listing 15.4:

Lines 1–3: Set up the data sets.

Lines 4–14: Study second- through fifth-order fits.

Line 5: Combines polyfit and polyval calls to compute the new y values.

Lines 6–12: Plot the results. Notice the use of sprintf(...) to make a dynamic title for the plots.

Listing 15.4 Higher-order fits

```
1. x = 0:5;
2. fine_x = 0:.1:5;
3. y = [0 20 60 68 77 110];
4. for order = 2:5
5.      y2=polyval(polyfit(x,y,order), fine_x);
6.      subplot(2,2,order-1)
7.      plot(x, y, 'o', fine_x, y2)
8.      axis([-1 7 -20 120])
9.      ttl = sprintf('Degree %d Polynomial Fit', ...
10.                     order );
11.     title(ttl)
12.     xlabel('Time (sec)')
13.     ylabel('Temperature (degrees F)')
14. end
```

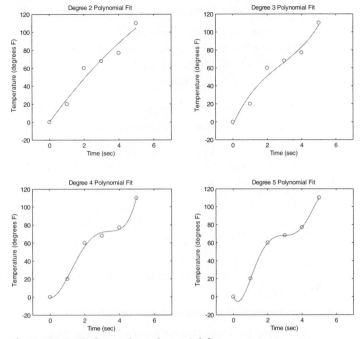

Figure 15.7 *Higher-order polynomial fits*

The results are shown in Figure 15.7. Notice that with six points, the fifth-order fit goes through all the data points.

15.2.3 Practical Application

We return briefly to the problem of replacing the blue sky in Chapter 13. The sky we used to replace the gray skies of Vienna has a power line we need to remove. We can use polynomial curve fitting to create an artificial sky with exactly the same color characteristics as the blue sky in the cottage picture, but without the wire. This is possible because each row of the image has so much data that define its color profile that the presence of the wire is a minor amount of "noise." We merely need to process each row of the sky, fit a second-order curve to it, interpolate a new sky row from the parameters, and replace the row in the sky. The code to perform this is shown in Listing 15.5.

In Listing 15.5:

> Line 1: Reads the original cottage picture.
> Line 2: Obtains its sizes.
> Line 3: The x values for the curve fitting.
> Line 4: Makes a copy of the original picture.
> Lines 5–12: Convert the top 700 rows where the sky is.
> Lines 6–11: Treat each color individually.

Listing 15.5 Removing the power line from the sky

```
 1. p = imread('Witney.jpg');
 2. [rows, cols, clrs] = size(p);
 3. x = 1:cols;
 4. sky = p;
 5. for row = 1:700
 6.     for color = 1:3
 7.         cv = double(p(row, :, color));
 8.         coef = polyfit(x, cv, 2);
 9.         ncr = polyval(coef, x);
10.         sky(row,:,color) = uint8(ncr);
11.     end
12. end
13. image(sky)
14. imwrite(sky, 'sky.jpg');
```

Line 7: The polynomial approximation needs each row as a double vector.

Lines 8–9: Compute a synthetic row.

Line 10: Puts the row into the new sky.

Lines 13 and 14: Show and save the new image.

Figure 15.8 shows the cottage picture updated with a smooth sky. Notice that the chimneys have been smeared off, but this does not affect the part of the sky needed for the Vienna picture. This synthetic sky is ready to be used in the script to replace the original sky (see Listing 13.1). Figure 15.9 shows the Vienna picture with a clear blue synthetic sky.

Figure 15.8 *Updated sky*

Figure 15.9 *Updated picture*

15.3 Numerical Integration

The integral of a function $f(x)$ over the interval $[a, b]$ is defined to be the area under the curve of $f(x)$ between a and b, as shown in Figure 15.10. If the value of this integral is K, the notation to represent the integral of $f(x)$ between a and b is as follows:

$$K = \int_a^b f(x)\, dx$$

For many functions, this integral can be computed analytically. However, for a number of functions, this is not possible, and we require a numerical technique to estimate its value. We look at two different scenarios:

- Two different techniques for computing the complete integral with various degrees of accuracy
- A technique for evaluating the continuous integral of $f(x)$

15.3.1 Determination of the Complete Integral

Two of the most common numerical integration techniques estimate $f(x)$ either with a set of piecewise linear functions or with a set of piecewise parabolic functions. If we use piecewise linear functions, we can compute the area of the trapezoids that compose the area under the piecewise linear function. This technique is called the **trapezoidal rule.** If we use piecewise quadratic functions, we can compute and add the areas of these components. This technique is called **Simpson's rule.**

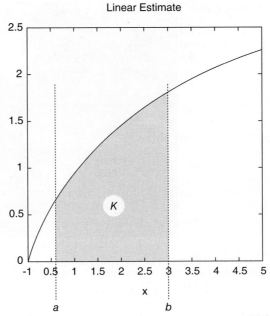

Figure 15.10 *Integration of f(x)*

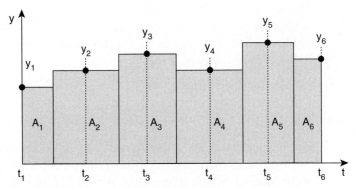

Figure 15.11 *Discrete integration*

The Trapezoidal Rule If we represent the area under a curve by trapezoids, as illustrated in Figure 15.11, and if the interval $[a, b]$ is divided into n equal sections, then the area can be approximated by the following formula:

$$K_T = \frac{b - a}{2n} (f(x_0) + 2f(x_1) + 2f(x_2) + \ldots + 2f(x_{n-1}) + f(x_n))$$

where the x_i values represent the end points of the trapezoids and where $x_0=a$ and $x_n=b$. Listing 15.6 shows a function that computes this integral.

Simpson's Rule If the area under a curve is represented by areas under quadratic sections of a curve, and if the interval $[a, b]$ is divided into

Listing 15.6 Trapezoidal integration

```
1. function K = trapezoid( v, a, b )
   % usage: K = trapezoid(v, a, b )
2. K = (b-a) * (v(1) + v(end) + ...
3. 2*sum(v(2:end-1))) / (2*(length(v) - 1) );
4.
```

$2n$ equal sections, then the area can be approximated by the formula (Simpson's rule):

$$K_s = \frac{h}{3}\left(f(x_0) + 4f(x_1) + 2f(x_2) + 4f(x_3) + \dots\right.$$

$$\left. + 2f(x_{2n-2}) + 4f(x_{2n-1}) + f(x_{2n})\right)$$

where the x_i values represent the end points of the sections, $x_0 = a$ and $x_{2n} = b$, and $h = (b - a) / (2n)$. Listing 15.7 shows a function to integrate using Simpson's rule.

15.3.2 Continuous Integration Problems

We now consider a slightly different scenario. If $f(t)$ is the rate of change of $F(t)$ defined as $f(t) = dF(t)/dt$, then given $f(t)$, we can find the indefinite integral $F(t)$ according to the following formula:

$$F(t) = \int_{t_0}^{t} f(x)\,dt$$

For example, we might be given data that represent the velocity of a sounding rocket, such as is plotted in Figure 15.12. We need to approximate the altitude of the rocket over time by integrating this data.

To perform this kind of integral, the MATLAB language provides the function F = cumsum(f) that computes the cumulative sum of the vector f. The result, F, is a vector of the same length as f where F(i) is the sum of f(1:i). If the data values, f, are regularly sampled at a rate Δt, the integral is found by multiplying cumsum(f) by the time interval, Δt. If they are not regularly sampled, you have to compute the cumsum(...) of the scalar product of f and the vector of time differences.

Listing 15.7 Simpson's rule integration

```
1. function K = simpson( v, a, b )
   % usage: K = simpson(v, a, b )
2. K = (b-a) * (v(1) + v(end) + ...
3.              4*sum(v(2:2:end-1)) + ...
4.              2*sum(v(3:2:end-2)) ) / (3*(length(v) - 1) );
```

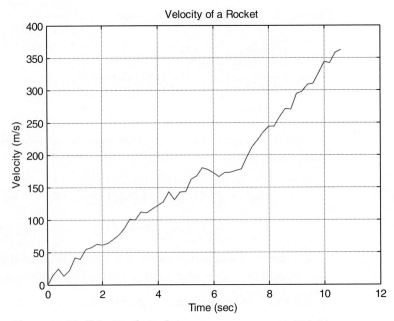

Figure 15.12 *Velocity of a rocket*

To compute a more accurate integral, especially if the samples are not regularly spaced along the independent axis, MATLAB also provides the function cumtrapz(t, f) where t is the independent parameter and f the dependent parameter. The function uses trapezoidal integration to calculate the indefinite integral F(t).

Listing 15.8 shows the function that computes this continuous integral, making use of cumsum(...).

Listing 15.8 Integrating rocket velocity

```
1. v =[ 0.0 15.1 25.1 13.7 22.2 41.7 ...
2.     39.8 54.8 57.6 62.6 61.6 63.9 69.6 ...
3.     76.2 86.7 101.2 99.8 112.2 111.0 ...
4.     116.8 122.6 127.7 143.4 131.3 143.0 ...
5.     144.0 162.7 167.8 180.3 177.6 172.6 ...
6.     166.6 173.1 173.3 176.0 178.5 ...
7.     196.5 213.0 223.6 235.9 244.2 244.5 ...
8.     259.4 271.4 270.5 294.5 297.6 ...
9.     308.7 310.5 326.6 344.1 342.0 358.2 362.7 ];
10. lv = length(v);
11. dt = 0.2;
12. t = (0:lv-1) * dt;
13. h = dt * cumsum(v);
14. plot(t, v)
15. hold on
16. plot(t, h/5,'k--')
17. legend({'velocity', 'altitude/5' })
```

continued on next page

```
18. title('velocity and altitude of a rocket')
19. xlabel('time (sec)'); ylabel('v (m/s), h(m/5)')
20. fprintf('cumsum height: %g\n', h(end) );
21. fprintf('trapezoidal height: %g\n', ...
22.              trapezoid(v, t(1), t(end) ));
23. fprintf('Simpson''s Rule height: %g\n', ...
24.              simpson(v, t(1), t(end) ));
```

In Listing 15.8:

> Lines 1–9: Generate the original velocity data.
>
> Lines 10–12: Parameters for plotting.
>
> Line 13: Performs the integration.
>
> Lines 14–19: Plot the results.
>
> Lines 20–24: Validate the three integration techniques by checking the results.

Figure 15.13 shows the resulting plot. The results displayed in the Command window are:

```
cumsum height: 1848.5
trapezoidal height: 1811.85
Simpson's Rule height: 1811.14
```

The continuous integration produces results within 2% of the "accurate" integration techniques.

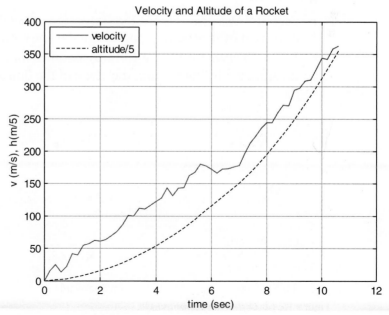

Figure 15.13 *Rocket velocity and altitude*

15.4 Numerical Differentiation

The derivative of a function $f(x)$ is defined to be a function $f'(x)$ that is equal to the rate of change of $f(x)$ with respect to x. The derivative can be expressed as a ratio, with the change in $f(x)$ indicated by $df(x)$ and the change in x indicated by dx, giving us the following:

$$f'(x) = \frac{df(x)}{dx}$$

There are many physical processes for which we want to measure the rate of change of a variable. For example, velocity is the rate of change of position (as in meters per second), and acceleration is the rate of change of velocity (as in meters per second squared).

The derivative $f'(x)$ can be described graphically as the slope of the function $f(x)$, which is defined to be the slope of the tangent line to the function at the specified point. Thus, the value of $f'(x)$ at the point a is $f'(a)$, and it is equal to the slope of the tangent line at the point a.

15.4.1 Difference Expressions

In general, numerical differentiation techniques estimate the derivative of a function at a point x_k by approximating the slope of the tangent line at x_k using values of the function at points near x_k. The approximation of the slope of the tangent line can be done in several ways, as shown in Figure 15.14.

- *Backward Difference:* Figure 15.14(a) assumes that the derivative at x_k is estimated by computing the slope of the line between $f(x_{k-1})$ and $f(x_k)$
- *Forward Difference:* Figure 15.14(b) assumes that the derivative at x_k is estimated by computing the slope of the line between $f(x_k)$ and $f(x_{k+1})$

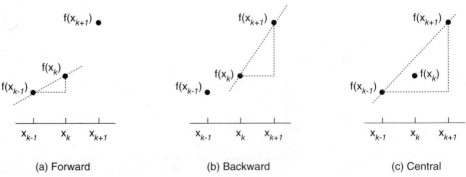

(a) Forward   (b) Backward   (c) Central

Figure 15.14 *Difference techniques*

- *Central Difference:* Figure 15.14(c) assumes that the derivative at x_k is estimated by computing the slope of the line between $f(x_{k-1})$ and $f(x_{k+1})$

The quality of all of these types of derivative computations depends on the distance between the points used to estimate the derivative; the estimate of the derivative improves as the distance between the two points decreases.

15.5 Analytical Operations

We return to the discussion of fitting a polynomial to some raw data in Section 15.2.2. We approximated a polynomial fit with the following expression:

$$f(x) = a_0 x^n + a_1 x^{n-1} + a_2 x^{n-2} + a_3 x^{n-3} + \dots a_{n-1} x + a_n$$

Since this is an analytical expression, even if some or all of the coefficients are complex, we can integrate it to estimate the integral of the raw data and differentiate it to estimate the slope of the raw data.

15.5.1 Analytical Integration

The expression for F(x), the integral of f(x) with respect to x, is given by:

$$F(x) = a_0 x^{n+1}/(n+1) + a_1 x^n/n + a_2 x^{n-1}/(n-1) + a_3 x^{n-2}/(n-2) + \dots$$
$$a_{n-1} x^2/2 + a_n x + K$$

Note that an arbitrary constant, K, is always required for analytical integration representing the starting value F(0).

15.5.2 Analytical Differentiation

The expression for f'(x), the integral of f(x) with respect to x, is given by:

$$f'(x) = n a_0 x^{n-1} + (n-1) a_1 x^{n-2} + (n-2) a_2 x^{n-3} + (n-3) a_3 x^{n-4} + \dots a_{n-1}$$

15.6 Implementation

To facilitate differentiation, the MATLAB language defines the `diff(...)` function, which computes differences between adjacent values in a vector, generating a new vector with one less value than the original:

```
dv = diff(V) returns [V(2)-V(1), V(3)-V(2), ..., V(n)-V(n-1)]
```

An approximate derivative dy/dx can be computed by using `diff(y)./ diff(x)`. Depending on the application, this can be used to compute the

Listing 15.9 Differentiating a function

```
 1. x = -7:0.1:9;
 2. f = polyval([0.0333,-0.3,-1.3333,16,0,-187.2,0], x);
 3. plot(x, f)
 4. hold on
 5. df = diff(f)./diff(x);
 6. plot(x(2:end), df, 'g')
 7. plot(x(1:end-1), df, 'r')
 8. xm = (x(2:end)+x(2:end)) / 2
 9. plot(xm, df, 'c')
10. grid on
11. legend({'f(x)', 'forward', 'backward', 'central'})
```

forward, backward, or central difference approximation. The solution to the forward difference is shown in Listing 15.9.

In Listing 15.9:

Lines 1–4: Establish and plot $f(x)$.

Line 5: The difference expression—returns a vector one shorter than the original.

Lines 6–11: Plot the forward, backward, and central differences.

The results are shown in Figure 15.15. Since the original data were generated from a series of coefficients, we could also plot the exact value of the slope using the result of Section 15.5.2.

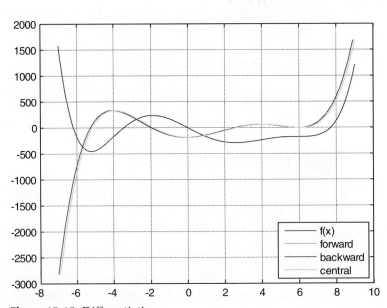

Figure 15.15 *Differentiation*

15.7 Engineering Example—Shaping the Synthesizer Notes

As discussed in Chapter 14, we can synthesize the frequency content of an instrument by selecting an appropriate number of coefficients from the energy spectrum, multiplying each by an appropriate sine or cosine wave and summing the results. This gives a time trace with constant amplitude, which is fine for an instrument like a trumpet, but notes played on other instruments like a piano have a very non-linear time profile as shown in Figure 15.16. That same figure has two overlays indicating how to develop the decay profile typical of a piano note. First, we choose a

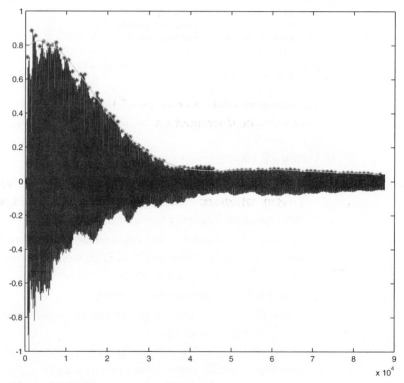

Figure 15.16 *Piano note time history*

modest number of samples that describe the envelope of the sound (marked by red * symbols). Then, we perform a high-order curve fit on that data and check its accuracy by plotting it as the solid line on the same figure.

To demonstrate the essence of this capability, we begin with Listing 14.6 from Chapter 14, reading the file 'instr_piano.wav' instead of 'instr_tpt.wav.' Now, we insert the code in Listing 15.10 in place of the last two lines of Listing 14.6.

Listing 15.10 Modifying sound amplitude

```
1. figure
2. plot(snd)
3. hold on
4. incr = 1000;
5. at = 1;
6. samples = [];
7. tm = [];
8. while at < (N - incr)
9.    val = max(snd(at:at+incr-1));
10.   samples = [samples val];
11.   tm = [tm at+incr/2];
12.   at = at + incr;
13. end
14. plot(tm, samples,'r*')
15. coeff = polyfit(tm, samples, 8);
16. samp = polyval(coeff, tm);
17. plot(tm, samp, 'c')
18. amult = polyval(coeff, 1:length(f));
19. f = f .* amult;
20. sf = f ./ max(f);
21. sound(sf, Fs)
```

In Listing 15.10:

> Lines 1–3: Plot the sound's time history in new figure window.
>
> Line 4: Arbitrarily choose a time sample increment to achieve a small but representative set of amplitude samples.
>
> Lines 8–13: A loop to compute and store the amplitude samples and the corresponding time indices. Each step calculates the maximum amplitude during its time window and saves it with the window location.
>
> Line 14: Plots the sample locations.
>
> Lines 15–17: Compute and plot the polynomial fit to the amplitudes using an eight-order fit.
>
> Lines 18–21: Modify the synthesized piano sound by multiplying by the amplitude profile determined in this script.

In conclusion, with these two engineering examples, we have shown how the essence of the sound of a musical instrument can be derived from the actual sound of an instrument and captured as a small set of complex amplitudes with their frequency value and an even smaller set of real coefficients of the function that multiplies the amplitude over time.

To construct from these data a real music synthesizer, one need only to detect that a keyboard note has been pressed, determine the required frequency, and play the synthesized note until the key is released. If the synthesizer is equipped to specify that the sustain pedal is depressed, the piano sound should not be cut off, but allowed to fade into silence.

Chapter Summary

In this chapter, we saw the implementations of four common numerical techniques:

- We can estimate data points between given data values using linear (interp1/2/3) or spline interpolation
- We can smooth noisy data by fitting polynomial curves of suitable order to the raw data
- Given, for example, the velocity of an object over time, we can determine its position by integrating using cumtrapz(...) or cumsum(...)
- We can differentiate to generate its acceleration

Special Characters, Reserved Words, and Functions

Special Characters, Reserved Words, and Functions	Description	Discussed in This Section
NaN	Not a number	15.1.1
cumsum(y)	Computes the integral of the function y(x), assuming that Δx is 1	15.3.2
cumtrapz(x,y)	Computes the integral of the function y(x), using the trapezoidal rule	15.3.2
diff(v)	Computes the differences between adjacent values in a vector	15.6
interp1(x, y, nx)	Computes linear and cubic interpolation	15.1.1
interp2(x, y, z, nx, ny)	Computes linear and cubic interpolation	15.1.1
interp3(x, y, z, v, nx, ny, nz)	Computes linear and cubic interpolation	15.1.1
polyfit(x, y, n)	Computes a least-squares polynomial	15.2.2
polyval(c, x)	Evaluates a polynomial	15.2.2
spline(x, y)	Spline interpolation	15.1.2

Self Test

Use the following questions to check your understanding of the material in this chapter:

True or False

1. All MATLAB functions permit extrapolation beyond the limits of the original independent variable.

T 2. The cubic spline is a series of parametric curves.

F 3. You cannot extrapolate the equations generated by curve fitting.

T 4. You should always match the order of a parametric curve fit to the underlying physics of the data.

T 5. Simpson's rule is more accurate than the trapezoidal rule for integrating a function.

F 6. Numerical differentiation produces a vector that is the ~~same~~ *shorter* length as the original vector.

Fill in the Blanks

1. _Interpolation_ is the technique by which we estimate a variable's value between known values.

2. Nth-order polynomial regression determines the _the equation_ *coefficients of* of order n that minimize the _sum of the_ between the line and the data points. *squared distances*

3. The _approximation_ *central difference* makes the slope at x_k the _slope_ of the line between x_{k-1} and x_{k+1}.

4. To compute the continuous integral of a data set that is not regularly sampled, you have to compute the _cumsum(...)_ of the _dot product_ of _the data vector_ and _a vector of time_ *difference*

5. If a(n) _critical point_ is defined by its polynomial coefficients, you can integrate or differentiate it by _differentiating_ the vector of coefficients.

Programming Projects

1. Do the following basic exercises with numerical methods.
    a. Define two vectors xi and yi of the same length where the xi values are monotonically increasing and the yi values are somehow related to the xi values. Then define a new vector x with closer spacing than xi and extending below and above the range of xi. Find the y values corresponding to the x values in xi by linear interpolation. On the same figure, plot the original yi vs. xi as red circles, and y vs. x as a black line. What do you observe about the visible range of the x values?
    b. Repeat the exercise in part a using the spline(...) function to interpolate. Explain the difference in the range of the resulting y vs. x plot.
    c. Use polyfit(...) to find the coefficients of the third-order polynomial that best fits the points represented by vectors xi and

yi and then use `polyval(...)` to evaluate that curve at the x points. As before, plot yi vs. xi as red circles and y vs. x as a black line.

d. Approximate the derivative, dxy = dy/dx, for the vectors xi and yi using the `diff(...)` function and plot yi vs. xi. Since `diff(...)` reduces the length of the vector by one, you will have to plot dxy vs. either xi(1:end−1), xi(2:end) or compute xm, the mid-points of xi.

e. Find yp, the cumulative sum of the elements in dxy, and add this to the plot of part d. With the exception of a constant offset, this curve ought to track the original plot of yi vs. xi.

f. Use `cumtrapz` to find the area under the curve represented by yp vs. xi with the trapezoidal method of approximation. Compare this result to the ending value of the yp curve.

2. Write a function, `bestFit`, that takes in a vector of x-coordinates and a vector of y-coordinates. Your function should fit a polynomial curve to the data. The degree of the polynomial should be the smallest degree polynomial with an average error (the average of the absolute value of the difference between the new y-coordinates and the original y-coordinates) less than 2. Your function should return:

- the vector of coefficients of your polynomial
- the vector of new y-coordinates, which is the polynomial evaluated at the original x-coordinates, and
- the vector of the error magnitudes of your polynomial.

Write a test program to provide reasonable data to your function and plot the original data (in blue), the curve-fitted data (in green), and the error (in red) on one figure. Title your plot and label your axes accordingly, including a legend.

3. You have been approached by the Rambling Wreck club to test the performance of the Rambling Wreck. You are provided with the test results of the car for 10 trial runs in the form of a vector d that contains the displacement of the car from the origin at that second. The first element is the displacement at the 0th second, the second element is the displacement at the 1st second, and so on. Write a script called `testWreck` that displays a plot of the speed of the Rambling Wreck over time during the test run. You could test your script using:

```
d = [0 20 35 50 60 55 30 25 15 5];
```

4. Engineers often use tabulated data for various calculations. An important method that any good engineer should be able to apply to tabulated data is interpolation. In thermodynamics, the properties of a gas can be known when two of its properties have been fixed.

You are required to come up with a continuous function being given the tabulated data below measured where the pressure is 0.10 MPa:

Temperature (deg C)	Specific Volume (cu meters/Kg)
99.63	1.694
100	1.696
120	1.793
160	1.984
200	2.172
240	2.359
280	2.546
320	2.732
360	2.917
400	3.103
440	3.288
500	3.565

Write a function called lookup that consumes three parameters: the above table in an array, a number value , and a logical control value getTemp. If getTemp is true, the function interpolates the value as a specific volume and returns the corresponding temperature. Otherwise, it interpolates the value as a temperature and returns the corresponding specific volume. Your function must not extrapolate the data (i.e., it should return NaN if the user tries to obtain values outside the range of the table values).

5.   Mathematically speaking, a critical point occurs when the derivative of a function equals zero. It is possible that a local minimum or a local maximum occurs at a critical point. A local minimum is a point where the function's value to the left and right of it is larger, and a local maximum is a point where the function's value to the left and right of it is smaller. You are going to write a function that finds the local minimum and maximum points of a set of data. Call the function find_points. It should take in vectors of x and y values and return two vectors. The first vector should contain the x values where the minimum points occur, while the second vector should contain the x values where the maximum points occur.

For example:

```
If x=linspace(-8,2,1000) and y=x.^2+6*x+3;
 [min_p max_p]=find_points(x,y) should return
        min_p = -3, max_p = []
If x=linspace(-5,5,1000) and y=x.^3-12*x;
 [min_p max_p]=find_points(x,y) should return:
        min_p = 2, max_p = -2
```

You should plot x and y to confirm the answers.

6. Now that we used the derivative it only makes sense that you are going to write a function that finds integrals. Call your function find_integral. Your function should take in a vector of x and y values as Problem 15.5 does and should plot the integral and also return the total area under the function. You are to use the trapezoidal rule to find the integrals.

For example:

```
If x=linspace(0,5,1000); and y=2*x+5;
find_integral(x,y) should return 50.0000
```

CHAPTER 16

Sorting

Chapter Objectives

This chapter discusses:

- A technique for comparing the performance of algorithms
- A range of algorithms for sorting a collection of data
- Application areas in which these algorithms are most appropriate

First, we will digress from the main thread of problem solving to discuss an "engineering algebra" for measuring the cost of an algorithm in terms of the amount of work done. Then we will consider a number of sorting algorithms, using this technique to assess their relative merits.

16.1 Measuring Algorithm Cost

How many times do you ask yourself, "Just how good is my algorithm?" Probably not very often, if ever. After all, we have been creating relatively simple programs that work on a small, finite set of data. Our functions execute and return an answer within a second or two (except for the recursive Fibonacci function on numbers over 25). You may have noticed that some of the image processing scripts take a number of seconds to run. However, as the problems become more complex and the volume of data increases, we need to consider whether we are solving the problem in the most efficient manner. In extreme cases, processes that manipulate huge amounts of data like the inventory of a large warehouse or a national telephone directory might be possible only with highly efficient algorithms.

Big O is an algebra that permits us to express how the amount of work done in solving a problem relates to the amount of data being processed. It is a gross simplification for software engineering analysis purposes, based on some sound but increasingly complex theory.

Technical Insight 16.1

Interested readers should look up little-O, Big-Ω, little-ω, and Big-Θ.

Big O is a means of estimating the worst case performance of a given algorithm when presented with a certain number of data items, usually referred to as N. In fact, the actual process attempts to determine the limit of the relationship between the work done by an algorithm and N as N approaches infinity.

We report the Big O of an algorithm as O (<expression in terms of N>). For example, O(1) describes the situation where the computing cost is independent of the size of the data, O(N) describes the situation where the computing cost is directly proportional to the size of the data, and $O(2^N)$ describes the situation where the computing cost doubles each time one more piece of data is added. At this point, we should also observe some simplifying assumptions:

- We are not concerned with constant multipliers on the Big O of an algorithm. As rapidly as processor performance and languages are improving, multiplicative improvements can be achieved merely by acquiring the latest hardware or software. Big O is a concept that reports qualitative algorithm improvement. Therefore, we choose to ignore constant multipliers on Big O analyses.

- We are concerned with the performance of algorithms as N approaches infinity. Consequently, when the Big O is expressed as the sum of multiple terms, we keep only the term with the fastest growth rate.

16.1.1 Specific Big O Examples

On the basis of algorithms we have already discussed, we will look at examples of the most common Big O cases.

O(1)—Independent of N O(1) describes the ideal case of an algorithm or logical step whose amount of work is independent of the amount of data. The most obvious example is accessing or modifying an entry in a vector. Since all good languages permit direct access to elements of a vector, the work of these simple operations is independent of the size of the vector.

O(N)—Linear with N O(N) describes an algorithm whose performance is linearly related to N. Copying a cell array of size N is an obvious example, as is searching for a specific piece of data in such a cell array. One might argue that occasionally one would find the data as the first element. There is an equal chance that we would be unlucky and find the item as the last element. On average, we would claim that the performance of this search is the mean of these numbers: (N+1) / 2. However, applying the simplification rules above, we first reject the 1 as being N to a lower power, leaving N/2, and then reject the constant multiplier, leaving O(N) for a linear search.

O(logN)—Binary Search Consider searching for a number—say, 86—in a sorted vector such as that shown in Figure 16.1. One could use a linear search without taking advantage of the ordering of the data. However, a better algorithm might be as follows:

1. Go to the middle of the vector (approximately) and compare that element (59) to the number being sought.
2. If this is the desired value, exit with the answer.
3. If the number sought is less than that element, since the data are ordered, we can reject the half of the array to the right of, and including the 59.
4. Similarly, if the number sought is greater than that element, we can reject the half of the array to the left of and including the 59.
5. Repeat these steps with the remaining half vector until either the number is found or the size of the remaining half is zero.

Now consider how much data can be covered by each test—a measure of the work done as shown in Table 16.1.

In general, we can state that the relationship is expressed as follows:

$$N = 2^W$$

| 7 | 12 | 42 | 59 | 71 | 86 | 104 | 212 |

Figure 16.1 *Binary search*

Table 16.1 Work done in a binary search	
Work	**N**
1	2
2	4
3	8
4	16
5	32
.	.
.	.
W	2^W

However, we need the expression for the work, W, as a function of N. Therefore, we take the log base 2 of each side so that:

```
W = log₂N
```

Now, we realize that we can convert $\log_2 N$ to $\log_x N$ merely by multiplying by $\log_2 x$, a constant that we are allowed to ignore. Consequently, we lose interest in representing the specific base of the logarithm, leaving the work for a binary search as O(log N).

$O(N^2)$**—Proportional to N^2** $O(N^2)$ describes an algorithm whose performance is proportional to the square of N. It is a special case of $O(N \times M)$, which describes any operation on an $N \times M$ array or image.

$O(2^N)$**—Exponential Growth or Worse** Occasionally we run across very nasty implementations of simple algorithms. For example, consider the recursive implementation of the Fibonacci algorithm we discussed in Section 9.6.2. In this implementation, fib(N) = fib(N − 1) + fib(N − 2). So each time we add another term, the previous two terms have to be calculated again, thereby doubling the amount of work. If we double the work when 1 is added to N, in general the Big O is $O(2^N)$. Of course, in the case of this particular algorithm, there is a simple iterative solution with a much preferable performance of O(N).

16.1.2 Analyzing Complex Algorithms

We can easily calculate the Big O of simple algorithms. For more complex algorithms, we determine the Big O by breaking the complex algorithm into simpler abstractions, as we saw in Chapter 10. We would continue that process until the abstractions can be characterized as simple operations on defined collections for which we can determine their Big Os. The Big O of the overall algorithm is then determined from the individual components by combining them according to the following rules:

- If two components are sequential (do A and then do B), you add their Big O expressions
- If components are nested (for each A, do B), you multiply their Big O expressions

For example, we will see the merge sort algorithm in Section 16.2.5. It can be abstracted as follows:

> Perform a binary division of the data (O(logN)) and *then for each* binary step (of which there are O(log(N)), merge all the data items (O(N)).

This has the general form:

> Do A, then for each B, do C

which, according to the rules above, should result in $O_A + O_B * O_C$. The overall algorithm therefore costs O(log N) + O(N) * O(log N). We remove the first term because its growth is slower, leaving O(N log N) as the overall algorithm cost.

16.2 Algorithms for Sorting Data

Generally, sorting a collection of data will organize the data items in such a way that it is possible to search for a specific item using a binary search rather than a linear search. This concept is nice in principle when dealing with simple collections like an array of numbers. However, it is more difficult in practice with real data. For example, telephone books are always sorted by the person's last name. This facilitates searching by last name, but it does not help if you are looking for the number of a neighbor whose name you do not know. That search would require sorting the data by street name.

There are many methods for sorting data. We present five representative samples selected from many sorting algorithms because each has a practical, engineering application. First we describe each algorithm, and then we compare their performance and suggest engineering circumstances in which you would apply each algorithm. Note that in all these algorithms, the comparisons are done using functions (e.g., `gt(...)`, `lt(...)`, or `equals(...)`) rather than mathematical operators. This permits collections containing arbitrarily complex objects to be sorted merely by customizing the comparison functions.

16.2.1 Insertion Sort

Insertion sort is perhaps the most obvious sorting technique. Given the original collection of objects to sort, it begins by initializing an empty

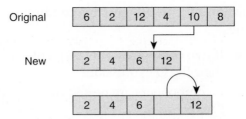

Figure 16.2 *Insertion sort in progress*

collection. For example, if the collection were a vector, you might allocate a new vector of the same size and initialize an "output index" to the start of that vector. Then the algorithm traverses the original vector, inserting each object from that vector in order into the new vector. This usually requires "shuffling" the objects in the new vector to make room for the new object.

Figure 16.2 illustrates the situation where the first four numbers of the original vector have been inserted into the new vector; the algorithm finds the place to insert the next number (10) and then moves the 12 across to make space for it.

Listing 16.1 shows the MATLAB code for insertion sort on a vector of numbers. The algorithm works for any data collection for which the function lt(A,B) compares two instances.

Listing 16.1 The insertion sort function

```
1. function b = insertionsort(a)
     % This function sorts a column vector,
     % using the insertion sort algorithm
2.      b = []; i = 1; sz = length(a);
3.      while i <= sz
4.          b = insert(b, a(i,1) );
5.          i = i + 1;
6.      end
7. end
8. function a = insert(a, v)
     % insert the value v into column vector a
9.      i = 1; sz = length(a); done = false;
10.     while i <= sz
11.         if lt(v, a(i,1))
12.             done = true;
13.             a = [a(1:i-1); v; a(i:end)];
14.             break;
15.         end
16.         i = i + 1;
17.     end
18.     if ~done
19.         a(sz+1, 1) = v;
20.     end
21. end
```

In Listing 16.1:

> Line 2: Initializes the result and the `while` loop parameters.
>
> Line 4: Calls the helper function to insert the latest value into the output vector.
>
> Lines 8–21: The helper function that inserts a new value into a vector and returns that vector.

Later we will refer to the selection sort algorithm that is similar in concept to insertion sort. Rather than sorting as the new data are put into the new vector, however, the selection sort algorithm repeatedly finds and deletes the smallest item in the original vector and puts it directly into the new vector.

Both insertion sort and selection sort are $O(N^2)$ if used to sort a whole vector.

16.2.2 Bubble Sort

Where insertion sort is easy to visualize, it is normally implemented by creating a new collection and growing that new collection as the algorithm proceeds. Bubble sort is conceptually the easiest sorting technique to visualize and is usually accomplished by rearranging the items in a collection in place. Given the original collection of N objects to sort, it makes $(N - 1)$ major passes through the data. The first major pass examines all N objects in a minor pass, and subsequent passes reduce the number of examinations by 1. On each minor pass through the data, beginning with the first data item and moving incrementally through the data, the algorithm checks to see whether the next item is smaller than the current one. If so, the two items are swapped in place in the array.

At the end of the first major pass, the largest item in the collection has been moved to the end of the collection. After each subsequent major pass, the largest remaining item is found at the end of the remaining items. The process repeats until on the last major pass, the first two items are compared and swapped if necessary. Figure 16.3 illustrates a bubble sort of a short vector. On the first pass, the value 98 is moved completely across the vector to the rightmost position. On the next pass, the 45 is moved into position. On the third pass, the 23 reaches the right position, and the last pass finishes the sort.

Listing 16.2 shows the MATLAB code for bubble sort on a vector of numbers. The algorithm works for any data type for which the function `gt(A,B)` compares two instances. Since bubble sort performs $(N - 1) * (N - 1)/2$ comparisons on the data, it is also $O(N^2)$. Some implementations use a flag to determine whether any swaps occurred on the last major pass and terminate the algorithm if none occurred. However, the efficiency

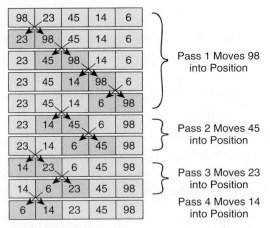

Figure 16.3 *Bubble sort*

Listing 16.2 Bubble sort

```
1. function bubblesort()
   %  This function sorts the column array b in place,
   %  using the bubble sort algorithm
2.      global b
3.      N = length(b);
4.      right = N-1;
5.      for in = 1:(N-1)
6.          for jn = 1:right
7.              if gt(b(jn), b(jn+1))
8.                  tmp = b(jn); % swap b(jn) with b(jn+1)
9.                  b(jn) = b(jn+1);
10.                 b(jn+1) = tmp;
11.             end
12.         end
13.         right = right - 1;
14.     end
15. end
```

gained by stopping the algorithm early has to be weighed against the cost of setting and testing a flag whenever a swap is accomplished.

In Listing 16.2:

Line 2: In order to be able to access the array in place, we pass it as a global variable instead of as a parameter.

Lines 3–4: Since each pass puts the largest element in place, we can reduce the item count by 1 each time. This initializes the size of the first pass.

Lines 4–14: Show the loop for the $N - 1$ major passes.

Lines 6–12: Show the loop for each major pass.

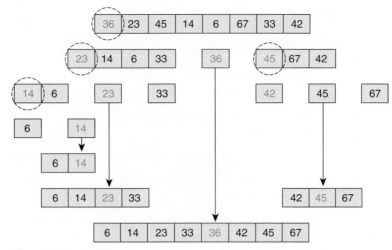

Figure 16.4 *Quick sort*

Lines 8–10: Swap the current item with its neighbor. By doing this in place, the largest item is always considered the current item until it reaches the end.

Line 13: Shortens the row after each major pass because the largest item in the last pass is placed at the right-hand end.

16.2.3 Quick Sort

As its name suggests, the quick sort algorithm is one of the fastest sorting algorithms. Like Bubble Sort, it is designed to sort an array "in place." The quick sort algorithm is recursive and uses an elegant approach to subdividing the original vector. Figure 16.4 illustrates this process. The algorithm proceeds as follows:

- The terminating condition occurs when the vector is of length 1, which is obviously sorted.
- A "pivot point" is then chosen. Some sophisticated versions go to a significant amount of effort to calculate the most effective pivot point. We are content to choose the first item in the vector.
- The vector is then subdivided by moving all of the items less than the pivot to its left and all those greater than the pivot to its right, thereby placing the pivot in its final location in the resulting vector.
- The items to the left and right of the pivot are then recursively sorted by the same algorithm.
- The algorithm always converges because these two halves are always shorter than the original vector.

Listing 16.3 shows the code for the quick sort algorithm. The partitioning algorithm looks a little messy, but it is just performing the

Listing 16.3 Quick sort

```
1. function a = quicksort(a, from, to)
   % This function sorts a column array,
   % using the quick sort algorithm
2.    if from < to
3.          [a p] = partition(a, from, to);
4.          a = quicksort(a, from, p);
5.          a = quicksort(a, p + 1, to);
6.       end
7. end
8. function [a lower] = partition(a, from, to)
   % This function partitions a column array
9.       pivot = a(from); i = from - 1; j = to + 1;
10.      while i < j
11.          i = i + 1;
12.          while lt(a(i), pivot)
13.              i = i + 1;
14.          end
15.          j = j - 1;
16.          while gt(a(j), pivot)
17.              j = j - 1;
18.          end
19.          if (i < j)
20.              temp = a(i); % this section swaps
21.              a(i) = a(j); % a(i) with a(j)
22.              a(j) = temp;
23.          end
24.      end
25.      lower = j;
26. end
27.
```

array adjustments. It starts with i and j outside the vector to the left and right. Then it keeps moving each toward the middle as long as the values at i and j are on the proper side of the pivot. When this process stops, i and j are the indices of data items that are out of order. They are swapped, and the process is repeated until i crosses past j. Quick sort is O(N log N). As with the previous techniques, this algorithm applies to collections of any data type for which the functions lt(A,B) and gt(A,B) compare two instances.

In Listing 16.3:

> Line 1: Each recursive call is provided with the vector to sort and the range of indices to sort. These are initially from = 1 and to = length(a).

> Line 2: The terminating condition for the recursion is when the vector to sort has size 1—that is, when from == to.

> Line 3: The partition function performs three roles—it places the pivot in the right place, moves the smaller and larger values to the

correct sides, and returns the location of the pivot to permit the recursive partitioning.

Lines 4 and 5: Show recursive calls to sort the left and right parts of the vector.

Lines 8–26: Show the helper function.

Line 9: Initializes the variables.

Lines 10–24: The outer loop continues until i passes j.

Lines 11–14: Skip i forward over all the items less than the pivot.

Lines 15–18: Skip j backward over all the elements greater than the pivot.

Lines 20–22: If i < j, i is indexing an item greater than the pivot, and j is indexing an item less than the pivot. By swapping the contents of a(i) and a(j), we rectify both inequities and can continue the inner loop.

Line 25: When the loop exits, both i and j are indexing the pivot.

There is one performance caution about quick sort. Its speed depends on the randomness of the data. If the data are mostly sorted, its performance reduces to $O(N^2)$.

16.2.4 Merge Sort

Merge sort is another $O(N \log N)$ algorithm that achieves speed by dividing the original vector into two "equal" halves. It is difficult at best to perform a merge sort in place in a collection. Equality, of course, is not possible when there is an odd number of objects to be sorted, in which case the length of the "halves" will differ by at most 1. The heart of the merge sort algorithm is the technique used to reunite two smaller sorted vectors. This function is called "merge." Its objective is to merge two vectors that have been previously sorted. Since the two vectors are sorted, the smallest object can only be at the front of one of these two vectors. The smallest item is removed from its place and added to the result vector. This merge process continues until one of the two halves is empty, in which case the remaining half (whose values all exceed those in the result vector) is copied into the result.

The merge sort algorithm is shown in Figure 16.5 and proceeds as follows:

- The terminating condition is a vector with length less than 2, which is, obviously, in order
- The recursive part invokes the merge function on the recursive call to merge the two halves of the vector
- The process converges because the halves are always smaller than the original vector

The code for merge sort is shown in Listing 16.4.

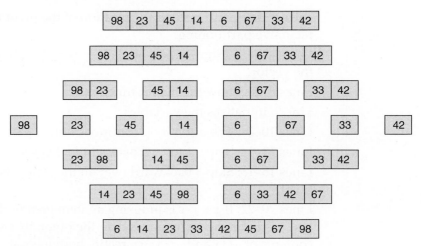

Figure 16.5 *Merge sort*

Listing 16.4 Merge sort

```
1. function b = mergesort(a)
   %  This function sorts a column array,
   %  using the merge sort algorithm
2.    b = a; sz = length(a);
3.    if sz > 1
4.        szb2 = floor(sz / 2);
5.        first = mergesort(a(1 : szb2));
6.        second = mergesort(a(szb2+1 : sz));
7.        b = merge(first, second);
8.    end
9. end
10. function b = merge(first, second)
    %   Merges two sorted arrays
11.     i1 = 1; i2 = 1; out = 1;
    % as long as neither i1 nor i2 past the end,
    % move the smaller element into a
12.     while (i1 <= length(first)) & (i2 <= length(second))
13.         if lt(first(i1), second(i2))
14.             b(out,1) = first(i1); i1 = i1 + 1;
15.         else
16.             b(out,1) = second(i2); i2 = i2 + 1;
17.         end
18.         out = out + 1;
19.     end
    % copy any remaining entries of the first array
20.     while i1 <= length(first)
21.         b(out,1) = first(i1); i1 = i1 + 1; out = out + 1;
22.     end
    % copy any remaining entries of the second array
23.     while i2 <= length(second)
24.         b(out,1) = second(i2); i2 = i2 + 1; out = out + 1;
25.     end
26. end
```

In Listing 16.4:

> Line 2: Initializes the parameters.
>
> Line 3: The terminating condition is an array of length 1, which does not need sorting.
>
> Line 4: Divides the array in half.
>
> Lines 5 and 6: Sort the halves of the array.
>
> Line 7: Merges the two sorted halves.
>
> Lines 10–26: Show the helper function to merge sorted arrays.
>
> Lines 12–19: This loop repeats until one of the two arrays is used up choosing and removing the smaller element out of the two arrays.
>
> Lines 20–25: Copy the remains of each array to the result.

16.2.5 Radix Sort

A discussion of sorting techniques would not be complete without discussing radix sort, commonly referred to as bucket sort. This is also an O(N log N) algorithm whose most obvious application is for sorting physical piles of papers, such as students' test papers. However, the same principle can be applied to sorting successively on the units, tens and hundreds digit of numbers (hence, the term radix sort). The process begins with a stack of unsorted papers, each with an identifier consisting of a number or a unique name. One pass is made through the stack separating the papers into piles based on the first digit or character of the identifier. Subsequent passes sort each of these piles by subsequent characters or digits until all the piles have a small number of papers that can be sorted by insertion or selection sorts. The piles can then be reassembled in order. Figure 16.6 illustrates the situation at the end of the second sorting pass when piles for the first digit have also been separated by the second digit.

There are a number of reasons why this technique is popular for sorting:

- There is a minimal amount of "paper shuffling" or bookkeeping
- The base of the logarithm in the O(N log N) is either 10 (numerical identifier) or 26 (alphabetic identifier), thereby providing a "constant multiplier" speed advantage
- Once the first sorting pass is complete, one can use multi-processing (in the form of extra people) to perform the remaining passes in parallel, thereby reducing the effective performance to O(N) (given sufficient parallel resources)

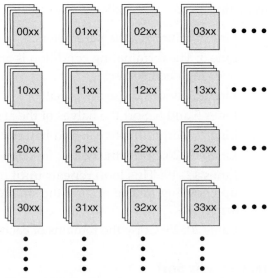

Figure 16.6 *Radix sort*

16.3 Performance Analysis

In order to perform a comparison of the performance of different algorithms, a script was written to perform each sort on a vector of increasing length containing random numbers. The script started with a length of 4 and continued doubling the length until it reached 262,144 (2^{18}). To obtain precise timing measurements, each sort technique was repeated a sufficient number of times to obtain moderately accurate timing measurements with the internal millisecond clock. In order to eliminate common computation costs, it was necessary to measure the overhead cost of the loops themselves and subtract that time from the times of each sort algorithm. Note that in order to show the results of the system internal sort on the same chart, its execution time was multiplied by 1,000.

Figure 16.7 shows a typical plot of the results of this analysis, illustrating the relative power of $O(N \log N)$ algorithms versus $O(N^2)$ algorithms. The plot on a log-log scale shows the relative time taken by the selection sort, insertion sort, bubble sort, merge sort, quick sort, and quick sort in place algorithms, together with the internal sort function. Also on the chart are plotted trend lines for $O(N^2)$ and $O(N \log N)$ processes. We can make the following observations from this chart:

- Since the scales are each logarithmic, it is tempting to claim that there is "not much difference" between $O(N^2)$ and $O(N \log N)$ algorithms. Looking closer, however, it is clear that for around 200,000 items, the $O(N^2)$ sorts are around 100,000 times slower than the $O(N \log N)$ algorithms.

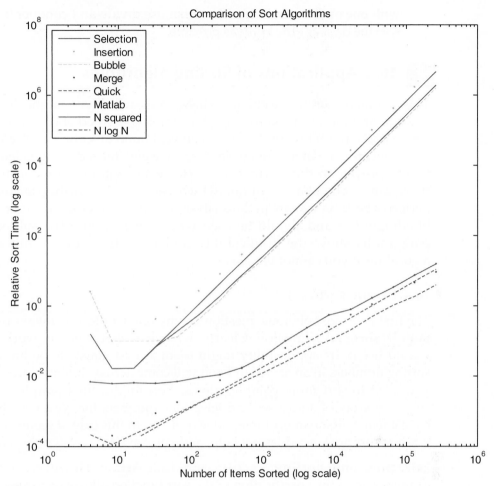

Figure 16.7 *Sort study results*

- The performance of most of the algorithms is extremely erratic below 100 items. If you are sorting small amounts of data, the algorithm does not matter.
- The selection sort, bubble sort, and insertion sort algorithms clearly demonstrate $O(N^2)$ behavior.
- The merge sort and quick sort algorithms seem to demonstrate $O(N \log N)$. Notice, however, that the performance of quick sort is slightly better than $O(N \log N)$. This slight improvement is due to the fact that once the pivot has been moved, it is in the right place and is eliminated from further sorting passes.
- Clearly, the internal sort function, in addition to being 1,000 times faster than any of the coded algorithms, is closely tracking the $O(N \log N)$ performance curve, indicating that it is programmed

with one of the many algorithms that use divide-and-conquer to sort the data as efficiently as possible.

16.4 Applications of Sorting Algorithms

This section discusses the circumstances under which you might choose to use one or another of the sorting algorithms presented above. We assert here without proof that the theoretical lower bound of sorting is O(N log N). Consequently, we should not be looking for a generalized sorting algorithm that improves on this performance. However, within those constraints, there are circumstances under which each of the sorting techniques performs best. As we saw in the analysis above, the internal sort function is blindingly fast and should be used whenever possible. The subsequent paragraphs show the applicability and limitations of the other sort algorithms if you cannot use sort(...).

16.4.1 Using sort(. . .)

The first and most obvious question is why one would not always use the built-in sort(...) function. Clearly, whenever that function works, you should use it. Its applicability might seem at first glance to be limited to sorting numbers in an array, and you will come across circumstances when you need to sort more complex items. You might, for example, have a structure array of addresses and telephone numbers that you wish to sort by last name, first name, or telephone number. In this case, it seems that the internal sort program does not help, and you have to create your own sort.

Extracting and Sorting Vectors and Cell Arrays However, a closer examination of the specification of the sort function allows us to generalize the application of sort(...) significantly. When you call sort(v), it actually offers you a second result that contains the indices used to sort v. So in the case where you have a cell array or a structure array and your sort criteria can be extracted into a vector, you can sort that vector and use the second result, the indexing order, to sort the original array. Furthermore, if you can extract character string data into a cell array of strings, the internal sort function will sort that cell array alphabetically.

For example, consider again the CD collection from Chapter 10. We might want to find the most expensive CD in our collection and then make a list of artists and titles ordered alphabetically by artist. We leave the details of this as an exercise for the reader.

16.4.2 Insertion Sort

Insertion sort is the fastest means of performing incremental sorting. If a small number of new items—say, M—are being added to a sorted collection of size N, the process will be O(M*N), which will be fastest as long as M < log N. For example, consider a national telephone directory with over a billion numbers that must frequently be updated with new listings. Adding a small number of entries (< 20) would be faster with insertion sort than with merge sort, and quick sort would be a disaster because the data are almost all sorted (see below).

16.4.3 Bubble Sort

Bubble sort is the simplest in-place sort to program and is fine for small amounts of data. The major advantage of bubble sort is that in a fine-grained multi-processor environment, if you have N/2 processors available with access to the original data, you can reduce the Big O to O(N).

16.4.4 Quick Sort

As its name suggests, this is the quickest of the sorting algorithms and should normally be used for a full sort. However, it has one significant disadvantage: its performance depends on a fairly high level of randomness in the distribution of the data in the original array. If there is a significant probability that your original data might be already sorted, or partially sorted, your quick sort is not going to be quick. You should use merge sort.

16.4.5 Merge Sort

Since its algorithm does not depend on any specific characteristics of the data, merge sort will always turn in a solid O(N log N) performance. You should use it whenever you suspect that quick sort might get in trouble.

16.4.6 Radix Sort

It is theoretically possible to write the radix sort algorithm to attempt to take advantage of its apparent performance improvements over the more conventional algorithms shown above. However, some practical problems arise:

- In practice, the manipulation of the arrays of arrays necessary to sort by this technique is quite complex
- The performance gained for manual sorts by "parallel processing" stacks using multiple people cannot be realized
- The logic for extracting the character or digit for sorting is going to detract from the overall performance

Therefore, absent some serious parallel processing machines, we recommend that the use of bucket sort be confined to manually sorting large numbers of physical objects.

16.5 Engineering Example—A Selection of Countries

In the Engineering Application problem in Section 10.5, we attempted to find the best country for a business expansion based on the rate of growth of the GNP for that country versus its population growth. The initial version of the program returned the suggestion that the company should move to Equatorial Guinea. However, when this was presented to the Board of Directors, it was turned down, and you were asked to bring them a list of the best 20 places to give them a good range of selection.

We should make two changes to the algorithm:

- Originally, we used a crude approximation to determine the slope of the population and GNP curves. However, now we know that `polyfit` can perform this slope computation accurately, and we will substitute that computation.

- We will use the internal sort function to find the 20 best countries. The code to accomplish this, a major revision of the code in Chapter 10, is shown in Listing 16.5.

Listing 16.5 Updated world data analysis

```
1. function doit
2.      worldData = buildData('World_data.xls');
3.      n = 20;
4.      bestn = findBestn(worldData, n);
5.      fprintf('best %d countries are:\n', n)
6.      for best = bestn(end:-1:1)
7.          fprintf('%s\n', worldData(best).name)
8.      end
9. end
10. function bestn = findBestn(worldData, n)
     % find the indices of the n best countries
     % according to the criterion in the function fold
     % we first map world data to add the field growth
11.     for ndx = 1:length(worldData)
12.         cntry = worldData(ndx);
13.         worldData(ndx).growth = fold(cntry);
14.     end
        % now, sort on this criterion
15.     values = [worldData.growth];
16.     [junk order] = sort(values);
        % filter these to keep the best 10
17.     bestn = order(end-n+1:end);
18. end
19. function ans = fold(st)
     % s1 is the rate of growth of population
20.     pop = st.pop(~isnan(st.pop));
21.     yr = st.year(~isnan(st.pop));
22.     s1 = slope(yr, pop)/mean(pop);
```

continued on next page

```
                % s2 is the rate of growth of the GDP
23.         gdp = st.gdp(~isnan(st.gdp));
24.         yr = st.year(~isnan(st.gdp));
25.         s2 = slope(yr, gdp)/mean(gdp);
                % Measure of merit is how much faster
                % the gdp grows than the population
26.         ans = s2 - s1;
27. end
28. function s1 = slope(x, y)
        % Estimate the slope of a curve
29.         if length(x) == 0 || x(end) == x(1)
30.             error('bad data')
31.         else
32.             coef = polyfit(x, y, 1);
33.             s1 = coef(1);
34.         end
35. end
```

In Listing 16.5:

> Line 1: Wraps the script in a pseudo-function to allow the helper functions to reside in the same file.
>
> Line 2: Reads in the world data.
>
> Line 3: Selects the number of countries to present.
>
> Line 4: Calls the function that will return the indices of the n best countries.
>
> Lines 5–8: Print the list of country names in reverse order (the best first).
>
> Lines 10–18: Show an updated version of the original function to return the indices of the n best countries.
>
> Lines 11–14: Map the worldData structure array, adding to each a field called growth that contains the criterion specified in the fold function.
>
> Lines 15 and 16: Extract and sort the values of growth for each country.
>
> Line 17: Returns the last n countries that will have the highest growth values.
>
> Lines 19–27: The fold function unchanged from Chapter 10.
>
> Lines 28–35: The modified slope function from Chapter 10.
>
> Lines 32 and 33: Use polyfit to compute an accurate slope and return it to the calling function.

Common Pitfalls 16.1

A deceptively simple question arises: Should you expect the worldData at line 6 of Listing 16.7 to contain the field growth? Actually, it will not. Although it appears that the function findBestn adds this field to worldData, it is working with a copy of the worldData structure array that is not returned to the calling script.

The results from running this version are shown in Table 16.2. This seems to be an acceptable list of possibilities to take back to the Board of Directors.

Table 16.2 Updated world data results	
Best 20 countries are:	
Estonia	Lebanon
St. Kitts & Nevis	Malta
Albania	Cyprus
Vietnam	Tajikistan
Croatia	Taiwan
Kazakhstan	Korea, Republic of
Azerbaijan	Grenada
Uzbekistan	Ireland
Georgia	Portugal
Dominica	Antigua

Chapter Summary

This chapter discussed:

- A technique for comparing the performance of algorithms
- A range of useful algorithms for sorting a collection of data
- Application areas in which these algorithms are most appropriate

Self Test

Use the following questions to check your understanding of the material in this chapter:

True or False

T 1. When computing the Big O of sequential operations, you retain only the term that grows fastest with N.

F 2. All search algorithms have O(N).

T 3. No sort algorithm can perform better than O(NlogN).

F 4. All sorting algorithms with O(N^2) traverse the complete data collection N times.

T 5. Quick sort in reality should be listed as O(N^2).

Fill in the Blanks

1. ___Big O___ is an algebra that permits us to express how the amount of ___work___ done in solving a problem relates to the amount ___data___ of being processed.

2. Any algorithm that traverses, maps, folds, or filters a collection is O(___N___).

3. ___Merge___ sort and ___Quick___ sort perform with O(NlogN).

4. ___Bubble___ sort and ___Quick___ sort are designed to sort the data in place.

5. The system internal `sort(...)` returns the _____ and a(n) _____ that allow you to sort any collection from whose elements one can derive a(n) _____ or _____.

Processing Graphs

Chapter Objectives

This chapter demonstrates algorithms that solve two problems: finding the minimum spanning tree for a graph and finding the best path through a graph. However, first we need to understand the following:

■ How to construct and use two special forms of data collection: queues and priority queues

■ How to build a model of a graph

■ How to traverse and search a graph

Introduction

The collections we have considered so far—vectors, arrays, structure arrays, and cell arrays—have essentially been collections whose elements are linearly related to each other by being organized in rows and columns. However, practical engineering frequently meets data that are not organized so easily. Graphs are one such data set. The ultimate goal of this chapter is to discuss this most general form of data structure. We need first to resolve the semantic problem of the name "graph." We typically think of a graph as a plot. However, in computer science, a **graph** is a collection of **nodes** connected by **edges**. A street map might be a useful mental model of a graph where the streets are the edges and the intersections are the nodes.

To process graphs effectively, we must first consider two simpler concepts: **queues** in general and **priority queues** in particular.

17.1 Queues

We first consider the nature and implementation of queues, special collections that enable us to process graphs efficiently. We experience the concept of a queue every day of our lives. A line of cars waiting for the light to turn green is a queue; when we stand in line at a store or send a print job to a printer, we experience typical queue behavior. In general, the first object entering a queue is the first one to exit the other end.

17.1.1 The Nature of a Queue

Formally, we refer to a queue as a first in/first out (FIFO) collection, as illustrated in Figure 17.1. The most general form of a queue is permitted to contain any kind of object, that is, an instance of any data type or class. A cell array, therefore, would be a good underlying structure upon which to build queue behavior.

Typically, operations on a queue are restricted to the following:

- enqueue puts an object into the queue
- dequeue removes an object from the queue
- peek copies the first object out of the queue without removing it
- isempty determines that there are no items in the queue

17.1.2 Implementing Queues

Although there are many ways to implement a queue, a cell array is a good choice because it is a linear collection of objects that may be of any type and can be extended or shortened without any apparent effort. If we establish a queue using a cell array, the implementation of the above behavior is trivial:

- enqueue concatenates data at the end of the cell array
- dequeue removes the item from the front of the cell array and returns that item to the user
- peek merely accesses the first item in the cell array
- isempty is the standard MATLAB test for the empty vector

Clearly, because all the cell array operations are also accessible to the programmer, nothing prevents an unscrupulous programmer from using other operations on the queue—for example, adding an item to the front of

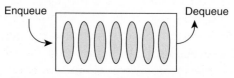

Figure 17.1 *A queue*

Listing 17.1 Enqueue and dequeue functions

```
1. function q = qEnq(q, data)
      % enqueue onto a queue
2.    q = [q {data}];
3. end
4. function [q ans] = qDeq(q)
      % dequeue
5.    ans = q{1};
6.    q = q(2:end);
7. end
```

the queue rather than the back to effectively "jump in line." There are implementations beyond the scope of this text that use object-oriented programming techniques to encapsulate the data and restrict the available operations on that data to those that implement the required functionality. However, for our purposes, the "open" cell array implementation is sufficient.

Functions that perform the enqueue and dequeue operations for a queue are shown in Listing 17.1.

In Listing 17.1:

> Line 1: Obviously, these two trivial functions should actually be in separate files. Both functions must return the updated queue because they receive copies of the original queue.
>
> Line 2: Concatenates the enqueued item in a cell (the braces) at the back of the cell array.
>
> Line 3: The dequeue function must return the new queue and the item being removed.
>
> Line 4: We return the first item on the cell array and remove it by returning the rest.

17.1.3 Priority Queues

There are times when we wish ordinary queues were priority queues. For example, at the printer where you wait an hour for one page while someone prints large sections of an encyclopedia and you wonder why the print queue can't put really small jobs ahead of really large jobs.

The only difference between an ordinary queue and a priority queue is in the enqueue algorithm. On a priority queue, the enqueue function involves adding the new item in order to the queue, as illustrated in Figure 17.2. For the enqueue function to add in order, there must be a means of comparing two objects. Here, we use the function is_before that generally should be able to compare any two objects.

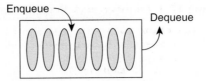

Figure 17.2 *A priority queue*

In this implementation, it is sufficient to be able to compare numbers or structures that contain either the fields key or NaN. Clearly, this can be extended as necessary to compare any two objects.

The code for is_before is shown in Listing 17.2.

In Listing 17.2:

> Line 1: Shows a function that consumes two objects and returns a Boolean result.
>
> Line 2: Captures the data type (class) of the first object.
>
> Line 3: Initializes the result.
>
> Line 4: Checks that the second object is the same data type—otherwise, the false answer is returned.
>
> Line 5: Decides how to compare the objects based on the data type.
>
> Lines 6 and 7: Numbers are easily compared.

Listing 17.2 Comparing two objects

```
 1. function ans = is_before(a, b)
    % comparing two objects
 2.     acl = class(a);
 3.     ans = false;
 4.     if isa(b, acl)
 5.         switch acl
 6.             case 'double'
 7.                 ans = a < b;
 8.             case 'struct'
 9.                 if isfield(a, 'key')
10.                     ans = a.key < b.key;
11.                 elseif isfield(a, 'dod')
12.                     ans = age(a) < age(b);
13.                 else
14.                     error('comparing unknown structures')
15.                 end
16.             otherwise
17.                 error(['can''t compare ' acl 's'])
18.         end
19.     end
20. end
```

Listing 17.3 Priority queue enqueue function

```
1. function pq = pqEnq(pq, item)
    % enqueue in order to a queue
2.      in = 1;
3.      at = length(pq)+1;
4.      while in <= length(pq)
5.          if is_before(item, pq{in})
6.              at = in;
7.              break;
8.          end
9.          in = in + 1;
10.     end
11.     pq = [pq(1:at-1) {item} pq(at:end)];
12. end
```

Line 8: Selects different structures to compare based on fields in the structure.

Lines 9 and 10: If the field key is present, compare these.

Lines 11 and 12: If the field age is present, compare these.

Lines 13–18: Show that an error exits.

The enqueue function that uses is_before(...) to compare objects for a priority queue is shown in Listing 17.3.

In Listing 17.3:

Line 1: Shows the same signature as the enqueue function for ordinary queues.

Lines 2 and 3: Initialize the while loop parameters.

Line 4: Moves the index in down the existing queue until it falls off the end of the cell array or finds something that the item to insert goes before. This second exit is implemented with a break statement.

Line 5: Checks whether the item is less than the current entry in the queue.

Lines 6 and 7: If so, mark the spot and exit the loop.

Lines 8 and 9: Otherwise, keep moving down the queue.

Line 11: Inserts the item in a container between the front part of the queue and the remains of the queue from at to the end.

17.1.4 Testing Queues

It is always advisable to test utility functions thoroughly before using them in complex algorithms. First we will build a simple utility for presenting the contents of any cell array, and then we will write a script to test the queues.

In order to observe the results from testing the queues, we need a function that will convert a cell array to a string for printing. Although it is tempting

Listing 17.4 Converting a cell array to a string

```
1. function str = CAToString(ca)
       % Traverse a cell array to make a string
2.     str = '';
3.     for in = 1:length(ca)
4.         str = [str toString(ca{in}) 13];
5.     end
6. end
```

to try to write a single function to accomplish this, we achieve more maintainable code by separating the cell array traversal from the details of converting each item to a string. The first function, CAToString, which traverses the cell array, is shown in Listing 17.4.

In Listing 17.4:

> Line 1: The function consumes any cell array and returns a string.
>
> Line 2: Initializes the string.
>
> Line 3: Traverses the cell array.
>
> Line 4: Extracts each item from the container, uses the toString utility function below to convert it to a string, and appends it to the end of the output string together with a new-line character (the ASCII value 13).

Of course, the real effort in creating this string is the second function that converts each individual item from the cell array to its string representation. This is shown in Listing 17.5.

In Listing 17.5:

> Line 1: Java programmers might recognize the concept of converting an object to its string equivalent.
>
> Lines 2 and 3: If the object is a string, surround it with single quotes.
>
> Lines 4–6: Individual scalar numbers are printed in %g form.
>
> Lines 7–12: Vectors are enclosed in braces.
>
> Line 14: Recursively uses toString to print the fields of a structure.
>
> Lines 15 and 16: A special case wherein if there is a name field in the structure, the value of that field is used for the string.
>
> Lines 18–23: Extract the field names and iterate through them one at a time, creating a string by appending each field name with its value and a new line.

Listing 17.6 illustrates a test script that exercises most of the available functions for queues and priority queues using numbers. However, a queue can contain any object you can display, and a priority queue can contain any object you can display and compare to another of the same type.

Listing 17.5 Converting any object to a string

```
1. function str = toString(item)
   % turn any object into its string representation
2.     if isa(item, 'char')
3.         str = ['''' item ''''];
4.     elseif isa(item, 'double')
5.         if length(item) == 1
6.             str = sprintf('%g', item );
7.         else
8.             str = '[';
9.             for in = 1:length(item)
10.                str = [str ...
11.                    sprintf(' %g', item(in) ) ];
12.            end
13.            str = [str ' ]'];
14.        end
15.    elseif isa(item, 'struct')
16.        if isfield(item, 'name')
17.            str = item.name;
18.        else
19.            nms = fieldnames(item);
20.            str = [];
21.            for in = 1:length(nms)
22.                nm = nms{in};
23.                str = [str nm ': ' ...
24.                    toString(item.(nm)) 13];
25.            end
26.        end
27.    else
28.        str = 'unknown data';
29.    end
30. end
```

Listing 17.6 Testing the queues

```
1. q = [];
2. for ix = 1:10
3.     q = qEnq(q, ix);
4. end
5. CAToString(q)
6. [q ans] = qDeq(q);
7. fprintf('dequeue -> %d leaving \n%s\n', ...
8.     ans, CAToString(q) );
9. fprintf('peek at queue -> %d leaving \n%s\n', ...
10.    q{1}, CAToString(q) );
11. pq = [];
12. for ix = 1:10
13.     value = floor(100*rand);
14.     fprintf(' %g:', value );
15.     pq = pqEnq(pq, value );
16. end
17. fprintf('\npriority queue is \n%s\n', ...
18.     CAToString(pq) );
```

In Listing 17.6:

> Line 1: Initializes a queue.
>
> Lines 2–4: Enqueue 10 numbers.
>
> Line 5: Displays the resulting queue.
>
> Lines 6–8: Dequeue and print one value and the remaining queue.
>
> Lines 9 and 10: Peek at the head of the queue and verify that we have not changed its contents.
>
> Line 11: Creates a priority queue.
>
> Lines 12–16: Enqueue 10 random integers.
>
> Lines 17 and 18: List the queue to show that they were enqueued in order.

A serious reader can verify that this indicates correct queue behavior.

17.2 Graphs

This chapter focuses on processing a graph—the most general form of dynamic data structure, an arbitrary collection of nodes connected by edges. The edges may be **directional** to indicate that the graph can be traversed along that edge in only one direction (like a one-way street). The edges may also have a value associated with them to indicate, for example, the cost of traversing that edge. We refer to this as a **weighted graph**. For a street map, this cost could either be the distance, or in a more sophisticated system, the travel time—a function of the distance, the speed limit, and the traffic congestion. Graphs are not required to be completely connected, and they may contain **cycles**—closed loops in which the unwary algorithm could become trapped. Graphs also have no obvious starting and stopping points. A **path** on a graph is a connected list of edges that is the result of traversing a graph.

17.2.1 Graph Examples

A simple graph is shown in Figure 17.3. In the figure, the connection points A . . . F are the nodes and the edges are the interconnecting lines, which are

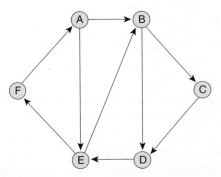

Figure 17.3 *A simple graph*

Figure 17.4 *A simple street map*

directional but not weighted. Graphs occur frequently in everyday life, as illustrated by the street map shown in Figure 17.4. Street maps can be conveniently represented as graphs where intersections are the nodes and streets are the edges. Streets can be directional (one-way), and they may have weights associated with them—either the transit time (a function of the length of the street and its speed limit) or with access to real-time traffic information, a more complex estimate of the transit time.

17.2.2 Processing Graphs

In designing algorithms that operate on graphs in general, we need to consider the following constraints:

- With cycles permitted in the data, there is no natural starting point like the beginning of a cell array. Consequently, the user must always specify a place on the graph to start as well as the place to stop.

- There are no natural "leaf nodes" where a search might have to stop and back up. Consequently, an algorithm processing a graph must have a means of determining that being at a given node is the "end of the line." Typically, this is accomplished by maintaining a collection of visited nodes as it progresses around the graph. Each time a node is considered, the algorithm must check to see whether that node is already in the visited collection. If so, it refuses to return to that node. The algorithm must backtrack if it reaches a node from which there is no edge to a node that has not already been visited.

- Whereas on a cell array there is only one feasible path from one node to another, there may be many possible paths between two nodes on a graph. The best algorithms that search for paths must take into account a comparison between paths to determine the best one.

For a simple, consistent example, consider the graph shown in Figure 17.5. We will use this simple example to demonstrate minimum spanning trees (MSTs) and finding paths through the graph.

17.2.3 Building Graphs

We need to consider graphs as two collections of data as follows:

- A list of n nodes with the properties of identity (a name) and position
- An n × n adjacency matrix that specifies the weight of the edge from each node to any other node

If one node is not reachable from another, by convention we will specify that weight as 0. This is actually a rather intimidating structure to build "by hand." In order to facilitate reliable construction of the adjacency matrix, we start with a simpler description of the graph shown in Figure 17.5. This graph can be described initially with the following data:

- `cost` a vector of size m × 1 containing the weights for each of m edges
- `dir` a vector of size m × 1 indicating the directionality of each edge as follows:
  - 2 two-way edge
  - 1 one way in a positive direction
  - −1 one way in the other direction
- `node` a matrix of size n × rows containing the edge indices for each node. For example, if `node(i, j)` contains x, it says that the ith node connects to the xth edge. If x is 0, there is no connection. The

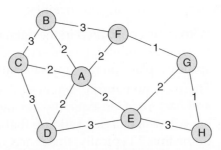

Figure 17.5 *A weighted graph*

value rows is the maximum number of nodes that can be reached from any other node.

- coord a matrix of size n × 2 containing the x-y coordinates of each node that is used only for the graphical representation of the graph.

The script shown in Listing 17.7 starts with the above representation of the graph and calls the function grAdjacency(...) to produce the adjacency matrix. We will save this script as the constructor script makeGraph.m. Again referencing Figure 17.5, the sequence of edges used in this script is:

A-B, A-C, A-D, A-E, A-F, B-F, B-C, C-D, D-E, F-G, E-G, G-H, E-H

Large adjacency matrices usually contain very little data relative to their size. Consequently, to store them as a conventional n × n array is to waste most of the storage space and may even cause memory problems for the processor. Recognizing this eventuality, the MATLAB language provides a special class, sparse, that stores a matrix as lists of row and column indices and the associated value. All normal array and matrix operations can be applied to a sparse matrix. The assumption is that any value not specifically allocated in a sparse matrix contains a zero. This is consistent with the earlier treatment of vectors and arrays where unknown values are filled with 0.

The function grAdjacency(...) that converts graph data from arrays of nodes, costs, and direction to the adjacency matrix form builds a sparse

Listing 17.7 Constructing a simple graph

```
      % edge weights
 1.   cost = [2 2 2 2 2 3 3 3 3 1 2 1 3];
      % edge directions
 2.   dir = [2 2 2 2 2 2 2 2 2 2 2 2 2];
      % connectivity
 3.   node = [ 1 2 3 4 5; ...      % edges from A
 4.            1 6 7 0 0; ...      % edges from B
 5.            2 7 8 0 0; ...      % edges from C
 6.            3 8 9 0 0; ...      % edges from D
 7.            4 11 13 9 0; ...    % edges from E
 8.            5 6 10 0 0; ...     % edges from F
 9.           10 11 12 0 0; ...    % edges from G
10.           12 13 0 0 0];        % edges from H
      % coordinates
11.   coord = [ 5 6; ...  % A
12.             3 9; ...  % B
13.             1 6; ...  % C
14.             3 1; ...  % D
15.             6 2; ...  % E
16.             6 8; ...  % F
17.             9 7; ...  % G
18.            10 2];     % H
19.   A = grAdjacency( node, cost, dir )
```

Listing 17.8 Creating an adjacency matrix

```
1. function A = grAdjacency( node, cost, dir )
   % compute an adjacency matrix.
   % it should contain the weight from one
   % node to another (0 if the nodes
   %                   are not connected)
2. [m cols] = size(node);
3. n = length(cost);
4. k = 0;
   % iterate across the edges
   %    finding the nodes at each end of the edge
5. for is = 1:n
6.     iv = 0;
7.     for ir = 1:m
8.         for ic = 1:cols
9.             if node(ir, ic) == is
10.                iv = iv + 1;
11.                if iv > 2
12.                    error(
                         'bad intersection matrix');
13.                end
14.                ij(iv) = ir;
15.            end
16.        end
17.    end
18.    if iv ~= 2
19.        error(sprintf(
            'didn't find both ends of edge %d', is));
20.    end
21.    t = cost(is);
22.    if dir(is) ~= -1
23.        k = k + 1;
24.        ip(k) = ij(1); jp(k) = ij(2); tp(k) = t;
25.    end
26.    if dir(is) ~= 1
27.        k = k + 1;
28.        ip(k) = ij(2); jp(k) = ij(1); tp(k) = t;
29.    end
30. end
31. A = sparse( ip, jp, tp );
32. end
```

matrix by establishing three vectors of the same length—the row index, the column index, and the value of each point in the sparse matrix. The code to accomplish this is shown in Listing 17.8.

In Listing 17.8:

> Line 1: Shows a function consuming the `node`, `cost`, and `direction` arrays defined above. The locations of the nodes are needed only for plotting.

> Lines 2–4: Show initial parameters, where `k` is the number of entries in the sparse matrix.

Line 5: Iterates down the list of edges.

Line 6: Initializes the number of nodes found connected to the edge.

Lines 7 and 8: Iterate across the nodes and columns of the node array, looking for the nodes connected to the edge.

Lines 9 and 10: When we find the edge value, we want to save that node index.

Lines 11–13: There can be only two ends to an edge; any more indicates a bad data set.

Line 14: Saves each end in the local variable `ij`.

Lines 18–20: When we finish the traversal, there must be a node at each end of the edge.

Line 21: Retrieves the cost of this edge.

Lines 22–25: Since bidirectional edges must be in the matrix twice, we check to see if the edge is bidirectional or forward, and enter the forward path in the sparse matrix.

Lines 26–28: Similarly, the reverse path is entered only if the edge is not forward.

Line 31: Constructs the sparse adjacency matrix.

17.2.4 Traversing Graphs

In its simplest form, the template for graph traversal is shown in Template 17.1.

In Template 17.1:

Line 1: This algorithm uses a queue to serialize the nodes to be considered. The first in/first out behavior of the queue causes the nearest nodes to emerge before the nodes farther away.

Template 17.1 Template for graph traversal

```
 1. < create a queue >
 2. < enqueue the start node >
 3. < initialize the result >
 4. while < the queue is not empty >
 5.      < dequeue a node >
 6.      < operate on the node >
 7.      < for each edge from this node >
 8.          < retrieve the other node >
 9.          if < not already used >
10.              < enqueue the other node >
11.          end
12.      end
13. end
14. < return the result >
```

Line 2: Since all nodes have equal status on a graph, graph traversal must be provided with the node from which to begin the traversal. We enqueue that node to begin the traversal.

Lines 3 and 4: Show the typical `while` loop traversal, initializing a result.

Lines 5 and 6: Extract and process one node.

Lines 7 and 8: Traverse the edges from this node. There must be an indication for each problem of which order to use in selecting the edges to the children of the current path.

Lines 9 and 10: Because the graph can contain cycles, the mechanism for preventing the algorithm from becoming trapped requires that we enqueue only those nodes that have not already been visited.

The choice of queue type governs the behavior of the traversal. If a simple queue is used, the traversal will happen like ripples on a pond from the starting node, touching all the nearest nodes before touching those farther away.

To illustrate the use of Template 17.1, we will print the names of all the nodes of the graph in Figure 17.5 in breadth-first order starting from node E, assuming that all edges are bidirectional. When choosing the edges to the next child node, the child nodes should be taken in alphabetical order:

- To make sure that a node is not revisited, we will keep a list of the visited nodes, beginning with the start node.
- We find the children from the non-zero entries in the adjacency matrix—because of the way we built the matrix, they are already in alphabetical order.
- We then traverse these children, adding to the queue those not found on the visited list and adding each to the visited list.

The script for this is shown in Listing 17.9.

In Listing 17.9:

Line 1: Invokes the script in Listing 17.7 to build the adjacency matrix.

Line 2: The user-defined starting node—E.

Line 3: Enqueues the starting node on a new queue.

Line 4: Initializes the visited list.

Line 5: Initializes the result—in this case, a printout.

Line 6: Shows the `while` loop.

Line 7: Dequeues a node.

Line 8: In this case, processing the node involves printing its label and a dash.

Listing 17.9 Breadth-first graph traversal

```
1. makeGraph
     % Constructs an adjacency matrix
2. start = 5;
     % start is a node number (in this case, 'E')
     % Create a queue and
     % enqueue a path containing home
3. q = qEnq([], start);
     % initialize the visited list
4. visited = start;
     % initialize the result
5. fprintf('trace: ')
     % While the queue is not empty
6. while ~isempty(q)
         % Dequeue a path
7.       [q thisNode] = qDeq(q);
         % Traverse the children of this node
8.       fprintf('%s - ', char('A'+thisNode-1) );
9.       children = find(A(thisNode,:) ~= 0);
10.      for aChild = children
             % If the child is not on the path
11.          if ~any(aChild == visited)
                 % Enqueue the new path
12.              q = qEnq(q, aChild);
                 % add to the visited list
13.              visited = [visited aChild];
14.          end % if ~any(eachchild == current)
15.      end % for eachchild = children
16. end % while q not empty
17. fprintf('\n');
18.
```

Line 9: The non-zero values from the row in the adjacency matrix corresponding to this edge give us the children of this node.

Line 10: Traverses the children.

Lines 11–13: If they are not already on the visited list, enqueue them and put them on the visited list.

Line 17: Completes the result when the queue is empty.

The results from this script are as follows:

```
trace: E - A - D - G - H - B - C - F -
```

which, referring to Figure 17.5, is a breadth-first traversal from node E outward, taking children in alphabetical order as specified.

17.2.5 Searching Graphs

Rather than traversing a graph, we frequently need to know whether a graph contains a specific node. Template 17.1 is easily modified to include a test to see if the current node is the one sought and to exit with success when it is, leaving the existing exit for the failure case.

17.3 Minimum Spanning Trees

We will consider two practical algorithms commonly found in a large range of engineering disciplines. The MST of a graph is used, for example, to calculate the shortest cable necessary to connect all the houses in a subdivision. Unlike path search, the second algorithm to be discussed later, a spanning tree may have multiple branches essentially modeling side streets in the subdivision.

While there may be a large number of spanning trees, and there may be mutiple MSTs in different configurations, they should all have the same total length. We will consider one of the two major algorithms for computing a MST—that commonly referred to as Prim's algorithm. The other, Kruscal's, is similar and will not be covered here.

Prim's algorithm finds the subset of the edges of the graph that connect every node exactly once and whose total cost is less than that of any other spanning tree.

Technical Insight 17.1

According to Wikipedia, this algorithm was developed in 1930 by Czech mathematician Vojtech Jarník and later independently by computer scientist Robert C. Prim in 1957 and rediscovered by Edsger Dijkstra in 1959. Therefore, it is also sometimes called the DJP algorithm, the Jarník algorithm, or the Prim–Jarník algorithm.

The algorithm continuously increases the size of a tree, one edge at a time, starting with a tree consisting of a single vertex, until it spans all the vertices. The resulting tree, V, is a collection of edges. It needs another collection, N, the nodes currently included in the MST.

Specifically, given a graph as defined above, Prim's algorithm proceeds as follows:

- Initialize the result V as an empty vector and N, the included nodes = {x}, where x is an arbitrary node chosen from the graph
- Repeat the following while there are available edges:
  - Choose an edge (u, v) with minimal weight such that u is in N and v is not (if there are multiple edges with the same weight, any of them may be picked)
  - Add v to N, and (u, v) to V.
- Report the contents of V as the resulting MST.

Listing 17.10 shows the code that extracts MST from our sample graph.

In Listing 17:10

Lines 1 and 2: Invoke the script that builds the graph.

| **Listing 17.10** Prim's Algorithm to compute a MST

```
 1. makeGraph
 2. start = 1;
 3. gplot(A, coord, 'ro-')
 4. hold on
 5. for index = 1:length(coord)
 6.        str = char('A' + index - 1);
 7.        text(coord(index,1) + 0.2, ...
 8.             coord(index,2) + 0.3, str);
 9. end
10. axis([0 11 0 10]); axis off; hold on
11. N = start;
12. running = true;
13. result = sparse([0]);
14. while running
           % find the smallest edge
15.     best = 10000;
16.     running = false;
17.     for ndx = 1:length(N)
18.         node = N(ndx);
19.         next = find(A(node,:) > 0);
20.         for nxt = 1:length(next)
21.             nxtn = next(nxt);
22.             if ~any(N == nxtn)
23.                 running = true;
24.                 if A(node, nxtn) < best
25.                     best = A(node, nxtn);
26.                     from = node;
27.                     to = nxtn;
28.                 end
29.             end
30.         end
31.     end
32.     if running
33.         N = [N to];
34.         result(from, to) = 1;
35.     end
36. end
37. gplot(result, coord, 'gx--')
```

Line 2: Sets the starting node (A).

Line 3: Plots the basic graph structure using the built-in `gplot(...)` function.

Lines 4–10: Add plot axes and labels for all the nodes.

Lines 11–13: Initialize the visited node list, `N`, a sparse matrix to store the result and the while condition.

Lines 14–37: Repeat as long as there are nodes to process.

Line 16: Establishes a large initial best node.

Line 17: Assumes failure to find a node.

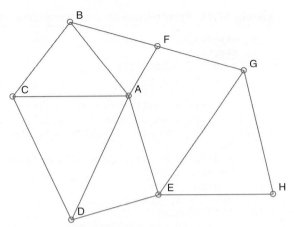

Figure 17.6 *MST result*

Line 18: Looks through all the visited nodes.

Line 19: Extracts a node.

Line 20: Extracts from the adjacency matrix the edges from that node. The indices with non-zero entries are the nodes to which the edge connects; the value in the adjacency matrix is the weight or cost of that edge.

Lines 21 and 22: Examine each of the edges for the node it reaches (`nxtn`).

Line 23: Only continues if this is not already on the visited list.

Lines 24–29: Report that an edge has been found, determine if it is shorter than the previous best, and if so store the new best value and the nodes at each end of the edge.

Lines 33–36: Add the new node to the visited list and the edge to the result array.

Line 38: Plots the MST as green dashed lines.

Figure 17.6 shows the MST resulting from this script. Note that if a different starting node is used, the specific tree might be different but its total edge length will be the same.

17.4 Finding Paths through a Graph

This section discusses three algorithms for finding a path from one node on the graph to another. The first two algorithms exhaustively search the graph to find the absolute best path between node pairs by different criteria. The third is one of many approximation algorithms typically used to compute a good enough route in circumstances where an exact solution is not feasible.

17.4.1 Exact Algorithms

In order to find a path rather than traverse it, we have to make the following changes to Template 17.1:

- Since we need to return the complete path between the start and target, the queue has to contain that path
- Rather than use a global visited list, we can use the path taken from the queue to determine whether a child node is causing a cycle
- The order of the nodes on the path has the starting node at the front of the path and the new node at the end

17.4.2 Breadth-First Search (BFS)

Frequently, we actually need the path with the smallest number of nodes between the starting and ending nodes. For example, because changing trains involves walking and waiting, the best path on a railway map (such as the street map in Figure 17.4) is that with the fewest changes, even if the resulting path is longer. The algorithm is based on Template 17.1 with the changes noted above.

To search for the path with the least nodes, we need a function that performs a Breadth-First Search (BFS) on a graph. In order to be able to use the built-in graph plotting program, the answer returned should be an adjacency matrix showing the computed path. The function to perform this search is shown in Listing 17.11.

Listing 17.11 Breadth-first graph search

```
1. function D = grBFS(A, home, target)
2.      q = qEnq([], home);
3.      while ~isempty(q)
4.          [q current] = qDeq(q);
5.          if current(end) == target % success exit
6.              D = sparse([0]);
7.              for ans = 1:length(current)-1
8.                  D(current(ans), current(ans+1)) = 1;
9.              end
10.             return; % exit the function
11.         end % if current == target
12.         thisNode = current(end);
13.         children = find(A(thisNode,:) ~= 0);
14.         for thisChild = children
15.             if ~any(thisChild == current)
16.                 q = qEnq(q, [current thisChild]);
17.             end % if ~any(thisChild == current)
18.         end % for thisChild = children
19.     end % while q not empty
        % if we reach here we never found a path
20.     D = [];
21. end
```

In Listing 17.11:

> Line 1: Shows a function consuming an adjacency matrix, the starting and destination node indices.
>
> Line 2: Initializes the queue.
>
> Line 3: Repeats to Line 19 until the queue is empty.
>
> Line 4: The queue now contains a vector of the node indices on the current path.
>
> Line 5: If the node dequeued (`current(end)`) is the target, the function creates a new adjacency matrix representing the path from the home node to the target.
>
> Line 6: Creates an empty sparse matrix.
>
> Lines 7–9: Add to it the edges between each node in the path.
>
> Line 10: Exits the function.
>
> Line 12: Otherwise, recovers the last node.
>
> Line 13: Retrieves its children.
>
> Lines 14–18: Traverse the children as before, checking for their presence on the current path. When a child is enqueued, it is appended to the end of the current path and the whole path is enqueued.

The BFS path from A to H is shown in Figure 17.7. Note that it found the path with the least number of nodes.

17.4.3 Dijkstra's Algorithm

Although the minimal number of nodes is sometimes the right answer, frequently there is a path that uses more nodes but has a smaller overall

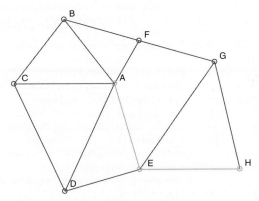

Figure 17.7 *Breadth-first result*

cost. This is evident from a quick glance at Figure 17.5: the path A–F–G–H has a lower cost than the A–E–H path found by the BFS algorithm, which actually ignores the edge weights. Many algorithms exist for finding the optimal path through a graph. Here we illustrate the algorithm attributed to the Dutch computer scientist Dr. Edsger Dijkstra. Perhaps it is not the most efficient algorithm; but for our purposes, this approach has the virtue of being a minor extension to the `while` loop algorithm described in Template 17.1.

- The major differences arise from the use of a priority queue in place of the normal queue used in the BFS algorithm. As previously noted, priority queues differ from basic queues only to the extent that the `enqueue` method puts the data in order, rather than at the tail.
- The ordering criterion required by the algorithm is to place the paths in increasing order of path cost (total weight).

The objects contained in the priority queue need to contain not only the path used for BFS, but also the total path weight. For this we will use a structure with fields `nodes` and `key`, and implement a small collection of helper functions. The helper functions to build a structure with a key and extract the key of the last path entry are shown in Listing 17.12.

In Listing 17.12:

Line 1: Shows a function to construct a path structure from its components.

Lines 2 and 3: Build the structure.

Line 5: Shows a function to retrieve the last node from a path.

Line 6: Since the path nodes start at the path origin, the last entry is the node we need.

The function that performs Dijkstra's algorithm is shown in Listing 17.13.

In Listing 17.13:

Line 1: Shows a function consuming an adjacency matrix, and the starting and destination node indices.

Listing 17.12 Helper functions for Dijkstra's algorithm

```
1. function ret = Path(nodes, len)
   % Path constructor
2.     ret.nodes = nodes;
3.     ret.key = len;
4. end
5. function ret = pthGetLast(apath)
   % Returns number of last node on a path
6.     ret = apath.nodes(end);
7. end
```

Listing 17.13 Code for Dijkstra's algorithm

```
1.  function D = grDijkstra(A, home, target)
2.      pq = pqEnq([], Path(home, 0));
3.      while ~isempty(pq)
4.          [pq current] = qDeq(pq);
5.          if pthGetLast(current) == target
6.              D = sparse(0);
7.              answer = current.nodes;
8.              for ans = 1:length(answer)-1
9.                  D(answer(ans), answer(ans+1)) = 1;
10.             end
11.             return;
12.         end % if last(current) == target
13.         endnode = pthGetLast(current);
14.         children = A(endnode,:);
15.         children = find(children ~= 0);
16.         for achild = children
17.             len = A(endnode, achild);
18.             if ~any(achild == current.nodes)
19.                 clone = Path( [clone.nodes achild] ...
20.                     current.key + len;
21.                 pq = pqEnq(pq, clone);
22.             end % if ~any child == current.nodes
23.         end % for achild = children
24.     end % if pq not empty
        % If we reach here we never found a path
25.     D = [];
26. end
```

Line 2: Initializes the priority queue with a starting node and zero cost.

Line 3: Continues repeating until the queue is empty.

Line 4: Shows that the queue now contains a path structure.

Lines 5–12: If the node dequeued is the target, the function creates a new adjacency matrix representing the path from the home node to the target.

Line 13: Otherwise, it recovers the last node.

Line 14: Retrieves its children.

Lines 15–23: Traverse the children as before, checking for their presence on the current path. When a child is enqueued, it is appended to the end of the current path, and the whole path is enqueued.

The optimal path from A to H is shown in Figure 17.8. Note that it found the path with the least cost.

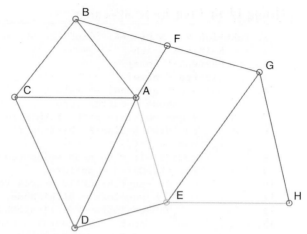

Figure 17.8 *Dijkstra's result*

17.4.4 Approximation Algorithm

When a graph is very large, the computation complexity of the exact solutions (roughly $O(N^2)$) becomes unmanageable. The A* algorithm is one of many popular approximation techniques that will produce a solution, but is not guaranteed to produce the best, and its computational complexity is roughly $O(N)$. This algorithm is quite simple:

1. Beginning at the starting node, it evaluates the result of traveling along each of the feasible edges to an adjacent node (eliminating cyclic paths). The evaluation takes the form of summing the cost of that edge and an estimate of the cost from that node to the destination. On a street map, for example, the estimated cost of each step would be the length of the edge and the straight-line distance from the new node to the destination.

2. It selects the step with the least cost, adds the node reached to the path, and repeats step 1 until the destination is reached.

3. Back-tracking is sometimes necessary if a node is reached from which there are no feasible paths, such as driving into a dead end street.

4. Complete failure is also possible, as it is for the other algorithms, if no physical path exists between the origin and destination nodes.

Listing 17.14 shows the code that implements the A* algorithm. Notice that some additional information is necessary to effectively compute the estimated cost from a node to the destination. In our example, we can use the location of each node, but in general, that location may not be readily available.

Listing 17.14 Code for A* algorithm

```
1. function D = A_Star(A, home, target, coord)
         % initial path
2.       current = home;
3.       visited = home;
4.       while current(end) ~= target
5.           thisNode = current(end);
             % get possible paths from here
6.           children = find(A(thisNode,:) ~= 0);
7.           best = inf;
8.           node = -1; % no node seleected yet
9.           for thisChild = children
10.              if ~any(thisChild == visited)
11.                  edgeCost = A(thisNode, thisChild);
12.                  estimate = dist(thisChild, target, coord);
13.                  cost = edgeCost + estimate;
14.                  if cost < best
15.                      best = cost;
16.                      node = thisChild;
17.                  end
18.              end % if ~any(thisChild == current)
19.          end % for thisChild = children
20.          if node == -1
                 % dead end -> back up one
21.              current = current(1:end-1);
22.              if length(current == 0)
23.                  error('path failed')
24.              end
25.          else
26.              current = [current node];
27.              visited = [visited node]; %
28.          end
29.      end
30.      D = sparse([0]);
31.      for it = 1:length(current)-1
32.          D(current(it), current(it+1)) = 1;
33.      end
34. end
35. function res = dist(a, b, coord)
36.      from = coord(a,:);
37.      to = coord(b,:);
38.      res = sqrt((from(1)-to(1)).^2 + (from(2)-to(2)).^2);
39. end
```

In Listing 17.14:

> Lines 2 and 3: We will maintain two lists—the current path and the visited list indicating all the nodes that have been visited. This provides for the case when back-tracking is necessary to avoid revisiting the dead end.

> Lines 4–29: Continue until the target node is reached.

Lines 5 and 6: Find the nodes that can be reached from the current node.

Lines 7 and 8: Initialize the storage for the best next step.

Lines 9–19: Iterate across all possibilities.

Line 10: Only considers nodes not on the visited list.

Lines 11–13: The cost of this step is the sum of the actual cost of one step and the estimate of the remaining cost given in this case by the distance between the nodes (invoking the helper function at lines 35–39).

Lines 14–17: Check for improvement in the best cost.

Lines 20 and 21: Check for a dead end.

Lines 22 and 23: Check for total failure—we have backed up beyond the starting node.

Lines 26 and 27: Add a successful node to the current path (from which it might later be remove by backing up) and the visited nodes from which it is never removed.

Lines 30–33: Prepare the results as a sparse matrix for plotting.

Lines 35–39: Helper function calculating the distance between the specified points.

The A* path from A to H is shown in Figure 17.9. Note that in this simple case, it found the same path as the BFS, but that is not necessarily the case in a more complex test.

17.4.5 Testing Graph Search Algorithms

The script that develops both search path solutions is shown in Listing 17.15. It requests the starting and ending node letters from the user and then

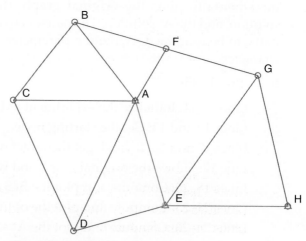

Figure 17.9 *A* result*

Listing 17.15 Testing graph search algorithms

```
1. makeGraph; % call script to make the graph:
2. start = 1;
3. while start > 0
4.     gplot(A, coord, 'ro-')
5.     hold on
6.     for index = 1:length(coord)
7.         str = char('A' + index - 1);
8.         text(coord(index,1) + 0.2, ...
9.             coord(index,2) + 0.3, str);
10.    end
11.    axis([0 11 0 10]); axis off; hold on
12.    ch = input('Starting node: ','s');
13.    start = ch - 'A' + 1;
14.    if start > 0
15.        ch = input('Target node: ','s');
16.        target = ch - 'A' + 1;
17.        disp('original graph'); pause
18.        D = grBFS( A, start, target);
19.        gplot(D, coord, 'go-')
20.        disp('BFS result'); pause
21.        D = grDijkstra( A, start, target);
22.        gplot(D, coord, 'bo-')
23.        disp('Optimal result'); pause
24.        D = A_Star( A, start, target, coord);
25.        gplot(D, coord, 'm^-')
26.        disp('A* result'); pause
27.        hold off
28.    end
29. end
```

incrementally plots the original graph, the BFS solution, the optimal solution, and the A* solution. The pause between plots allows the individual paths to be examined. Without a parameter, pause waits for any keyboard character.

In Listing 17.15:

> Lines 1–11: Initialize the experiment as before.
>
> Lines 12 and 13: Get the starting node.
>
> Lines 15 and 16: If valid, get the target node.
>
> Line 17: Shows the original graph and waits for a character.
>
> Lines 18–20: Compute and plot the BFS solution.
>
> Lines 21–23: Compute and plot the optimal solution.
>
> Lines 24–26: Compute and plot the A* solution.
>
> Lines 27 and 28: Repeat as necessary.

17.5 Engineering Applications

Many practical engineering problems can be characterized as graph search problems.

17.5.1 Simple Applications

MSTs are used by utility companies to find the least amount of cable that must be used to wire a subdivision.

Approximate path finding is used, for example, in navigation systems that use GPS to find the current position of the vehicle and an approximate algorithm like A* to determine the route to a destination.

Exact path finding is used to optimize the flight profile of commercial aircraft outside FAA-managed air space and can save as much as 10% of the fuel burned on every flight.

17.5.2 Complex Extensions

In addition to the obvious examples above, consider these examples:

- designing printed circuit boards is a complex extension of path finding
- stresses in a redundant structure like an aircraft wing seek a path that is in some sense optimal, and
- the "traveling salesperson problem" is an unpleasant extension of path finding in which the objective is to find the shorted linear path that connects all of the nodes of a graph visiting each exactly once. For example, designing routes for garbage collection or school buses.

Each of these belongs to a large class of problems called N-P Complete problems, a continued topic of research in many communities.

 Chapter Summary

This chapter demonstrated effective algorithms for finding good paths through a graph, and included the following:

- How to construct and use queues and priority queues as the underlying mechanism for graph traversal
- The basic use of an adjacency matrix for defining a graph
- Prim's algorithm for finding the minimum spanning tree of a graph
- Breadth-first and Dijkstra's algorithms for finding exact paths through a graph
- The A* algorithm for finding approximate paths that are "good enough"

Programming Project

1. We would like to validate the assertion that the street map is designed to have at most two train changes between any pair of stations. Using the methodology of Section 17.2.3 and the picture in Figure 17.4, construct a graph representing the major routes in that system. You will not need all the stations identified for this exercise—only one station per track segment between transfer stations.

    a. Write a function that will determine the number of train changes to travel between any pair of stations using a breadth-first search to minimize the number of changes.

    b. Iterate across every pair of stations and find the station pair with the maximum number of train changes.

MATLAB Special Characters, Reserved Words, and Functions

Special Characters	Description
<...>	Used to indicate template parameters—data to be supplied
%	Indicates a comment in an m-file
{...}	Defines a cell array
[ ]	The empty vector
[...]	Concatenates data, vectors, and arrays
( )	Used to override operator precedence
( )	Used to identify the formal and actual parameters of a function
(...)	Used to index an array
(<variable>)	Used to allow a variable to be used as a structure field
'abc'	Encloses a literal character string
'	Transposes an array
;	Suppresses output when used in commands
;	Separates rows in an array definition
:	Specifies a vector in the form <from:incr:to>
:	Used in slicing vectors and arrays
.	Used to access fields of a structure
...	Used to continue a MATLAB command to the next line

Mathematical Operators	Description
=	Assignment operator—assigns a value to a variable (memory location); not the same as an equality test
+	Scalar and array addition
−	Scalar and array subtraction
−	Unary negation
*	Matrix multiplication
.*	Element-by-element multiplication
/	Matrix division
./	Element-by-element division
^	Matrix exponentiation
.^	Element-by-element exponentiation

Logical Operators	Description
<	Less than
<=	Less than or equal to
>	Greater than
>=	Greater than or equal to
==	Equal to
~=	Not equal to
&	Element-by-element logical AND
&&	Short-circuit logical AND (scalar)
|	Element-by-element logical OR (vectors)
||	Short-circuit logical OR (scalar)
~	Unary not

Logical Functions	Description
all(a)	True if all the values in a (a logical vector) are true
and(a, b)	True if both a and b are true
any(a)	True if any of the values in a (a logical vector) are true
not(a)	True if a is false; false if a is true
or(a, b)	True if either a or b is true

File Input and Output	Description
[nums txt raw] = csvread(<file>)	Read comma-separated text files
csvread(<file>)	Read comma-separated text files
csvwrite(<file>, <data>)	Write comma-separated text files
dlmread (<file>, < dlm>)	Read text files separated by the given delimiting character(s)
dlmwrite(<file>, <data>, <dlm>)	Write text files separated by the given delimiting character(s)
fclose(<handle>)	Close a text file
fgetl(<handle>)	Read a line omitting the new-line character
fgets(<handle>)	Read a line including the new-line character
fh = fopen (<handle>, <why>)	Open a text file for reading or writing
fprintf (<handle>, ...)	Write to the console, or to plain text files (when <handle> is present
imread(<file>)	Read an image file
imwrite(<data>, <file>, <format>)	Write an image file
load <file>	Load the current workspace from a file

`save <file>`	Save workspace variables in a file
`[tk rest] = strtok(<str>, <dlm>)`	Extract a token from a string and return the remainder of the string
`ca = textscan (<handle>, <format>)`	Acquire and scan a line of text according to a specific format and save the data in a cell array
`[data Fs nb] = wavread(<file>)`	Read a sound file in .wav format
`wavwrite(<data>, <Fs>, <nb>,<file>)`	Write a sound file in .wav format
`[nums, txt, raw] = xlsread(<file>)`	Read an Excel spreadsheet
`xlswrite(<file>, <data>, <sheet>, <range>)`	Write an Excel spreadsheet in a specific row/column range

Format Control	Description
`%<m>.<n>e`	Exponential notation
`%<m>.<n>f`	Fixed point or decimal notation
`%<m>.<n>g`	Fixed point or exponential notation
`%q`	A quoted string delimited by double quotes
`%<n>s`	Character string
`\b`	Backspace
`\n`	New Line
`\t`	Tab

Display Formatting	Description
`format compact`	Set format to compact form
`format long`	Set format to 14 decimal places
`format long e`	Set format to 14 exponential places
`format loose`	Set format back to default, non-compact form
`format short`	Set format back to default, 4 decimal places
`format short e`	Set format to 4 exponential places

User Interface Management	Description
`ans`	Default variable name for results of calculations
`clc`	Clear the interactions window
`clear <selection>`	Remove all (or slected) variables from the workspace
`clf`	Clear the current figure

continued on next page

`close all`	Close all graphics windows
`exit`	Terminate the user interface system
`help <topic or function>`	Invoke the help utility
`load <file>`	Load the current workspace from a file
`quit`	Terminate the user interface system
`save <file>`	Save workspace variables in a file
`who`	List variables in the workspace
`whos`	List variables and their sizes

Special Constants	**Description**
`eps`	Smallest possible difference between two floating point numbers
`false`	Logical false
`inf`	Infinity
`NaN`	Not a number
`pi`	Ratio of the circumference of a circle to its diameter
`true`	Logical true

Basic Mathematical Functions	**Description**
`abs(x)`	Compute the absolute value
`ceil(x)`	Round x to the nearest integer toward positive infinity
`cross(a, b)`	Vector cross product
`exp(x)`	Compute e to the power x
`fix(x)`	Round x to the nearest integer toward zero
`floor(x)`	Round x to the nearest integer toward minus infinity
`log(x)`	Compute the natural log of x
`log10(x)`	Compute the log base 10 of x
`mod(x, a)`	Compute the remainder when x is divided by a
`rem(x, a)`	Compute the remainder when x is divided by a
`round(x)`	Round x to the nearest integer
`sqrt(x)`	Calculate the square root of x

Trigonometry	**Description**
`acos(x)`	Compute the inverse cosine (arcsine) of x
`asin(x)`	Compute the inverse sine (arcsine) of x
`atan(x)`	Compute the inverse tangent (arctan) of x
`atan2(y, x)`	Compute the inverse tangent given the x and y values (4 quadrant resolution)
`cos(x)`	Compute the cosine of x
`sin(x)`	Compute the sine of x
`tan(x)`	Compute the tangent of x

Vector, Array, and Matrix Operations	Description
cumsum(v)	Compute a cumulative sum of the values in v
deal(...)	Distribute cell array results among variables
det(a)	Compute the determinant of a matrix
diag(a)	Extract the diagonal from a matrix or (if provided a is a vector) construct a matrix with a as the diagonal
eye(n)	Generate the identity matrix of size n × n
find(<logical a>)	Compute a linear list of the locations of the true values in a logical array
fliplr(a)	Flip a matrix from left to right
inv(a)	Compute the inverse of a matrix
length(a)	Determine the largest dimension of an array
linspace(from, to, n)	Define a linearly spaced vector
magic(n)	Generate a magic square of size n × n
[v,in] = max(a)	Find the maximum value and its position in a
mean(a)	Compute the average of the elements in a
meshgrid(x, y)	Map each of two vectors into separate 2-D arrays
[v,in] = min(a)	Find the minimum value and its position in a
ones(r, c)	Generate an array filled with the value 1
prod(x)	Compute the product of all the items in x
rand(r, c)	Calculate an r × c array of evenly distributed random numbers in the range 0...1
randn(r, c)	Calculate an r × c array of normally distributed random numbers in the range 0...1
size(a)	Determine the dimensions of an array
sparse	Define a sparse matrix
[v,in] = sort(v)	Sort the vector v (a vector or a cell array of strings)
sum(a)	Find the sum of an array
zeros(r, c)	Build an array filled with the value 0

2-D Plotting	Description
bar	Generate a bar graph
barh	Generate a horizontal bar graph
contour	Generate a contour plot
hist	Draw a histogram
loglog	Generate an x-y plot, with both axes scaled logarithmically
pie	Generate a pie chart
plot	Create an x-y plot
polar	Create a polar plot
semilogx	Generate an x-y plot, with the x-axis scaled logarithmically
semilogy	Generate an x-y plot, with the y-axis scaled logarithmically

3-D Plotting	Description
bar3	Generate a 3-D bar graph
barh3	Generate a horizontal 3-D bar graph
gplot	Plot a graph
mesh	Generate a mesh plot of a surface
meshc	Generate a mesh plot of a surface with contours
meshz	Generate a mesh plot of a surface with a skirt
meshgrid(r, c)	Create a plaid for 3-D plots
peaks	Create a sample matrix used to demonstrate graphing functions
pie3	Generate a 3-D pie chart
plot3	Generate a 3-D line plot
sphere	Example function used to demonstrate graphing
surf	Generate a surface plot
surfc	Generate a combination surface and contour plot
waterfall	Generate a mesh plot of a surface with one skirt edge

Plot Appearance Line Type Control	Description
−	Solid
:	Dotted
−.	Dash-dot
− −	Dashed
.	Point
o	Circle
x	x-mark
+	Plus
*	Star
s	Square
d	Diamond
⌄	Triangle down
^	Triangle up
<	Triangle left
>	Triangle right
p	Pentagram
h	Hexagram

Color Control Character	Description
b	Blue
c	Cyan
g	Green
k	Black
m	Magenta

r	Red
w	White
y	Yellow

Figure Control	Description
axis	Freezes the current axis scaling for the current plot or specifies the axis dimensions
figure <n>	Open a new figure window. If present, <n> specifies a figure number
grid off/on	Turn the grid off or on
hold off/on	If hold is not set, erase figure contents before the next plotting instruction
legend(ca)	Add a legend to a graph
shading <value>	Shade a surface plot with one color per grid section
subplot(plts, n)	Divide the graphics window up into sections available for plotting
text(x,y,str)	Add text to a plot
title(str)	Add a title to a plot
xlabel(str)	Add a label to the x-axis
ylabel(str)	Add a label to the y-axis
zlabel(str)	Add a label to the z-axis

Color Map Values	Description
autumn	yellow, orange, and red colors
bone	shades of gray
colorcube	multiple multi-color bands
cool	light blue to purple
copper	shades of red-brown
flag	multiple red, white, and blue bands
hot	deep red through orange to white
hsv	single spectrum from red to purple
jet	(default) rainbow from blue to red
pink	from dark to light pink
prism	multiple bands of spectrum colors
spring	from purple to yellow
summer	from dark green to yellow
white	all white
winter	from dark blue to light green

String Operations	Description
disp(...)	Display matrix or text
fprintf(...)	Print formatted information
input(...)	Prompt the user to enter a value and parse the result
int2str(a)	Convert an integer to its numerical representation

continued on next page

`num2str(a,n)`	Convert a number to its numerical representation with n decimal places
`sprintf(...)`	Format a string result
`sscanf(...)`	Formatted input conversion
`strcmp(s1, s2)`	Compare two strings—returns `true` if equal
`strcmpi(s1, s2)`	Compare two strings without regard to case—returns `true` if equal
`textscan`	Scan a text string

Time-Related Functions	Description
`clock`	Determine the current time on the CPU clock
`etime`	Find elapsed time
`pause`	Pause the execution of a program, either until any key is hit or for a specified number of seconds
`tic`	Start a timing sequence
`toc`	Stop a timing sequence and returns the elapsed time

Numerical Methods	Description
`diff(v)`	Compute the differences between adjacent values in a vector
`interp1`	Compute linear and cubic interpolation
`interp2`	Compute linear and cubic interpolation
`interp3`	Compute linear and cubic interpolation
`polyfit(x, y, n)`	Compute a least-squares polynomial
`polyval(c, x)`	Evaluate a polynomial
`spline(x, y)`	Spline interpolation

Program Control	Description
`break`	A command within a loop module that forces control to the statement following the innermost loop
`case`	A specific value alternative within a `switch` statement
`catch`	End of a suspect code block where the exception is trapped
`continue`	Skip to the end of the innermost loop, but remains inside it
`else`	Within an `if` statement, begin the code block executed when the condition is false
`elseif <expression>`	Within an `if` statement, begin a subsequent test when the result of the previous test is false
`end`	Terminate a function specification or an `if`, `switch`, `for`, `while`, or `catch` block.
`end`	When indexing, the value of the last element in an index vector
`for var = v`	A code block repeated as many times as there are elements in the vector `v`
`function`	Identify an m-file as a function or begin a helper function within a function file

`error(str)`	Throw an exception to announce an error with the string provided
`global var`	Define a variable as globally accessible
`if <expression>`	Begin a conditional module—the following code block is executed if the logical expression is true
`lasterror`	Provide a structure describing the environment from which an exception was thrown
`nargin`	Determine the number of input parameters actually supplied by a function's caller
`nargout`	Determine the number of output parameters actually requested by a function's caller
`otherwise`	Catch-all code block at the end of a `switch` statement
`switch <variable>`	Begin a code module selecting specific values of the `variable` (must be countable)
`try`	Begin a block of suspect code from which an exception might be thrown
`while <expression>`	A code module repeated as long as the logical expression is true

Data Class Operations	Description
`char(...)`	Cast to a character type
`class(<object>)`	Determine the data type of an object
`double(a)`	Cast a to type `double`
`int8/16/32/64(a)`	Cast a to integer type with the specified number of bits
`uint8/16/32/64(a)`	Cast a to unsigned integer type with the specified number of bits
`isa(obj, str)`	Test for a given data type
`ischar(ch)`	Determine whether the given object is of type `char`
`iscell(...)`	Determine whether the given object is a cell
`isempty(a)`	Test for the empty vector [ ]
`islogical(a)`	Determine whether the given object is of type `logical`
`isnumeric(a)`	Determine whether the given object is of type `double`
`isspace(a)`	Test for the space character
`isstruct(a)`	Determine whether the given object is a structure

Structure Operations	Description
`fieldnames(str)`	Return a cell array containing strings that are the names of the fields in the structure
`getfield(str, field)`	Extract the value of the field
`isfield(str, field)`	Return true if the string is a field in the specified structure
`str = rmfield (str, field)`	Return a copy of the given structure with the given field removed
`str = setfield (str, field, value)`	Construct a structure in which the value of the field has been changed to the given value
`struct(...)`	Construct a structure from `<fieldname>` `<value>` pairs of parameters

The ASCII Character Set

Originally, the American Standard Code for Information Interchange (ASCII) specified the meaning of code numbers transmitted across telephone lines one byte at a time. Frequently, the data were also stored on paper tape. These data controlled communication between two simple devices like a teletype machines. They had to not only deliver characters, but also manage the communications link and control the behavior of the teletype by forcing the print mechanism back to the first column (Carriage Return, CR), advancing the platen to the next print row (Line Feed, LF) or skipping to the column whose number was the next multiple of 8 (tabbing, HT). The first 32 values were set aside as non-printable characters that performed these control tasks. While most of the control characters are now unused, we still make use of the three mentioned above as '\r', '\n', and '\t' to control the behavior of text presented in a window or on a document.

The original ASCII table defined a mapping, whereby a specific set of printable characters was assigned the numerical values 32–126. This was sufficient to represent the number symbols, the lowercase and uppercase alphabet, and all the common punctuation marks. However, as the need arose to represent more international characters, this numerical range was inadequate, and the next 128 values were assigned to meet this need. There is no universal agreement on this second mapping. The following table shows the first 128 values used by the MATLAB language.

When a still broader set of characters was required by the international community, it became necessary to use multiple bytes to encode the symbols. A Unicode Character Set was defined, followed by an international agreement on how to transmit these codes efficiently called UTF-8, the UCS Transformation Format.

Two totally irrelevant historical observations:

1. Astute observers will note that the values 0–127 occupy only the lower 7 bits of one byte of data. The 8th bit was used as an error detection bit during transmission. An agreement was required in transmitting between two machines as to the *parity* of the transmission. Even parity meant that there would always be an

	0	1	2	3	4	5	6	7	8	9	10	11	12	13	14	15
0	NUL	SOH	STX	ETX	EOT	ENQ	ACK	BEL	BS	HT	LF	VT	FF	CR	SO	SI
16	DLE	DCI	DC2	DC3	DC4	NAK	SYN	ETB	CAN	EM	SUB	ESC	FS	GS	RS	US
32		!	"	#	$	%	&	'	(	)	*	+	,	-	.	/
48	0	1	2	3	4	5	6	7	8	9	:	;	<	=	>	?
64	@	A	B	C	D	E	F	G	H	I	J	K	L	M	N	O
80	P	Q	R	S	T	U	V	W	X	Y	Z	[	\	]	^	_
96	`	a	b	c	d	e	f	g	h	i	j	k	l	m	n	o
112	p	q	r	s	t	u	v	w	x	y	z	{	|	}	~	DEL

even number of bits set, and the 8th bit was set or reset to ensure that this was true. If there were an odd number of bits set in a byte, the system knew that the data had been corrupted.

2. ASCII 127 is another non-printing control character used when editing paper tape. Since the value 127 has all the bits set and a hole in the tape signified 1, if operators made a mistake when typing a message, they would back the tape up in the punch and hit DEL to make holes all across the byte, thereby erasing the erroneous character.

Internal Number Representation

There are two different techniques whereby most computers today store the values of numbers: integer and floating-point. Integer storage has the nice property that it represents the exact value of the number stored; floating-point storage only guarantees a certain number of digits of precision. There is an upper limit to the values that can be stored in both integer and floating-point form. However, significantly larger numbers can be stored in floating-point storage than in integer storage.

By default, MATLAB sets the storage of numbers to double-precision floating-point representation. However, operations like reading images into MATLAB present the large volume of data in the more compact unsigned integer form.

Integers

Integers are represented in computer memory by blocks of data bits of various sizes. Memory is allocated in 8-bit increments, usually referred to as bytes; therefore, it is not surprising that integer storage comes in the same size increments. For a given size, the values of the data bits are represented in two different ways—signed or unsigned. Normally, of course, we expect a number to have both positive and negative values, and when the number of bits is large, this does not seem to have much impact. However, when a small number of bits are used to store a value, one of those bits must be used to show that the number is positive or negative. The range of numbers that can be stored is therefore reduced by 1 bit, a factor of 2. The following figure illustrates the internal storage of 8-bit unsigned and signed values.

Clearly, for 8 bits, the maximum value is 127 signed, or 255 unsigned. If this is not sufficient storage, numbers can be stored in 16-, 32-, or 64-bit words, with the corresponding increase in the maximum stored size.

Floating-Point Numbers

Floating-point numbers are stored in single precision (32 bits) or double precision (64 bits) using the IEEE 754 standard. As the name suggests, the storage format includes a mantissa and an exponent, each expressed internally in a manner similar to integer storage. The fixed size of the mantissa leads to the fixed amount of precision of each storage type. The float data type gives 7 significant decimal digits; the double data type gives 15 significant decimal digits.[1]

For details of these storage types, search the Web for "IEEE 754 standard." At the time of writing, there was a good explanation at: http://www. geocities.com/SiliconValley/Pines/6639/docs/fp_summary.html

Parameters of Each Storage Type

The following table describes the most commonly used storage types available in MATLAB, their minimum and maximum values, and their equivalent names in C.

MATLAB Name	Size (Bytes)	Minimum Value	Maximum Value	C Name
uint8	1	0	255	unsigned char
int8	1	−128	127	char
uint16	2	0	65,536	unsigned short
int16	2	−32,768	32,767	short
uint32	4	0	4,294,967,295	unsigned int
int32	4	−2,147,483,648	2,147,483,647	int
float	4	~ −3.4E+38	~ 3.4E+38	float
double	8	~ −1.7E+308	~ 1.7E+308	Double

---

[1]Note that although this seems to be a large amount of precision, you must always design your programs to preserve that precision. If, for example, you were to subtract two numbers almost equal in value, the precision of the result would be significantly worse than that of the original numbers.

Answers to True or False and Fill in the Blanks

Chapter 1

Answers to True or False

1. True.
2. False. Although Charles Babbage is usually credited with the design of the first computer, one could argue that the counting boards in use in 500 BC from which the abacus was derived would qualify as a computer design.
3. False. Operating systems arrived on the scene quite late in the development of computers. Before then, the computer ran one application that did all the work, and this is still possible today.
4. False. The driver is just a pluggable operating system component.
5. True. For a computer to be useful, there has to be hardware to carry data to and from the processor.
6. True.
7. False. A solution solves the whole problem by assembling solutions to manageable subproblems. An algorithm is a series of steps to solve a small subproblem.

Answers to Fill in the Blanks

1. theoretical; practical
2. the Von Neumann architecture
3. virtual memory
4. utilities
5. application programs
6. logic
7. solutions to subproblems
8. states; states

Chapter 2

Answers to True or False

1. True.
2. False. Written correctly, algorithms can be generalized to solve a range of subproblems.
3. True. Both functional and object-oriented programs require procedural components to function on a processor.
4. True.
5. False. This is merely the assignment of the sum of x and y to z; you cannot make any inference about the value of y from this expression.
6. False. Untyped languages merely leave the programmer free of needing to define the type of data. The CPU has to have information about the nature of each data item in order to process it correctly.
7. True.

8. False. In general, especially in MATLAB, the class of an item refers to its data type. The more restrictive definition combining the data type with the operations performed on it is an OOP restriction.
9. False. You must use scripts for permanent command storage.
10. True.
11. True. Clicking the icon to the left brings up the Document window.
12. False. Double-clicking a file name opens the file in the editor.
13. True.
14. True.
15. False. The asterisk indicates that the file has been changed since it was saved.
16. False. Comments appear only in the text of the script for human understanding of the logic.
17. False. Only the F5 hot key saves before executing.

Answers to Fill in the Blanks

1. Abstraction
2. An algorithm
3. side effects
4. a numeric character
5. name; type
6. class; object; class
7. perform calculations; perform calculations
8. double-click; repeat the execution
9. name; current value; data type
10. double-click
11. double-click; variable name
12. automatically; MATLAB command
13. percent sign (%)
14. ignore; the end of the current line

Chapter 3

Answers to True or False

1. False. Homogeneous collections must consist of data of the same type. This could be `double`, `logical`, `char`, or any of the types you saw in this text.
2. True.
3. False. Because a column vector has more columns than rows, it returns the number of columns.
4. True. Regrettably, you can. This is the array linearization. Should you use this? No.
5. False. Either array can be a scalar quantity (a 1 × 1 array).
6. True, as long as the indices in the index vector do not exceed the dimensions of A.
7. False. The position of the values in the logical index vector corresponds to the position of values in the vector being indexed. Longer logical index vectors are reaching beyond the end of the original vector.
8. True.

Answers to Fill in the Blanks

1. numerical value; position in the vector
2. starting value; increment; ending value
3. elements; true values
4. parentheses

5. have the same dimensions; a scalar
6. the empty vector, []; complete rows or columns
7. bad; logical difficulties; indexing; copy the rows and columns you want to keep

Chapter 4

Answers to True or False

1. False. Comments are colored green; keywords that control execution are colored blue.
2. False. The MATLAB editor inserts indentation only to clarify for the reader the flow of control in a script.
3. True. If the `if` statement has no `else` clause, or the `switch` statement has no `otherwise` clause and the data provided matches none of the specified cases.
4. True.
5. False. The result that invalidates all other `&&` expressions is `false`.
6. True. But you can still use `break` to exit the loop early.
7. False. But it ought to be. This is really bad programming practice.
8. False. The expression specifies the reason to stay in the loop.

Answers to Fill in the Blanks

1. key command words
2. `all(...)`
3. `otherwise`
4. `true`
5. variable; values of data
6. `for` or `while`; innermost containing

Chapter 5

Answers to True or False

1. False. Functions have access to all the system data and functions and can also reach `global` data directly.
2. False. Although this ought to be True. MATLAB calls user-defined functions by the name of the m-file, and ignores the name specified there.
3. True.
4. False. Functions can be defined with no parameters required.
5. False. Any result for which a variable is not provided by the caller is ignored.
6. False. This is merely a convention suggested to clarify the source of their definition.

Answers to Fill in the Blanks

1. Procedural abstraction
2. actual; formal
3. vector-like container of variable names
4. Local Scope
5. first; first function; other auxiliary functions in the same file

Chapter 6

Answers to True or False

1. False. Casting changes the way the computer views a piece of data without changing it.
2. True.

3. False. It can be represented within a string by inserting two successive quote marks: (' ').
4. False. MATLAB will automatically cast the string to its ASCII values first.
5. True. But they have to be explicitly converted to characters and concatenated into one string.
6. False. Unequal length strings are reported as not being equal.
7. True.

Answers to Fill in the Blanks

1. a special internal representation
2. characters; numbers; punctuation marks; 0–127
3. `uint8(...)`; each letter
4. format control string; value parameters
5. `if`; cannot
6. `char(...)`; pads them with blanks

Chapter 7

Answers to True or False

1. False. None of the collective operations defined for numerical arrays can be applied to cell arrays or structures.
2. True.
3. True.
4. True.
5. False. It returns a new structure with the field and value removed.
6. True.
7. False. If stra is a structure array with the field data, the expression `{stra.data}` will extract all the values into a cell array.

Answers to Fill in the Blanks

1. extracted one at a time; replaced
2. arrays; containers
3. cell containing 42
4. `str.(field) = 42`
5. `struct(...)`; field name as a string; cell array of field contents

Chapter 8

Answers to True or False

1. True. Although the actual storage technique on a hard drive may have blocks of characters distributed randomly on its surface, the software that reads and writes the disk serializes the characters.
2. False. You save the variable names and their current values, not the programs that generated the data.
3. False. While some applications permit delimited strings to be embedded in comma- or tab-delimited files, MATLAB's readers read only numerical data into arrays.
4. False. You can use the qualifier `'a'` to indicate that you will append to the end of an existing file.
5. True. If you read past the end of a file, a numerical –1 is returned.

Answers to Fill in the Blanks

1. values; organization
2. numerical values; double array; text data; cell array; both string and numerical data; cell array

3. numerical array; filled with zero
4. system dependent (for example, in the standard version on a PC, this is indicated by returning a file handle of –1)

Chapter 9
Answers to True or False

1. True.
2. False. If that function or any function it calls throws an exception, all the frames down to the function containing a `try ... catch` block are popped off the stack.
3. False. Tail recursive functions perform the math "on the way in."
4. True. But this is a bad practice.
5. False. MATLAB actually does not care what the name of the file is. When a function is called, MATLAB finds the function by file name and starts the first function in that file whatever it is called. Local functions in the file must be called from that first function.

Answers to Fill in the Blanks

1. an alternative technique
2. wrapper function; check for erroneous data
3. runtime errors; programming errors; bad data
4. any tests or setup; as a helper to the main function call
5. compute; estimating the answer; recursive function.

Chapter 10
Answers to True or False

1. True.
2. False. All the elements might fail a test you apply to determine whether to change them or not.
3. False. Filtering might remove elements from the collection, but those that remain are not changed.
4. False. It really is folding because the two results are different attributes of the same element of the collection.
5. True. The `break` statement allows you to exit a `for` loop early; the code is a little obscure if written this way.
6. False. Sorting requires some criterion for deciding that one element must precede another—alphabetical order is a good example.

Answers to Fill in the Blanks

1. character of the data; basic operation(s) we are asked to perform
2. beginning with an empty collection; inserting elements one at a time
3. two or more collections
4. filter
5. folding
6. finding what you seek; failing to find it
7. traverse; writing

Chapter 11
Answers to True or False

1. True. If the `x` vector is omitted, 1:N is assumed for the independent parameter, and if the `str` is omitted, a solid blue line is used.

2. False. To apply to a specific data plot, the enhancement functions must follow the plotting function.
3. False. Any area not provided with a plot remains blank.
4. True.
5. False. Bodies of rotation, for example, use one of the axis directions as an independent parameter.
6. False. It is the x and z axes (those axes not the axis of rotation).
7. False. The curve does not need to be continuous.
8. False. You can rotate the data to align an arbitrary axis with the x-axis, perform the body of rotation there, and invert the rotation.

Answers to Fill in the Blanks

1. new figure; the next higher
2. `clf; close all`
3. dependent; separate; independent
4. z; an x-y plaid
5. plaid; angles
6. linear curve; specified axis

Chapter 12

Answers to True or False

1. True. Even the most primitive data members encapsulate their data and control the operations that can be performed on the data.
2. False. It also works if one or both of the matrices are scalar.
3. True, only if one is a scalar; otherwise, False. If A and B are not square, one will fail; even if they are square, they will have different answers.
4. True.
5. False. It is equivalent to back dividing: `A \ B`.
6. True.

Answers to Fill in the Blanks

1. data; procedural
2. column; row
3. translate the object; perform the rotation; translate the rotated object back to P
4. N independent; N unknown; N * (N + 1) constant

Chapter 13

Answers to True or False

1. False. 0 is the absence of light, which will give a black screen.
2. True. `imread(...)` can be adapted to read any supported image file, returning different results for different image styles.
3. True.
4. False. For two reasons—it only works for 2-D arrays, and the rotation is counter-clockwise.
5. True. Consider Figure 13.18. The original number of $1600 \times 1200 \times 3$ pixels has been reduced to a smattering of pixels of interest.

Answers to Fill in the Blanks

1. three; `uint8`; 0–255
2. pixel; `uint8`
3. decoded; true color; three color layers.

4. figure window; image(...)
5. Cropping; shrinking; stretching
6. transpose; major diagonal

Chapter 14

Answers to True or False

1. True.
2. False. Removing samples raises the frequency.
3. False. The number of bits in the recording has no significant effect on an untrained ear.
4. True.
5. True.

Answers to Fill in the Blanks

1. amplitude; frequency
2. A/D; D/A; pressure
3. 7; 5; 2; 12
4. sound energy; frequency band

Chapter 15

Answers to True or False

1. True. The provision is that while the linear interpolation does not give an error, it returns NaN for data points that are out of range.
2. True. There is a unique cubic parametric curve between each pair of points. The curve is parametric rather than a function of the independent variable in order to permit the curve to "double back" if necessary for smoothness.
3. False. All curve fitting does is provide the coefficients of a polynomial. You can insert any value of the independent variable.
4. True.
5. True. Simpson's rule better captures fluctuations in the function being integrated.
6. False. The diff(...) function shortens the vector by one element.

Answers to Fill in the Blanks

1. Interpolation
2. coefficients of the equation; sum of the squared distances
3. central difference approximation; slope
4. cumsum(...); dot product; the data vector; a vector of time differences
5. critical point; differentiating

Chapter 16

Answers to True or False

1. True. First we perform all the algebra to reduce the compound expression to a sequential series of O(...) values, and then we add them and remove any terms that increase more slowly with N than other terms.
2. False. Linear search algorithms are O(N), but binary search is O(log N).
3. True. Mathematicians have proven that one cannot sort with a faster Big O. However, better algorithms can provide a constant multiplier improvement.
4. False. Most of them have some kind of optimization that reduces the length of the minor passes.

5. True. Since Big O should reflect the worst case performance, and quick sort on a sorted collection is O(N2).

Answers to Fill in the Blanks

1. Big O; work; data
2. N
3. Merge; quick
4. Bubble; Quick
5. ad at the end; or string

Index